D1251741

Party Competition between Unequals

Why do some political parties flourish while others flounder? In this book, Bonnie M. Meguid examines variation in the electoral trajectories of the new set of single-issue parties: green, radical right, and ethnoterritorial parties. Instead of being dictated by electoral institutions or the socio-economic climate, as the dominant theories contend, the fortunes of these niche parties, she argues, are shaped by the strategic responses of mainstream parties. She advances a new theory of party competition in which mainstream parties facing unequal competitors have access to a wider and more effective set of strategies than posited by standard spatial models. Combining statistical analyses with in-depth case studies from Western Europe, the book explores how and why established parties undermine niche parties or turn them into weapons against their mainstream party opponents. This study of competition between unequals thus provides broader insights into the nature and outcome of competition between political equals.

Bonnie M. Meguid is an associate professor of political science at the University of Rochester. Her research on party competition has been published in the *American Political Science Review*. Her research has been funded by grants from the National Science Foundation and the Krupp Foundation, and her doctoral dissertation was awarded the Samuel H. Beer Prize for Best PhD Dissertation on British Politics by the British Politics Group.

Cambridge Studies in Comparative Politics

General Editor
Margaret Levi *University of Washington, Seattle*

Assistant General Editors
Kathleen Thelen *Massachusetts Institute of Technology*
Erik Wibbels *Duke University*

Associate Editors
Robert H. Bates *Harvard University*
Stephen Hanson *University of Washington, Seattle*
Torben Iversen *Harvard University*
Stathis Kalyvas *Yale University*
Peter Lange *Duke University*
Helen Milner *Princeton University*
Frances Rosenbluth *Yale University*
Susan Stokes *Yale University*

Other Books in the Series

David Austen-Smith, Jeffry A. Frieden, Miriam A. Golden, Karl Ove Moene, and Adam Przeworski, eds., *Selected Works of Michael Wallerstein: The Political Economy of Inequality, Unions, and Social Democracy*
Andy Baker, *The Market and the Masses in Latin America: Policy Reform and Consumption in Liberalizing Economies*
Lisa Baldez, *Why Women Protest? Women's Movements in Chile*
Stefano Bartolini, *The Political Mobilization of the European Left, 1860–1980: The Class Cleavage*
Robert Bates, *When Things Fell Apart: State Failure in Late-Century Africa*
Mark Beissinger, *Nationalist Mobilization and the Collapse of the Soviet State*
Nancy Bermeo, ed., *Unemployment in the New Europe*
Carles Boix, *Democracy and Redistribution*
Carles Boix, *Political Parties, Growth, and Equality: Conservative and Social Democratic Economic Strategies in the World Economy*
Catherine Boone, *Merchant Capital and the Roots of State Power in Senegal, 1930–1985*
Catherine Boone, *Political Topographies of the African State: Territorial Authority and Institutional Change*
Michael Bratton, Robert Mattes, and E. Gyimah-Boadi, *Public Opinion, Democracy, and Market Reform in Africa*

Continued on pages following the Index

To Michael and in Memory of my Grandmothers

Party Competition between Unequals

STRATEGIES AND ELECTORAL FORTUNES IN WESTERN EUROPE

BONNIE M. MEGUID

University of Rochester

CAMBRIDGE
UNIVERSITY PRESS

CAMBRIDGE UNIVERSITY PRESS
Cambridge, New York, Melbourne, Madrid, Cape Town, Singapore,
São Paulo, Delhi, Dubai, Tokyo

Cambridge University Press
32 Avenue of the Americas, New York, NY 10013-2473, USA

www.cambridge.org
Information on this title: www.cambridge.org/9780521169080

First published 2008
First paperback edition 2010

Printed in the United States of America

A catalog record for this publication is available from the British Library.

Library of Congress Cataloging in Publication Data

Meguid, Bonnie M., 1973–
Party competition between unequals : strategies and electoral fortunes in Western
Europe / Bonnie M. Meguid.
  p.   cm. – (Cambridge studies in comparative politics)
Includes bibliographical references and index.
ISBN 978-0-521-88765-6 (hardback)
1. Political parties – Europe, Western – Case studies. 2. Power (Social sciences) –
Europe, Western – Case studies. 3. Europe, Western – Politics and government –
1989– I. Title. II. Series.
JN94.A979M44   2007
324.2094–dc22   2007036840

ISBN 978-0-521-88765-6 Hardback
ISBN 978-0-521-16908-0 Paperback

Contents

List of Tables and Figures

FIGURES

List of Abbreviations and Acronyms

POLITICAL PARTY ABBREVIATIONS AND ACRONYMS

AGALEV   Anders Gaan Leven (Live Differently [Flemish Greens]), Belgium

AN   Alleanza Nazionale (National Alliance), Italy

AP   Alianza Popular (Popular Alliance), Spain

CDC   Convergència Democràtica de Catalunya (Democratic Convergence of Catalonia), Spain

CDU   Christlich Demokratische Union (Christian Democratic Union), Germany

CiU   Convergència i Unió (Convergence and Unity), Spain

CSU   Christlich Soziale Union (Christian Social Union), Germany

CSV   Chrëschtlech Sozial Vollekspartei (Christian Social Party), Luxembourg

CVP/PDC   Christlichdemokratische Volkspartei (Christian Democratic People's Party [German])/Parti démocrate-chrétien suisse (Swiss Christian Democratic Party [French]), Switzerland

DC   Democrazia Cristiana (Christian Democrats), Italy

DNA   Det Norske Arbeiderparti (Norwegian Labor Party), Norway

DVU   Deutsche Volksunion (German People's Union), Germany

Ecolo   Écologistes (Ecologists [French]), Belgium

ERC   Esquerra Republicana de Catalunya (Catalan Republican Left), Spain

FDF   Front Démocratique des Francophones (Francophone Democratic Front), Belgium

FDP   Freie Demokratische Partei (Free Democratic Party), Germany

FN   Front National (National Front), France

FPÖ   Freiheitliche Partei Österreichs (Austrian Freedom Party), Austria

GE   Génération Écologie (Ecology Generation), France

H	Høyre (Conservatives), Norway
HB	Herri Batasuna (United People), Spain
KF	Konservative Folkeparti (Conservative People's Party), Denmark
KOK	Kansallinen Kokoomus (National Coalition), Finland
LN	Lega Nord per l'indipendenza della Padania (Northern League for the Independence of Padania), Italy
LSAP	Lëtzebuerger Sozialistesch Arbechterpartei (Luxembourg Socialist Workers' Party), Luxembourg
M	Moderata Samlingspartiet (Moderate Unity Party), Sweden
MSI	Movimento Sociale Italiano (Italian Social Movement), Italy
ND	Nea Demokratia (New Democracy), Greece
NF	National Front, U.K.
OIKIPA	Ikologiko Kinima Politikis Anagennisis (Ecological Movement – Political Resistance), Greece
ÖVP	Österreichische Volkspartei (Austrian People's Party), Austria
PASOK	Panhellinio Sosialistiko Kinima (Pan-Hellenic Socialist Movement), Greece
PC	Plaid Cymru (Party of Wales), U.K.
PCF	Parti communiste français (French Communist Party), France
PCI	Partito Comunista Italiano (Italian Communist Party), Italy
PNV	Partido Nacionalista Vasco (Basque Nationalist Party), Spain
PP	Partido Popular (Popular Party), Spain
PRL/PVV	Parti réformateur libéral (Liberal Reform Party [French])/Partij voor Vrijheid en Vooruitgang (Party of Liberty and Progress [Flemish]), Belgium
PS	Parti socialiste (Socialist Party), France
PS/SP	Parti socialiste (Socialist Party [French])/Socialistische Partij (Socialist Party [Flemish]), Belgium
PSC	Partit dels Socialistes de Catalunya (Socialist Party of Catalonia), Spain
PSD	Partido Social Democráta (Portuguese Social Democractic Party), Portugal
PSOE	Partido Socialista Obrero Español (Spanish Socialist Workers' Party), Spain
PSP	Partido Socialista Português (Portuguese Socialist Party), Portugal
PvdA	Partij van de Arbeid (Labor Party), Netherlands
RPR	Rassemblement pour la république (Rally for the Republic), France
RW	Rassemblement Wallon (Walloon Rally), Belgium
SAP	Sveriges Socialdemokratiska Arbetareparti (Swedish Social Democratic Party), Sweden
SD	Socialdemokratiet (Social Democratic Party), Denmark
SNP	Scottish National Party, U.K.

SPD   Sozialdemokratische Partei Deutschlands (German Social
            Democratic Party), Germany
SPÖ   Sozialistische Partei Österreichs (Austrian Socialist Party),
            Austria
SPS/PSS   Sozialdemokratische Partei der Schweiz (Swiss Social
            Democratic Party [German])/Parti socialiste suisse (Swiss
            Socialist Party [French]), Switzerland
SSDP   Suomen Sosialidemokraattinen Puolue (Finnish Social
            Democratic Party), Finland
UDB   Union Démocratique Bretonne (Breton Democratic Union),
            France
UDC   Unió Democràtica de Catalunya (Democratic Union of
            Catalonia), Spain
UDF   Union pour la démocratie française (Union for French
            Democracy), France
UPC   Unione di u Populu Corsu (Corsican People's Union), France
VGÖ   Vereinte Grüne Österreichs (United Greens of Austria), Austria
VVD   Volkspartij voor Vrijheid en Democratie (People's Party for
            Freedom and Democracy), Netherlands

DATA SOURCE ABBREVIATIONS AND ACRONYMS

CCO   Conservative Central Office, London, United Kingdom
CEVIPOF   Centre d'études de la vie politique française (Center for the
            Study of French Political Life), Paris, France
CPA   Conservative Party Archives, Bodleian Library, Oxford, United
            Kingdom
CRAPS   Centre de recherches administratives, politiques et sociales
            (Center for Administrative, Political, and Social Research),
            Lille, France
CRD   Conservative Research Department
FNSP   Fondation nationale des sciences politiques (National
            Foundation of Political Sciences), Paris, France
IFOP   Institut français d'opinion publique (French Institute of Public
            Opinion), Paris, France
LCC   Leader's Consultative Committee, also known as the Shadow
            Cabinet, British Conservative Party
LPA   Labour Party Archives, National Museum of Labour History,
            Manchester, United Kingdom
NEC   National Executive Committee, British Labour Party
OURS   Office universitaire de recherche socialiste (Academic Office of
            Socialist Research), Paris, France
SOFRES   Société française d'enquêtes par sondage (French Society of
            Polling Inquiries), France

Acknowledgments

This project has benefited from the guidance and assistance of many people and organizations. I would like to start by thanking my dissertation committee, Peter Hall, Torben Iversen, and Jorge Domínguez, who first shaped my ideas about the competition of mainstream and niche parties during my doctoral work at Harvard. Peter Hall has been a generous and inspiring mentor. His countless thought-provoking comments and suggestions both during and since the dissertation phase have influenced my ideas, my writing, and the scope of this project. Torben Iversen introduced me to the field of party competition and spatial modeling and provided invaluable feedback on both my theoretical and empirical arguments. Jorge Domínguez repeatedly amazed me with his knowledge of European party politics and provided new perspectives along with detailed comments and thoughtful advice.

Many others have been critical to the articulation and execution of this project. I am extremely grateful to James Adams and Michael Laver for reading the entire manuscript and offering suggestions for revisions. I am also thankful to the many other scholars who have read and provided helpful comments and critiques on various parts of the project and manuscript over the years. Although the number of people in this group is too long to list, I particularly thank Jim Alt, Éric Bélanger, Ted Brader, Barry Burden, Kevin Clarke, Mark Duckenfield, Mark Fey, Matt Golder, Sona N. Golder, Anna Grzymala-Busse, Tim Hellwig, Gretchen Helmke, Sunshine Hillygus, Michael Jones-Correa, Tasos Kalandrakis, Orit Kedar, Gary King, Miki Caul Kittilson, Ken Kollman, Gary Marks, Tony Messina, Dick Niemi, Susan Pharr, Bing Powell, David Primo, Susan Scarrow, Ethan Scheiner, Cindy Skach, Jae-Jae Spoon, Josh Tucker, and Carolyn Warner. Participants in various workshops and seminars at Harvard University, the Kellogg Institute at the University of Notre Dame, the University of Michigan, Princeton University, and Wesleyan University provided stimulating questions and useful feedback on many parts of this project. I am also grateful to the anonymous reviewers of my manuscript for their comments and critiques, to Margaret Levi for her suggestions and encouragement, and to Lewis Bateman at Cambridge

University Press for his support throughout the publication process. Needless to say, any shortcomings of the book are my own responsibility.

The field research for this book could not have been conducted without the help and support of many scholars, colleagues, and friends in Europe. In particular, I would like to thank Bruno Cautrès, Nicole Catala, Gérard Grunberg, Pascal Perrineau, and Patrick Weil in France and Virginia Bottomley, David McCrone, Robert McLean, and John Mellon in Great Britain. I am grateful to the librarians and members of research departments in Paris, Fontainebleau, Oxford, and Manchester who helped me navigate party and governmental archives. They include Robert Bird, Frédéric Cépède, Jill Davidson, Andrew Flinn, Odile Gaultier-Voiturier, Mireille Jean, Martine Jouneau, Jeremy McIlwaine, James Walsh, and Sheridan Westlake. I am indebted to the CEPIC in Paris and the Politics Department at Birkbeck College in London for providing me with institutional homes and intellectual environments during my field research. And I am grateful to Margaret Paquês, Sabine Weidlich, and Hervé Demangue in France and Camilla and John Brown, Gil Lea, Andrew Pearson, Tim and June Perfect, Margaret Tabor, and Jane Tinkler in England for their friendship and support. I also would like to thank the countless members – voters and elite – of British and French political parties who generously met with me, answered my questions, and taught me about their organizations.

The research and writing of this book were made possible by financial support from many sources. For the funding of my field research, I would like to thank the National Science Foundation Graduate Fellowship program and the Krupp Foundation. Grants from the Mellon Foundation, the Program for the Study of Germany and Europe at the Center for European Studies at Harvard University, the Program in Empirical Policy Research at the Wallis Institute, and the Charles E. Lanni Memorial Fund at the University of Rochester provided generous support for writing and additional research. I would like to especially thank Gerald Gamm and the Department of Political Science at the University of Rochester for the leave time and research support needed to complete the research and writing of this book.

For assistance with securing access to data sets, I thank Bruno Cautrès and the Banque des Données Socio-Politiques, Russ Dalton, Gérard Grunberg, Murray Goot, Robert Harmel, Sophie Holloway and the Australian Social Science Data Archive, Kenneth Janda, Sol Lebovic and Cassandra Marks of Newspoll, Ann Marshall, Andrea Volkens, and Bernard Wessels. For their help in the final stages of the manuscript preparation, I am thankful for the research assistance of Tanya Bagashka, Jon Sabella, and Susanna Supalla. I am also grateful for the assistance of Peter Dorey, Jane Green, Janet Laible, Fabiana Machado, Susan Scarrow, and Jae-Jae Spoon in gathering party logos for the cover art. I thank Becky Hornyak for her preparation of the index.

Material from parts of Chapters 11, 22, and 33 was previously published in "Competition Between Unequals: The Role of Mainstream Party Strategy in Niche Party Success." *American Political Science Review* 99:3 (2005): 347–59 and is reprinted here with the permission of Cambridge University Press.

Last, but certainly not least, I offer my gratitude to my family. I thank my parents and brother for their support of my academic pursuits. My parents were my first academic role models. They taught me to embrace challenges and to always persevere, for which I am grateful. My grandmothers provided much needed physical and emotional respite during my years of study in the United States and in Europe. They never saw the final product of that work, but they were critical to its achievement. My deepest thanks go to my husband, Michael. He has been a tireless advocate of my work since the very beginning. He has read countless drafts of this book and the papers and dissertation that came before it. My theory and analyses have benefited immensely from the thought-provoking comments and questions that he wrote in the margins of those many drafts. This project and my life would have been much less rich and much more difficult without his intellectual support, love, and general encouragement. I dedicate this book to him and to the memory of my grandmothers.

1

The Niche Party Phenomenon

Running under the slogan "defend the French," a new political party known as the Front National (FN) first fielded candidates in the 1973 French national legislative elections.[1] Over the next three decades, the FN, fearful of the contamination and erosion of the French national identity, advocated a ban on further immigration and called for the (forced) repatriation of immigrants and the restoration of traditional French family values. Initially, the FN's promotion of this new set of issues was met with little electoral enthusiasm; in its first decade of existence, the party received less than 1 percent of the national vote per legislative election. Its charismatic leader, Jean-Marie Le Pen, also fared poorly, capturing a mere 0.7 percent in the 1974 presidential election.

Although political observers and scholars at the time discounted the prospects of this minor party – especially in an electoral environment thought to disadvantage nonmainstream parties – the FN emerged as one of the strongest radical right parties in Western Europe by 2000.[2] Even though large-scale immigration to France had been banned officially since 1974 and the percentage of foreign citizens had been stabilizing and even falling, the anti-immigrant FN won an average of more than 9 percent of the vote across national legislative elections in the 1980s and 1990s and ended the millennium with a peak vote of 14.9 percent in 1997. Once on the margins of the French political scene, the Front National would surpass the Communist Party to become the number three party in France.

Just as the French radical right party was flourishing under inauspicious institutional and sociological conditions, other parties were struggling under supposedly propitious ones. The Swedish Ecology Party (Miljöpartiet) first contested national elections in 1981, calling for the elimination of Sweden's nuclear power plants and the reduction of environmental pollution.[3] Despite the fact that

---

[1] Front National, *Défendre les Français*, 1973, cited in Mayer and Sineau 2002: 71.
[2] As will be discussed later in this chapter, France's restrictive two-ballot plurality electoral system is thought to discourage voting for smaller parties.
[3] In 1985, the party would rename itself Miljöpartiet de Gröna.

Sweden had electoral and socio-economic conditions thought to benefit small parties, and environmental parties in particular, the Ecology Party captured a mere 1.7 percent of the vote in that first election.[4] Its vote share would increase to 5.5 percent in 1988, but this lifetime peak vote was hardly consistent with the strong environmental priorities of the Swedish electorate. In a poll taken in 1988, "53% of respondents believed that a sound environmental policy was more important than whether one or [an]other of the main party groups achieved power."[5] The Ecology Party, however, would never gain the support of half of the electorate; indeed, it would not surpass the 5 percent mark in any of the next three elections. Contrary to scholarly expectations, permissive institutional and socio-economic environments matched with strong Swedish environmentalist demands failed to produce a strong green party.

Across Western European political landscapes over the past thirty years, stories of new party successes and failures abound. Green parties have succeeded electorally in Belgium but failed in Italy. Radical right parties have done well in Denmark but struggled in Sweden. Ethnoterritorial parties have captured significant percentages of the vote in Flanders and Scotland but fared less well in Brittany and Ticino. And these disparities are not limited to cross-country cases, as the strength of the German Greens and the weakness of their radical right compatriots, the Republikaner and Deutsche Volksunion (DVU), illustrate. Why have some parties flourished while others have floundered? In other words, what determines variation in the electoral success of niche (green, radical right, and ethnoterritorial) parties?

These questions have typically been answered with institutional and sociological explanations. Scholars have looked to a country's electoral rules and state structure or its levels of postmaterialism, unemployment, and immigrants to account for party success and failure. Yet, although popular, these explanations are insufficient. Static institutions cannot account for variation in a party's support over time. And, as suggested by the "surprising" but not unusual cases of the French FN's success and the electoral stagnation of the Swedish Miljöpartiet, neither institutional nor sociological conditions are determinative of new parties' vote share.

By emphasizing the context in which party competition takes place, the existing literature has curiously downplayed the behavior of the competitors. This book brings parties back into the analysis of party success. It demonstrates the critical role that the most powerful set of party actors – mainstream parties of the center-left and center-right – plays in shaping the competitiveness of new political dimensions and the electoral fortunes of the niche parties competing on them. Recognizing that mainstream parties have access to a greater range of strategies

---

[4] Sweden's Sainte-Laguë electoral system is considered favorable to minor parties. Moreover, Sweden had low levels of unemployment and high rates of postmaterialism, factors that sociological theories posit encourage green party support.

[5] Poll conducted by Research Group for Social and Informational Studies, cited in O'Neill 1997: 397.

than previously outlined by the strategic literature, I explain how and why niche parties became (or were made into) electoral superstars under often inhospitable institutional and sociological circumstances and minor electoral figures under supposedly favorable ones. In doing so, this book not only sheds light on the nature of competition between these fundamentally different and unequal sets of parties, but its comparative analysis of mainstream party strategies and niche party fortunes also provides insights into the character of competition between mainstream political equals, the survival of mainstream party actors, and the longevity of the party system.

THE NICHE PARTY PHENOMENON

Since 1960, countries from Western Europe and North America to Australasia and Latin America have experienced an explosion in the number of new parties. In Western Europe alone, that number has exceeded 250. This rapid multiplication of the number of political options exacerbated an already tumultuous political environment; in many of these countries, class cleavages were weakening (Franklin et al. 1992; Inglehart 1997; Särlvik and Crewe 1983), and voter loyalty was declining (Dalton 2000). Traditional bases of party support were called into question, and voter volatility was on the rise.[6] The flood of new parties thus further increased the competitiveness of these unstable political arenas.[7] In some countries, these new parties even caused a sea change in the identity of the governments and the nature of the political systems.

Along with exacerbating these system-level changes, what is remarkable about this wave of new parties is the presence of a set of political actors quite unlike those seen before. Although many of the new political organizations are variants of the existing socialist, liberal, and conservative parties, the new group of parties includes green, radical right, and ethnoterritorial parties. While these actors, which I call *niche parties*, have typically been studied individually in the literature, they share three characteristics that differentiate them from both their fellow neophytes and mainstream parties.

First, niche parties reject the traditional class-based orientation of politics. Instead of prioritizing economic demands, these parties politicize sets of issues that were previously outside the dimensions of party competition. Ethnoterritorial parties, for example, entered political arenas in the 1960s and 1970s to promote regional and ethnic identities over class ones. Green parties followed on their heels in the 1970s, echoing their calls for locally oriented action but

---

[6] As recorded by Anderson (1998: 579), Bartolini and Mair (1990: Appendix), Pedersen (1979: 202), and others, voter volatility rates across Western Europe increased between the 1960s and the mid-1990s. These increases in the net electoral shifts between political parties were accompanied by, and often thought to be a result of, a decline in voter partisanship and a weakening of social cleavages.

[7] Not only did the new parties increase the number of political options available to the voters, but in many countries, they also attracted significant voter support. This is one reason for the increase in the effective number of parties seen in all advanced industrial democracies, except the Netherlands, since World War II (Dalton et al. 2000: 43).

placing the emphasis on the underdiscussed issues of environmental protection, nuclear disarmament, and the elimination of nuclear power. The most recent wave of new political actors, the parties of the radical right, prioritizes (patriarchal) family values and the protection of a nationally oriented, immigrant-free way of life. Despite differences in the substance of their demands, these parties similarly challenge the economic content of the political debate.

Second, the issues raised by the niche parties are not only novel, but they also often do not coincide with the existing, "left-right" lines of political division. Niche parties appeal to groups of voters that may crosscut – and undermine – traditional patterns of partisan alignment.[8] And with the class-based political cleavages already beginning to weaken by the period of niche party emergence, the niche parties' issue appeals resulted in the creation of new types of political coalition. Where niche parties compete, cases of voter defection between "unlikely" party pairs have occurred. The defection of former British Conservative voters to the Green Party in 1989 and former French Communist Party voters to the radical right Front National in 1986 are typical examples.

Third, niche parties further differentiate themselves by limiting their issue appeals. They eschew the comprehensive policy platforms common to their mainstream party peers, instead adopting positions on and prioritizing only a restricted set of issues. Even as the number of issues covered in their manifestos has increased over the parties' lifetimes, they have still been perceived largely as single-issue parties by the voters and other parties. While this image is a simplification of reality, research has shown – and the case studies in this book will reveal – that each of these parties is best known for one issue (Lubbers et al. 2002: 350),[9] and that those voting for niche parties share few policy preferences besides those on the niche party's single issue (Ivarsflaten 2005).[10] Unable to benefit from pre-existing partisan allegiances or the broad allure of comprehensive ideological positions, niche parties rely heavily on the salience and attractiveness of their one policy stance for voter support.

The countries and political systems of Western Europe have been most profoundly affected by this phenomenon. Over the past forty years, approximately 110 niche parties have contested national elections in eighteen countries in Western Europe.[11] This group has included women's, peace, environmental, ethnoterritorial, and radical right parties, with the last three being the most common types. As shown in Table 1.1, no country has been spared from the niche party

---

[8] Even though the introduction of a new issue axis does not necessarily result in the reorganization of party competition around that dimension, the electoral participation of the niche parties did lead to an increase in public awareness of, and eventually electoral support for, their issues.

[9] This point is highlighted by Lubbers et al. (2002: 350) in their analysis of radical right parties: "If there is one issue with which the extreme right wing has made itself heard, it has been a restrictive position towards immigration."

[10] Not all scholars of new parties share this perspective, as evidenced by Mudde (1999) and Kitschelt (1994, 1995).

[11] These countries are Austria, Belgium, Denmark, Finland, France, Germany, Greece, Iceland, Ireland, Italy, Luxembourg, the Netherlands, Norway, Portugal, Spain, Sweden, Switzerland, and the United Kingdom.

TABLE 1.1. *Niche Parties in Western European Countries, 1960–2000*

Country	Number of Niche Parties	Number with Peak National Vote Greater than 5 Percent	Number with Seat in National Legislature
Austria	4	2	2
Belgium	12	6	8
Denmark	5	1	3
Finland	4	2	3
France	6	1	2
Germany	7	1	1
Greece	6	0	3
Iceland	3	2	3
Ireland	1	0	1
Italy	20	3	10
Luxembourg	5	2	3
Netherlands	4	1	3
Norway	3	1	2
Portugal	2	0	1
Spain	14	1	13
Sweden	2	2	2
Switzerland	8	2	8
United Kingdom[a]	6	0	2

[a] The information on U.K. niche parties in this table, as in the rest of the book, does not include Northern Ireland.

Sources: Binghamton Election Results Archive; Mackie and Rose (1991, 1997); Mair (1999).

phenomenon. The number of parties competing in national-level elections has varied, however, from a single example in Ireland to twenty in Italy (Mackie and Rose 1991, 1997).[12] Given that some parties participate only in local and municipal elections, the actual number of niche parties to form is probably much higher. Niche party electoral success has also varied, with 24 percent achieving a peak national vote of over 5 percent and 63 percent holding a seat in a national legislature. This electoral success is not concentrated in a few countries; fourteen countries have had at least one niche party surpass the 5 percent threshold, and all eighteen have had at least one niche party officeholder.[13]

The influence of niche parties is not limited to vote and seat percentages. These parties have shaped the nature of governments and the electoral fortunes of other parties. Almost 12 percent of niche parties have participated in coalition governments, and the participation of over half of those parties was pivotal to the formation of majority governments (Woldendorp, Keman, and Budge 1998). Even in those cases where niche parties have not gained many or any seats, their electoral strength has influenced the vote level of others. The role of the

[12] These numbers are based on those parties reported in a country's official election statistics.
[13] The four countries lacking a niche party with a peak national vote greater than 5 percent are Greece, Ireland, Portugal, and the United Kingdom.

French FN in the legislative victory of the Socialist Party (and the defeat of the Gaullists) in 1997 is just one of many similar examples. Less dramatic but more pervasive, the niche parties' introduction of new issues has changed the content of the political debate and altered the careers of mainstream parties. For instance, the environment and immigration have become standard campaign topics in most Western European countries, topics that the mainstream parties continue to address even in cases where the niche parties that introduced them have disappeared.

STANDARD RESPONSES TO VARIATION IN NEW PARTY ELECTORAL SUCCESS AND THEIR LIMITATIONS

Variation in niche party electoral and legislative strength across Western Europe presents us with a puzzle. Why have some niche parties gained more electoral support than others? Moreover, what determines the timing of the peaks and troughs in the electoral trajectories of these noneconomic, single-issue parties? Although there is no scholarship on the electoral success and failure of niche parties as a *category* of party actors per se, a significant literature has developed to account for the electoral fortunes of parties in general and specific types of niche party (e.g., green, radical right, or ethnoterritorial) in particular. This work focuses on two sets of factors: institutional and sociological conditions.

Institutional Approaches

Based on their role in shaping the political and electoral environment in which a party competes, institutions have earned a prominent place in theories of party systems and individual party success. They provide incentives – opportunities and costs – that are thought to influence voter and elite behavior and, consequently, party support. Proponents of this approach have concentrated mainly on the effect of electoral rules and, to a lesser extent, state structure and governmental type.

Consistent with the work of Duverger (1954), Lijphart (1994), Ordeshook and Shvetsova (1994), and Cox (1997), scholars of green and radical right parties have posited a connection between electoral systems and party success. Applying the logic of Duverger's Law and Hypothesis for party systems to the fortunes of individual parties, Müller-Rommel (1989), Jackman and Volpert (1996), and Golder (2003b) argue that the number of votes received by single-issue parties is positively related to the permissiveness of the electoral rules.[14] Plurality electoral rules reduce the likelihood of third parties obtaining office, thus providing disincentives for voters to support, and elites to serve as candidates for, those minor parties. Proportional representation (PR) rules, conversely, increase the

---

[14] Duverger's Law states, "The simple-majority, single-ballot [i.e., simple plurality rule] system favors the two party system" (Duverger 1954: 217). His more tentative Hypothesis reads as follows: "the simple-majority system with second ballot and proportional representation favor multipartism" (Ibid., 239).

likelihood of minor party seat attainment and, thus, provide incentives for sincere minor party voting. Consequently, green and radical right parties are expected to receive lower vote shares in systems with low district magnitudes and high electoral thresholds and, conversely, higher vote shares in systems with high district magnitudes and low electoral thresholds.[15]

An oft-overlooked exception to Duverger's Law has led to different expectations about the relationship between electoral rules and ethnoterritorial party support. Rae (1971: 95) notes that a two-party system should not emerge "where strong local minorities exist."[16] Sartori (1986: 59) further explains this anomaly:

> Conversely, a two-party format is *impossible* – under whatever electoral system – if racial, linguistic, ideologically alienated, single-issue, or otherwise incoercible minorities (which cannot be represented by two major mass parties) are concentrated in above-plurality proportions in particular constituencies or geographic pockets. If so, the effect of a plurality system will only be reductive vis-à-vis the third parties which do not represent incoercible minorities.

Thus, while most parties are expected to prosper only under permissive electoral systems, this correction suggests that those single-issue parties representing regionally concentrated groups are likely to flourish under more restrictive plurality rules. De Winter (1998: 219) consequently hypothesizes that ethnoterritorial parties gain greater shares of the vote under plurality than PR systems.

Although it is less common, institutional accounts have also considered other system features, such as state structure (unitary vs. federal states) and governmental type (presidentialism vs. parliamentarism), in their explanations of new party fortunes. Harmel and Robertson (1985) and Willey (1998: 93) argue that federal systems are more conducive to minor party success than unitary ones. Their logic is as follows: under federal systems – where governmental power is shared between multiple levels (i.e., local, regional, and national) – there are more elected offices and consequently more opportunities for minor parties to obtain office. The multiplication of representative offices also increases the familiarity of those elected parties with governance, thereby increasing the quality of their candidates. Furthermore, it allows new competitors, such as niche parties, to build up their bases of electoral support and, with that support, their credibility before tackling a national-level seat (Willey 1998: 57). In unitary states, on the other hand, party competition is restricted to the national-level arena, where minor parties do not necessarily have the reputation and degree of grassroots support needed to succeed.

Approaching this question from the study of party system formation, Chhibber and Kollman (2004) similarly expect a positive relationship between federalism and party support, but for different reasons and only for regionally oriented parties. They argue that where political and fiscal authority rests with subnational

---

[15] In contrast to the others, Müller-Rommel (1989) more closely follows Duverger's original dichotomization of electoral systems and focuses on the broad distinction between plurality and PR systems.

[16] A similar argument is made in Riker (1982b: 760).

governments, as is the case in a decentralizing or federal system, there are fewer incentives for parties to coordinate or aggregate across districts and regions to win national office.[17] The result is the emergence of regional party systems and stronger regional parties than in unitary states.[18]

These positive predictions are challenged by scholars of ethnoterritorial parties. According to Levi and Hechter (1985), ethnoterritorial parties, like all niche parties, can benefit from the increased political opportunities and patronage available in a federal or highly decentralized system. They note, however, that because decentralization is a policy goal of ethnoterritorial party actors, the implementation of federalism should appease ethnoterritorial party voters, leading them to abandon the niche party. Jolly (2006) likewise believes in the appeasement effect of decentralization on ethnoterritorial parties, but he argues that a curvilinear relationship exists. Voter mobilization and support for regionalist parties will be lowest, he posits, at middling levels of decentralization, where demands for some regional autonomy have effectively been met. A lack of decentralization and extensive decentralization both will spur voter support for ethnoterritorial parties.

The case for the influence of governmental type on party success is the least well developed or examined in the new party literature. However, the basic argument evident in Shugart and Carey (1992), Lijphart (1994), and Cox (1997) and applied specifically to the question of new party vote in Willey (1998: 58, 94) is that presidentialism depresses support for minor parties in legislative elections because voters do not want to support a candidate whose party is perceived to have no reasonable chance of winning the presidency. This suggests that niche party vote should be higher in parliamentary systems where (1) there are no winner-take-all executive elections and (2) the frequency of coalitions increases the likelihood of niche party politicians' being in government.

Inconsistent Findings. The literature on green, radical right, and, to a lesser extent, ethnoterritorial parties has explored (some of) these general relationships, with conflicting conclusions. In analyses of radical right party vote in Western Europe, Jackman and Volpert (1996), Golder (2003a, 2003b), and Swank and Betz (2003) find that party vote is significantly and positively correlated with the permissiveness of the electoral rules.[19] Similar patterns in the success of green parties come out of the more descriptive work by Müller-Rommel (1989) and

---

[17] Unlike most institutional accounts, Chhibber and Kollman (2004) argue that the actual implementation of an institutional change is not necessary for its effects to be felt; a credible commitment by a government to adopt federalism or to decentralize is all that is necessary for a regional party's vote to increase.

[18] Their prediction applies to all regionalist parties, including but not limited to ethnoterritorial parties. Regional versions of green or radical right parties in decentralizing or federal systems should also be included in this group of parties.

[19] These three studies employ different measures of electoral systems in their statistical analyses. Golder (2003a) argues, however, that Jackman and Volpert (1996) would find little evidence that lower electoral thresholds are positively related to the electoral success of radical right parties if they took conditional standard errors into account.

Taggart (1996). Regarding ethnoterritorial parties, case study analyses by De Winter (1998: 219) find the reverse relationship; as predicted by Rae's correction to Duverger's Law, regionalist actors perform better under plurality than PR rules.

Yet, the existence of causal relationships between institutions and party vote share are challenged by others. Carter's (2005) examination of radical right party support in Western Europe finds little support for these claims; she concludes that neither the effective electoral threshold nor the disproportionality index of an electoral system has any significant effect on the support of these parties. Swank and Betz arrive at similar conclusions in their 1995 and 1996 studies of radical right party support when they test the effect of electoral thresholds and an ordinal measure of proportionality on the vote share of radical right parties. Kitschelt (1989: 25) downplays the centrality of electoral institutions to the success of left-libertarian parties (including green parties):

> The correlation between voting systems and left-libertarian parties is not very neat, since at least five countries with proportional representation do not have significant left-libertarian parties ... although plurality rules do create an impediment to left-libertarian parties, this factor should not be overemphasized.

The limited statistical examination of ethnoterritorial party vote (see Pereira, Villodres, and Nieto 2003) also offers little support for the consistent and determinative role of electoral institutions.[20]

The few analyses that explore the relationship between vote and state structure also provide mixed support for the institutionalist claims.[21] Whereas Jolly (2006) discovers a nonlinear relationship between decentralization and ethnoterritorial party vote, Chhibber and Kollman (2004) find support for a somewhat contradictory claim that regional parties in Canada, Britain (including the Scottish National Party [SNP] in Scotland), India, and the United States receive more support in times of decentralization – both periods of middling and full-fledged federalism – than in times of centralization. Harmel and Robertson (1985) conclude that federalism plays no appreciable role in explaining new party success in general in Western Europe, Canada, the United States, New Zealand, and Australia. And Willey's (1998) analysis of new party cases in Western Europe reveals that federalism, contrary to expectation, actually *decreases* new party support.[22] To my knowledge, no study examines the effect of government type on green, radical right, or ethnoterritorial party vote share in Western Europe.

Accompanying the empirical ambiguities evident in these analyses are the theoretical limitations of institutional approaches for explaining niche party fortunes.

---

[20] The negative relationship between proportional systems and ethnoterritorial party vote that Pereira, Villodres, and Nieto (2003) find in bivariate analysis disappears when they examine specific aspects of these electoral systems in multivariate analysis.

[21] Being a theoretical piece, the Levi and Hechter (1985) chapter does not test this hypothesis.

[22] Unlike the other scholars, Willey (1998) measures new party support as seat percentage in the national legislature. This discrepancy must be taken into consideration when weighing his unexpected findings.

As some of the empirical analyses demonstrate, differences in electoral rules and possibly in the degree of state centralization may help to explain the poor performance of a green, radical right, or ethnoterritorial party in one country and the strong performance of its counterpart in another. However, these institutions are unable to account for two key dimensions of the niche party story: variation in electoral success across a party's lifetime and variation in the electoral success across parties in one country. As largely static factors, these institutions cannot explain why, for example, voter support for the Swedish green party changed over time, or why support for the radical right Austrian Freedom Party (FPÖ) was higher than for its green party compatriots.

There are, of course, exceptions to the fixed nature of institutions; electoral rules or state structure do change – or rather, are changed. In France, the two-ballot plurality system was replaced by PR for the 1986 legislative elections, an institutional change that played a role in the sharp increase in the radical right Front National's vote in that election. Yet, while the changeability of these factors may overcome the aforementioned shortcoming in some cases, this mutability serves to highlight another limitation of the institutional approach. Namely, institutions are not as exogenous to electoral competition as generally portrayed by this literature (e.g., Chhibber and Kollman 2004; Cox 1997; Lijphart 1994; Samuels 2002).[23] Rather, they are chosen by parties and governments over other options for specific purposes. They are neither neutral nor independent of the process.[24] As this book argues, institutions are part of a party's strategic repertoire. To the extent that institutions alter or are designed to alter niche party support, they cannot be separated from strategic theories of party fortune.

Sociological Approaches

Whereas institutional arguments view party support as a function of the independent structure of the electoral and political system, a second set of theories, which I term *sociological theories*, locate the determinants of party success in the salience of the party's issue(s). This approach has been widely used in the research on green, radical right, and ethnoterritorial parties, often in conjunction with institutional factors. According to these theories, the vote share received by a green, radical right, or ethnoterritorial party depends on the resonance of its issue position with a particular electorate, where voter receptivity is a direct product of the objective cultural and socio-economic conditions of a society and its population.

---

[23] Although there is a recent literature exploring why electoral institutions are adopted (e.g., Andrews and Jackman 2005; Benoit 2004; Boix 1998), its insights about institutional endogeneity have not yet been incorporated into the work on new party fortunes. Earlier work by Levi and Hechter (1985) on the emergence and success of ethnoterritorial parties did consider how the state (and its government) could use decentralization schemes to alter the electoral support of these regionalist niche parties. Some of their insights on the use of institutions as policy appeasement strategies inform the model of competition between unequals discussed in this book.

[24] I borrow this language of institutional nonneutrality from Huber (1996: 1).

Issue salience, and thus niche party vote, is thought to be exogenous to political competition.

Researchers have looked to measures of economic prosperity, value orientation, and immigrant prevalence to determine the size of a niche party's electorate and to ascertain the auspiciousness of a political environment for party success. In contrast to institutional explanations, the predictions of this literature (and even the preferred indicators of these economic conditions) vary by type of niche party. Based on the belief that quality of life issues, such as the environment, will become salient only when societies or no longer preoccupied with mere economic survival, green party vote is expected to be positively correlated with high gross domestic product (GDP) per captia and, to a lesser extent, low unemployment (Müller-Rommel 1996; Taggart 1996). This same relationship suggests that green party vote will be drawn disproportionately from the more economically prosperous segments of a society (Kitschelt 1988).

Conversely, the immigration issue becomes more salient – and radical right parties, more electorally attractive – under conditions of economic insecurity, most often defined as high unemployment (Jackman and Volpert 1996; Lubbers et al. 2002; Swank and Betz 2003). This hypothesis stems from two related claims. First, support for radical right parties is thought to be drawn disproportionately from the economically and socially marginalized, which includes the unemployed (Kitschelt 1995: 21). The second contention is that radical right voters believe that immigration and immigrants cause unemployment; thus, an increase in unemployment will positively influence support for these anti-immigrant parties.[25] Based on the latter claim, Golder (2003b) proposes a revision to the direct connection expected between unemployment and radical right party vote. He argues that the effect of unemployment is conditional on the percentage of foreign citizens in a country, and he expects that unemployment should have a positive influence on radical right party support only when immigrant levels are high.

Conflicting expectations about the effects of economic health on vote emerge from the work on ethnoterritorial parties. Like the research on green and radical right party vote, this literature views economic conditions as shaping the priorities of the electorate. However, a disagreement exists over whether ethnoterritorial party vote share is encouraged by the relative economic deprivation or relative economic prosperity of a region and ethnic group. According to the theory of internal colonialism (e.g., Hechter 1975), regional, or "peripheral," identities develop in reaction to economic repression from the "core." It follows that ethnic mobilization and, by extension, vote for an ethnoterritorial party should be higher in regions that are poorer (lower GDP per capita and higher unemployment)

[25] As Golder (2003b: 438) notes, "there is little theoretical or empirical evidence to support the claim that immigration actually causes unemployment." However, as he further argues, it is perception rather than fact that drives voters' behavior. Immigrants become easy scapegoats for those facing unemployment.

than the capital or the country as a whole. Proponents of the theory of overtaxed development (Fearon and van Houten 2002; Gourevitch 1979; Jolly 2006), on the other hand, posit that voters will demand greater regional autonomy and support a niche party that promotes autonomy when their region is economically better off than the country as a whole.[26]

Beyond direct measures of the economy, theories of green party vote, in particular, have also considered the indirect effects of economic prosperity on an individual's, or country's, value orientation and vote. Starting with the ideas formulated by Maslow, Inglehart (1971, 1994, 1997) claims that adolescent socialization under conditions of material and physical security has resulted in "the shift away from *materialist* concerns . . . toward greater emphasis on freedom, self expression, and quality of life, or *post-materialist* values" (Inglehart 1994: 336). Individuals possessing postmaterialist values are more receptive than materialists to the political messages offered by social movements and, thus, should form the natural electorate of green parties.[27] Consequently, Inglehart (1997), Taggart (1996), and Müller-Rommel (1996) expect that the level of postmaterialism in a country should be positively correlated with green party vote.[28]

Just as scholars of green parties have focused on value orientation as an indicator of voter receptivity to environmental programs and their political advocates, researchers of radical right parties have considered how the prevalence of immigrants alters voter support for anti-immigrant parties. While each measures the independent variable slightly differently, Swank and Betz (2003), Givens (2005), Golder (2003b), and Lubbers et al. (2002) all argue that radical right party vote should be positively related to the degree of immigrant presence in a country.[29]

Limitations of Sociological Theories. Although more amenable to explaining changes in electoral support over time than their institutional counterparts, sociological theories also have their explanatory limitations. First, empirical analyses of these claims have yielded conflicting results. Following the expectations

---

[26] The overtaxed development argument typically frames the situation as one in which a region pays more taxes to the national government than it receives back in the form of subventions.

[27] Other proponents of this theory include Taggart 1996 and Müller-Rommel 1996. The association of postmaterialism with environmental support is criticized, however, by Kreuzer in his 1990 study of the factors leading to the emergence and electoral advancement of the Swiss and Austrian Greens.

[28] An extension of this argument is that radical right party support, being predicated on economic insecurities, should be higher among materialists. This is consistent with the claim that radical right parties developed as a backlash against postmaterialism (see Ignazi 1992; Kitschelt 1995). However, this argument is rarely advocated or tested by scholars of radical right vote (note its absence in Carter 2005; Givens 2005; Golder 2003a, 2003b; Jackman and Volpert 1996). The literature expresses no expectation about the relationship between value orientation and ethnoterritorial party vote.

[29] Golder (2003b) and Givens (2005) use measures of the percentage of foreign citizens in a country's population, whereas Lubbers et al. (2002) and Swank and Betz (2003) focus their analyses on the percentage of non–European Union citizens and percentage of refugees and asylum seekers, respectively, in a population.

of this class of theories, Taggart (1996) and Müller-Rommel (1996) find green party support to be positively correlated with GDP per capita, and Jackman and Volpert (1996) conclude that radical right party support increases with the level of unemployment. Work by Jolly (2006) also suggests the power of economic variables, specifically, the power of the overtaxed development theory; he finds that ethnoterritorial party support is higher in relatively prosperous regions.

However, the analyses performed by Swank and Betz (2003) and Givens (2005) reveal that the relationships between economic conditions and radical right party vote hold only under limited circumstances. The former finds that the positive effect is produced by youth unemployment, not unemployment in general. According to the latter, unemployment proves a significant predictor of vote in Austria and France but not in Germany. Similarly, Golder (2003b) finds support for the positive effect of unemployment but only for the populist subset of radical right parties and only when immigrant prevalence is high. His results show that unemployment actually *reduces* the vote share of neofascist parties when the percentage of foreign citizens is low. More troubling for the theory, Lubbers et al. (2002) find, in an examination of the full set of radical right parties in the European Union (EU) and Norway, that unemployment has a *negative* effect on anti-immigrant party vote.

The results are more favorable for the other two sociological factors. Descriptive studies by Inglehart (1997), Dalton (1996), and Müller-Rommel (1996) conclude that postmaterialism positively affects support for green parties. Likewise, a number of scholars (Givens 2005; Lubbers et al. 2002; Swank and Betz 2003) conclude that higher percentages of foreign citizens in a country lead to higher levels of radical right party vote. Golder (2003b) finds, however, that this positive result applies only to populist radical right parties.

The lack of consistent findings, especially across analyses of radical right party support, is troubling. Also problematic for this set of explanations is the fact that the mechanism by which sociological variables affect vote and voter behavior is not well specified in this literature. An assumption is made that objective societal conditions automatically translate into voter preferences for specific parties. Yet, why should an increase in economic prosperity naturally lead voters to cast ballots for environmental parties, parties that explicitly eschew economic platforms? Why should increasing unemployment translate into greater support for radical right parties? There is no empirical evidence corroborating the claim that unemployment is linked to immigrant levels (Golder 2003b), so why do so many voters believe it and vote for anti-immigrant parties when unemployment rises?

The answers to these questions lie in the behavior of political actors. In contrast to the claims of sociological theories, the connections between societal conditions and vote choice do not form naturally; they are forged by political slogans such as "2 million unemployed, 2 million immigrants" or the even more obvious "eliminate unemployment, stop immigration" (Betz 1990). That is, they are the product of party behavior. And as research on political campaigns (Kingdon 1995; Petrocik 1996; Zaller 1992) has taught us, these linkages are therefore subject to manipulation and appropriation by others.

A STRATEGIC PARTY EXPLANATION OF NICHE PARTY FORTUNE

This book picks up the story of niche party success and failure where institutional and sociological explanations end. The limitations of these dominant approaches suggest that niche party vote is not simply the product of the electoral rules, state structure, and socio-economic conditions of a country. This book looks to the role of political actors and, specifically, the strategic behavior of the mainstream parties. While niche parties are not completely unaccountable for their performances, their fates are not independent of the actions of others.[30] The central argument of this study is that the strategies of the electorally dominant, governmental parties of the center-left and center-right are critical determinants of niche party fortunes.

Although consideration of the strategic behavior of parties is relatively rare in studies of new party success,[31] an extensive literature on strategic behavior (e.g., Adams et al. 2005; Downs 1957; Enelow and Hinich 1984) has long recognized that political parties can alter the attractiveness and distinctiveness of themselves and others. Focused almost exclusively on interaction between equal-sized, economically oriented mainstream parties, standard spatial approaches typically view party fortune as a function of policy positions; a party increases or decreases its vote share and the vote shares of its competitors by moving along an existing issue dimension or within a fixed issue space.

This prolific literature has been useful in explaining how mainstream parties spar with their mainstream party opponents. However, niche parties are fundamentally different from their mainstream party competitors. The emergence of these parties promoting previously undiscussed single issues has highlighted the fact that parties, and mainstream parties in particular, have access to additional tools – overlooked by standard spatial theories – with which to shape the competitiveness of their opponents and themselves. This book recognizes that in addition to shifting their position on a given issue dimension, parties also compete by altering the salience and ownership of issue dimensions in the political arena.

---

[30] Generalizable theories about the role of niche parties in their own electoral fortunes have not been articulated in the literature. However, individual works on green, radical right, or ethnoterritorial parties (e.g., Carter 2005; Kitschelt 1989; O'Neill 1997) have identified specific party characteristics as contributing to party electoral failure, the most commonly mentioned being a party's organizational disunity. Yet, while internal party divisions can cause incoherent party campaigns and even lead to splits in the original parties, these niche party characteristics are not necessarily independent of the actions of other parties in the political arena; they can be exacerbated or even created by others. For example, the conflict within many green parties in Western Europe over whether to pursue a more pragmatic, conciliatory "realo" approach as opposed to a purist "fundi" path of isolation was typically provoked by a mainstream party's offer of coalition formation. This suggests that, to find the explanation for neophyte fortunes, one must look beyond the niche party to the dominant parties in the system.

[31] Among hundreds of works on new party success, the few that discuss strategic approaches include Bale 2003, Carter 2005, Givens 2005, Harmel and Svasand 1997, Hug 2001, Kitschelt 1994, and Rohrschneider 1993.

Niche parties are particularly vulnerable to such tactics by mainstream parties. First, as niche parties advance only one issue, their support turns on the salience, attractiveness, and ownership of that single issue. Unlike mainstream parties espousing multiple issues, therefore, niche parties cannot boost their vote by emphasizing another issue already in their platform. Second, studies suggest that the niche party's position on that one issue is relatively fixed. Adams et al. (2006) find that green, radical right, and communist parties tend to move less than mainstream parties, and that when they do, they are punished more electorally than their more mobile, established party opponents.[32] Although this does not mean that niche parties have no capacity for strategy, it does indicate that their ability to respond to mainstream party tactics on their single issue dimension is limited.[33] According to Adams et al. (2006: 526), these parties are "'prisoners of their ideologies' – they have no real choice other than to cling to the policy ground they have staked out for themselves."

Niche party susceptibility is further exacerbated by the electoral, governmental, and media dominance of their mainstream party competitors. First, mainstream parties have more legislative experience and governmental effectiveness than niche parties and therefore are more likely to gain ownership of an issue. Second, the established parties generally benefit from greater access to the voters, whether through traditional means such as formal associations with unions or more modern conduits including party or governmental control over the media. As a result, the mainstream parties are able to publicize their issue positions more easily and influence voter perceptions of issue salience and ownership. Even in countries where these formal linkages do not exist, the preponderance of mainstream over niche party activists generally ensures that the message, or strategy, of the mainstream party dominates that of the niche party.[34]

With niche parties especially vulnerable to the manipulation of issue salience and ownership by mainstream parties, my new conception of party strategies has significant ramifications for competition between political unequals and niche party vote. If parties can increase or decrease the importance of specific issues for voter decisions and can undermine or reinforce the credibility of parties' positions on those issues (i.e., their issue ownership), competition is no longer limited to

[32] While only one indicator, their relative policy immobility suggests that niche parties may be policy- rather than vote- or office-seekers.

[33] A niche party may be strategic in its choice of policy stance or even its issue. Alternatively, a niche party could try to level the playing field by fundamentally changing its identity. With mainstream parties able to undermine niche party vote by dismissing the importance of its single issue or co-opting the issue position and ownership of its single issue, a strategic niche party might be encouraged to adopt positions on additional issue dimensions, thus transforming itself into a multi-issue party. However, there is currently no evidence of such fundamental transformations of niche parties in advanced industrial democracies. And it is not clear that ideological diversification would be a successful tactic for boosting the competitiveness of the niche parties. Further research into this possible path of party strategy is needed, especially as the niche party phenomenon ages.

[34] Mainstream party activists are also generally better integrated into society than those of the neophyte party.

programmatically proximal parties. Contrary to the claims of standard spatial theories, mainstream parties can respond to and affect the electoral fortunes of niche parties anywhere in the political space. Consequently, a niche party's success can be shaped by the behavior of multiple – proximal *and* nonproximal – mainstream parties. This theoretical insight allows us to finally understand why certain niche parties have been successful despite the co-optative efforts of their political neighbors.

Furthermore, my modified spatial theory of party interaction – the Position, Salience, and Ownership (PSO) theory – implies that mainstream parties are not using strategies only to undermine those niche parties threatening their vote. Mainstream parties can also bolster the support of niche parties who threaten the vote of their mainstream party opponents. Thus, niche parties are either targets themselves or weapons used to hurt other, typically larger, parties. This study therefore provides a new mechanism by which mainstream parties shape the electoral fortunes of their political equals as well as their political unequals.

In addition to revising the standard spatial conception of party competition, this book also examines the motivation and capability of political parties to adopt and implement these strategies. One finding of this study is that the tactical response of a mainstream party is not simply a reflection of the niche party's national vote share. A niche party's electoral threat and thus the behavior of the mainstream parties depend on the percentage of votes the niche party is stealing from one mainstream party relative to another and the importance of those votes to the established parties. Consequently, this study can explain, for example, why the British Labour and Conservative parties would pursue costly strategies against a radical right competitor, the National Front, that garnered an average of only 0.2 percent nationally. However, this book also shows that strategies are not adopted in a void. A mainstream party's choice of a particular strategy is constrained by both the tactical maneuvering of other parties in the system and the capacity of the strategizing party to overcome internal division and decision-making impasses.

METHODOLOGY AND CASE SELECTION

To understand the how and the why of niche party success and failure, this book explores the electoral trajectories of green, radical right, and ethnoterritorial parties in Western Europe. These parties are the archetypal single-issue actors to have emerged around the world over the last thirty years. Their high concentration, long history, and variation in electoral and governmental success across and within the countries of Western Europe provide a critical opportunity for evaluating the PSO strategic theory of niche party fortune.

With the goal of explaining general trends across niche parties as well as specific niche party puzzles, this study brings together two complementary approaches that are typically employed separately in the parties literature: it marries cross-national statistical analyses of niche party support with in-depth case studies of green, radical right, and ethnoterritorial parties. To test the predictions of my

PSO theory of strategic competition, I conduct a statistical analysis of niche party vote share using an original data set covering the tactics of thirty-five mainstream parties toward fifty-five niche parties in seventeen Western European countries from 1970 to 1998.[35] The data set also includes information on institutional and sociological conditions, allowing me to test the dominant alternative explanations. Whereas most of the work on single-issue parties consists of one-party or one-country qualitative studies, and the existing quantitative research restricts its cross-national examinations to one type of niche party, [36] the statistical analyses of this new data set permit broad conclusions to be drawn about the determinants of niche party support across niche party types, in addition to across countries and over time.

Complementing the statistical analyses are comparative case studies of green, radical right, and ethnoterritorial parties in Britain and France. Whereas the large-N analyses allow us to examine the effect of strategies, the detailed examinations of competition between unequals reveal why parties adopted particular tactics, thus permitting the testing of my theory of strategic choice. Information drawn from party and governmental archives and interviews with political party elite plus electoral and survey data are used to uncover the motivations of the mainstream parties and the constraints they faced in their interactions with the niche parties over multiple rounds of elections. Not only is this information critical to understanding the choices made by the established parties, but it also supplements the findings of the statistical analyses on the effects and effectiveness of the chosen strategies on niche party success.

Furthermore, the case studies provide an additional means to test the power of the PSO theory of party competition.[37] Although the quantitative analyses are able to show that certain tactics lead to an increase or decrease in a niche party's vote, they cannot test *how* that happens. The detailed accounts of mainstream party–niche party interaction allow me to examine explicitly the mechanism linking strategies to niche party support. Using public opinion data, I can determine, for each election, whether mainstream tactics affect the new party's vote by altering levels of issue salience and ownership in addition to shifting party policy positions. In other words, I can directly test whether strategies follow my modified spatial or the standard spatial logic.

Reliance on case studies to test theories and determine causal factors requires close consideration of case selection. As Mill (1843), Lijphart (1975), and Eckstein (1975) have taught us, case studies are useful for testing propositions only if they can yield conclusive findings, unmuddied by multiple causal mechanisms or intervening variables. With this goal in mind, the book explores in-depth three

---

[35] An eighteenth country, Iceland, is excluded from the statistical analyses because its green party did not contest multiple, consecutive elections in the period under investigation.

[36] The exceptions are Harmel and Robertson (1985) and Hug (2001), who examine the emergence and, to a lesser extent, the success of all new parties, which include, but are not restricted to, niche parties.

[37] These case studies also reveal differences in the specific forms of tactics employed by established parties – a level of detail that cannot be captured in the statistical analysis.

niche parties in two countries: the Green Party and the ethnoterritorial Scottish National Party in Britain and the radical right Front National in France.[38]

Niche parties from Britain and France were selected to maximize the similarity of their institutional environments – following the most similar systems research design – and to represent "hard cases" for my strategic theory.[39] Of the six Western European countries with all three types of single-issue parties, Britain and France emerge as one of the structurally similar pairs.[40] Both countries have restrictive electoral systems with district magnitudes of one[41] and highly unitary state structures that were eventually decentralized during our period of study. Also relevant to this study, the mainstream party landscapes of these countries are comparable: both possess center-left, center, and center-right parties with developed party organizations.

These institutional similarities increase the likelihood of isolating and ascertaining the effect of strategic variables across the cases. But, according to the alternative explanations, their restrictive electoral climates also make these countries least likely environments in which to see niche party success, to witness the effects of mainstream party strategies on niche party vote, or even to observe mainstream parties reacting at all. In other words, these countries were chosen in order to test the strategic theory of niche party vote under the most difficult circumstances. According to the institutional theories, not only are nonregionally based niche parties *not* expected to emerge under these conditions, but in the event that these parties develop, the restrictiveness of the electoral environment should discourage mainstream parties from pursuing costly strategies against them; where niche parties are not expected to flourish, it is thought that such behavior is unnecessary and unlikely to affect the already disadvantaged niche parties. And yet, as the electoral results of the British and French niche parties in Table 1.2 suggest and the case analyses in the book will discuss, niche parties develop, often engender costly and extensive responses from the mainstream parties in Britain and France, and are sometimes successful. Such results in these "hard cases" of mainstream party–niche party interaction suggest that strategies will matter in the "more likely" cases as well (Eckstein 1975: 118).

To understand better how British and French single-issue parties succeeded (and failed) under sometimes hostile conditions, I chose three niche party cases

---

[38] Comparisons are made in Chapter 8 to the French Green, British radical right (National Front), and French ethnoterritorial (Union Démocratique Bretonne) parties.

[39] Although the institutional features of Britain and France are fairly similar, the two countries would ideally also possess similar sociological conditions to control for those factors. When compared with countries in other regions of the world and even some countries in Western Europe, the economic health of these two countries is comparable. However, there are some differences in their absolute levels of GDP per capita and unemployment between 1970 and 1998. Given the party literature's greater focus on institutional factors, I have chosen to prioritize institutional similarities when selecting my comparative cases. The relevance of these sociological differences for accounting for variation in niche party success across countries will be addressed in the case studies and Chapter 8.

[40] The six countries are Belgium, France, Italy, Spain, Switzerland, and the United Kingdom.

[41] The 1986 French national assembly elections conducted under PR rules being the exception.

TABLE 1.2. *Electoral Fortunes of Niche Parties in Britain and France, 1970–2000*

Country	Niche Party	Average National Vote in Legislative Elections	Peak Vote (year)
Britain	Green Party	0.2%[a]	0.5% (1992)
	National Front	0.2%[a]	0.6% (1979)
	Scottish National Party	1.7%, or 18.8% of Scottish vote	2.9%, or 30.4% of Scottish vote (October 1974)
	Plaid Cymru	0.5%, or 9.4% of Welsh vote	0.6%, or 11.5% of Welsh vote (1970)
France	Les Verts/La Génération Écologie	3.2%	7.7% (1993)
	Front National	8.0%	14.9% (1997)
	Union Démocratique Bretonne	0.03%, or 0.6% of Breton vote	0.07%, or 1.27% of Breton vote (1997)
	Unione di u Populu Corsu	0.05%, or 9.8% of Corsican vote	0.1%, or 21% of Corsican vote (1993)

[a] Especially in the British cases, the nonregional niche parties did not always contest all constituencies. Considering the votes of these parties from only those constituencies contested, the vote average and peak vote of the parties are as follows: British Green Party: average vote (1.0%) and peak vote (1.4% in 1987); British National Front: average vote (1.8%) and peak vote (3.6% in 1970).

Sources: Author's files; BDSP; Butler and Butler 2000; http://elections.figaro.net/popup_2004/accueil.html; Mackie and Rose 1991, 1997.

that maximize variation on the dependent variable. The British Green Party, with an average national vote of 0.2 percent and a peak vote of only 0.5 percent, never escaped electoral marginality; the French Front National captured an average score of 8 percent and rose to be the number three party in France; and the Scottish National Party, with a peak score of 30.4 percent and an average of 18.8 percent of the Scottish vote, edged out the Conservatives to become the second-place party in the region.[42] Further variation exists in the shape of their electoral trajectories. While the vote shares of the British Greens rose then fell and those of the Scottish National Party peaked, declined, and then grew again, the French Front National increased monotonically across the 1980s and 1990s. That a supposedly disadvantaged radical right party gained high levels of continually rising vote shares while a similarly "disadvantaged" nonregional green party failed to achieve minimal levels of support poses a puzzle. Add to that the waxing and waning of the vote level of an institutionally "advantaged" ethnoterritorial party, and these cases become important testing grounds for strategic theories of mainstream party behavior and niche party vote.

[42] Throughout the book, with the exception of Table 1.1, I will cite the percentage of *regional* vote when I am discussing the vote share obtained by ethnoterritorial parties.

ORGANIZATION OF THE BOOK

To solve the puzzles of niche party success and failure, the book explores the strategic tools available to mainstream parties and how they use strategies to shape both the electoral fortunes of niche parties and their own electoral security. In Chapter 2, I develop the PSO theory of party competition, which recognizes that mainstream parties facing unequal competitors have access to a wider and more effective set of strategies than that posited by standard spatial models. Rather than being restricted to policy moves on existing issue dimensions, mainstream parties, I argue, can also manipulate the salience of the niche party's new issue and the ownership of its position on that dimension. Several ramifications follow, leading to a conception of competition in which mainstream parties can either eliminate a threatening niche party opponent or bolster the niche party's support to use it as a weapon against mainstream party opponents. The chapter concludes with the PSO theory's testable hypotheses of the effects of these reconceptualized strategies on niche party vote.

Using evidence from political parties in seventeen Western European countries from 1970 to 1998, Chapter 3 tests the ability of my strategic interaction model to predict the electoral fortunes of niche parties. The analysis also measures the explanatory power of my model against that of competing institutional, sociological, and other strategic theories. These cross-sectional time-series analyses confirm that the strategic behavior of mainstream parties better accounts for intertemporal variations in support within and across the set of green, radical right, and ethnoterritorial parties than the dominant institutional and sociological explanations. Moreover, the evidence suggests that my reconceptualized view of strategies outperforms spatial models of party interaction, better capturing how mainstream parties undermine and bolster niche party electoral performance. By recognizing that strategies are not just designed to alter a party's issue position, this chapter unravels some of the mysteries of niche party failure and success that have been heretofore unexplained.

Having ascertained that strategies matter, I turn to the next logical question: under what conditions do established parties adopt and implement particular strategies? In Chapter 4, I develop a theory of strategic choice based on the relative threat posed by a niche party to one mainstream party over another in a given electoral system. One implication of this model is that a niche party drawing 5 percent of a mainstream party's vote may be more threatening and merit a more active mainstream party strategic response than a niche party taking 10 percent. In addition, this theory explicitly recognizes that party leaders do not choose strategies in a vacuum. Following a game theoretic logic, the chapter examines how the choice of a particular strategy is constrained by both the tactical maneuvering of other parties in the system and a party's own capacity to overcome internal division.

Chapters 5 through 7 examine in detail the electoral trajectories of the Green Party in Britain, the French Front National, and the Scottish National Party. These case studies provide a testing ground for the theory of strategic choice.

Drawing on survey data and interview and archival material from extensive field research, these chapters uncover the strategic responses of British and French mainstream parties to the green, radical right, and ethnoterritorial parties, revealing the motivations of the mainstream parties and the internal party features that constrained their actions.

These in-depth case studies also confirm the central role of mainstream party tactics in shaping the electoral trajectories of the British Green Party, the French Front National, and the Scottish National Party. Chapters 5 through 7 elucidate the mechanism by which my modified spatial strategies work. Chapter 5 demonstrates how the consistent implementation of accommodative tactics transfers issue ownership away from the Green Party, ultimately reducing its support. However, as the cases of the French Front National and Scottish National Party emphasize, the effectiveness of strategies is subject to internal and external constraints. Internal factionalism undermines an accommodative party's short- *and* long-term prospects of capturing issue ownership. Strategic out-maneuvering by a mainstream party opponent likewise mitigates or even erases the intended impact of an established party's behavior.

The findings of these chapters match the expectations of my strategic PSO theory: changes in the political importance of the environmental, anti-immigrant, and decentralization issues and their niche party proponents result primarily from the strategic behavior of the mainstream parties, not institutional or sociological conditions. Moreover, in contrast to the claims of standard spatial theories, the success of niche parties depends on the strategic interaction of ideologically proximal and distant mainstream parties and their position-, salience-, and ownership-altering tactics.

Chapter 8 tests the generalizability of my findings within and across regions. Comparisons of the three cases examined in Chapters 5 through 7 to other British and French niche parties confirm the central role of mainstream party behavior in niche party vote. I also extend my analyses of the PSO theory to party competition and niche party fortunes in other, non-European advanced industrial democracies, specifically examining the influence of mainstream party strategy on the electoral trajectories of the Green Party in the United States and the radical right One Nation party in Australia.

Chapter 9 presents a summary of the book's argument and its main findings on the electoral success of niche parties. It then concludes with a discussion of the larger implications of this study of political unequals for the long-run competition between mainstream party *equals*.

2

Position, Salience, and Ownership

A Strategic Theory of Niche Party Success

The varied electoral success of green, radical right, and ethnoterritorial parties across Western Europe is the result of mainstream party strategies. This is the thesis introduced in Chapter 1. Contrary to the dominant literature, I argue that the electoral trajectories of niche parties are not mere reflections of the institutional or sociological characteristics of a country. These successes and failures are rather the result of deliberate attempts by center-left and center-right political actors to quell new political threats and bolster their own electoral competitiveness. Niche party fortunes are, in many respects, the by-products of competition between mainstream parties.

And yet existing strategic theories of party competition prove ill-suited for understanding the nature of interaction between mainstream parties and their neophyte competitors. Unlike their mainstream party opponents, niche parties refuse to compete within the given policy dimensions, instead promoting and competing on new issues that often cut across existing partisan lines. Consequently, mainstream party reactions are not limited to the standard spatial tools of policy convergence and divergence – i.e., movement toward and away from a competitor – on an established issue dimension. Rather, mainstream parties can also alter niche party electoral support by manipulating the salience and ownership of the neophyte's new issue for political competition.

In this chapter, I challenge the standard spatial approach to party interaction by developing a theory of party competition based on this expanded conception of party strategies. I argue that, by manipulating the importance and perceived ownership of issue dimensions, mainstream parties have access to a wider and more effective range of tactics than previously thought. In addition, competition is no longer restricted to ideologically proximal parties; parties can affect the competitiveness of challengers anywhere in the political arena. I then spell out the implications of this theory for the electoral fortunes of niche parties, noting the constraints to the effectiveness of mainstream party strategies. I conclude the chapter with a summary of the testable hypotheses of my PSO theory of competition between unequals.

UNDERSTANDING PARTY INTERACTION

A logical place to start an analysis of any type of competition is with the following questions: Who are the players? What tools are available to them? And what are the effects of these tools? The first question has already been addressed in Chapter 1: to understand the electoral trajectories of niche parties, I argue that we need to examine the behavior of the mainstream parties; their dominance in the electoral, governmental, and even media arenas provides them with credibility and voter access unavailable to niche parties. In other words, the focus of this analysis is on competition between the dominant parties of the center-left and center-right and their niche party opponents.

However, the answers to the next two questions are less obvious. Although these questions have been repeatedly asked and answered with regard to competition between equals, the development of niche parties has altered the nature of party interaction. Lacking significant numbers of partisans, niche parties have attracted voters largely on the basis of issues, not pre-existing party loyalties.[1] And in a period of declining partisan loyalties (Dalton 2000), the presence of policy-peddling niche parties has reinforced the importance of issues in voter decisions for all parties (Franklin et al. 1992).[2] Also, within issue-based competition, the niche parties' new policy dimensions are challenging the perceived primacy of the standard, economically defined Left-Right spectrum. In sum, voters are rejecting the traditional partisanship and economic bases of party selection – factors that have shaped mainstream party behavior in the past. In light of these changes, we cannot assume that mainstream parties facing niche parties are restricted to the same set of tools that they have relied on, or have been thought to rely on, in competition with other mainstream parties. Moreover, we cannot assume that the effectiveness of the existing tactics will be the same when employed against a niche party. A re-examination of party tactics is in order.

Bases of Voter Support

An exploration of the range and effectiveness of party tactics begins by considering the factors governing voter decisions. This step is important because understanding why a voter supports a given party provides clues as to how party success can be manipulated. Or, seen from a different perspective, knowing why a niche party gains votes helps us understand better how mainstream parties can alter neophyte competitiveness.

In situations of issue-based party competition – such as those developing in Western Europe since 1970 – where voters cast their ballots based on policies,

---

[1] Evidence of the primacy of issue-based support – and, specifically, single-issue-based support – for niche parties can be found, for example, in Ivarsflaten (2005) and Lubbers et al. (2002) and will be presented in Chapters 5 through 7.

[2] While not the only cause, niche parties have facilitated the decline of partisan politics because they provided dealigned voters with previously unavailable electoral choices.

rather than class loyalties or partisanship,[3] voter support for a party depends on three conditions:

1. The party's issue is considered salient, or important.
2. The party's position on a given issue is attractive.
3. The party is perceived to be the rightful "owner" of that policy stance.

If any of these conditions fails to hold – if the party's issue dimension is considered irrelevant, its issue position is unappealing, or the party lacks credibility on that issue position – the voter will not support the party on the basis of that issue. Where a party professes policy stances on several issues, a voter might repeat this assessment for each of those issue dimensions before arriving at a decision. However, should the party take a stand or be known for its stand on only *one* issue, as is the case for a niche party, then failure to fulfill the three criteria on that one dimension will cost the party electoral support.

Facets of Party Strategy

Altering Party Position. Traditional theories of party strategy have focused almost exclusively on how mainstream parties can affect the second of these necessary conditions; their attention has been drawn to how parties manipulate the attractiveness of their issue positions. According to Downsian spatial theory (Downs 1957), the most renowned strategic approach to party competition, party behavior is limited to movement along existing policy dimensions. Based on the assumption that voters are rational and will support the party with policy preferences most similar to their own, political parties will choose policy positions that minimize the distance between themselves and the voters.[4]

In this framework, parties are faced with two possible strategies: movement toward (policy convergence) or movement away from (policy divergence) a specific competitor. Considered the primary tool in party interaction, policy convergence, or what I call an *accommodative strategy*, is typically employed by parties hoping to draw voters away from a threatening competitor.[5] At its extreme, such behavior can result in the obliteration of the threatening party.[6] Conversely, by increasing the policy distance between parties, policy divergence, or what I term an *adversarial strategy*, encourages voter flight to the competing party.

Altering Issue Salience. The positional conception of party behavior has become the dominant lens through which to understand political competition. However,

---

[3] Dalton 2000; Franklin et al. 1992.

[4] The degree to which parties will move depends on whether they are vote- or office-seeking. For a more extensive discussion of the different implications of these goals, see Strøm 1990.

[5] The term *accommodation* has its origins in the literature on ethnoterritorial parties. I follow its use of the word: accommodation is behavior designed to satisfy or pacify a competitor in order to reduce its threat to the political party and party system (Rudolph and Thompson 1989).

[6] To quote Downs (1957: 118), when faced with a threatening party challenger, "Party B must adopt some of Party C's policies, thus . . . taking the wind out of Party C's sails. This will cause Party C to collapse."

it is not without limitations. As discussed earlier in this chapter, voters' decisions do not turn solely on the proximity of political parties on a given issue dimension. The salience, or perceived importance, of the issue dimensions defining the political space also matters. Voters will discount the attractiveness of a party's position if they find the overall issue to be unimportant; proximity, therefore, becomes irrelevant if the underlying policy dimension is not salient.

Although spatial theorists have considered the ramifications of unequally weighted issue dimensions for voting and party fortunes (see, for example, Enelow and Hinich 1984; Hinich and Munger 1997), they generally have not drawn any connection between issue salience and party strategy. Questions posed about whether a party moves closer to or farther away from an electoral competitor on a given issue have not been preceded by the cognitively prior question of whether a party recognizes and validates the issue dimension presented by that competitor. Standard spatial approaches explicitly assume that the salience of those issue axes is exogenously given and remains fixed during party competition.

Yet research calls into question the validity of these assumptions. Issue salience is neither an inherent property of a topic, nor – contra the claims of sociological theories – a direct reflection of the characteristics and conditions of a society.[7] Rather, the importance of an issue dimension is subject to manipulation.

This view of salience as a dimension of party strategy has been the focus of theoretical and empirical work that has arisen over the last thirty years in reaction to spatial theories. Studies of party competition have shown that parties themselves can enhance or undermine the salience of the political dimensions (Budge, Robertson, and Hearl 1987; Rabinowitz and Macdonald 1989; Riker 1982a, 1986, 1996). In their examination of electoral campaigns in Britain and the United States, Budge and Farlie (1983a, 1983b) observe that political parties do not compete on all issues in the political space in every election. Rather, parties emphasize those issues on which they hold an advantage and downplay those that disadvantage them;[8] this is the central claim of their saliency theory of party competition. As shown by Riker (1982a, 1986, 1996) in his work on heresthetics, parties can even accentuate issues that were previously not part of the political discussion. By choosing which issues to compete on in a given election, parties can shape the perceived importance of policy dimensions. Because voters, who often take their cues from political parties, discount the attractiveness of policies on issues they find irrelevant, a party's ability to downplay or highlight issues influences party fortunes.

While the existing literature has focused on the role of issue salience in interactions between mainstream party equals, this facet of party strategy has particular

---

[7] Those who view salience as an inherent characteristic of a topic cannot explain, for example, why the significance of an issue varies over time. While proponents of sociological approaches overcome this limitation by identifying plausible factors that could alter the salience of an issue, they do not provide a mechanism by which those conditions could affect voter perceptions.

[8] This is consistent with the findings of Budge, Robertson, and Hearl (1987: 39) that "parties compete by accentuating issues on which they have an undoubted advantage, rather than putting forward contrasting policies on the same issues."

relevance to competition between mainstream and niche parties. Unlike mainstream parties, which draw on multiple issues to appeal to voters, niche parties, as single-issue actors, are dependent on the importance of their one issue dimension. Indeed, it is the only dimension along which they compete with mainstream parties. Reduction in the salience of their one issue translates directly into the loss of voters. And the issues introduced by niche parties tend to be more susceptible to salience manipulation in general because they are not the core economic axes around which the political system is built and on which most mainstream parties are founded.

Altering Issue Ownership. The positional conception of party tactics is further challenged by the role of issue ownership in voter decision making. A relatively undertheorized phenomenon, issue ownership, or issue credibility, has been overlooked by standard spatial theories of voting and party competition, which claim that voter decisions depend only on ideological proximity.[9] However, in a situation where voters face parties that are equally distant from them on a substantive policy issue, the standard spatial claim that voters are actually indifferent between their political options does not seem reasonable (Downs 1957; Enelow and Hinich 1984); common sense tells us that voter decisions are rarely dictated by the flip of a coin. Just as partisan identification has been shown to influence voter decision making in highly aligned political environments, a party's issue credibility, or ownership, plays a key role in issue-based voting (Budge and Farlie 1983a, 1983b; Petrocik 1996; Trilling 1976). According to Petrocik's ownership theory and Budge and Farlie's saliency theory, voters accord their support to the most credible proponent of a particular issue or issue position.[10]

While these theories suggest that who owns an issue affects voter decisions among any set of parties, the significance of issue ownership increases when that vote choice is between mainstream and niche parties. Once again, the single-issue identity of the niche party constrains its electoral prospects. The new party must be deemed owner of that one issue in order to receive voter support. This means convincing the voters both that it is committed to a given policy stance and that it is the party best able to implement such a policy. Niche parties are further

---

[9] An exception is the growing literature on valence issues, which, to use the language of issue ownership, focuses on how a party's ownership of or advantage on nonpolicy issues – such as integrity and intelligence – affects party competition (e.g., Ansolabehere and Snyder 2000; Groseclose 2001; Schofield 2003). The theory of party competition developed in this book follows the work of Budge and Farlie (1983a, 1983b) and Petrocik (1996) by applying the concept of issue ownership to *policy* dimensions. I consider how a party's ownership of, or credibility advantage on, a particular policy position, separate from its stated position on that issue, affects its fortune.

[10] Most work on issue ownership (Budge and Farlie 1983a, 1983b; Petrocik 1996) focuses on a party's capacity to own valence issues, which are defined as issues on which all actors share a common policy stance but may disagree about the means of achieving them (Stokes 1963, 1966). Despite the current focus of the "valence literature" on candidate and party qualities (see n. 9 in this chapter), Stokes's valence category includes policy issues such as crime and education. However, the concept of issue ownership can be equally applied to policy stances on position issues. Thus, on issues where there is no commonly agreed on policy goal, it is conceivable that one party may be known as the owner of one position and another as the owner of the opposite stance. The niche party issue of immigration is one example; there are pro- and anti-immigration issue owners.

disadvantaged in the battle for issue ownership by their relative inexperience in governmental office and by the electorate's unfamiliarity with them relative to the established parties.

The importance of a party's ideological reputation to its electoral support introduces the possibility of an additional facet to party strategy and political competition. Although initial research on issue ownership assumed the long-term stability of this characteristic (Budge and Farlie 1983a, 1983b), more recent observations confirm that policy reputations are not static (Bélanger 2003; King 2001; Sanders 1999). Through their campaign efforts, parties have reinforced or undermined linkages between political actors – themselves and others – and specific issue dimensions (Budge, Robertson, and Hearl 1987). Issue ownership, therefore, is subject to party manipulation.

From this analysis of the factors governing voter decisions, it is clear that the nature of party interaction under issue-based competition is not adequately addressed by existing theories. This discussion has suggested that, in contrast to the claims of standard spatial approaches, party behavior is not limited to policy movement in a fixed policy space. Whereas saliency and ownership theories have taken an important step by recognizing that parties can manipulate the salience of issues, especially those that they own, these theories still treat ownership as though it were fixed. It seems clear, however, that parties can compete by altering three factors: policy position, issue salience, and issue ownership. In the next section, I spell out the implications of this new conception of strategies for a theory of party competition between unequals, where the mainstream parties compete with the niche party using strategies restricted to the new issue dimension.[11] As the discussion reveals, not only does recognition of the salience- and ownership-altering properties of strategies fundamentally expand the form and the utility of tactics available to mainstream parties, but it also changes the nature and objectives of party competition; when trying to understand the electoral success of niche parties, the rules of party engagement postulated by existing strategic theories are no longer adequate.[12]

THE POSITION, SALIENCE, AND OWNERSHIP THEORY OF PARTY COMPETITION

An Expanded Tool Kit

In moving to a definition of strategies as position-, salience-, and ownership-altering tools, our understanding of the range and effectiveness of party tactics

[11] This constraint is consistent with the nature of the interaction observed between mainstream and niche parties, and it also allows us to avoid the problems of modeling competition between multiple players in multiple dimensions (Enelow and Hinich 1984).

[12] In the rest of this chapter and book, my main focus will be on the differences between my modified spatial theory and the standard spatial theory. Not only have spatial theories become dominant in the field, but they offer a more developed and precise conception of the strategies available for party competition on any given issue dimension. Moreover, the saliency theory does not articulate a set of expectations distinct from the spatial model for parties competing on common, "unowned" issue dimensions.

increases. Whereas standard spatial theories emphasize party movement on a given issue dimension, my Position, Salience, and Ownership theory suggests strategic behavior starts one step earlier – with the decision regarding *mainstream party* entry onto a new issue dimension.[13] Established parties must actively decide whether to recognize and respond to the issue introduced by the niche party. Party presence on a specific policy dimension, such as the environment, immigration, or decentralization, is not a given.[14]

Parties finding an issue unimportant or too difficult to address can decide to ignore it. Rather than indicating a party's failure to react, this previously over-looked "nonaction" is a deliberate tactic that I call a *dismissive strategy*.[15] By not taking a position on the niche party's issue, the mainstream party signals to voters that the issue lacks merit.[16] The party does not validate its inclusion within the political debate and urges voters to similarly dismiss it as irrelevant. If voters are persuaded that the niche party's issue dimension is insignificant, they will not vote for the neophyte. Thus, even though a dismissive strategy does not challenge the distinctiveness or ownership of the niche party's issue position, its salience-reducing effect will lead to niche party vote loss.

Conversely, parties can actively compete with the new party by adopting a position on its issue dimension. The salience of that issue increases as the main-stream party acknowledges the legitimacy of the issue and signals its prioritization of that policy dimension for electoral competition. Given that the adoption of a new policy position is a costly endeavor for a political party, requiring a diversion of its resources away from existing policy commitments, this action should be viewed as a credible signal of the issue's importance to the party.[17] Depending on the position that the mainstream party adopts upon entering the new issue space, this response is either an accommodative or an adversarial strategy.

Although both boost issue salience, the similarities between accommodative and adversarial tactics end there. In an accommodative strategy, the mainstream party adopts a position similar to the niche party's. This tactic thus undermines the distinctiveness of the new party's issue position, providing like-minded voters

---

[13] In contrast, most spatial models of multiparty competition (Palfrey 1984; Shepsle 1991) assume that the *new* party is the actor entering an established policy space.

[14] The work on party realignment does recognize that political actors might not take positions on all issue dimensions. And Kitschelt (1994: 124) hints at the possibility that mainstream parties may need to enter a new policy space. However, neither Kitschelt nor the party realignment literature (e.g., Rohrschneider 1993) includes the decision to ignore new issue dimensions in their repertoires of party strategy.

[15] This tactic is similar in effect to the downplaying of issues owned by an opponent in the saliency theory of competition. However, in my dismissive strategy, unlike in the saliency model, main-stream parties are not assumed to have a policy position on the issue dimension they downplay.

[16] Although researchers often look for significance in the content of an actor's response, the dismissive tactic suggests that critical information can also be gleaned from the absence of any statement.

[17] The costs include the time, money, and manpower associated with researching the new topic and preparing party materials on that new policy. And, there are also less-visible opportunity costs. Given that a party's resources are finite, the adoption of a new issue position means fewer resources can be devoted to the other issues. In addition to the more obvious resource of money, the older issues receive less time in campaign speeches and fewer pages in party documents.

with a choice between similar parties. Consistent with standard spatial models, those voters closer to the accommodating mainstream party on the new issue will desert the niche party. But, according to my theory, even those voters who are (programmatically) indifferent between the two parties may be persuaded to leave the new party. By challenging the exclusivity of the niche party's policy stance, the accommodative mainstream party is trying to undermine the new party's issue ownership and become the rightful owner of the issue.

If niche parties typically introduce new issues to the political spectrum, why should voters prefer the accommodating mainstream party "copy" to the niche party "original"? In contrast to actors in competition between equals, parties in this situation are not evenly matched. As noted in Chapter 1, mainstream parties are aided in this process by their greater legislative experience and governmental efficacy than niche parties. Issue voters who care about the implementation of party proposals into law are more likely to favor the party with legislative experience. In addition, mainstream parties generally have more access to the voters than niche parties, allowing them to publicize their issue positions and establish name recognition. Niche parties are consequently disadvantaged because voters will not support a party if they are unaware of its position.

In addition to strengthening the already powerful tool of policy convergence, the salience and ownership dimensions also empower the commonly neglected spatial strategy of policy divergence. When a party adopts an adversarial strategy – taking a position on the new issue dimension opposite to the niche party's – it declares its hostility toward the niche party's policy stance. This behavior deliberately calls attention to that challenger and its issue dimension, leaving voters primed to cast their ballots on the basis of this new issue. The adversarial strategy also reinforces the niche party's issue ownership by defining the mainstream party's issue position in juxtaposition to that of the new party. It strengthens the link in the public's mind between that issue stance and the niche party as its primary proponent. As a result, the adversarial strategy encourages niche party electoral support.[18]

The predicted effects of this expanded set of party strategies on issue salience, ownership, party programmatic position, and, in turn, niche party electoral support are summarized in Table 2.1. Because a niche party's support depends on a single issue, any tactic that undermines the perceived relevance of that issue or the distinctiveness or credibility of the niche party's position on that dimension will result in niche party vote loss. Assuming that voters find the niche party's policy stance attractive, mainstream parties can undermine niche party vote with dismissive or accommodative tactics and boost it with adversarial tactics.[19]

---

[18] The innovative utility of this strategy will be explored in detail later in this chapter.

[19] In order for the predicted effects of the strategies to be realized, at least some voters must share the niche party's policy preference. Moreover, it is assumed in this model, as in most spatial models, that voter distribution is fixed. Parties cannot alter the policy preferences of the voters. Rather mainstream parties alter the voting behavior of the electorate by changing the salience and ownership of the new issue and the position of the mainstream party relative to the niche party on that dimension.

TABLE 2.1. *Predicted Effects of the PSO Theory's Issue-based Strategies (in Isolation)*

	Mechanism			
Strategies	**Issue Salience**	**Issue Position**	**Issue Ownership**	**Niche Party Electoral Support**
Dismissive	Decreases	No movement	No effect	**Decreases**
Accommodative	Increases	Converges	Transfers to mainstream party	**Decreases**
Adversarial	Increases	Diverges	Reinforces niche party's ownership	**Increases**

Non-Issue-based Strategies

As the preceding discussion has argued, mainstream parties have access to a greater and more powerful range of strategies than previously recognized. Policy movement (or lack thereof) has implications for the salience and ownership of the dimensions of party competition. And the power imbalance between the mainstream and niche parties in issue-based competition means that these issue salience– and issue ownership–altering tactics are particularly effective at shaping the fortunes of these single-issue parties. These issue-based strategies are the dominant tools employed in competition between unequals, but the power differential between the mainstream and niche parties also opens up other arenas for strategic maneuvering. Specifically, mainstream parties facing weaker political competitors have their choice of organizational and institutional tools as well as the ideological ones.

Organizational Tactics. Organizational strategies allow mainstream parties to alter the viability of the niche party as an independent electoral contestant. Instead of pacifying a niche party through programmatic accommodation, an established party can co-opt the neophyte's leader or elite. Through offers of greater job security and the possibility of advancement in a "winning" organization, the mainstream party may be able to hollow out the threatening party. In addition to luring away the elite or even the rank-and-file members of the party, the mainstream party can propose the formation of electoral pacts or formal coalitions with the new party. These acts of linking the mainstream party to the niche party in the minds of the voters – whether by co-opting niche party elite or officially connecting the parties on the ballot or in government – may facilitate the "contagion effect." By this I mean that the mainstream party will be perceived to be a credible supporter of the niche party's position. Assuming that the niche party, or its elite, has been formerly recognized as the owner of its single issue, organizational accommodation can result in a transfer of (some) issue ownership, with the mainstream party taking on a green, ethnic, or xenophobic tint, depending on the niche party's issue of choice.[20] Like issue-based forms of accommodation, this tactic is expected to lead to a reduction in the electoral support of the niche party.

If, on the other hand, a mainstream party wishes to boost the niche party's support, organizational tactics analogous to a programmatic adversarial strategy can be employed. A mainstream party can verbally denigrate the niche party and its elite or forbid the establishment of electoral or formal coalitions between the parties at local, regional, national, and even supranational (e.g., EU) levels. These tactics are designed to demonize the niche party in the eyes of the public, while simultaneously reinforcing that niche party's independent organizational legitimacy. By focusing negative attention on the new party and its issue position, this form of organizational strategy – like that of the issue-based adversarial tactic – publicizes the niche party and strengthens its claim to issue ownership and its attractiveness to like-minded voters.

Institutional Tactics. Institutional strategies, like organizational tactics, allow the more powerful governing parties to shape the competitiveness of niche party challengers. However, instead of manipulating the ownership of issue positions, institutional strategies let mainstream parties directly affect niche party access to the electoral arena. As discussed previously, a mainstream party employs accommodative tactics to decrease the electoral support of a niche party competitor. Mainstream parties can achieve similar results by altering the institutional environment – for example, by raising the electoral threshold necessary for office attainment, tightening campaign finance restrictions, and limiting niche party media access.[21] In extreme cases, established parties may propose laws forbidding the electoral participation or even existence of a niche party.[22] Conversely, institutional strategies can also be used to facilitate niche party access to the electoral arena. Analogous to issue-based adversarial tactics in their effects on

---

[20] The French Parti socialiste (PS) employed an organizational strategy in 1988 when it created a junior ministry for the environment and named a leader of the Greens, Brice Lalonde, as its first placeholder; in 1991, the PS government made Lalonde the first Minister of the Environment. The Socialists hoped Lalonde would help them to acquire a more environmentally friendly image.

[21] An electoral pact also directly decreases niche party access to the electoral arena by removing the party from the ballot in specific districts. However, it has been classified as an organizational strategy because, like other organizational tactics and unlike institutional ones, its effectiveness depends on the perceived credibility of the strategizing mainstream party. Supporters of niche parties, for instance, can refuse to follow the pact and vote for rogue niche party candidates rather than for a noncredible mainstream party.

[22] Article 21, Section 2 of the German Basic Law is an example of an institutional form of accommodative strategy. When proposed, this constitutional clause was designed to target fascist parties. The wording is as follows: "Parties which, by reason of their aims or the behavior of their adherents, seek to impair or destroy the free democratic basic order or to endanger the existence of the Federal Republic of Germany shall be unconstitutional. The Federal Constitutional Court decides on the question of unconstitutionality." Article 21, Section 2 of the German Basic Law, amended December 21, 1983. From http://www.jura.uni-sb.de/law/GG/gg2.htm.

niche party vote, these institutional reforms include decreasing electoral system thresholds, loosening campaign finance restrictions, and increasing niche party media access.[23]

It is important to note that the feasibility and effectiveness of these institutional strategies are dependent on the relative power of the strategizing party. Institutional changes are unlikely to be enacted if the mainstream party strategizer does not maintain a legislative advantage over its target party – whether that be the niche party or a mainstream party opponent; indeed, the similar electoral and governmental strengths of competing mainstream parties explain why such tactics are typically ignored by traditional theories of party interaction and not often seen in competition between mainstream parties. Once successfully implemented, these strategies directly alter the competitiveness of the target party and the overall electoral arena. Thus, unlike the issue-based and organizational strategies, the institutional tactic's impact on voter behavior is not dependent on the perceived credibility of the strategizing mainstream party.

Changing the Nature of Party Competition: The Critical Role of Nonproximal Parties

In the PSO theory of competition between unequals, mainstream parties have access to an expanded and more effective set of strategic tools than previously thought. Not only can the established actors alter the competitiveness of their niche party opponents by manipulating the relevance, attractiveness, and credibility of the new issues and issue proponents, but they also can change the organizational integrity of niche parties and their institutional access to the electoral arena. In other words, the competitiveness of the political space and that of the niche parties competing within it are endogenous to the strategic behavior of mainstream parties.

But the implications of this revision extend far beyond the size of the political party's tool kit. They call into question the very rules of party interaction propounded by spatial models. Recall that in the standard spatial conception of strategies, parties can only affect the electoral support of neighboring parties; in a unidimensional space, this means that movement by a center-left party away from a center-right party cannot influence the electoral support of a right flank party. If instead strategies can also alter issue salience and ownership, then parties can target opponents *anywhere* on that dimension. Ideological proximity is no longer a requirement.

While it may be obvious that institutional and even organizational strategies can be used against any niche party opponent regardless of its spatial location, it is not necessarily clear how this applies to issue-based tactics. To appreciate the irrelevance of spatial proximity for strategic effectiveness, consider the effects and utility of the adversarial strategy. Given that political opponents are

---

[23] As will be shown in the case study chapters, these institutional strategies may be combined with other forms of adversarial behavior.

generally viewed as threats, it might seem counterintuitive to suggest, as I do, that a party would seek to heighten the political visibility and electoral strength of a competitor. Indeed, in a two-party system, where politics is a zero-sum game, political parties are unlikely to employ adversarial tactics. When competition occurs between three or more players on a single dimension, however, such a vote-boosting strategy might be used against a competitor at the opposite end of the issue axis.[24] Although spatial theorists would argue that such strategic behavior toward a nonproximal party is unnecessary, costly, and, ultimately, ineffective,[25] the salience- and ownership-altering facets of the adversarial strategy allow mainstream parties who are not directly threatened by the niche party to use it as a *weapon* against their own mainstream party opponents. This is the political embodiment of the adage "the enemy of my enemy is my friend"; the mainstream party helps the niche party – the enemy of its enemy in this case – gain votes from the other mainstream party. With adversarial strategies, the new single-issue party becomes a pawn in the larger political competition between mainstream parties.

By highlighting the nontraditional use of policy divergence in my reconceptualized repertoire of party strategies, this example clearly demonstrates that party competition is not restricted to interaction between ideological neighbors. In this case and others, nonproximal parties have the ability and motivation to alter the electoral fortunes of their political friends and enemies. Failure to consider the effects of their behavior on party competitors could lead to faulty predictions about the outcome of party interaction. Consequently, spatial models of party competition that restrict analysis to proximal parties must be traded for a model in which party success turns on the interaction of strategies pursued by both proximal and distant parties.

HYPOTHESES OF THE POSITION, SALIENCE, AND OWNERSHIP THEORY

Table 2.2 contains the predictions of the PSO theory of party competition for niche party success. These hypotheses are based on the behavior of multiple mainstream parties on one dimension – the niche party's new issue dimension. For ease of presentation, I assume that there are only three parties in the political system: mainstream party A, mainstream party B, and the niche party.[26] Because the effect of each tactic is theorized to be independent of the identity of the strategizing mainstream party, six distinct strategic combinations emerge: dismissive-dismissive (DIDI), dismissive-accommodative (DIAC), dismissive-adversarial (DIAD), accommodative-accommodative (ACAC), accommodative-adversarial

---

[24] According to the theory of strategic choice that will be outlined in Chapter 4, it would be rational for a mainstream party to employ an adversarial strategy in this situation – i.e., against a niche party that threatens its mainstream party opponent but not itself.

[25] Note that under the tenets of spatial theory, policy convergence and divergence only reduce or increase the electoral support of the most proximal party. They have no impact on the electoral strength of parties on the other side of their spatial neighbors.

[26] This restriction does not represent an intrinsic limitation of the theory.

TABLE 2.2. *Predicted Effects of Mainstream Party Strategic Combinations on Niche Party Electoral Support*

		Mainstream Party B		
		Dismissive	Accommodative	Adversarial
Mainstream Party A	Dismissive	Niche party vote loss	Niche party vote loss	Niche party vote gain
	Accommodative	Niche party vote loss	Niche party vote loss	If AC > AD, Niche party vote loss If AD > AC, Niche party vote gain
	Adversarial	Niche party vote gain	If AC > AD, Niche party vote loss If AD > AC, Niche party vote gain	Niche party vote gain

(ACAD), and adversarial-adversarial (ADAD). The predictions for each strategic combination recorded in Table 2.2 represent the combined effects of the individual tactics from Table 2.1 on niche party support.

The reconceptualization of party strategies has a profound impact on the expected outcomes of party competition. As demonstrated in Table 2.2, parties have multiple means of undermining or bolstering the electoral support of a competitor. Instead of being limited to accommodative (AC) strategies as suggested by spatial theories, mainstream parties can also lower the niche party's vote by employing simple, salience-reducing dismissive (DI) tactics.[27]

Moreover, the electoral fortune of a niche party is shaped by the behavior of multiple mainstream parties. The predictions captured in Table 2.2 suggest that one party's behavior alone is rarely determinative of niche party support. Rather, mainstream parties can use strategies to thwart the strategic efforts of their mainstream competitor. For example, I posit that mainstream party B's adversarial strategy (AD) will decrease the effectiveness of mainstream party A's vote-reducing dismissive and accommodative tactics. In the case of a DIAD combination, the salience, ownership, and positional effects of the active adversarial strategy are expected to overpower the simple salience-reducing impact of the dismissive strategy. To the dismay of the threatened mainstream party A, the result will be a more popular niche party with strengthened issue ownership.

The expected outcome of the ACAD strategy is contingent on the relative intensity of the two mainstream parties' strategies, where intensity is a function of the prioritization, frequency, and duration of a party's programmatic, organizational, and institutional tactics against a niche party. In this situation, best described as a battle of opposing forces, the mainstream party employing the greatest number of tactics consistently for the longest period of time will

---

[27] Although the effect may be the same, it is important to remember that the strategic mechanisms are different.

prevail. If the accommodative strategy is more intense than the adversarial one, the niche party will lose ownership of the issue and issue-based voters to the accommodating party. On the other hand, if the adversarial tactic is stronger and more consistently employed, then the issue ownership of the niche party will be strengthened, and its electoral support will increase.

CONTEXTUALIZING PARTY BEHAVIOR: CONSTRAINTS
TO STRATEGIC EFFECTIVENESS

According to my modified spatial conception of party strategies, tactics work by manipulating the programmatic positions of parties and the perceived salience and ownership of the underlying issue dimensions. In a broader sense, therefore, parties compete by trying to alter the policy reputations of themselves and others. However, reputational changes take time, and the success of such attempts – i.e., the effectiveness of party strategies – depends on both past and future party behavior. Thus, the predicted effects of strategic combinations presented in Table 2.2 are subject to constraints, the two most important being policy inconsistency and policy hesitation.

The Need to Be "Responsible"

Spatial theories of party interaction (e.g., Downs 1957) claim that a party's positioning on a particular issue is dictated by the positions of other existing actors and the distribution of voters rather than any specific ideological party mandate. While there is growing evidence to support the proposition that parties, especially catch-all parties, have relative flexibility in choosing their issue positions, there are still important limitations to party strategies. For example, it remains problematic for parties to hold contradictory policy positions simultaneously. The emergence of antisystem parties in Western Europe highlights this predicament. By attracting voter support through anticlientelist appeals, these new parties are challenging the political system utilized, and often created, by the dominant parties (Kitschelt 1995; 2000). Thus, mainstream party accommodative tactics designed to stem voter defection to the antisystem parties will lack credibility and be less effective; ownership of the antisystem issue will not be easily transferred to the very mainstream parties that constructed or perpetuate the system under debate. As demonstrated by this example, the current policy positions of mainstream parties limit their simultaneous co-optation of a contradictory policy stance.

Just as mainstream parties are restricted from accommodating parties with positions opposite to their own, mainstream parties cannot pursue policy positions that conflict with their previous positions on the same issue. Although a party can credibly move from downplaying the issue (i.e., pursuing a dismissive strategy) to taking an active (accommodative or adversarial) stance on it, shifts between accommodative and adversarial stances on the same issue raise doubts among the voters about the credibility of the strategizing actor. In fact, one of the few constraints to party movement imposed by Downs (1957: 105) is this idea that parties needed to be "responsible," proposing policies that are consistent from one period to the next.[28]

A party's programmatic "irresponsibility" has ramifications for issue ownership. By wildly switching issue positions from one period to the next, a mainstream party undermines its ability to establish either itself (when being accommodative) or the niche party (when being adversarial) as the only true proponent of the issue.[29] The electorate is likely to perceive the party as a strategic actor indifferent to the programmatic merits of the particular policy position, and, in an electoral environment in which parties attract voters on the basis of their issues and image as policy seekers, mainstream parties demonstrating policy fickleness will not be rewarded with electoral support. Accommodative tactics will not lead to a transfer of issue ownership when interspersed with adversarial messages. Nor will the issue ownership of the niche party be reinforced when a mainstream party's adversarial behavior alternates with its own attempts at issue co-optation.

Strategy inconsistency proves less costly, however, when a party is employing institutional tactics. Whereas the effectiveness of issue-based tactics relies on the perceived credibility of the strategizing party, the potency of institutional strategies depends merely on legislative approval and governmental enforcement. Although voters could, in the long run, punish the party for its strategic manipulation of electoral institutions, the short-term impact of an institutional strategy on niche party fortune is generally unaffected by any voter disapproval of that strategy.[30]

Organizational tactics are also somewhat insulated from the effects of policy inconsistency because, by using them, parties can benefit from issue contagion without actually adopting the issue position in question. For example, a party can form a coalition with a niche party competitor even if the two parties have divergent policy stances. That said, the greater the policy differences between the parties, the less likely it is that the established party will be able to obtain ownership of the niche party's issue. Adversarial forms of organizational tactics are similarly affected by policy inconsistencies. Although a mainstream party can effectively ban coalitions with a niche party despite having pursued these arrangements in the past, this contradictory behavior might not result in the successful reinforcement of the niche party's issue ownership.

---

[28] This preoccupation with policy consistency across time is not limited to spatial models. Although it frames the discussion differently, the literature on party ideology likewise recognizes the constraining effect of past party actions and decisions – one way in which a party's ideology is manifested – on future party behavior (see Sani and Sartori 1983; von Beyme 1985; Ware 1996).

[29] The costs of policy inconsistency to party reputation and strategic effectiveness are discussed at length by Alesina (1988), Bowler (1990), Downs (1957), Przeworski and Sprague (1986), and Robertson (1976).

[30] For example, whether the French electorate doubted the Socialists' motives for reforming the electoral system in 1986 did not alter the fact that a vote for a niche party "counted more" in that election than in previous ones.

The Need to Be Timely

Policy inconsistency either within or between periods can be costly for a main-stream party, but the solution is not necessarily to delay adopting an accommoda-tive or adversarial issue-based tactic for fear of the "lock-in effect." Just as some strategies are not credible when implemented after their tactical opposites, so too certain strategies lose their effectiveness at later stages in mainstream party–niche party interaction. The strategy most sensitive to the competition life cycle is accommodation. As discussed earlier, accommodative policy tactics are success-ful because they transfer issue ownership from the niche party to the mainstream actor. However, this transfer is impeded by the failure of the mainstream party to initiate co-optative measures shortly after the emergence of the niche party on the electoral scene.[31] Once the niche party has gained a reputation as the sole proponent of the issue, the advocacy of a similar policy position by other parties will be judged less credible; hesitation will cause the mainstream party to be denounced as a mere "copy" of the niche party "original."[32] Adversarial tactics, on the other hand, are designed to reinforce a niche party's association with the issue. Barring the counteracting effects of another mainstream party's tactics, a delay in the implementation of an adversarial tactic will only strengthen its intended effect on niche party ownership and vote.[33]

My reconception of strategies as issue-ownership-altering devices therefore introduces a timing dimension to party competition. The effectiveness of an accommodative strategy is dependent on its implementation during a window of *ownership* opportunity: issue linkage can be altered only in the early stages of the issue's politicization. Once voters identify the niche party as the sole proponent of the issue, the costs involved in undermining that perceived ownership render its likelihood slim.

The key factor controlling the size of the window of opportunity is time – specifically, the amount of time that has elapsed between a niche party's electoral emergence and the active response of the mainstream party to it and its issue. In unitary states, electoral emergence is marked by the niche party's first con-testation of a national election; in more federal systems, that first election could be participation in subnational elections. In addition to the neophyte's partici-pation in elections, other factors, such as the nature of the electoral system and the degree of media attention a niche party receives, also influence how fast a

---

[31] Elite factionalism and lack of party discipline are the main factors leading to the delayed imple-mentation of a party's policy. These factors are discussed in greater detail in Chapter 4.

[32] When hesitating, mainstream parties are typically pursuing dismissive tactics. These tactics have a low short-term cost because they do not commit a party to a future strategic position. How-ever, because dismissive tactics do not alter issue ownership, they undermine the future ability of accommodative tactics to co-opt issue ownership and reduce niche party support.

[33] The effect of a delayed adversarial tactic will be mitigated by the tactics employed by other parties in its absence. Failure to employ an adversarial strategy until after a mainstream competitor has adopted an accommodative tactic will reduce the adversarial party's ability to reinforce the niche party's issue ownership.

reputation is established. For instance, one might expect to see a smaller window under more permissive electoral systems in which, on average, niche parties are considered more viable governmental actors and thus more credible policy owners.[34] Regardless of the exact size of the window, the same mechanism applies: mainstream party issue co-optation will be more effective when niche party reputations are in flux than after they become established. Hesitation undermines the potency of these reconceptualized programmatic strategies.

With the closing of the window of opportunity, issue-based co-optation is expected to be traded for forms of accommodation less reliant on altering issue ownership. Organizational tactics, such as coalition formation or incorporation of niche party leadership, remain effective. In fact, the impact of "stealing" a party figurehead on a mainstream party's issue credibility is stronger once the niche party has been recognized as the owner of an issue position. Because they do not work by altering issue ownership, institutional strategies are relatively insensitive to the closing of the ownership window. Such tactics as outlawing a party or simply increasing the electoral threshold will prove effective at altering niche party support levels even in the case of delayed implementation.

To summarize, the effectiveness of mainstream parties' strategies is limited by policy inconsistency and delay in implementation. Failure to be "responsible," in the Downsian sense, within and across electoral periods reduces the impact of a party's accommodative and adversarial strategies on niche party support. However, avoiding the "lock-in effect" by delaying before adopting a strategy is not a costless solution. Once the niche party's reputation as the credible issue owner is established, programmatic accommodation, which works by altering issue linkages, becomes less effective, and parties are forced to turn to less-sensitive organizational and institutional tactics.

CONCLUSION

This chapter has presented a strategic answer to the puzzle of niche party success and failure across Western Europe since 1970. Instead of merely reflecting the institutional or sociological characteristics of a society, the electoral trajectories of these new parties are, I argue, the product of strategic behavior. Specifically, niche party fortunes are shaped by the deliberate actions of the dominant mainstream parties of the political arena.

While strategic explanations of party success abound, the exigencies of competition between *unequals* alter the nature of party interaction and therefore call for the construction of a new theory of party competition, the PSO theory. Where party success depends on the perceived relevance, attractiveness, and credibility of its issue and issue position, party strategies are no longer limited to programmatic movement in an existing policy space, as assumed by spatial theories. They

---

[34] This claim rests on the tendency for sincere voting to be more common in less-restrictive electoral systems (Riker 1982b).

TABLE 2.3. *Testable Hypotheses of the PSO Theory of Party Competition*

H2.1: When confronting niche parties in issue-based competition, mainstream parties have access to a wider and more effective set of programmatic strategies.

H2.1a: Dismissive tactics reduce issue salience, thereby decreasing the electoral support of a niche party.

H2.1b: Accommodative strategies increase issue salience. However, by adopting a niche party's policy position and transferring ownership of that issue to itself, an accommodating mainstream party reduces the electoral support of the niche party.

H2.1c: Adversarial strategies bolster issue salience while reinforcing the distinctiveness and ownership of a niche party's policy position. These effects increase the electoral support of the niche party.

H2.2: In addition to issue-based tactics, mainstream parties can use organizational and institutional tactics to manipulate – undermine or bolster – the competitiveness of less-powerful niche parties.

H2.3: The electoral trajectory of a niche party is shaped by the effects of the strategies of multiple – proximal and nonproximal – mainstream parties.

H2.4: Policy inconsistency both within and between electoral periods lowers the effectiveness of accommodative and adversarial strategies.

H2.5: Implementation of accommodative strategies after the reputational entrenchment of the niche party decreases their effectiveness.

---

are also not limited to shifting the salience of issue dimensions with fixed owners, as argued by saliency and ownership theories. Rather, parties can manipulate electoral support by altering their position on and the salience and ownership of issues new to political competition.

Several implications follow. These are presented as testable hypotheses in Table 2.3. First, this expanded conception of party behavior increases the number and effectiveness of strategies. Mainstream parties have multiple means of undermining or bolstering the electoral competitiveness of their niche party opponents; instead of being limited to the traditional spatial tools of policy convergence and divergence, parties have access to the newly recognized dismissive tactic, more potent accommodative and adversarial strategies, and even organizational and institutional tools. Second, the availability of salience- and ownership-altering tools means that competition is no longer restricted to spatially proximal parties. Mainstream parties not directly threatened by a niche party have the ability and the motivation – as will be argued in Chapter 4 – to alter the neophyte's electoral prospects. Third, it follows that niche party electoral success is shaped by the strategies of multiple mainstream parties.

When these three propositions are combined with hypotheses H2.4 and H2.5 (see Table 2.3), it is clear that my PSO theory does not signal inevitable doom for all new parties. Consistent with the wide variation in the electoral fortunes of niche parties observed across Western Europe, this strategic theory of competition between unequals can explain niche party success as well as the more commonly expected niche party failure. As this chapter has argued, these outcomes can be the result of intended strategies or the by-product of suboptimal behavior. Policy inconsistency within or between time periods limits the potency of party tactics. Timing also matters: hesitation undermines accommodation. And even if the conditions are favorable, not all mainstream parties desire the elimination of a niche party challenger. This theory's recognition of niche parties as weapons against mainstream party opponents indicates that the fortunes of these neophytes are not divorced from the fortunes of their mainstream party counterparts. Competition between unequals is shaped by but also affects competition between equals.

Having formulated and specified a modified spatial theory of party behavior, I turn to its testing. In Chapter 3, I perform cross-sectional, time-series analyses of niche party vote across seventeen Western European countries from 1970 to 1998. This quantitative examination of fifty-five niche party fortunes across countries and over time allows me to systematically test the implications of my PSO theory against the claims of competing institutional, sociological, and standard strategic theories and to provide conclusive, generalizable results about the role and effectiveness of mainstream party behavior.

3

An Analysis of Niche Party Fortunes in Western Europe

Tales of electoral disparity characterize the niche party experience. Across Western Europe between 1970 and 2000, niche parties promoting the same issues achieved wildly different levels of support. In Germany, the Grünen captured a peak vote of 8.3 percent and rivaled the centrist Free Democratic Party (FDP) for the title of the third largest party, whereas in equally environmentally friendly Denmark, the Green Party cobbled together a mere 1.4 percent of the vote in its most auspicious electoral performance. Similar tales can be told about the divergent fortunes of different niche parties within a given country. The strength of Spanish ethnoterritorial parties stands in sharp contrast to the electoral marginalization of their environmental compatriot, Los Verdes. Variation in niche party fortunes has also been witnessed across party life-spans. Voter support for the Greek green party peaked early and faded away, while the attractiveness of the Austrian Freedom Party continued to increase over the decades.

The goal of this chapter is to account for the variations in niche party fortunes across Western Europe. In Chapter 2, I argued that the solution to this puzzle of varying neophyte support can be found in the behavior of the mainstream parties. Rather than being solely or even primarily determined by the permissiveness of the electoral system or the rate of unemployment or economic growth in a country, the competitiveness of a niche party is largely a function of mainstream party strategic interaction. Faced with electorally threatening political challengers, established parties adopt issue-based, organizational, and institutional strategies to increase their own relative electoral security. In the process, these tactics alter the salience and ownership of the niche party's issue for competition, ultimately leading to changes in the neophyte's vote share.

In the following pages, I test the explanatory power of the PSO theory against the competing institutional, sociological, and standard spatial competition theories. This analysis takes as given the observed strategies of the mainstream parties, without assessing either their rationality or the underlying reasons for their implementation; those issues will be the subject of Chapter 4.[1] The focus of this chapter is on the determinants of green, radical right, and ethnoterritorial party support levels.[2] Drawing on evidence from seventeen Western European countries between 1970 and 1998, I perform a series of cross-sectional time-series analyses of niche party vote. In a field often dominated by single-party case studies, this statistical approach facilitates comparative analysis of electoral success across three types of niche party. Its use of data from all countries in the region over approximately three decades further strengthens the weight of its findings. Chapters 5 through 7 complement this broad analysis with more detailed accounts of mainstream parties' behavior, its causes, and its effects on green, radical right, and ethnoterritorial party success in Great Britain and France.

This chapter is divided into five main sections. The first discusses the operationalization of the dependent and explanatory variables. This section is followed by the results of statistical tests of the competing institutional, sociological, and strategic theories and my strategic theory on green and radical right party vote and an analysis of these findings in the short and long terms. In a third section, these regression results are broken down by niche party type to examine differences in the application and the effectiveness of mainstream strategies toward green and radical right parties. I then extend the analyses to a less-common and less-commonly studied set of niche parties – ethnoterritorial parties – to see if mainstream party tactics play similar roles in shaping their regional vote shares in national legislative elections. In the concluding section, I construct typical cases of mainstream party–niche party interaction to demonstrate the power of my reconceptualized strategic variables and the overall fit of the PSO model. When compared to the actual cases that they mirror, these simulations lend support to the salience- and ownership-altering mechanisms posited by my modified spatial theory to link mainstream party strategy to niche party electoral support.

OPERATIONALIZATION OF VARIABLES

As suggested in Chapter 1, the goal of this study is to understand the varying electoral fortunes of niche parties across and within Western European countries over time. To this end, I develop models of niche party support to test the effects of mainstream party strategy, institutions, and sociological conditions on the vote share of these single-issue parties. These independent and dependent variables are discussed in the next sections.

Dependent Variable

Niche Party Electoral Support. Although single-issue party success has been the subject of numerous analyses, none has recognized or examined the wide range

---

[1] Because parties' behavior is not always rational, the analysis in this chapter presents a tough test of the explanatory power of the strategic theories.
[2] The new parties examined in this study represent the more prominent and ubiquitous party families to have emerged in Western European countries over the last thirty years. This latter characteristic accounts for the absence of women's and peace parties from the sample.

of parties that are classified under the rubric of "niche party"; most existing cross-national studies on new party electoral success have focused solely on one type of new party.[3] This analysis, on the other hand, examines the electoral trajectories of multiple single-issue parties. The examination begins by focusing on the most common set of niche parties: environmental and radical right parties. Unlike their peace party or even ethnoterritorial party counterparts, these parties are present in the majority of Western European countries and typically contest electoral districts nationwide rather than competing in only a handful of districts.[4] The dependent variable of this analysis is operationalized as the percentage of votes received nationally by a given niche party in a national-level legislative election.[5] For those countries in which two or more green parties contest a given election, the value of the dependent variable for that country-party-election-year observation is the sum of those parties' votes.[6] The same adjustment is made for countries with multiple radical right parties.

Following from my original description of niche parties in Chapter 1, I categorize individual parties on the basis of their primary issue positions.[7] Those parties prioritizing a strong pro-environmental stance are labeled green parties. Using the expert survey data from Laver and Hunt (1992) on party prioritization of and position on an environmental policy scale,[8] these characteristics correspond to a party's having a high positive score on the importance scale and a strongly negative score on the leaders' policy position scale.[9] This set of high

---

[3] Recent work by Adams et al. (2006) and Ezrow (forthcoming) comes closest by examining the effects of party movement on the fortunes of communist, green, and radical right parties versus mainstream parties in Western Europe. However, even their cross-party analyses do not include the other significant actors in the niche party category: ethnoterritorial parties.

[4] Later in this chapter, I extend the analysis to the smaller set of ethnoterritorial parties. Because ethnoterritorial parties generally compete in only one region in a country, the appropriate measure of their electoral support is their regional vote share, rather than the national vote share measure used for green and radical right parties. The means of these two sets of dependent variables differ significantly enough to render problematic the inclusion of all three party types in the same statistical analysis.

[5] Data on the dependent variable come from Mackie and Rose (1991, 1997) and Caramani (2000). My examination of national-level legislative scores allows us to compare niche party success across a wide range of political and electoral systems – parliamentary and presidential, and unitary and federal political arrangements. While pertinent to the model of party strategic choice discussed in Chapter 4, niche party electoral scores in European Parliament elections are excluded from this analysis in order to preserve the comparability of niche party cases in EU and non-EU member states.

[6] With the data organized as niche party panels, the separate inclusion of multiple green or multiple radical right parties from the same country would violate the assumed independence of the observations. It would introduce the possibility that the electoral success of a green party simply reflects the failure of a different green party in the same country.

[7] Thus, I explicitly exclude those smaller economically focused mainstream parties that are often included with green and radical right parties in left-libertarian or right-authoritarian categories (e.g., Kitschelt 1994).

[8] The environment position scale runs from "support protection of environment, even at the cost of economic growth" to "support economic growth, even at the cost of damage to environment" (Laver and Hunt 1992: 124).

[9] Parties that scored a mean score of 1.05 and higher on the importance scale of -1.38 (Finnish Pensioner's Party) to 2.38 (Portuguese Greens) and a mean score of -1.40 and lower on the position

priority–strong position criteria serves to distinguish environmentally focused, single-issue green parties from economically focused mainstream parties that also hold pro-environmental positions. The resulting classification is consistent with the list of green parties identified by O'Neill (1997) and Müller-Rommel (1989) for this same set of countries and time period. I thus consulted these sources to classify other parties that were not included in the Laver and Hunt study, either because the party or country was excluded or the party emerged after the survey was administered.

Parties emphasizing strong pro-law-and-order and anti-immigration stances are deemed radical right parties. Unfortunately, there was no comparable measure of these issues in Laver and Hunt (1992) or other expert surveys conducted during the period under examination. I thus largely followed the classification, which focused on populist and neofascist parties, employed by other scholars of radical right parties for this time period (Carter 2005; Golder 2003b; Kitschelt 1995).[10] The main exception to this coding involved the categorization of regionalist parties, specifically the Lega Nord and the Lega dei Ticinesi. Based on these parties' prioritization of regional autonomy issues, I follow the work of Caramani (2004), De Winter and Türsan (1998), Fearon and van Houten (2002), Gomez-Reino Cachafeiro (2002), Gordin (2001), Jolly (2006), and Pereira et al. (2003) and classify them as ethnoterritorial parties.[11] I conducted validity checks of my overall categorization of radical right parties using Benoit and Laver's (2006) more recent expert survey data on the prioritization and position of parties on the immigration dimension.[12] While Carter and Golder do not conceptualize radical right parties in this manner, i.e., specifically as single-issue anti-immigration

scale of -1.75 (French Greens) to 1.54 (Norwegian Progress Party) were identified as green parties. The one exception involved the Herri Batasuna (HB) party in Spain. Although it scored 1.17 on the importance and -1.49 on the positional dimensions of the environmental scale, it is properly classified as an ethnoterritorial party (see De Winter and Türsan 1998; Jolly 2006; Müller-Rommel 1998). This judgment is consistent with additional information from Laver and Hunt (1992); in their surveys, HB received a higher importance score on the issue of decentralization (1.29) than on the environment. Herri Batasuna is examined with the group of ethnoterritorial parties later in this chapter.

[10] I agree with Carter's decision to classify the successor to the Italian MSI, the Alleanza Nazionale, as a radical right party. Whereas some scholars have argued that it was moving away from its neofascist MSI roots (e.g., Ignazi 2003; Newell 2000), this is not alleged to have begun until 1998 (Gallagher 2000: 82–3) – after the last Italian election in my analysis – and even then, Ignazi (2003: 223) notes that the old ideological preferences were still strong among midlevel elite and party members. In fact, the Benoit and Laver (2006) expert survey data still report the AN as being a quite strong promoter and supporter of the anti-immigration position when their data were collected in 2002–2003. Conversely, I exclude the Greek EPEN party from the radical right category on the basis of both its formation and continued identification as an explicitly single-issue party for the amnesty of the Greek military junta leaders (Ignazi 2003: 193; Mackie and Rose 1991).

[11] These parties are discussed in the analysis of ethnoterritorial party fortunes later in this chapter.

[12] Those parties with high scores on the immigration importance scale and high scores on the immigration position scale are deemed radical right parties. The position scale runs from "favors policies designed to help asylum seekers and immigrants integrate into [country name] society" to "favors policies designed to help asylum seekers and immigrants return to their country of origin" (Benoit and Laver 2006: 173).

TABLE 3.1. *Niche Parties in Western Europe*

Country	Environmental Party	Radical Right Party
Austria	Die Grüne Alternative, VGÖ	FPÖ
Belgium	Ecolo, AGALEV	Vlaams Blok, Front National, Agir
Denmark	De Grønne	Fremskridtspartiet
Finland	Vihreät/Vihreä Liitto	–
France	Les Verts, Génération Écologie	Front National
Germany	Die Grünen	Die Republikaner, Deutsche Volksunion
Greece	OIKIPA	–
Ireland	Comhaontas Glas	–
Italy	Liste Verdi	Movimento Sociale Italiano/Alleanza Nazionale
Luxembourg	Di Grëng Alternative, Greng Lëscht Ekologesch Initiativ	Lëtzebuerg fir de Letzebuerger National Bewegong
Netherlands	Groen Links, De Groenen	Centrumdemocraten, Centrumpartij/ Centrumpartij '86
Norway	Miljøpartiet de Grønne	Fremskrittspartiet
Portugal	Os Verdes	Partido da Democracia Crista
Spain	Los Verdes	–
Sweden	Miljöpartiet de Gröna	Ny Demokrati
Switzerland	Grüne Partei der Schweiz (Parti écologiste suisse), Grünes Bündnis der Schweiz (Alliance socialiste verte)	Nationale Aktion (Action nationale)/Schweizerische Demokraten (Démocrates suisses), Vigilance, Schweizer Auto Partei (Parti automobiliste suisse)
United Kingdom	Green Party	National Front, British National Party

Note: The French names of the Swiss parties are in parentheses. The names of parties that change are indicated with a slash.
Sources: Mackie and Rose (1991, 1997).

parties, their categorization is remarkably consistent with this coding scheme based only on a party's prioritization of a strong anti-immigration policy position.

Given that mainstream party strategies are implemented only after niche party challengers have developed, the cases in this analysis are limited to those instances of green and radical right party emergence.[13] Even with this restriction, the data set includes a more diverse set of party cases than those examined in single-issue party analyses. As summarized in Table 3.1, the analysis includes the electoral trajectories of forty-three single-issue parties across seventeen Western European

[13] This is different from sociological models, in which observed rates of unemployment can be used to impute latent green or radical right party support in the absence of party formation (Golder 2003a, 2003b; Jackman and Volpert 1996; Swank and Betz 2003). This chapter, therefore, assesses the impact of the explanatory variables on niche party vote conditional on niche party entry.

countries and 120 national elections.[14] This group consists of the green and radical right parties that contest multiple consecutive national legislative elections,
regardless of their peak vote share, as listed in Mackie and Rose (1991, 1997).
The electoral trajectories of the niche parties are examined from 1970 to 1998,
a period that encompasses the life-spans of the majority of these niche parties to
the end of the twentieth century.[15]

Independent Variables

What factors alter the electoral trajectories of these new parties? The electoral
success of niche parties has been linked to three sets of variables: party strategies,
institutions, and sociological conditions.

Mainstream Party Strategies. This book argues that the competitiveness of
niche parties is shaped by the behavior of their fellow political contestants.
Although the political arena may contain up to thirty party competitors in any one
national legislative election, this analysis focuses on the tactics of a subset of political actors: the mainstream parties of the center-left and center-right.[16] Defined
by both their location on the Left-Right political dimension and their electoral
dominance of that left or right ideological bloc, mainstream parties are typically
governmental actors. As discussed in previous chapters, their name recognition
and status as governmental players provide them with strategic tools unavailable
to smaller, less-prominent political parties. Their co-optation of issues is seen as
being more credible. Their offers to form electoral and permanent coalitions with
niche parties are more credible and enticing. Furthermore, these stronger mainstream parties typically have greater media access, facilitating the communication
of their strategic message to the electorate.

Mainstream parties from the seventeen countries were initially chosen according to their position on the Left-Right axis. Based on the expert survey party
classification data from Castles and Mair (1984: 83), I defined mainstream parties
of the center-left, or "Moderate Left," as those parties with scores of 1.25 to 3.75
on a scale of 0 to 10. Mainstream parties of the center-right, Castles and Mair's
"Moderate Right" parties, were those parties with positions of 6.25 to 8.75.[17]
Where more than one party met the same criterion in any given country, the party
with the highest electoral average from 1970 to 2000 was chosen.[18] This system

---

[14] Information on these forty-three parties is represented in the data set by thirty niche party panels,
or one panel per niche party type per country.

[15] More detailed information on the electoral history of these niche parties is found in Tables A3.1
and A3.2 in this chapter's Appendix.

[16] I later expand the number of mainstream party actors in the analysis to include centrist mainstream
parties.

[17] With an average score of 5.4, Italy's commonly recognized center-right party, Democrazia Cristiana (DC), was the exception. See Castles and Mair 1984: 80.

[18] It is assumed that the party with the strongest electoral record will have greater voter recognition,
more credibility as a governmental actor, and, thus, more access to the strategic advantage inherent
to mainstream parties.

TABLE 3.2. *Mainstream Parties in Western Europe*

Country	Center-Left	Center-Right
Austria	SPÖ	ÖVP
Belgium	PS/SP	PRL/PVV
Denmark	SD	KF
Finland	SSDP	KOK
France	PS	RPR
Germany	SPD	CDU
Greece	PASOK	Nea Dimokratia
Ireland	Labour	Fianna Fáil, Fine Gael
Italy	PCI	DC
Luxembourg	LSAP	CSV
Netherlands	PvdA	VVD
Norway	DNA	H
Portugal	PSP	PSD
Spain	PSOE	AP/PP
Sweden	SAP	M
Switzerland	SPS/PSS	CVP/PDC
United Kingdom	Labour	Conservative

Sources: Castles and Mair (1984); Laver and Hunt (1992).

yielded one mainstream center-left and one mainstream center-right party in each country, with one exception: Ireland is recognized as having two center-right parties.[19] The resulting classifications are consistent with the rank ordering of parties reported in Laver and Hunt (1992). The mainstream parties included in the study are listed in Table 3.2.

Having identified the strategic actors, we turn our attention to the measurement of their tactical behavior. As argued in Chapter 2, in competition between unequals, mainstream parties have access to three strategies – dismissive, accommodative, and adversarial. In light of this new conception of mainstream party responses, the few existing data sets with measures of party strategies are not appropriate.[20] Instead, I developed and implemented a coding scheme to capture the established parties' behavior using data from the Comparative Manifestos

[19] The dominance of a noneconomic dimension in Irish politics means that Fianna Fáil and Fine Gael are largely indistinguishable on the Left-Right spectrum.

[20] The only article that has employed a somewhat similar coding procedure for mainstream party behavior in a subset of countries is Rohrschneider (1993). But his omission of a dismissive category from the range of tactics – a decision consistent with standard spatial models – alters the number of possible strategic combinations, biasing the values of the explanatory variable and their effects on niche party electoral success. Specifically, in dividing party strategies between policy convergence and policy divergence categories, Rohrschneider assumes that all mainstream parties have actively recognized and validated the niche party's issue. As such, he accords the new parties a higher degree of importance in the political arena than they necessarily deserve. The same limitation would be apparent in strategies coded from any expert survey that does not allow respondents to refuse to place mainstream parties on a niche party's new issue dimension (see Laver and Hunt 1992; Lubbers et al. 2002).

Project (CMP) (Budge et al. 2001) supplemented with information from primary and secondary sources.

The CMP data set offers several advantages over other data sets. First, this data set records a party's general support for *and* prioritization of a set of issue positions based on the content of the political party's election manifestos.[21] This second piece of information distinguishes the CMP data set from other data sources and allows us to measure the centrality of a given issue to the mainstream party's agenda – information critical to the coding of modified spatial strategies. Second, these data are available on the oft-overlooked noneconomic issues championed by green and radical right parties. Third, this information is available for every mainstream party and almost every election in my analysis.[22] The CMP data, therefore, better capture changes in an established party's response to a niche party across elections than expert surveys of party location, which are conducted less frequently and only code party position (and not prioritization of those positions) on a limited number of issues (e.g., Benoit and Laver 2006; Laver and Hunt 1992).

Based on CMP measures of party policy related to the niche party's new issue axis, I coded the strategies of individual mainstream parties as dismissive, accommodative, or adversarial.[23] Support for a niche party's issue position in an election manifesto was deemed indicative of mainstream party accommodation.[24] Mainstream party adversarial tactics were signaled by opposition to a niche party's issue position. A party neither supporting nor opposing a niche party's issue, as indicated by the presence of little to no discussion of that topic in its election manifesto, was categorized as engaging in dismissive behavior.[25] This coding

---

[21] Though there is disagreement in the literature as to whether precise spatial positions can be derived from CMP data, it is not necessary to join that debate here; information about the exact spatial position of a mainstream party on a particular issue is not necessary for my coding of party behavior.

[22] The CMP data set does not include information on mainstream party political manifestos from the 1996 election in Spain, the 1997 election in Norway, and the 1998 election in Denmark (Budge et al. 2001: 221); the data set merely substitutes the results from the previous national election. Because of the lack of data on mainstream party strategies for these elections, these observations are excluded from the analysis.

[23] These measures of strategy capture the behavior of parties, not the effects of those tactics on voter perceptions of the salience and ownership of the niche party's issue. Because the predictions of the standard and modified spatial theories are not observationally equivalent, conclusions about the relative explanatory power of these strategic theories can be drawn without looking at the microlevel mechanism. The microlevel mechanism by which these tools alter niche party support will be directly examined in the case studies in Chapters 5 through 8.

[24] For a strategy to be coded accommodative, a party's pronounced support of a neophyte's issue position could be accompanied by few references in opposition to that policy stance. A similar confirmatory procedure was employed when coding the adversarial tactics.

[25] As with the accommodative and adversarial tactics, a confirmatory procedure was used when coding the dismissive strategies. In the event that a mainstream party's manifesto contained both statements in support of and in opposition to the niche party's policy position, as indicated by sentences in both the AC and AD categories discussed previously, the response was coded as being dismissive unless other information to the contrary was available from primary and secondary sources.

procedure was conducted for each mainstream party for each national-level election between 1970 and 1998, the last election year for which the data were available.[26]

However, the Comparative Manifestos Project data have certain limitations that affect the coding of mainstream party responses. As noted by Laver and Garry (2000: 621) and Laver, Benoit, and Garry (2003), not all issues coded in the data set are presented as position issues, or topics with positive and negative stances to them. Critical to this analysis, the main coding categories for the single issues of green and radical right parties – the "environment" and "law and order" – refer only to support for these issues (Budge et al. 2001: Appendix III).[27] No category directly measures opposition to environmental protection or to immigration restrictions. In addition, the CMP coding process is vulnerable to the problem of "seepage" (Benoit, Laver, and Mikhailov 2007: 13–14), whereby manifesto sentences on one topic could be miscoded into one of multiple, related, and not mutually exclusive coding categories.[28]

To mitigate these limitations and arrive at more reliable measures, I drew on several related topics in the CMP data set to derive information about the mainstream parties' positions on the niche parties' issues. Support for law and order (variable 605), a national(istic) way of life (601), and traditional morality (603), and opposition to multiculturalism (608) were deemed indicative of mainstream party accommodation of radical right parties.[29] Mainstream adversarial tactics were signaled by opposition to both a national(istic) way of life (602) and traditional morality (604), and support for multiculturalism (607) and underprivileged minority groups (705). Low levels of measures for or against these categories signified a dismissive tactic.

The Comparative Manifesto Project provides fewer appropriate measures for coding strategies toward green parties. The variables of environmental protection (501) and anti-growth economy (416) explicitly mention support for the environment, and thus, manifesto coverage of these topics was considered reflective of

---

[26] Manifestos for a particular national-level election reflect the strategies adopted by mainstream parties sometime after the previous election but before the one being contested.

[27] The creation of this unipolar classification structure reflects the theoretical motivations behind the Comparative Manifestos Project. According to the saliency theory supported by the CMP's principal investigators, party competition is a series of salience-altering, not position-altering, maneuvers. Parties compete by promoting the unipolar, or "valence" issues that they own. Given the researchers' assumption that certain issues have only one acceptable position, the coding scheme was designed to measure party intensity on those unipolar issues, not parties' positive and negative positioning on those topics.

[28] Volkens (2001: 100) notes that the most common coding errors of this type included coding "quasi-sentences" on precise policy positions (such as "Economic Growth") in more general categories (such as "General Economic Goals") and vice versa. However, in more recent work (Klingemann et al. 2006: 115), the CMP researchers report that overlaps, or seepage, also occurred across nonnested related topics.

[29] The grouping of these closely related categories is consistent with the recommendation of Klingemann et al. (2006: 113–15) in order to arrive at measures that are "more stable and reliable than any one of their components." The wording of the individual CMP variable categories can be found in Appendix Table A3.5.

TABLE 3.3. *Incidence of Mainstream Party*
Strategies toward Green and Radical Right
Parties per Electoral Period from 1970 to 1998

Mainstream Party Strategies	Frequency of the Strategic Combination
DIDI	41
ACAC	13
DIAC	27
DIAD	4
ADAD	2
ACAD AC > AD	27
ACAD AD > AC	6
N	120[30]

mainstream party accommodation of green parties. In the absence of any variable recording explicit opposition to environmental protection, I used support for free enterprise (401) and agriculture and farmers (703), and opposition to internationalism (109) to capture adversarial strategies toward green parties.[31]

Given the broad nature of some of these issue classification categories, the resulting coding decisions were checked against mainstream party policy deliberations and pronouncements about the niche party and its issue recorded in archival materials, contemporaneous news sources, and secondary analyses.[32]

From the individual coding of mainstream party tactics for each electoral period, I find occurrences of each of the six possible strategic combinations in the data (see Table 3.3). I model DIDI, DIAC, DIAD, ACAC, and ADAD as simple dummy variables. The effect of the sixth strategic combination, ACAD, on niche party vote depends on the relative intensity of the constituent strategies.[33] I code the ACAD variable -1 when the intensity of the AC tactic is greater and $+1$ when the intensity of the AD tactic is greater.

As currently modeled, the strategic variables capture the effect of the strategies in a given electoral period, independent of the tactics pursued in previous time

[30] The increase in N over the data analyzed in Meguid 2005 (where $N = 114$) reflects the availability of economic data for an additional year and the inclusion of previously missing observations for the Austrian greens and the Dutch radical right.

[31] As seen in Appendix Table A3.5a, this last category is included because it refers to opposition to "world planning of resources" (Budge et al. 2001: 222–3).

[32] The resources consulted include the following: Labour and Conservative Party Archives and French Socialist Party Archives; *Keesing's Record of World Events, CD-ROM* 1999; Betz and Immerfall 1998; Taggart 1996; Kitschelt 1994, 1995; Norris 2005; O'Neill 1997; Hainsworth 2000. These sources also supplement the programmatically focused CMP data with information on the organizational dimension of the mainstream parties' tactics.

[33] Based on the definition offered in Chapter 2, the intensity of a mainstream party's strategy is a function of the number of tactics (programmatic and organizational) employed against the niche party and the prioritization of the niche party's issue in the party's election manifesto as measured by the percentage of each party's manifesto devoted to the issue position.

periods. However, the PSO theory posits the importance of policy consistency and timeliness for the effectiveness of mainstream party strategies. Accommodative tactics will not lead to a reduction (or as much of a reduction) in niche party support if that mainstream party previously pursued an adversarial strategy toward the neophyte. The vote-boosting effect of adversarial tactics is also expected to be compromised if that mainstream party was accommodative in the previous electoral period. Likewise, active, especially accommodative, strategies will prove less effective if implemented after successive periods of dismissive tactics; a mainstream party's ability to acquire issue ownership – the key mechanism of accommodation – is severely limited once the window of ownership opportunity is closed and the niche party's reputation as the rightful issue owner is entrenched.

A review of mainstream party strategies in my data set reveals that policy hesitation occurs more frequently than policy inconsistency in mainstream party–niche party interaction in Western Europe. Of the 120 observations, there are eight cases of mainstream parties employing accommodative tactics (ACAC or DIAC) after two or more successive periods of dismissive strategies following the niche party's emergence.[34] Because there are only two instances of a mainstream party switching between AC and AD tactics in successive electoral periods in my data, I model only policy delay. I create time-sensitive dummy variables for DIAC and ACAC strategies, where the variables are coded 1 when the strategy was implemented after two or more successive periods of dismissive tactics by a given mainstream party.[35]

Institutional Factors. The existing literature on single-issue parties holds as central to party success the institutional environment in which the party competes (Givens 2005; Golder 2003b; Jackman and Volpert 1996; Müller-Rommel 1996). As discussed more fully in Chapter 1, barriers to office attainment not only affect a party's ability to turn votes into seats but are also thought to alter a voter's incentives to support a given party. Proponents of this theoretical approach have identified three critical institutional factors that are purported to alter party vote both directly and indirectly: electoral laws, state structure, and type of government. I include measures of the first two variables in the regression analysis. The third factor – whether a country has a parliamentary or presidential system of government – is excluded from the study because of the limited range of governmental types across Western European countries[36] and disagreement within the discipline over the defining characteristics of a semipresidential system (Lijphart 1984: 70; Shugart and Carey 1992; Skach 1999).

---

[34] In the previous version of the data set, the hesitation variables were incorrectly calculated, leading to the inclusion of nondelayed cases of accommodation with delayed. This has now been corrected.

[35] For example, following this coding rule, the accommodative party would need to have been dismissive for two or more successive electoral periods in the past for the subsequent DIAC combination to be coded "delayed."

[36] There is no pure presidential system in the region.

ELECTORAL RULES. Based on its popularity in election studies and strong performance as a determinant of party success, I employ a measure of district magnitude to test the impact of electoral rules on niche party vote level.[37] Following
the practices of Amorim Neto and Cox (1997) and Golder (2003b), this variable
was operationalized as the logged magnitude of the median legislator's district.[38]
The expectation is that, as district magnitude increases, niche party support will
increase, with the marginal effect decreasing as the district magnitude becomes
large.

STATE STRUCTURE. Although less-commonly examined, the concentration of
political power in a state is also posited to influence the electoral success of parties,
especially new competitors lacking entrenched bases of national support. To test
the claims of Harmel and Robertson (1985) and Willey (1998) that third party
support at the national level will be higher in countries with more opportunities
for elected office at the subnational level, I include a state structure dummy
variable, where 1 signifies a unitary state and 0 signifies a federal state.[39] As the
variable is operationalized, we expect a negative relationship; green and radical
right party vote levels should be lower in unitary than in federal systems.

Sociological Factors. Second only to institutional factors in their popularity in
election studies, the sociological or socio-economic characteristics of a country are regularly touted as determinants of a party's fortune (e.g., Dalton 1996;
Givens 2005; Golder 2003b; Inglehart 1997; Jackman and Volpert 1996; Kitschelt
1994, 1995; Müller-Rommel 1989). As outlined previously, this group of theories
claims that individual-level characteristics and societal conditions influence the
perceived salience of specific political issues. Support for a given party turns on
the resonance of that party's issues in the existing sociological climate. To capture the auspiciousness of a political environment for party success, researchers
of green and radical right parties have examined a series of measures, including
a society's economic health, value orientation, and percentage of immigrants.

ECONOMIC HEALTH. Following the practices of sociological analyses of green
and radical right party support (e.g., Golder 2003b; Jackman and Volpert 1996;
Taggart 1996), I use two measures of economic health: the current level of GDP
per capita and the current rate of unemployment in a given election year.[40] Unlike

---

[37] Although the multiple dimensions of an electoral system cannot be fully captured by its district
magnitude, institutionalists defend this choice of variable specification. Ordeshook and Shvetsova
(1994: 105) claim: "It is by now agreed in the comparative elections literature that *the* critical
institutional variable influencing the formation and maintenance of parties is district magnitude."
Sartori (1986: 53) agrees: "[district magnitude] affects the proportionality of PR more than do
the various mathematical translation formulas ... [and in] this regard the rule of thumb is that the
smaller the district the lesser the proportionality and, conversely, the larger the district the greater
the proportionality."

[38] Data from Golder 2003b.

[39] Information on state structure was obtained from Elazar (1995) and Watts (1996).

[40] GDP per capita, reported at current prices and current purchasing power parity (PPP) in thousands
of U.S. dollars, was obtained from the *OECD Factbook 2006: Economic, Environmental and Social
Statistics*. The unemployment rate, measured as a percentage of the total labor force, was obtained
from the *OECD Statistical Compendium CD-ROM 2000*.

the effect of institutional variables, the predicted effect of these economic factors varies by niche party family. Green party vote is expected to be positively correlated with GDP per capita and negatively correlated with unemployment (Taggart 1996). The relationships are the opposite for radical right party support (Golder 2003b; Jackman and Volpert 1996). To allow for these party-specific effects, I model the economic variables as a series of party-specific terms.

VALUE ORIENTATION. While the health of the economy has been considered an important factor in determining the success of both green and radical right parties, interest in the explanatory power of a society's value orientation has come mainly from scholars of environmental parties. I model value orientation as the percentage of postmaterialists in a country during the current election year, as computed from the European Communities Study and subsequent Eurobarometer surveys. Consistent time-series data are available for only eleven of the seventeen countries in my analysis.[41] Despite the missing data problems, the postmaterialism measure is retained because no suitable proxy for anti-materialist concerns exists.[42] According to Inglehart (1977), Dalton (1996), and Müller-Rommel (1989), higher levels of postmaterialism should lead to higher levels of green party support. Postmaterialism is included as a green-party-specific variable.

PERCENTAGE OF IMMIGRANTS. Just as the level of postmaterialism is viewed as a predictor of a country's support for the issue appeals of a green party, the prevalence of immigrants in a country has been thought to affect a society's endorsement of the anti-immigrant platform of radical right parties. I include a variable measuring the percentage of foreign citizens in a national population to test the relationship between immigrant percentage and support for radical right parties. In light of the claim by Golder (2003b) that the effect of immigrants on radical right vote is conditional on the level of unemployment in a country, I also include an immigrant percentage–unemployment interactive term. Data for both the nonconditional and conditional formulations of the immigrant percentage variable come from SOPEMI and national census data collected by Golder (2003b).[43] The lack of data for nine elections across five countries in this data set introduces problems of omitted cases, but in the absence of appropriate proxies,

[41] The surveys were only administered in European Economic Community and later European Union member states (Inglehart et al. 1994). Consequently, there is no postmaterialism measure for Switzerland and only limited information for Austria, Finland, Sweden, Norway, and Spain. Switching to the three waves of the World Values Surveys (Inglehart et al. 2000) does not significantly alleviate these problems, as these studies provide only one observation per country per decade for a limited number of the countries in my analysis.

[42] The demographic variables typically thought to be associated with postmaterialist values – age and education – are not appropriate substitutes for the value orientation variable. Although age is negatively correlated with postmaterialism and green party support, it is also negatively correlated with materialist values and radical right support (Taggart 1996). Moreover, education is found to have no relationship with green party vote when other factors are taken into account (Bürklin 1987). Inclusion of these demographic variables would therefore not measure the underlying support for postmaterialist values in a country.

[43] As discussed in Golder (2003b: 463), data on immigrant percentages were either available for the specific election years or were extrapolated from the existing SOPEMI or census data. For more information on the collection of this data, see Golder 2003b.

the immigrant variables are included nonetheless.[44] According to previous studies, for example, Givens (2005), Golder (2003b), and Swank and Betz (2003), the percentage of immigrants in a country is expected to be positively correlated with radical right party vote, regardless of whether the relationship is conditional on unemployment.[45] The immigrant variables are modeled as radical-right-specific terms.

MODELS AND ANALYSIS

To explain the magnitude, shape, and timing of niche party electoral support, I employ pooled cross-sectional time-series analysis. Specifically, I ran ordinary least squares (OLS) regressions with lagged dependent variables and panel-corrected standard errors. As recommended by Beck and Katz (1995, 1996), the lagged dependent variable (LDV) was added to eliminate autocorrelation in the underlying data. This specification is supported by the results of Lagrange multiplier tests.[46]

My analysis of niche party support starts with an assessment of the non-strategy-focused theories of vote share dominant in the literature. Following the extant research on green and radical right parties, Model Ia includes only institutional and sociological factors. The sociological variables of postmaterialism, immigrant percentage, and the interaction of immigrant percentage and unemployment are excluded from this first regression because of the severe data restrictions that they impose. These variables are included in Model Ib. Given that postmaterialism and GDP per capita are highly correlated, the GDP per capita variables were excluded from this second equation.[47] The results of these nonstrategic models are reported in Table 3.4, with the predicted signs of the explanatory variables listed in column two. The statistical significance of the coefficients is measured with one-tailed t-tests due to the directional nature of the institutional and sociological hypotheses.

Findings of the Nonstrategic Models

The regression results in Table 3.4 suggest that the electoral trajectories of niche parties are not mere reflections of the institutional and sociological climate. Contrary to the expectations of institutionalists, electoral rules do not emerge

---

[44] Data on the following elections were missing: Denmark 1971; Italy 1972, 1976; Norway 1973; Portugal 1999; and the United Kingdom 1970, February 1974, October 1974, 1979. With immigrant data lacking for half of the British elections in the time period under examination, the case of the British radical right party is effectively excluded from the analysis. Consequently, any regressions using this variable, including those found in Golder (2003b), will suffer from some selection bias.

[45] Golder's conclusion about the positive effect of immigrant percentage on vote share is limited to a populist subset of radical right parties.

[46] The tests for the models without the LDV specification indicated that we could reject the null hypothesis of the serial independence of the errors. With the addition of the lagged dependent variables to the models, the tests now show that we cannot reject the null hypothesis.

[47] The correlation between these variables is 0.92.

TABLE 3.4. *Multivariate Analyses of Niche Party Vote Percentage: Nonstrategic Models*

	Predicted Sign	Niche Party Vote Model Ia	Niche Party Vote (geographically restricted version) Model Ib
Institutional			
Ln Median District Magnitude	+	−0.07	0.12
		(0.14)	(0.29)
State Structure	−	−1.17**	−1.77*
		(0.44)	(0.89)
Sociological			
GDP/Capita *by Niche Party* (in thousands)			
Green Party	+	0.09*	
		(0.04)	
Radical Right Party	−	0.07	
		(0.04)	
Unemployment *by Niche Party*			
Green Party	−	−0.03	−0.10
		(0.05)	(0.09)
Radical Right Party	+	0.08	−0.16
		(0.09)	(0.17)
Postmaterialism (Green Party)	+		0.01
			(0.04)
Immigrant Percentage (Radical Right Party)	+		1.60*
			(0.74)
Immigrant Percentage × Unemployment (Radical Right Party)	+		−0.14
			(0.07)
Past Performance			
NP Vote $_{t-1}$		0.82***	0.78***
		(0.09)	(0.12)
Constant		0.91	3.07**
		(0.82)	(1.09)
Adjusted R²		0.6871	0.6636
N		120	56

***$p < .001$; **$p < .01$; *$p < .1$ (one-tailed tests). Panel-corrected standard errors are in parentheses.

as strong or statistically significant determinants of niche party vote.[48] Likewise, these results indicate little consistent support for the hypotheses linking green or radical right vote levels to a country's economic health, immigrant percentage, or value orientation. Of the factors used to test the institutional and sociological claims, only state structure has a statistically significant and correctly signed coefficient in both models; consistent with the often-overlooked claim by Harmel and

---

[48] The results are robust to the use of logged average district magnitude instead of logged median district magnitude.

Robertson (1985) and Willey (1998), the vote of green and radical right parties is found to be lower in unitary than federal systems.

Looking at the variables that meet these requirements (statistical significance and correct sign) in one of the two models, we have GDP per capita for green parties in Model Ia and percentage of immigrants in the geographically restricted Model Ib.[49] With regard to the immigrant percentage variable, even this limited support for the immigrant hypothesis is mixed. Although a strong, positive relationship emerges between percentage of immigrants and radical right party vote, the sign of the interactive term runs counter to Golder's prediction; the influence of immigrants on voter support is found to *decrease*, rather than increase, with rising levels of unemployment.[50]

Thus, while these analyses offer some support for the proposed relationships between niche party vote and state structure and GDP per capita (the latter only in the case of green parties), they do not signal the predominance of nonstrategic factors of party support. Rather, the regression results confirm the findings by others that general economic performance (Swank and Betz 2003) and electoral rules (Swank and Betz 1995, 1996; Carter 2005) have little independent impact on single-issue party support.[51]

The weak results of these standard, nonstrategic models imply that other factors – either in combination with the institutional and sociological variables or by themselves – are shaping niche party vote. Models IIa and IIb test the claim of my PSO theory that mainstream party strategies are those driving forces. The models include the six strategic variables in addition to the two "delayed" strategic variables. The competing sociological measures are also included: GDP per capita and unemployment in Model IIa; and unemployment, postmaterialism, immigrant percentage, and the interacted immigrant percentage–unemployment term in the geographically restricted Model IIb.

The result of a joint F-test supports the inclusion of country dummy variables in these models. Not only do these variables help to minimize country-level heteroskedasticity, which is not addressed by the niche-party-panel-level standard error correction of the models, but they also reflect country differences unaccounted for by the independent variables. These differences include, most importantly, variation in the distribution of voters' positions in the policy space – a variable for which no cross-country, time-series measure exists, yet which is critical to the predicted effect of mainstream party strategies on niche party support. However, as noted by Beck and Katz (2001: 492), the inclusion of these

---

[49] Although its effect on niche party vote is substantively significant, the GDP per capita coefficient for radical right parties in Model Ia has a sign that runs counter to the predictions of the sociological theories and fails to be statistically significant at $p < .1$ in either one-tailed or two-tailed tests.

[50] While it would be necessary to calculate the full range of conditional coefficients to determine when the interactive relationship between immigrant percentage and unemployment has a statistically significant effect on radical right party vote (see Friedrich 1982; Golder 2003b on interactive effects), the negative sign of the interactive term constitutes sufficient evidence that the direction of the modifying effect does not follow Golder's expectation.

[51] According to Golder (2003a, 2003b: 461), the data of Jackman and Volpert (1996) likewise support the finding that electoral institutions – specifically electoral thresholds – do not influence radical right party support.

country fixed effects in the model "means that any independent variable that does not vary temporally cannot be used as an explanatory variable."[52] Therefore, the largely static electoral rules and state structure variables are excluded from the equations.[53]

Findings of the Strategic Models

The regression results of the strategic models are reported in Table 3.5, with the predicted signs of the independent variables listed in column two. The statistical significance of the coefficients is measured with one-tailed t-tests due to the directional nature of the sociological and strategic hypotheses. For ease of presentation, the estimates of the seventeen country dummies are not shown.[54]

The regression results reinforce the conclusions of the previous models that the electoral trajectories of niche parties are not solely determined by – or, in some cases, even critically influenced by – sociological factors. Rather, the findings offer support for the central claim of the book that mainstream party tactics play a critical role in niche party vote. They exert statistically and substantively significant effects on the vote of green and radical right parties in both the full and geographically restricted models.[55] The strong influence of the strategic variables stands in contrast to the generally weaker roles, both statistically and substantively, played by the traditional sociological factors. Of the measures of economic health, value orientation, and immigrant prevalence used to test the competing theories, only GDP per capita in green party cases (in Model IIa) and immigrant percentage in radical right party cases (in Model IIb) emerge as statistically significant and correctly signed predictors of niche party vote.[56]

---

[52] This modeling limitation is not taken into consideration by the few existing quantitative analyses of single-issue party support, including Meguid 2005.

[53] The state structure variable is temporally invariant in all but one of the seventeen countries for the elections included in the analysis. Although exhibiting more variation within a country over time, the electoral rules variable, *Ln Median District Magnitude*, is still temporally invariant in seven of the seventeen countries, or in sixteen of the thirty niche party panels. The fact that the electoral variable was found to be statistically and substantively insignificant in the alternative models advocated by proponents of institutionalist theories (Models Ia and Ib) lessens my concerns about being unable to test its explanatory power in the strategic models.

[54] In Model IIa, ten of the seventeen country dummy variables were statistically significant at $p < .1$ in two-tailed tests. The number of country dummy coefficients reaching that significance level was eight out of fifteen in Model IIb. While the country dummy variables were included to account for unmeasurable country-level characteristics like voter distribution, the sign and magnitude of the specific country coefficients are not, in and of themselves, of interest here. The role that such unmeasured national-level factors play in niche party vote will be explored more in the British and French case studies of Chapters 5 through 7.

[55] Although there is some variation in the statistical significance of individual strategies across Models IIa and IIb, F-tests conducted for both the full and geographically restricted models support the rejection of the null hypothesis of the joint insignificance of all the strategic variables.

[56] In Model IIb, the variables of postmaterialism and the interacted immigrant percentage – unemployment term are not significant at $p < .1$ according to one-tailed tests based on the literature's directional hypotheses. The negative coefficient of the interaction term is statistically significant at this level if we disregard the predicted positive relationship and employ a two-tailed test instead. The coefficient of the postmaterialism variable remains insignificant at $p < .1$ if we employ a two-tailed test.

TABLE 3.5. *Multivariate Analyses of Niche Party Vote Percentage: Strategic Models*

	Predicted Sign	Niche Party Vote Model IIa	Niche Party Vote (geographically restricted version) Model IIb
Strategic			
Mainstream Party:			
DIDI	−	−1.10*	−1.46*
		(0.75)	(1.02)
ACAC	−	−0.89	−2.84*
		(1.00)	(1.47)
DIAC	−	−1.34*	−1.71*
		(0.85)	(1.21)
DIAD	+	5.58***	9.68***
		(1.36)	(1.37)
ADAD	+	6.29**	0.93
		(2.12)	(1.93)
ACAD with Relative Intensity[a]	+	1.43***	2.71***
		(0.39)	(0.70)
Delayed ACAC	+	1.17	3.30**
		(0.95)	(1.10)
Delayed DIAC	+	2.89*	NA[b]
		(1.72)	
Past Performance			
NP Vote$_{t-1}$		0.71***	0.66***
		(0.07)	(0.16)
Sociological			
GDP/Capita *by Niche Party* (in thousands)			
Green Party	+	0.06*	
		(0.04)	
Radical Right Party	−	0.02	
		(0.05)	
Unemployment *by Niche Party*			
Green Party	−	−0.09	0.04
		(0.08)	(0.17)
Radical Right Party	+	0.00	−0.03
		(0.09)	(0.18)
Postmaterialism (Green Party)	+		−0.09
			(0.06)
Immigrant Percentage (Radical Right Party)	+		0.87*
			(0.60)
Immigrant Percentage × Unemployment (Radical Right Party)	+		−0.11
			(0.05)
Country Dummies		Included	Included
Adjusted R²		0.8844	0.9104
N		120	56

***p < .001; **p < .01; *p < .1 (one-tailed tests). Panel-corrected standard errors are in parentheses.

[a] The coefficient of the variable ACAD with Relative Intensity is reported in terms of the adversarial strategy being stronger than the accommodative one. Where AC > AD, the sign of the beta is the opposite.

[b] This strategic variable was eliminated from the regression model because it was not observed within the population of mainstream party tactical responses.

These results are similar to those observed in Models Ia and Ib, models in which mainstream party strategies are not controlled for. Yet, just as in Model Ib, the explanatory power of the immigrant percentage variable in the strategic model is weakened by the surprisingly negative effect of the immigrant percentage–unemployment interaction term.

Beyond demonstrating the statistical strength of strategic behavior over standard sociological factors, the analysis confirms that mainstream parties can use strategies either to reduce or to strengthen niche party electoral support. Consistent with the predictions of the PSO theory, the results of Model IIa show that joint dismissive (DIDI) and dismissive-accommodative (DIAC) strategies decrease, and dismissive-adversarial (DIAD) and joint adversarial (ADAD) tactical combinations increase, niche party support. Although not statistically significant in Model IIa, the effect of the joint accommodative (ACAC) tactic is negative as predicted.[57] Per the expectations of my model, the impact of accommodative-adversarial (ACAD) tactics depends on the relative intensity of the constituent strategies. When adversarial tactics are dominant (ACAD = +1), this strategic combination leads to an increase in niche party vote. When accommodative actions are stronger (ACAD = −1), niche party support declines.

Support for the claim that hesitation mitigates the vote-reducing power of accommodative tactics is more mixed. Whereas in Model IIa the signs of both delayed strategic combinations are positive as predicted, only the Delayed DIAC variable is statistically significant. That result, however, demonstrates the strong influence of successive periods of dismissive tactics on the subsequent effect of mainstream party accommodation. Whereas the timely implementation of a DIAC tactic reduces a niche party's vote by 1.34 percentage points, the delayed use of a DIAC tactic *increases* its vote by 1.55 percentage points.[58]

The results of the geographically restricted Model IIb demonstrate the robustness of the findings.[59] Even though the lack of data on postmaterialism and immigrant percentage led to the elimination of more than half of the original observations from the analysis, mainstream party tactics remain critical determinants of niche party vote. All strategic variables have the expected signs, and the coefficients of all four vote-reducing (DIDI, ACAC, DIAC, and ACAD when AC > AD) and two vote-boosting (DIAD and ACAD when AD > AC)

---

[57] The strong negative and statistically significant effect of this variable is seen in the geographically restricted Model IIb.

[58] The effect of a delayed DIAC tactic is calculated by summing the coefficients for DIAC and Delayed DIAC.

[59] The effects of the strategic variables are also relatively robust to the addition of the tactics of a third set of mainstream parties – the centrist parties – to Model IIa. When the strategic responses of the center-left and center-right mainstream parties are controlled for, centrist party tactics generally prove insignificant. That said, there are some statistical costs to the incorporation of the centrist parties' strategies into the regression. The number of observations in the model drops to eighty-nine because only twelve of the seventeen countries have centrist parties (criteria based on Castles and Mair 1984). And the ADAD strategy is eliminated from that analysis since, during the time period under investigation, it is only employed in Austria, one of the countries lacking a centrist party.

combinations are statistically and substantively significant.[60] Like Model IIa, this regression provides some support for the mediating role of hesitation on strategic effectiveness; although the net effect of delay is smaller than that observed for DIAC in Model IIa, the normally vote-reducing ACAC strategic combination strengthens niche party vote when it is employed after two or more successive periods of dismissive strategies.

In both models, therefore, mainstream parties' behavior plays a statistically significant role in shaping the competitiveness of their single-issue competitors. And, as suggested by the coefficient values in Table 3.5, the impact of these strategies on the magnitude of a niche party's vote is also sizeable. Mainstream parties can alter the absolute level of niche party support in an election by between 1.1 and 6.3 percentage points, according to Model IIa, or between 1.5 and 9.7 percentage points, based on Model IIb's estimates.[61] And the effects of the sociological variables cannot erase the impact of mainstream party behavior.[62] With the mean niche party vote being 4.7 percent, mainstream party strategies emerge as a major force determining niche party fortunes.[63]

Comparing the Explanatory Power of the PSO and Standard Spatial Theories

On the whole, then, the regression results provide strong support for my strategic theory of niche party success over the competing institutional and sociological theories. Do they, however, contradict the claims of the traditional spatial theories of party interaction? Can we conclude that strategies follow the microlevel mechanism of the PSO theory whereby tactics alter issue salience and ownership, not just party programmatic position? Because the predictions of the standard spatial and PSO theories are not observationally equivalent, conclusions about their relative explanatory power can be drawn without looking at the microlevel mechanism, but by simply examining the effects of the strategies.[64] Thus, I have summarized in Table 3.6 the expected impact of each strategy in a unidimensional space according to the standard spatial theory along with the strategy's observed effect from the regression results of Model IIa. Adjacent to the effect of each strategic combination on niche party vote in the next election, I also present the

---

[60] Although its coefficient still has the predicted positive sign, the marked change in the substantive and statistical significance of the ADAD variable in Model IIb is a result of the paucity of time-series data on immigrant prevalence and postmaterialist values for Austria, the only country in which this strategy is employed.

[61] I exclude the coefficient values of the statistically insignificant strategic variables from this range.

[62] Whether calculated at their means or one standard deviation above or below, the effects of the sociological variables on niche party vote in each model are smaller than those of most, if not all, of the strategic variables.

[63] The lagged dependent variable accounts, on average, for 3.2 percentage points of a niche party's vote in a given election. Although this amount may in some cases overshadow the effect of current mainstream party tactics, it should not be forgotten that a critical determinant of the lagged vote, i.e., niche party vote in the previous election, is also mainstream party tactics.

[64] Direct tests of the issue position, salience, and ownership mechanism behind the PSO strategic theory are conducted in the case studies of Chapters 5 through 8.

TABLE 3.6. *Predicted versus Observed Effects of Strategies on Niche Party Vote Percentage: Assessing the Standard Spatial Theory's Predictions*

Predicted Effect on Vote According to the Standard Spatial Theory	Strategies		Observed Effect on Vote in Next Election (coefficients from Model IIa)	Effect on Long-Run Equilibrium Vote (calculated from Model IIa)
?	Dismissive	{ DIDI	−1.10	−3.79
Decrease	Accommodative	{ ACAC	−0.89	−3.07
		DIAC	−1.34	−4.62
		ACAD AC >	−1.43	−4.93
		ACAD AD >	+1.43	+4.93
Increase	Adversarial	{ DIAD	+5.58	+19.24
		ADAD	+6.29	+21.69

impact of the permanent adoption of each strategic combination on the long-run equilibrium niche party vote level.[65]

To compare the observed effects of the mainstream strategic combinations to the predictions of the standard spatial theory, one must recall that the actions of a nonproximal party are considered irrelevant by the standard spatial theory. Thus, if we focus only on the behavior of the mainstream party closest to the niche party on this new issue, we can reduce the set of six different strategic combinations to three: those where there is no proximal party (DIDI), those where the proximal party is accommodative (ACAC, DIAC, and ACAD where AC > AD or where AD > AC), and those where the proximal party is adversarial (DIAD and ADAD).[66] These three strategic groupings are presented in column two of Table 3.6.

A comparison of the predicted and observed effects of these strategies offers some support for the standard spatial theory. As anticipated by that theory for unidimensional competition, adversarial tactics employed by the proximal party – represented by DIAD and ADAD in the original set of mainstream party responses – lead to neophyte vote gain. Accommodative strategies, in general,

---

[65] The effect of the repeated use of mainstream party strategies on long-run equilibrium niche party vote was calculated from the following equation: (coefficient of the strategy of interest)/ (1-[coefficient of the lagged dependent variable]), or $b_0 Strategy/1-\alpha$. Johnston and DiNardo 1997: 244–6. Implicit within this model is the assumption that, over time, niche party support will reach a natural limit, or equilibrium level. The marginal impact of an additional electoral period of a given strategy will decrease over time.

[66] Proximity to the niche party in this unidimensional space is determined by the position adopted by a mainstream party upon entering the new issue dimension. A party acting accommodatively is proximal to the niche party on the new issue. The adversarial party is considered to be nonproximal unless no other mainstream party is accommodative; in that case, the adversarial party is considered proximal. Where both parties refuse to take a position on the new issue dimension (i.e., both act dismissively), there is no proximal party.

also have the expected effect: niche party vote loss. The standard spatial theory offers no clear predictions about the impact of dismissive tactics, or not taking a position along the new policy dimension, on target party vote levels.

But the shortcomings of the standard spatial theory begin to surface when we compare the effects of strategies within each of these three categories. No two of the combinations containing accommodative or adversarial strategies have regression coefficients of the same value. Greater inconsistencies emerge when we compare the long-term effects of each of the strategic combinations within the accommodative category or, especially, the adversarial category. Consideration of the confidence intervals around these point estimates reduces the perceived differences between the strategies within each of the three categories, but several discrepancies remain.[67] When an accommodative tactic is paired with a dismissive tactic (i.e., DIAC strategy), it reduces niche party support in the next election by 1.34 percentage points. Yet, when accommodation is joined with a more intense adversarial tactic (ACAD where AD > AC), niche party vote *increases* by 1.43 percentage points.[68] The difference in their effects on the equilibrium vote level is even starker; the former leads to a decrease in niche party vote of 4.62 percentage points, whereas the latter results in an increase of 4.93 percentage points. The power of the "irrelevant" nonproximal party is also evident when we compare the effect of the accommodatively dominant (AC > AD) and the adversarially dominant (AD > AC) versions of ACAD strategies. According to the standard spatial theory, the effect of these strategies should be the same. Yet there is a significant difference in niche party vote obtained after their implementation whether in the short or long terms – a difference expected by my modified spatial theory. These findings clearly demonstrate that the behavior of the *distant* party matters. Based on this comparison of the observationally distinct predictions of the two strategic theories, it seems that the logic of the PSO theory captures competition between unequals better than that of the standard spatial theory.

FROM ONE MODEL TO MANY: DISAGGREGATING THE NICHE PARTY CATEGORY

Whether analyzed in the short or long term, the strategies of mainstream political players strongly alter the electoral support of their niche party competitors. But to what extent are these tactical weapons deployed equally toward all new parties? Moreover, is there variation in the effectiveness of these tools across the range of niche parties? Do the strategies that prove effective at shaping green and radical right trajectories together influence the vote shares of each type separately?

Up to this point, the analysis has focused on similarities in the application and impact of mainstream party strategies across green and radical right party cases.

---

[67] As expected, based on the similarity of their coefficient estimates, 90 percent confidence intervals around the ACAC, DIAC, and ACAD AC > strategic combinations overlap with each other. The same is true for the DIAD and ADAD strategic combinations.

[68] The 90 percent confidence intervals of these two strategic combinations do not overlap.

TABLE 3.7. *Incidence of Mainstream Party Strategies by Niche Party Family as Measured per Electoral Period from 1970 to 1998*

Mainstream Party Strategies	Frequency of the Strategic Combination Toward	
	Green Parties	Radical Right Parties
DIDI	20	20
ACAC	10	3
DIAC	17	9
DIAD	1	3
ADAD	0	2
ACAD with AC > AD	11	15
ACAD with AD > AC	2	3
N	61	55

As will be discussed at greater length in Chapter 4, the mainstream party's choice between an accommodative and adversarial strategy depends on the relative electoral threat posed by a niche party, not the identity of that niche party. Likewise, the impact of that strategy should be the same whether the niche party advocates environmental protection or xenophobia.

Yet the prevalence of single-party-family case studies and their implicit concerns about the universality and comparability of strategies across party families suggest the need for a more detailed, disaggregated examination of the relationship between mainstream party behavior and niche party electoral strength. Table 3.7 contains the frequency of the mainstream party strategic combinations broken down by niche party type.[69] A quick glance reveals that not all cells are filled; strategic combinations are, as many have suspected, unequally applied toward niche parties. Although used against radical right parties, ADAD tactics were never implemented against the green parties in my sample. DIAD tactics were infrequently employed against either niche party type.

These specifics aside, however, neither niche party type was unexposed to dismissive, accommodative, or adversarial strategies. In contrast to the views of many scholars,[70] not all mainstream parties supported the environmental stance of green parties or opposed the anti-immigrant position of radical right parties. Green parties were treated to adversarial tactics, and radical right parties were targets of mainstream parties' accommodative strategies.

[69] The frequencies in Table 3.7 reflect the observations that are included in the party-specific models, Models III and IV, in Table 3.8.

[70] For example, Budge and Farlie (1983a, 1983b) and other proponents of the saliency theory believe that there is one acceptable position on some issues. As the coding schema used in the Comparative Manifestos Project highlights, the environment and law and order are supposedly two such issues (Budge et al. 2001).

Party-Specific Models and Analysis

Given the somewhat uneven application of strategic combinations toward niche parties, one is left to wonder if the effectiveness of these tactical pairs also differs by party type. Indeed, it is not outlandish to posit that the mainstream parties may be less successful at co-opting an anti-immigrant platform than a pro-environmental one.

To answer this question, a second set of regression analyses was performed with one regression for each niche party family. The models were again estimated using OLS regression with lagged dependent variables and panel-corrected standard errors. The dependent variable remains percentage of niche party vote. The regressions took the same form as that of the strategic Model IIa in Table 3.5; to test my strategic hypotheses, I include the strategies of the mainstream center-left and center-right parties. In addition to the GDP per capita and unemployment variables, the green and radical right party literatures have proposed other sociological factors to more directly capture support for the niche parties. Because these variables introduce geographic and temporal restrictions to the analyses that are particularly problematic for these already taxed party-specific models, I include only the ones that were statistically and substantively significant in the niche party models in Table 3.5.[71] As before, the models include country fixed effects.[72] The regression results are reported in Table 3.8.

Findings of the Party-Specific Models. In contrast to the straightforward findings of the full-data models, the results of these party-specific regressions indicate the presence of a more nuanced and less-uniform explanation of the electoral successes and failures of niche parties. First, as noted in the previous section, strategies were not equally applied toward green and radical right parties. Not only does this mean that certain strategies were excluded from the analysis – specifically, the joint adversarial tactics in the green party regression – but it also means that the estimates of the included strategic combinations are based on fewer observations. The smaller number of observations and the reduced variation in the values of the included strategic variables serve to increase uncertainty in the estimates of the coefficients (Achen 1982; King 1998).

Second and a related point, the relative substantive and statistical significance of those tactics in shaping niche party electoral support also varied. In the green party model, three tactics prove critical to niche party electoral support.[73] DIDI, Delayed ACAC, and Delayed DIAC strategic combinations all exhibit

[71] Consequently, the immigrant percentage and the interacted immigrant percentage–unemployment variables were added to the radical right party model.

[72] To simplify the presentation, the coefficients of the country dummies are not displayed in Table 3.8. In the green party vote model, seventeen country dummies were included. Five of them were found to be significant at $p < .1$ in two-tailed tests. A country dummy for each of the thirteen countries with radical right parties was included in Model IV. Five were significant at $p < .1$ in two-tailed tests.

[73] That said, an F-test rejects the null hypothesis of the joint insignificance of all the strategic variables in the model.

TABLE 3.8. *Multivariate Analyses of Niche Party Vote Percentage: Party-Specific Strategic Models*

	Predicted Sign	Green Party Vote Model III	Radical Right Party Vote Model IV
Strategic			
DIDI	−	−1.74*	−2.75*
		(0.87)	(1.23)
ACAC	−	−0.09	−0.92
		(0.92)	(2.32)
DIAC	−	−0.35	−3.28*
		(0.92)	(1.48)
DIAD	+	−0.02	5.12***
		(0.79)	(1.47)
ADAD	+	NA^a	0.01
			(2.02)
ACAD with Relative Intensity^b	+	0.41	2.90**
		(0.65)	(0.92)
Delayed ACAC	+	−2.99	1.70
		(1.24)	(2.70)
Delayed DIAC	+	−4.87	4.37**
		(1.30)	(1.53)
Past Performance			
NP Vote$_{t-1}$		0.07	0.54***
		(0.16)	(0.11)
Sociological			
GDP/Capita (in thousands)			
Green	+	0.28***	-0.01
Radical Right	−	(0.09)	(0.07)
Unemployment			
Green	−	−0.04	−0.28
Radical Right	+	(0.07)	(0.29)
Immigrant Percentage	+		−0.26
			(0.49)
Immigrant Percentage × Unemployment	+		0.06*
			(0.04)
Country Dummies		Included	Included
Adjusted R^2		0.8975	0.9263
N		61	55

***$p < .001$; **$p < .01$; *$p < .1$ (one-tailed tests). Panel-corrected standard errors are in parentheses.

^{a} This strategic variable was not observed within the population of mainstream party tactical responses.

^{b} The coefficient of the variable ACAD with Relative Intensity is reported in terms of the adversarial strategy being stronger than the accommodative one. Where AC > AD, the sign of the beta is the opposite.

substantively significant negative effects on green party vote and are statistically significant in two-tailed tests.[74] As predicted by the PSO theory, the DIDI strategy decreases environmental party vote, at a one-tailed significance level of $p = .02$. But the strong negative effects of the other two variables suggest, counter to my predictions, that hesitation is not sufficient to weaken the vote-reducing force of mainstream party accommodation.[75] Whether delayed or timely, the ACAC and DIAC strategic combinations lead to the undermining of green party vote.[76]

If the power of my PSO strategic theory is less clear in the green party regression,[77] its theoretical and empirical relevance is reinforced by the findings of the radical right party analysis. Five strategic combinations are statistically significant, substantively powerful, and supportive of the strategic hypotheses presented in Chapter 2.[78] DIDI and DIAC strategies decrease radical right party support, whereas DIAD and Delayed DIAC tactics increase it. As expected, ACAD strategies are estimated to boost niche party support when adversarial tactics are stronger and weaken niche party vote when accommodative tactics are more intense.

These regression results demonstrate that mainstream parties have tools to both heighten and diminish the support levels of radical right parties. And, unlike the results of the green model, which do not allow us to differentiate between the applicability of the standard and modified spatial theories, the results of the radical right model indicate that a standard spatial logic is not at work. The differences between the effects of DIAC and ACAD where AD > AC and between the effects of the accommodatively dominant (AC > AD) and the adversarially dominant (AD > AC) forms of the ACAD strategies suggest that the behavior of nonproximal parties matters. These findings are inconsistent with the standard spatial model but expected by my PSO approach. Competition between mainstream and radical right parties appears to be governed by a modified spatial logic.

The results of these two regressions also offer some support for select sociological explanations of niche party vote. As is consistent with the findings of Models Ia and IIa in Tables 3.4 and 3.5, GDP per capita stands out as a positive

---

[74] In two-tailed tests, the coefficient of the Delayed ACAC variable was statistically significant at $p = .02$ and that of the Delayed DIAC variable was statistically significant at $p = .000$.

[75] The mechanism by which hesitation influences strategic effectiveness against green parties will be explored further in the British Green Party case study in Chapter 5.

[76] The coefficients of the timely ACAC and DIAC tactics, although also negative, were much weaker than the delayed versions of these strategies. And, unlike the delayed versions, they did not attain statistical significance.

[77] Given that the effects of the strategies in the green-party-specific model are consistent with the mechanisms posited by both the standard spatial and the modified spatial PSO theories, more evidence is needed to ascertain whether the strategies employed against the environmental parties follow the position-, salience-, and ownership-altering logic of my model. Some of that evidence is examined in the discussion of the microlevel mechanism behind the tactics of the British mainstream parties toward the Green Party in Chapter 5.

[78] An F-test of the entire set of strategic variables in the model allows us to reject the null hypothesis of their joint insignificance.

and substantively and statistically significant predictor of green party support. The immigrant percentage–unemployment interaction term also emerges as a correctly signed and significant determinant of vote for radical right parties. Yet, the force of this second finding is reduced by the fact that its constituent variables – unemployment and immigrant percentage – are not only not statistically significant but also have signs that run counter to those expected by the literature (see Golder 2003b).[79] In other words, while there is some evidence in support of sociological theories of green party vote, I find little for similar theories of radical right party support.

This disaggregation of the analysis by niche party family has posed a tough test for the strategic theories of niche party vote. As is clear from the results, the effects of the strategic variables were not as robust as they were in the combined data set. That said, mainstream party strategies did emerge as statistically and substantively significant predictors of niche party success and failure; the magnitude of these strategies' effects consistently eclipsed that of the alternative sociological factors. The relative resilience of the strategic variables is especially notable given that these reduced models are vulnerable to the methodological problems caused by subsetting the data.[80] Moreover, in light of the large number of regressors in models with a limited number of observations, it is encouraging to see that many of the variables performed as well as they did. One can therefore be confident in the conclusion that the responses of mainstream parties are critical to the electoral fortunes of both green and radical right parties. Furthermore, whereas the evidence in the green party cases supports the predictions of both the standard and modified spatial theories, the estimated effects of the strategies in the radical right cases suggest that party competition is not being driven by a standard spatial logic. Mainstream parties from across the political spectrum can positively and negatively shape the electoral trajectory of their less-established competitors. These findings are supportive of the PSO theory.

EXTENSION TO ETHNOTERRITORIAL PARTIES

Up to this point, I have examined the determinants of the vote share of the most common niche parties – the green and radical right parties. Yet, as this book has already discussed, the single-issue party phenomenon has included other examples. In this section, I extend the analyses to the electoral trajectories of ethnoterritorial parties. Like their environmental and anti-immigration counterparts, these parties are distinguished from mainstream parties by their rejection

---

[79] The coefficients of the unemployment and immigrant percentage variables are not statistically significant at $p < .1$ in either one-tailed tests based on hypotheses of their positive effects or two-tailed tests based on hypotheses of their nonzero effects on radical right party vote.

[80] As noted previously, these include increased uncertainty in the estimates caused by both the small number of observations in each regression and the reduction in the variation of the values of the strategic variables – a result of the uneven application of strategic combinations across the niche party types (Achen 1982; King 1998). The general effects of the strategic variables are more difficult to identify under these conditions.

of an economically oriented political space and their advocacy of an often cross-cutting single issue. For ethnoterritorial parties, that primary issue is regional autonomy. However, in contrast to the ubiquitous green and radical right parties, ethnoterritorial parties have developed in only a handful of Western European countries. And, within those countries, their electoral participation, as their party name and regionalist platforms suggest, is typically restricted to a particular sub-national region.[81]

In light of these differences, do mainstream party strategies also shape the electoral trajectories of ethnoterritorial actors? If so, can we conclude that a modified, rather than a traditional, spatial logic of competition is at work? To answer these questions and ascertain the generalizability and power of my theory across niche parties, I examine the electoral trajectories of those ethnoterritorial parties that contested multiple consecutive national-level legislative elections from 1970 to 1998.[82] Given that these parties generally compete in only one region in a country, the dependent variable is operationalized as the percentage of the regional vote received by a given ethnoterritorial party in a national-level legislative election.[83] For those countries in which multiple ethnic parties contest the *same* electoral districts, the value of the dependent variable for that observation is the sum of those parties' votes.[84]

Ethnoterritorial parties are defined as those parties championing regional autonomy in its varying degrees; following Müller-Rommel's (1998) definition of ethnoregionalist parties and consistent with my conception of niche parties, this issue should be the primary focus of the party. The resulting categorization of Western European parties is based on De Winter and Türsan (1998), Gordin (2001), and Caramani (2004) and confirmed by the admittedly limited data on strong party promoters of pro-decentralization positions from Laver and Hunt's (1992) expert surveys.[85] It should be noted that, although all ethnoterritorial parties are regionalist parties as defined by their policy platforms and typically their geographically limited electoral participation, the converse is not necessarily true – not all regionalist parties are ethnoterritorial. Because the focus of this analysis is on noneconomic, single-issue parties prioritizing regional autonomy, I explicitly exclude from the ethnoterritorial party category regional versions of

[81] Exceptions exist involving regionally concentrated parties that, as they gain in popularity, expand their areas of competition. Interestingly, these parties often compete in regions beyond the areas for which they demand autonomy. The Lega Nord (LN) in Italy is one case in point.

[82] Due to the lack of available data on the sociological variables, the analyses will only include observations from a subset of these years.

[83] The tendency of the Lega Nord of Italy to contest districts throughout the country caused some practical problems for the statistical analysis and ultimately led to the party's exclusion. Namely, although the LN's vote share across all contested districts could be used in place of a regional vote share, no simple cross-district substitute is available for the relative regional sociological variables included in the analysis.

[84] This is the case for the two ethnoterritorial parties in the Basque Country and the two in Catalonia in the data set.

[85] As noted earlier in this chapter, the Laver and Hunt data do not include all countries in Western Europe or all parties contesting elections during the late 1980s. Understandably, that data set also does not include parties that emerged after its surveys were administered.

mainstream parties, such as the Christian Social Union (CSU) in Germany and the Socialist Party of Catalonia (PSC) in Spain, and regionalist versions of other niche parties, such as the Flemish Greens (AGALEV) and radical right Vlaams Blok in Belgium.[86]

Based on this definition, six Western European countries have ethnoterritorial parties: Belgium, France, Italy, Spain, Switzerland, and the United Kingdom.[87] Whereas it is somewhat unusual for a country to have more than one green party or more than one radical right party, the mean number of ethnoterritorial parties in each of these countries is three. In contrast to the data analyzed previously, the inclusion of multiple ethnoterritorial parties (i.e., multiple ethnoterritorial party panels) from the same country is not problematic as long as they are contesting separate districts.

Given the greater difficulty of obtaining data – electoral and strategic – on ethnoterritorial parties than on green and radical right parties,[88] my analysis involves a subset of the existing ethnoterritorial parties.[89] Inclusion of a given party in the data set is not, however, correlated with its peak or mean vote level.[90] The twelve parties in the analysis are listed in Table 3.9.[91]

Mainstream Party Strategies

The PSO theory claims that issue salience- and ownership-altering strategies shape the electoral support of political parties. To test these hypotheses as they relate to ethnoterritorial parties, we again examine the strategic behavior of mainstream parties of the center-left and center-right. In coding mainstream party responses to ethnoterritorial parties, the CMP data present limitations that are

---

[86] Based on its low prioritization of decentralization (12.3 out of 20), especially relative to economic and other issues (see Benoit and Laver 2006), and the party's self-identification as a "moderate liberal party active in all sectors of politics" (http://www.sfp.fi/eng/), the Swedish People's Party (SFP) of Finland is also excluded from the ethnoterritorial party category.

[87] The Swiss ethnoterritorial party, Lega dei Ticinesi, is ultimately excluded from the final regression analysis because of the lack of time-series data for the sociological variables.

[88] The vote shares of small parties – a category that often includes ethnoterritorial parties – are neither consistently available nor broken down by individual parties in the main sources of Western European electoral data (e.g., Caramani 2000; Mackie and Rose 1991, 1997). In some countries, even the official national election statistics do not report the vote shares of these parties separately; they are aggregated into an "Other" category. In addition, there are fewer secondary sources available about the interaction of mainstream parties with ethnoterritorial parties.

[89] Excluded parties include Movimento Friuli (IT), Partito Sardo d'Azione (IT), Union Valdôtaine (IT), Lista per Trieste (IT), Lega Nord (IT), Agrupacion Independientes de Canarias (ES), Bloque Nacional Popular Galego (ES), Unio Valenciana (ES), and Lega dei Ticinesi (CH). IT, ES, and CH stand for Italy, Spain, and Switzerland, respectively.

[90] The parties included in the analysis obtained peak regional vote levels that range from 1.27 percent to 39.6 percent, with an average peak vote per party of 22.3 percent. Based on the available data, the peak regional vote levels of those excluded range from 4.3 percent to 55.2 percent, with an average peak vote per party of 21.8 percent. The average mean vote percentage for an included party is 16.1 percent as opposed to 17.4 percent for an excluded party. These means are statistically indistinguishable.

[91] More detailed information on the electoral history of these niche parties is presented in Table A3.3 in this chapter's Appendix.

TABLE 3.9. *Ethnoterritorial Parties of Western Europe Included in the Analysis*

Country	Ethnoterritorial Party
Belgium	Volksunie, Front Démocratique des Francophones (FDF), Rassemblement Wallon (RW)
France	Union Démocratique Bretonne (UDB), Unione di u Populu Corsu (UPC)
Italy	Südtiroler Volkspartei
Spain	Herri Batasuna, Partido Nacionalista Vasco (PNV), Convergència i Unió (CiU), Esquerra Republicana de Catalunya (ERC)
United Kingdom	Scottish National Party, Plaid Cymru

different from those experienced with the other niche parties. In contrast to its treatment of the issues raised by the green and radical right parties, the CMP data set does include both measures capturing support for and opposition to the eth-noterritorial party issue of regional autonomy: variable 301 measures support for decentralization, and variable 302 measures support for centralization. The former is suggestive of mainstream party accommodation; the latter, of mainstream party adversarial tactics. Little to no discussion of either position is indicative of a dismissive response.

However, the presence of multiple ethnoterritorial parties in a given coun-try – each advocating regional autonomy for a different region with a different history – means that the CMP variables are more likely to reflect a mainstream party's *average* attitude toward decentralization rather than its strategies toward any particular ethnoterritorial party. This would not be problematic if a main-stream party responded identically to all niche parties calling for greater regional political and fiscal independence in its country, but a survey of ethnoterritorial politics demonstrates the rarity of this scenario.[92] Spanish parties have reacted differently to the Basque and the Canary Island regionalist movements; Italian parties have privileged the party of the historically German enclave of the South Tyrol in a way that is not replicated in their tactics toward the Lega Nord; and even Belgian parties, which eventually accommodated their ethnoterritorial rivals by establishing a federal state structure, did not co-opt the message of each niche party simultaneously. Thus, information from party documents and secondary

[92] A comparison of the 1997 CMP data for British parties to the data coded by Agasøster (2001) for district-level party manifestos in Scotland for that same year reveals sizeable differences in mainstream party emphases. Thus, relying solely on the CMP's national-level manifesto data to code mainstream party strategies toward specific ethnoterritorial parties, as Jolly (2006) does, can be misleading and raises questions about the conclusions of the tests of strategic models that he performs.

TABLE 3.10. *Incidence of Mainstream Party Strategies toward Ethnoterritorial Parties as Measured per Electoral Period from 1970 to 1996*[93]

Mainstream Party Strategies	Frequency of the Strategic Combination toward Ethnoterritorial Parties
DIDI	15
ACAC	2
DIAC	6
DIAD	0
ADAD	0
ACAD with AC > AD	4
ACAD with AD > AC	2
N	29

sources, such as party histories, was consulted in conjunction with the CMP data to provide accurate codings of strategies toward the ethnoterritorial parties.[94]

The resulting distribution of strategic combinations employed toward the ethnoterritorial parties is presented in Table 3.10. These variables are modeled as dummy variables, following the specification discussed earlier in this chapter. As seen with mainstream party reactions to the other niche parties, not all accommodative strategies were employed in a timely fashion. There were two cases of mainstream parties using DIAC tactics after two or more successive periods of dismissive strategies, so a "Delayed DIAC" dummy variable was included in the analysis.[95]

Institutional and Sociological Factors

In addition to these strategic variables, I examine the effect of institutional and sociological factors identified by previous research as relevant to ethnoterritorial party success. Some of these factors are captured by the measures of district magnitude, state structure, GDP per capita, and unemployment I used in the green and radical right party models. But the existing literature both suggests

[93] As will be discussed in the next section, the scarcity of data on the sociological variables means that the analysis is limited to strategies implemented until 1996.

[94] These sources include Balfour 1996; Colomer 1999; Conversi 1997; Dewachter 1987; De Winter and Türsan 1998; Gibbons 1999; Gomez-Reino Cachafeiro 2002; Gras and Livet 1977; Gundle and Parker 1996; Gunther, Sani, and Shabad 1988; Hossay 2004; Keating 1998; Laible 2001; Loughlin and Mazey 1995; Mazzoleni 1999; McRoberts 2001; Newman 1996; Ramsay 1983; van Houten 2003; Zariski 1989; and Zolberg 1977. The greater reliance on non-CMP data for the coding of mainstream party strategies toward the ethnoterritorial parties means that the absence of CMP data for Spain 1996 poses less of a problem for this coding than for the coding of mainstream party tactics toward the green and radical right parties. Consequently, the analyses of ethnoterritorial party vote include the observations for the Basque and Catalan parties in 1996.

[95] The effects of the strategic variables do not change when the Delayed DIAC variable is omitted from the model.

additional measures and advances different predictions for the effect of these factors.

Institutional Variables. The literature identifies electoral rules and state structure as the institutions expected to influence ethnoterritorial party vote. I therefore include the two measures used in the green and radical right party analyses: the logged magnitude of the median legislator's district and a dummy variable indicating a unitary (as opposed to a federal) state structure.

Unlike green and radical right parties, which tend to compete nationwide, parties that appeal to regionally concentrated groups, like ethnoterritorial parties, are not predicted to be disadvantaged by plurality electoral rules. Based on the claims of Rae (1971) and Sartori (1986), a negative relationship is expected between the measure of district magnitude and ethnoterritorial party vote.

The literature yields two, opposite predictions about the relationship between state structure and ethnoterritorial vote. According to Chhibber and Kollman (2004), regionalist parties should receive more votes in federal systems where resources and policy-making powers are located at the regional level; therefore, a negative relationship is expected between unitary state structure and vote.[96] In contrast, Levi and Hechter (1985) suggest that ethnoterritorial parties calling for greater regional autonomy may attract more votes in unitary countries than in those that are already federal. The logic behind this prediction of a positive relationship is that an ethnoterritorial party's vote is influenced more by the novelty of its pro-decentralization policy in a unitary state than by the absence of subnational elected offices from which to build future party support.[97] It is worth noting that this latter institutional relationship is also anticipated by my PSO theory. As Chapter 7 will demonstrate, decentralization is the institutional embodiment of issue-based accommodation used by mainstream parties to undermine ethnoterritorial party support.

Sociological Variables. To assess the significance of the sociological climate for ethnoterritorial party support, I turn to measures of economic health. Like sociological analyses of green and radical right party success, the few existing quantitative, cross-national studies of ethnoterritorial success (Gordin 2001; Jolly 2006) employ variables capturing wealth and unemployment. Following the belief that a voter's ethnoterritorial identity, and thus ethnoterritorial party support, develops

---

[96] As noted in Chapter 1, Chhibber and Kollman also expect increases in regionalist party vote during periods of state decentralization, steps short of the formal implementation of federalism. Because of the nuanced nature of their coding decisions and the availability of their data for only one country in my analysis, I cannot fully test the implications of their theory for ethnoterritorial party support. The predictions of their full theory are examined in the SNP case study analysis in Chapter 7.

[97] Recall that Jolly (2006) proposes an alternate hypothesis; he posits that a curvilinear relationship should exist, whereby voter support for ethnoterritorial parties will be higher in unitary and federal countries than it will in countries with middling levels of decentralization. Due to the nature of my state structure variables, the presence of this more complex relationship cannot be directly tested in the statistical analysis.

as a reaction to the economic prosperity or poverty of a group or region relative to the national average, the economic variables are constructed as relative measures.[98]

I include relative regional measures of GDP per capita and unemployment rate defined as regional GDP per capita/national GDP per capita and regional unemployment rate/national unemployment rate.[99] This set of variables is constructed from the Eurostat REGIO database and reflects the values for the largest geographic regions below the national level in which the ethnoterritorial party competes.[100] Unfortunately, such regional data are only available consistently for EU member states and, even then, only for a subset of years in the 1970–98 period. Specifically, relative regional GDP per capita measures are available as early as 1975 for some countries and regions, but are generally available for all observations from the early 1980s until 1996. Data on relative regional unemployment rates are available from 1983 to 1998.

As discussed in Chapter 1, the two dominant theories of ethnoterritorial party support have opposite expectations about the effects of these economic variables. If the internal colonialism argument is true, then niche party vote levels should increase with regional economic deprivation – that is, as relative GDP per capita falls and relative unemployment rates increase. The overtaxed development argument yields opposite predictions.

MODELS AND ANALYSIS OF ETHNOTERRITORIAL PARTY VOTE

To estimate the effect of these institutional, sociological, and strategic variables on ethnoterritorial party vote, I again employ pooled cross-sectional time-series analysis. Consistent with the previous regressions, I ran OLS regressions with lagged dependent variables and panel-corrected standard errors. Table 3.11 presents the results of two models. Model V includes the institutional and sociological predictors of ethnoterritorial party vote, similar to Model Ia in the pooled analysis. In Model VI, I add the mainstream party strategic variables. An F-test supports the inclusion of country dummies in the latter model, so they have been added, and the time-invariant, institutional variables have been removed.[101] As before, the statistical significance of the institutional and strategic coefficients is measured with one-tailed tests due to the directional nature of the hypotheses. Two-tailed tests are used for the sociological variables.

---

[98] Given the literature's silence on the relationship between ethnoterritorial party vote and *national* levels of GDP per capita and unemployment, these economic measures are not included in the analyses.

[99] The relative regional variables will have scores greater than one when the region has higher levels of GDP per capita or unemployment than the country as a whole. Data from the REGIO database of *Eurostat Statistics* 2003.

[100] In the language of the REGIO database, this is typically NUTS level 1, where NUTS stands for Nomenclature of Territorial Units for Statistics.

[101] For ease of presentation, the coefficients of the country dummies are not displayed in Table 3.11. The coefficients of four of the five country dummies are statistically significant at $p < .1$ in two-tailed tests.

TABLE 3.11. *Multivariate Analyses of Ethnoterritorial Party Regional Vote Percentage*

	Predicted Sign	Ethnoterritorial Party Vote Model V (nonstrategic)	Ethnoterritorial Party Vote Model VI (strategic)
Strategic			
DIDI	−		−5.82*
			(2.96)
ACAC	−		−2.24
			(3.91)
DIAC	−		−7.50**
			(3.12)
ACAD with Relative	+		5.46*
Intensity[a]			(2.85)
Delayed DIAC	+		0.54
			(2.26)
Past Performance			
NP Vote$_{t-1}$		1.00***	0.42**
		(0.07)	(0.15)
Institutional			
Ln Median District	−	−2.08*	
Magnitude		(1.08)	
State Structure	+ or −	−0.15	
		(1.76)	
Sociological			
Relative Regional	+ or −	−0.21	5.51*
GDP/Capita		(5.00)	(3.27)
Relative Regional	− or +	−5.04	−6.08
Unemployment		(3.83)	(4.22)
Constant		7.83	
		(7.33)	
Country Dummies		Not included	Included
Adjusted R²		0.8862	0.9690
N		29	29

***$p < .001$; **$p < .01$; *$p < .1$ (one-tailed tests for all variables except the sociological, for which two-tailed tests are used). Panel-corrected standard errors are in parentheses. DIAD, ADAD, and Delayed ACAC were excluded from the regression models because they were not observed within the population of mainstream party tactical responses.

[a] The coefficient of the variable ACAD with Relative Intensity is reported in terms of the adversarial strategy being stronger than the accommodative one. Where AC > AD, the sign of the beta is the opposite.

Findings

Although caution is in order given the small number of observations and short time period of the analysis, the regression results in Table 3.11 paint a picture of niche party support similar to that seen in the previous analyses in this chapter. Certain institutional and sociological factors are relevant to the vote share of ethnoterritorial parties, but they do not preclude the power of a strategic explanation. The behavior of mainstream parties is critical to determining eth-noterritorial parties' electoral fortunes.

Focusing first on Model V, electoral rules emerge as a strong and statistically significant predictor of ethnoterritorial party vote.[102] Supporting the revision to Duverger's Law, the vote share of these geographically concentrated parties is estimated to be lower in electoral systems with high district magnitudes, such as PR, than in the single-member districts commonly used with plurality rules. None of the other institutional and sociological variables, however, has both a statistically and a substantively significant effect on niche party support. While additional information is needed to fully test the nuanced Jolly (2006) and Chhib-ber and Kollman (2004) hypotheses about the influence of state structure, the evidence suggests, contrary to Levi and Hechter's claim, that a country's unitary status does not positively influence niche party support.[103]

If Model V reveals the weak explanatory power of the nonstrategic variables, with the notable exception of electoral rules, Model VI indicates the strong role of mainstream party actors in the electoral success and failure of regionalist par-ties.[104] Consistent with the predictions of my modified spatial theory, DIDI, DIAC, and accommodatively dominant ACAD tactics decrease the vote of the ethnoterritorial parties.[105] As expected, adversarially dominant ACAD tactics increase the vote of these parties.[106] Not only do these findings reveal that main-stream parties can both weaken and strengthen these niche party opponents,[107] but differences in the effect of strategic combinations in which proximal par-ties act identically suggest that a modified spatial logic is at work. As also seen in the pooled green and radical right party models, there are significant differ-ences between the effect of DIAC and adversarially dominant ACAD tactics, and the effect of accommodatively dominant and adversarially dominant ACAD tactics. These differences are unexpected by the standard spatial model of party competition.

Despite the influence of the strategic variables, we cannot conclude from Model VI that sociological factors are irrelevant to understanding ethnoterri-torial party support. The results provide evidence of the importance of rela-tive regional GDP per capita for conditioning the environment in which parties

---

[102] The results are the same if the logged average district magnitude is used instead of the logged median district magnitude.

[103] While my analysis does not directly test Jolly's (2006) hypothesis, the lack of a statistically signif-icant finding for the state variable introduces the possibility that degree of federalism could have a curvilinear relationship with ethnoterritorial party vote, as he predicts.

[104] The result of an F-test supports the rejection of the null hypothesis of the joint insignificance of the strategic variables.

[105] Although its coefficient is negative as predicted, the effect of joint accommodative strategies is not statistically significant.

[106] There is no support, however, for the hypothesis that delayed DIAC tactics boost niche party support. It should be noted that this estimate was based on two observations.

[107] The effect of the permanent adoption of each strategic combination on the long-term equilibrium level of niche party vote in percentage points is as follows: DIDI (-10.03); ACAC (-3.86); DIAC (-12.93); ACAD when AC > AD (-9.41); ACAD when AD > AC ($+9.41$).

interact. Following the prediction of the overtaxed development argument and consistent with the findings of Jolly (2006), ethnoterritorial parties have higher vote levels in regions that are relatively prosperous (i.e., higher GDP per capita than the national average) than in regions that are relatively impoverished.[108]

FROM ONE ELECTION TO MANY: EXPLAINING A NICHE PARTY'S ELECTORAL TRAJECTORY

The regression parameter estimates presented in this chapter offer support for the core claim of my strategic approach: mainstream party behavior affects the electoral strength of niche parties. The statistical analyses have demonstrated how tactics can change a niche party's vote in the next election. We have also learned about the effects of the repeated use of strategies on the long-term equilibrium level of the niche party's electoral fortune. The reader will recall that an initial goal of this research, one that separated it from institutional approaches, was also to account for the waxing and waning of a party's electoral fortunes over its lifetime. What can this model tell us about the shape of a niche party's electoral trajectory when, as is commonly the case, mainstream parties employ different strategies over time?

In the following sections, I provide answers to this question by estimating the effects of mainstream party responses on the vote of two hypothetical niche parties. Here I discuss the effects of strategies on the vote share of a radical right and an ethnoterritorial party over several elections, under various institutional and sociological conditions. The hypotheticals are then compared to actual trajectories of Western European radical right and ethnoterritorial parties, demonstrating the fit of the regression models. As this discussion will show, strategies – specifically, tactics consistent with a modified spatial logic – are critical for shaping niche party support over time.

Radical Right Party Electoral Trajectory

In Table 3.12, I present the predicted electoral trajectory for a radical right party calculated from the pooled niche party Model IIa in Table 3.5.[109] In this example, the electoral support levels are evaluated under plurality electoral rules in a centralized state with all sociological variables held constant at their means.[110]

---

[108] Although the coefficient is not statistically significant at $p < .1$ in a two-tailed test, the sign of the relative regional unemployment variable is also consistent with the expectations of the overtaxed development argument.

[109] The shape of the radical right party trajectory is the same whether the pooled-niche-party model or the niche-party-specific model is used. With GDP per capita, unemployment, and immigrant percentage held constant at their means and the value of the interacted immigrant percentage – unemployment variable a product of those means, the radical right party vote calculated from Model IV in Table 3.8 is as follows: 2.20 (period 1); 9.64 (period 2); 11.44 (period 3); 12.42 (period 4); and 7.16 (period 5).

[110] Although institutional variables are not directly included in Model IIa, this institutional configuration approximately matches the electoral rules and state structure of France and the United

TABLE 3.12. *Electoral Trajectory of a Radical Right Party*

	Cumulative Electoral Support Level (%)	Change in Electoral Support (in percentage points)
Party Emerged: Base Level Vote (*Exogenous to Model*)	3.00	
Period 1: DIDI	4.10	+1.10
Period 2: DIAD	11.56	+7.46
Period 3: ACAD (where AD > AC)	12.69	+1.13
Period 4: ACAD (where AD > AC)	13.49	+0.80
Period 5: ACAD (where AC > AD)	11.20	−2.29

Note: Values calculated with sociological variables held constant at their means. The French country dummy variable is coded 1.

An electoral score of 3 percent was chosen to represent the niche party's opening electoral performance.[111]

Although a mainstream party's initial strategy is contingent on a neophyte's degree of electoral threat, a survey of the data shows that most implement cautious, low-cost dismissive tactics in the first electoral period.[112] Following the second electoral showing of the niche party, mainstream parties often take more active measures. Here a dismissive-adversarial tactic is depicted, a combination that almost triples the vote level of the radical right party and transforms it from a minor irritant into a significant electoral threat. In the subsequent elections, the accommodative behavior of the proximal party helps to temper the vote-boosting effect of the distant party's stronger adversarial tactics, slowing the rate of niche party vote gain. However, an actual reduction in the radical right party's support materializes only when the intensity of the co-optative tactics surpasses that of the adversarial ones.

Far from being a mere hypothetical, this scenario closely resembles the set of strategies employed by the French mainstream Socialist (PS) and Gaullist (RPR) parties toward the radical right Front National from 1978 to 1997.[113] As will be discussed at greater length in Chapter 6, the Socialist party adopted an early, adversarial stance toward the niche party. The internally divided Gaullist Party, on the other hand, was slow to respond actively to the threatening anti-immigrant party; the RPR pursued a co-optative strategy only as of 1986, *after*

Kingdom. As mentioned previously, missing data on the percentage of immigrants in the United Kingdom caused the British radical right party case effectively to be dropped from the niche-party-specific analysis. Thus, in order to compare the fitted values of the radical right party trajectory from the pooled and niche-party-specific models, in this example, I modeled the French case; the fitted values were calculated with the French country dummy variable coded 1.

[111] After the initial starting value, the value of the lagged dependent variable is endogenous to the model in the hypothetical.

[112] The rationale behind these strategic choices is more closely examined in Chapter 4.

[113] Between 1976 and 2002, the official name of the Gaullists' party was "Rassemblement pour la république," or RPR.

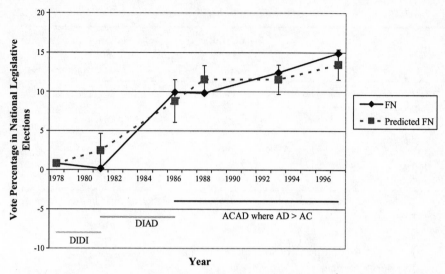

FIGURE 3.1. Electoral Trajectory of the French Front National: Actual versus Predicted (with 95 percent confidence intervals). *Note:* Predictions calculated for GDP/Capita, unemployment rates, and lagged FN vote as observed in France. The French country dummy variable is coded 1.

the electoral and reputational entrenchment of the Front National. In contrast to the hypothetical presented in Table 3.12, the RPR's accommodative strategy remained weaker than the PS's adversarial tactics throughout the time period under investigation.

A comparison of the predicted effects of these mainstream party strategies with the niche party's actual electoral trajectory demonstrates the explanatory power of my model. In Figure 3.1, I plot these trajectories, with the model's predictions of Front National support from 1981 to 1997 based on the set of mainstream party strategies, sociological conditions, and lagged FN vote observed in France. As the figure reveals, in four of the five predicted elections, the 95 percent two-tailed confidence intervals around the point estimate encompass the actual FN vote share. Although we cannot ignore how GDP per capita and unemployment rates varied during this time period, the significant electoral gains made by the FN cannot be attributed to these sociological variables. In each of these elections, the joint effect of the sociological variables was minimal; the magnitude of their effect on the FN's vote share ranged from +0.22 percentage points (in 1981) to +0.45 percentage points (in 1997). The strategic maneuvering of the French Socialists and Gaullists served as the workhorse of the FN's electoral success.

Beyond confirming the power of mainstream party strategies, this comparison also calls attention to the role played by each established party in altering niche party success. In my model – and in the actual FN electoral trajectory – the increases in niche party electoral support came largely at the hands of traditionally ignored, nonproximal party actors. Indeed, as Chapter 6 will discuss, it is readily accepted by French scholars and journalists alike that the niche party's high vote percentages were the direct result of the PS's adversarial behavior (Faux et al. 1994). Being the "enemy of the PS's enemy," therefore, proved electorally fruitful for the Front National. In contrast, the proximal Gaullist party was relatively ineffective at containing the radical right party's support. The vote-diminishing influence of its dismissive and accommodative tactics was repeatedly overwhelmed by the adversarial behavior of its Socialist counterparts. Had we assumed that meaningful interaction only occurs between proximal actors, as claimed by the standard spatial models of party competition, we would have predicted FN electoral failure and would have been at a loss to explain its patent success.

Ethnoterritorial Party Electoral Trajectory

A look at the electoral trajectory of a typical ethnoterritorial party provides similar support for the modified spatial strategic story of niche party success. Based on the regression results in Model VI of Table 3.11, I calculate the vote of an ethnoterritorial party under permissive electoral rules in a federal country with the relative regional economic variables held constant at their means.[114] The initial vote share of the niche party is set at 16.2 percent, the mean vote share received by an ethnoterritorial party in its first election in the data analysis.[115]

In Table 3.13, I present a set of mainstream party responses to an ethnoterritorial party and its estimated effect on that neophyte's vote over several elections. In contrast to their competition with green and radical right parties, mainstream parties facing ethnoterritorial parties often employ active strategies in the first electoral period. As will be discussed more in Chapter 7, the emergence of parties demanding radical changes to the state structure is unlikely to be met with indifference. For the first three electoral periods, I have modeled ACAD strategic combinations with varying levels of AC and AD intensity. Niche party vote shares jump up when adversarial tactics dominate and decline when accommodative tactics are stronger. Although the niche party is far from being eliminated electorally, its threat level diminishes consistently under the combination of accommodative and dismissive tactics (i.e., ACAC, DIAC, and DIDI) employed in periods four through six.

---

[114] The institutional configuration of the hypothetical case describes that found in Spain and Belgium. For this hypothetical, I have coded the Spanish country dummy 1. The shape of the resulting electoral trajectory is the same if the scenario is modeled for Belgium.

[115] The shape of the resulting electoral trajectory is identical if the starting value is changed to 18.6 percent, the average vote percentage received by an ethnoterritorial party in the first election it contested starting in 1970. The difference between these starting values reflects the limited availability of the sociological measures for the 1970–96 time period. With an initial vote set at 18.6 percent and with relative GDP per capita and relative unemployment held constant at their means, the ethnoterritorial party vote is as follows: 39.60 (period 1); 37.52 (period 2); 47.56 (period 3); 44.08 (period 4); 37.36 (period 5); and 36.21 (period 6).

TABLE 3.13. *Electoral Trajectory of an Ethnoterritorial Party*

	Cumulative Electoral Support Level (%)	Change in Electoral Support (in percentage points)
Party Emerged: Base Level Vote (*Exogenous to Model*)	16.20	
Period 1: ACAD (where AD > AC)	38.59	+22.39
Period 2: ACAD (where AC > AD)	37.09	−1.50
Period 3: ACAD (where AD > AC)	47.38	+10.29
Period 4: ACAC	44.01	−3.37
Period 5: DIAC	37.33	−6.68
Period 6: DIDI	36.20	−1.13

Note: Values calculated with sociological variables held constant at their means. The Spanish country dummy variable is coded 1.

This hypothetical incorporates the strategies used by the Spanish Socialists (PSOE) and Conservatives (AP/PP) against the Basque Country ethnoterritorial parties of the PNV and Herri Batasuna from 1977 to 1996.[116] Long-standing advocates of a federal system for Spain since before the transition to democracy, the Socialists adopted an accommodative stance toward these niche parties. The party embraced the creation of an autonomous communities system with special concessions for "historical regions" that would allow for at least some of the regional autonomy desired by the Basque parties.[117] The Spanish Conservatives, on the other hand, actively opposed the pro-decentralization stance of the Basque parties, only to switch to an accommodative strategy later when the niche parties could provide them needed electoral support in regional and, eventually, national elections. The individual mainstream parties' commitment to accommodation would fluctuate between 1986 and 1996. In contrast to the pattern of tactics modeled in the hypothetical, the PSOE and AP/PP alternated between joint accommodative and various combinations of dismissive tactics over these four electoral periods.[118]

How well do the predicted effects of these strategies explain the electoral trajectory of the Basque parties? In Figure 3.2, I plot the regional vote share of the Basque parties from 1977 to 1996, with the strategic combination pursued by the PSOE and AP/PP noted at the bottom. A visual comparison of the hypothesized

---

[116] Given that the PNV was founded in 1931 and had contested elections before the Franco regime, the mainstream parties reacted to the Basque party starting with the campaign for the first post-Franco democratic elections, in 1977.

[117] The strength and unity of the PSOE's support for the Basque parties' autonomist demands varied across electoral periods, as reflected in the relative intensity of the AC strategies in the ACAD strategic combinations employed between the run-up to the 1977 election and the 1982 election. For more details on this case, see Gibbons 1999; Zariski 1989.

[118] The sequence of strategic combinations adopted by the mainstream parties from the run-up to the 1986 election to the 1996 election was ACAC, DIDI, ACAC, and DIAC.

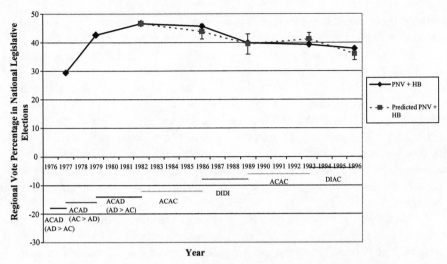

FIGURE 3.2. Electoral Trajectory of the Basque Parties (PNV and HB): Actual versus Predicted (with 95 percent confidence intervals). *Note:* Predictions calculated for the relative regional GDP/Capita, relative regional unemployment rates, and lagged Basque parties' vote as observed. The Spanish country dummy variable is coded 1.

effects of these strategies with the increases and decreases in the electoral support of the ethnoterritorial parties, with a few exceptions, provides evidence of the power of my PSO theory. The observed vote of the Basque parties increased in the 1982 election following an adversarially dominant ACAD strategy and decreased in elections after accommodative and dismissive tactics had been employed. For those elections for which relative regional GDP per capita and unemployment figures were available (1986–96), I calculate the strategic model's predicted vote share for the Basque parties and plot it in Figure 3.2. In three of those four elections, the regression results correctly predict the direction of change in the niche parties' vote. In all four elections, 95 percent confidence intervals around the point estimate encompass the actual Basque parties' vote.

Strategies clearly emerge as an important force driving changes in ethnoterritorial party support. This case also reminds us that the political and economic climate in which competition occurs cannot be ignored. As shown in Figure 3.2 by the gain in actual support for the Basque parties after a period of vote-diminishing ACAD (where AC > AD) tactics and the gain in my model's predicted support for the Basque parties after a period of ACAC tactics, contextual factors can mitigate and even erase the effects of mainstream party behavior. In these instances, the likely culprits are not just the sociological characteristics of the country, but also the country itself.[119] The strong, positive coefficient of the Spanish

---

[119] Because regional economic data are not available in my data set for 1979, it is unclear whether sociological factors helped determine the increase in ethnoterritorial vote in that election. For the 1993 election, however, we know that these variables do not fully account for the predicted

country dummy indicates that there are unmeasured aspects of the Spanish political environment that decrease the effectiveness of vote-reducing mainstream party tactics. Among the possible explanatory factors, voter distribution stands out. With the predicted impact of strategies dependent on their rationality as well as their credibility, it follows that the spatial location of voters alters the observed effect of mainstream party behavior on niche party vote. Further analysis is necessary to determine voter distribution on the decentralization issue and ascertain the precise role that it played in the Spanish niche parties' trajectory, but this case suggests that background conditions matter. This is not necessarily because they directly influence niche party vote, as argued by the institutional and sociological theories; they could simply alter the effectiveness of strategies.

As illustrated by these niche party electoral trajectories, mainstream party behavior is responsible for the electoral lows and highs of the neophyte competitors. But beyond revealing the limitations of sociological models of party success, the hypotheticals also challenge the traditional spatial conception of strategic interaction. The impact of nonproximal party tactics on both the radical right and ethnoterritorial party vote levels suggests that a different logic of party interaction is at work, a logic consistent with the PSO theory presented in Chapter 2.

CONCLUSION

By focusing on electoral rules, state structure, and the economic health, value orientation, and immigrant concentration of a society, theories of new party electoral strength have prioritized the structure of the competitive arena over the behavior of the actors within it. The evidence presented in this chapter suggests that party strategies should not be overlooked. Cross-sectional time-series analyses confirm that the strategies of the electorally and governmentally dominant parties shape the electoral fortunes of green, radical right, and ethnoterritorial parties. While there is some variation in the application and effectiveness of mainstream party strategic combinations across the niche party types, mainstream party behavior emerges as the strongest and most consistently statistically significant set of explanatory variables common to all my models of niche party fortune.[120]

The standard institutional and sociological factors, conversely, fail to exhibit a consistently significant effect on vote levels across all niche parties – whether analyzed in isolation or when mainstream party tactics are controlled for. My analysis does reveal the influence of certain variables on particular parties, such as state structure on green and radical right parties, GDP per capita on green parties,

---

vote increase; the joint effect of the sociological variables on the value of the dependent variable was a mere +0.23 percentage points.

[120] The strength of these findings is even more significant if one recalls that, in these models of niche party vote, we are not able to control for the rationality of the strategies employed by the mainstream parties.

and district magnitude and relative regional GDP per capita on ethnoterritorial parties. However, the prevailing claims about the explanatory dominance of, for example, electoral institutions or unemployment for the electoral success of *all* types of niche party is not supported by this study.

The findings in this chapter also challenge the sufficiency of the standard spatial conception of party strategies. Additional survey data on voter perceptions of the salience and ownership of the niche parties' issues are needed to examine explicitly the microlevel mechanism behind party tactics;[121] such data will be examined in the case studies in Chapters 5 through 8. But the regression results in this chapter already suggest that mainstream parties competing with a niche actor are not merely altering their positions along established policy dimensions with fixed salience. Rather, the results are consistent with the logic of my PSO theory, whereby mainstream parties also manipulate the salience and ownership of the new party's issue. It follows that competition is not restricted to interaction between ideological neighbors, as the standard spatial theory claims; nonproximal parties play a critical role in the success and failure of Western Europe's niche parties.

Chapter 4 takes the next step in understanding competition between unequals: positing the conditions under which particular strategies are adopted. Recall that the question of a strategy's rationality was put aside for the quantitative analyses in this chapter. Country dummy variables were included to capture some of the effects of voter distributions, but there was no direct measure of voter positions and, therefore, no direct measure of the appropriateness of the mainstream parties' tactics. Chapter 4 turns to this question of rationality, providing insight into why mainstream parties adopt vote-reducing tactics and, perhaps more surprisingly, why they adopt vote-bolstering strategies. Once this theory of strategic choice is presented, our attention will return to empirics with an analysis of party interaction and niche party success in Britain and France.

---

[121] Regular and consistent survey measures of issue salience and ownership do not exist for all Western European countries over the thirty-year period.

Appendix

TABLE A3.1. *Green Parties of Western Europe Included in the Analysis, 1970–98*

Country	Green Party	Date of First Election Contested	Peak National Percentage of Legislative Vote (year)
Austria	Vereinte Grünen Österreichs (VGÖ)	1983	2.0 (1990)
	Die Grüne Alternative (GA)	1986	7.3 (1994)
Belgium	Flemish Green Party (AGALEV)	1977	4.9 (1991)
	Wallonian Green Party (Ecolo)	1977	5.1 (1991)
Denmark	De Grønne	1987	1.4 (1988)
Finland	Vihreät/Vihreä Liitto	1983	6.8 (1991)
France	Les Verts	1978[a]	4.1 (1993)
	Génération Écologie		3.7 (1993)
Germany	Die Grünen	1980	8.3 (1987)
Greece	Ikologiko Kinima Politikis Anagennisis (OIKIPA)	1989	0.8 (1990)
Ireland	Comhaontas Glas	1982	2.8 (1997)
Italy	Liste Verdi	1987	2.8 (1992)
Luxembourg	Di Gréng Alternativ	1984	9.9 (1994)[b]
	Greng Lëscht Ekologesch Initiativ	1989	
Netherlands	Groen Links	1989	7.3 (1998)
	De Groenen	1989	0.4 (1989)
Norway	Miljøpartiet De Grønne	1989	0.4 (1989)
Portugal	Os Verdes	1983	1.0 (1991)
Spain	Los Verdes	1986	1.7 (1993)
Sweden	Miljöpartiet de Gröna	1982	5.5 (1988)
Switzerland	Grüne Partei der Schweiz (Parti écologiste suisse)	1979	6.1 (1991)
	Grünes Bündnis der Schweiz (Alliance socialiste verte)	1983	2.7 (1987)
United Kingdom	Green Party	1974	0.5 (1992)

[a] The date listed for the French green party signifies the first election contested by a loose group of environmentalists calling themselves the Ecologists. This group of activists would split many times to later form the two dominant French green parties: les Verts and la Génération Écologie.
[b] These two parties merged in 1994 (O'Neill 1997: 133).
Sources: Mackie and Rose (1991, 1997) and O'Neill (1997).

TABLE A3.2. *Radical Right Parties of Western Europe Included in the Analysis, 1970–98*

Country	Radical Right Party	Date of First Election Contested	Peak National Percentage of Legislative Vote (year)
Austria	Freiheitliche Partei Österreichs	1986[a]	22.4 (1994)
Belgium	Vlaams Blok	1978	7.8 (1995)
	Front National	1987	2.3 (1995)
	Agir	1991	0.3 (1995)
Denmark	Fremskridtspartiet	1973	15.9 (1973)
France	Front National	1978	14.9 (1997)
Germany	Die Republikaner	1990	2.1 (1990)
	Deutsche Volksunion	1987	1.2 (1998)
Italy	Movimento Sociale Italiano/ Alleanza Nazionale	1948	15.7 (1996)
Luxembourg	Lëtzebuerg fir de Letzebuerger National Bewegong	1989	2.6 (1994)
Netherlands	Centrumpartij/Centrumpartij '86	1981	0.8 (1982)
	Centrumdemocraten	1986	2.5 (1994)
Norway	Fremskrittspartiet	1973	15.3 (1997)
Portugal	Partido da Democracia Crista	1976	1.1 (1979)
Sweden	Ny Demokrati	1991	6.7 (1991)
Switzerland	Nationale Aktion (Action nationale)/Schweizerische Demokraten (Démocrates suisses)	1967	3.3 (1991)
	Vigilance	1967	0.5 (1983)
	Schweizer Auto Partei (Parti automobiliste suisse)	1987	5.1 (1991)
United Kingdom	National Front	1970	0.6 (1979)
	British National Party	1983	0.1 (1997)

[a] The date listed for the Austrian FPÖ signifies the first election contested by the party under the leadership of Jörg Haider.

Sources: Betz and Immerfall (1998); Kitschelt (1995); Mackie and Rose (1991, 1997).

TABLE A3.3. *Ethnoterritorial Parties of Western Europe Included in the Analysis, 1970–96*

Country	Ethnoterritorial Party	Date of First Election Contested	Peak Regional Percentage of National Legislative Vote (year)
Belgium	Volksunie	1954[a]	18.8 (1971)
	Rassemblement Wallon	1968	20.9 (1971)
	Front Démocratique des Francophones	1965	39.6 (1974)
France	Union Démocratique Bretonne	1967	1.27 (1997)
	Unione di u Populu Corsu	1967	20.8 (1993)
Italy	Südtiroler Volkspartei	1948	35.8 (1979)
Spain	Herri Batasuna	1979	17.8 (1986)
	Partido Nacionalista Vasco	1931/1977	31.9 (1982)
	Convergència i Unió	1979[b]	32.7 (1989)
	Esquerra Republicana de Catalunya	1931/1977	5.1 (1993)[c]
United Kingdom	Scottish National Party	1929	30.4 (October 1974)
	Plaid Cymru	1929	11.5 (1970)

[a] The party was named Volksunie in 1960.
[b] CiU was formed in 1979 as a coalition of the Convergència Democràtica de Catalunya (CDC) and the Unió Democràtica de Catalunya (UDC), which had formed and run separately in 1977.
[c] This represents the ERC's peak vote in the post-Franco period of 1977 to 1996.

Sources: Caramani (2000); De Winter and Türsan (1998); Lancelot (1998); Mackie and Rose (1991, 1997); Newman (1996).

TABLE A3.4a. *Descriptive Statistics for Select Variables from the Pooled Analysis of Green and Radical Right Party Vote (from Tables 3.4 and 3.5)*

Variable	Observations	Mean (standard deviation)	Min.	Max.
Niche Party Electoral Support$_t$ (National%)	120 elections across 30 party panels and 17 countries	4.66 (4.67)	0	22.4
Past Performance: Niche Party Vote$_{t-1}$	120 elections across 30 party panels and 17 countries	3.99 (4.29)	0	22.4
Ln Median District Magnitude	120 elections across 30 party panels and 17 countries	2.02 (1.39)	0	5.01
State Organization (1 = Unitary, 0 = Federal)	120 elections across 30 party panels and 17 countries	0.70 (0.46)	0	1
GDP/Capita for Green Party Observations (in thousands)	61 elections across 17 party panels and 17 countries	17.08 (5.41)	5.49	31.58
GDP/Capita for Radical Right Party Observations (in thousands)	59 elections across 13 party panels and 13 countries	15.49 (6.48)	4.65	31.58
Unemployment Rate for Green Party Observations	61 elections across 17 party panels and 17 countries	8.24 (4.37)	0.68	22.22
Unemployment Rate for Radical Right Party Observations	59 elections across 13 party panels and 13 countries	7.36 (3.33)	0.28	12.90
Postmaterialism Level for Green Party Observations	29 elections across 14 party panels and 14 countries	15.31 (6.91)	4	30
Immigrant Percentage for Radical Right Party Observations	27 elections across 9 party panels and 9 countries	3.75 (2.82)	0.5	9.1
Strategic Variables				
DIDI	120 elections across 30 party panels and 17 countries	0.34 (0.48)	0	1
ACAC	120 elections across 30 party panels and 17 countries	0.11 (0.31)	0	1
DIAC	120 elections across 30 party panels and 17 countries	0.23 (0.42)	0	1
DIAD	120 elections across 30 party panels and 17 countries	0.03 (0.18)	0	1
ADAD	120 elections across 30 party panels and 17 countries	0.02 (0.13)	0	1
ACAD with Relative Intensity	120 elections across 30 party panels and 17 countries	−0.18 (0.50)	−1	1
Delayed ACAC	120 elections across 30 party panels and 17 countries	0.04 (0.20)	0	1
Delayed DIAC	120 elections across 30 party panels and 17 countries	0.03 (0.16)	0	1

TABLE A3.4b. *Descriptive Statistics for Select Variables from the Analysis of Ethnoterritorial Party Vote (from Table 3.11)*

Variable	Observations	Mean (standard deviation)	Min.	Max.
Niche Party Electoral Support$_t$ (Regional%)	29 elections across 10 party panels and 5 countries	18.75 (14.48)	0.15	45.7
Past Performance: Niche Party Vote$_{t-1}$	29 elections across 10 party panels and 5 countries	19.11 (14.65)	0.15	46.7
Ln Median District Magnitude	29 elections across 10 party panels and 5 countries	1.40 (1.07)	0	3.18
State Organization (1 = Unitary, 0 = Federal)	29 elections across 10 party panels and 5 countries	0.45 (0.51)	0	1
Relative Regional GDP/Capita	29 elections across 10 party panels and 5 countries	1.07 (0.24)	0.78	1.61
Relative Regional Unemployment Rate	29 elections across 10 party panels and 5 countries	0.98 (0.22)	0.36	1.33
Strategic Variables				
DIDI	29 elections across 10 party panels and 5 countries	0.52 (0.51)	0	1
ACAC	29 elections across 10 party panels and 5 countries	0.07 (0.26)	0	1
DIAC	29 elections across 10 party panels and 5 countries	0.21 (0.41)	0	1
ACAD with Relative Intensity	29 elections across 10 party panels and 5 countries	−0.07 (0.46)	−1	1
Delayed DIAC	29 elections across 10 party panels and 5 countries	0.07 (0.26)	0	1

TABLE A3.5a. *Definitions of the CMP Variables Used to Capture Mainstream Party Strategies toward Green Parties*

Variable Name	Variable Number	Definition
Environmental Protection	501	Preservation of countryside, forests, etc.; general preservation of natural resources against selfish interests; proper use of national parks; soil banks, etc.; environmental improvement
Anti-Growth Economy	416	Favourable mention of anti-growth politics and steady state economy; ecologism; "Green politics"; sustainable development
Free Enterprise	401	Favourable mentions of free enterprise capitalism; superiority of individual enterprise over state and control systems; favourable mentions of private property rights, personal enterprise, and initiative; need for unhampered individual enterprises
Agriculture and Farmers	703	Support for agriculture and farmers; any policy aimed specifically at benefiting these
Internationalism: Negative	109	Favourable mentions of national independence and sovereignty as opposed to internationalism; otherwise as 107, but negative. *NB: The definition for variable 107 is: Need for international co-operation; co-operation with specific countries other than those coded in 101; need for aid to developing countries; need for world planning of resources; need for international courts; support for any international goal or world state; support for UN.*

Source: Budge et al. 2001: 222–4, 226–7.

TABLE A3.5b. *Definitions of the CMP Variables Used to Capture Mainstream Party Strategies toward Radical Right Parties*

Variable Name	Variable Number	Definition
Law and Order	605	Enforcement of all laws; actions against crime; support and resources for police; tougher attitudes in courts
National Way of Life: Positive	601	Appeals to patriotism and/or nationalism; suspension of some freedoms in order to protect the state against subversion; support for established national ideas
National Way of Life: Negative	602	Against patriotism and/or nationalism; opposition to the existing national state; otherwise as 601, but negative
Traditional Morality: Positive	603	Favourable mentions of traditional moral values; prohibition, censorship and suppression of immorality and unseemly behaviour; maintenance and stability of family; religion
Traditional Morality: Negative	604	Opposition to traditional moral values; support for divorce, abortion, etc.; otherwise as 603, but negative
Multiculturalism: Positive	607	Cultural diversity, communalism, cultural plurality, and pillarisation; preservation of autonomy of religious, linguistic heritages within the country including special educational provisions
Multiculturalism: Negative	608	Enforcement or encouragement of cultural integration; otherwise as 607, but negative
Underprivileged Minority Groups	705	Favourable references to underprivileged minorities who are defined neither in economic nor in demographic terms, e.g., the handicapped, disabled, homosexuals, immigrants, refugees, etc.

Source: Budge et al. 2001: 226–8.

TABLE A3.5c. *Definitions of the CMP Variables Used to Capture Mainstream Party Strategies toward Ethnoterritorial Parties*

Variable Name	Variable Number	Definition
Decentralisation	301	Support for federalism or devolution; more regional autonomy for policy or economy; support for keeping up local and regional customs and symbols; favourable mentions of special consideration for local areas; deference to local expertise
Centralisation	302	Opposition to political decision-making at lower political levels; support for more centralisation in political and administrative procedures; otherwise as 301, but negative

Source: Budge et al. 2001: 223.

4

A Theory of Strategic Choice

In 1970, calling for the protection of "our British Native stock" against "colored immigration," the National Front fielded candidates in its first parliamentary election.[1] Formed four years earlier by a merger of the League of Empire Loyalists and the British National Party, the National Front criticized the absence of the immigration issue from mainstream party political debate. Over the next decade, this xenophobic niche party would try to force the issue onto the political agenda with its repeated calls for the immediate cessation of immigration to the United Kingdom and repatriation of all nonwhite foreigners.

Although it garnered an average vote of less than 4 percent across contested districts, or a scant 0.3 percent average nationwide during the 1970s, the National Front did not go unnoticed by the British mainstream parties. The Conservative Party reacted with intense accommodative tactics to the defection of some of its voters to the niche party. Adopted by the Heath government as early as 1973, the Tories' accommodative proposals included the strengthening of immigration controls and the retraction of British citizenship obligations to immigrants from former Commonwealth nations. Conservative politicians, including party leader and future Prime Minister Margaret Thatcher, even invoked the National Front's xenophobic imagery of Britain as "a crowded island" being "swamped" by foreigners to try to win (back) anti-immigrant voters.[2]

Although not unscathed by the flight of voters to the National Front, the Labour Party did not follow in the Conservatives' footsteps. Instead of wooing back its sizeable group of defecting working-class voters, the Labour Party by

[1] National Front references taken from Holmes 1991: 57.
[2] In 1973, Robert Carr, Secretary of State in the Home Office, elucidated the guiding principles of Conservative immigration policy (Carr 1973: 3): "The recognition that Britain is a crowded island with a labour force which for the moment at least appears ample to her needs. Hence the restriction of all permanent settlement to what I described as the inescapable minimum and the establishment of effective controls to achieve this." As described in the text, four years later, Margaret Thatcher made an even more blatant appeal to xenophobic voters during an interview on the television program "World in Action" (Taylor 1982: 144).

the mid-1970s pursued a costly adversarial strategy of promoting race relations and denouncing the anti-immigrant positions of its niche party opponent. The strategy garnered the Labour Party little added support and failed to halt further voter loss to the xenophobic party, but it did help to reinforce the legitimacy of the National Front as the credible owner of the anti-immigration issue position.

The regression results of Chapter 3 suggest that this combination of stronger accommodative and weaker adversarial tactics will lead to the electoral decline of the niche party. Indeed, this is what happened to the British National Front. By the end of the 1970s, the party was capturing just over 1 percent of the vote in contested districts. Yet, while we can make predictions about the effects of particular strategic combinations, this book has not thus far examined when and why those strategies are employed. Why, for example, did the British Labour Party risk vote loss among its working-class supporters to boost the electoral support of a radical right party? And why did the Conservatives, when faced with a relatively unthreatening new party, eschew low-cost dismissive tactics for costly accommodative strategies? What were the parties' motivations for choosing these particular tactics? Did Labour and the Conservatives choose the most rational options available to them, and, if not, what were the obstacles to the adoption of those optimal tactics?

To answer these questions, I develop a theory of strategic choice. I argue that the strategic response of a mainstream party depends crucially on the intensity of the niche party threat, where threat is measured by the ratio of its vote losses to the niche party relative to its mainstream party opponent's vote losses. But a party's strategic choice is not made in a vacuum. First, the permissiveness of the electoral environment alters the frequency and form of the tactics employed. Second, the behavior of one party is influenced by the behavior of others. Third, even if a party identifies its optimal strategy in light of the electoral environment and what other actors might do, the successful adoption of that tactic is subject to organizational and reputational constraints. Elite factionalism and decentralized policy making reduce the credibility of the party's strategy, delay its adoption, and, in some cases, even inhibit the selection of the ideal tactic. Past policy decisions likewise constrain future strategic behavior.

This chapter opens by reviewing the nature of competition between un-equals – its players, their tactical choices, and the stakes of the game. Based on these characteristics and the findings of Chapter 3, I identify the conditions and constraints that shape party decision making. Whereas precise estimates of a party's actions depend on the contextual factors specific to a given historical case, this chapter provides general predictions of the individual variables' effects on strategic choice; these factors are combined into fully specified models of mainstream party–niche party interaction in the subsequent, in-depth case studies of Chapters 5 through 8.

THE NATURE OF COMPETITION BETWEEN UNEQUALS

At the heart of any model of strategic choice is a game, a game defined by its players, their choices, and their stakes in the interaction. As the opening story of the British National Front suggests, competition between mainstream and niche parties is a slightly different game than the standard Downsian interaction of equally matched opponents. In this new game, mainstream parties are faced with relatively inexperienced political actors who appeal to voters on the basis of one new issue. In contrast to the assumptions of spatial models of new party entry (e.g., Greenberg and Shepsle 1987; Palfrey 1984), these single-issue parties are not entering an existing policy space dominated by established party actors; they are instead adding a new dimension to the political arena. It is the mainstream parties who become the potential entrants confronting an entrenched niche party opponent with a fixed policy position. The appropriate economic analogy is, thus, not that of the chain store model, where a new actor decides whether to enter an established market (Selten 1978), but rather the lesser known story of market expansion, where established firms decide whether to enter a new market developed by a novice firm (Aron and Lazear 1987, 1990).

Because niche parties attract votes on the basis of their single issues, competition between unequals is confined to interaction on the one, new policy axis.[3] In this situation, mainstream parties have access to three strategic options. As discussed in Chapter 2, the established party can remain outside of the new policy dimension (dismissive tactic), enter the new policy dimension and approximate the niche party's position (accommodative tactic), or enter and adopt an opposite stance on the new issue (adversarial tactic).

Each of these tactics has costs and benefits. Starting with the benefits, the data analysis in Chapter 3 supports the claim that both dismissive and accommodative strategies lead to decreases in niche party support. However, according to my PSO theory, their mechanisms and, thus, their effectiveness differ. Dismissive strategies only decrease the salience of the issue, whereas accommodative tactics have the potential to be more potent because they work by increasing issue salience and challenging the ownership of the niche party's issue position. Adversarial tactics also boost issue salience, but, unlike AC strategies, they reinforce the niche party's issue ownership to lead to an increase in niche party vote. Note that adversarial tactics do not necessarily result in a direct increase in the vote of the strategizing mainstream party.

Just as the mechanisms of these strategies differ, so too do their costs. The dismissive option is the least costly of the three, especially in the short term, requiring the mainstream party to make no new policy statements or commitments to a particular stance on the niche party's issue. As a result, parties switching to a more active (accommodative or adversarial) strategy in the future avoid the reputational costs associated with having adopted contradictory positions on a given issue. That said, dismissive strategies are not cost free in the long term; there is

---

[3] For the purpose of this analysis, I assume that the position of the mainstream parties on the Left-Right dimension remains fixed during their interaction with the niche party. Party competition between the mainstream and niche parties therefore occurs in a one-dimensional space. Although this is a simplification of reality, survey data presented in Chapters 5 to 7 demonstrate that niche party voters are unfamiliar or unconcerned with the neophyte's position on other dimensions, and, thus, their vote choice for the green, radical right, and ethnoterritorial parties turns mainly on the one issue of the environment, immigration, and decentralization, respectively.

evidence, albeit mixed, from Chapter 3 that the effectiveness of accommodative strategies decreases after prolonged use of dismissive strategies.

Adoption of accommodative or adversarial tactics, on the other hand, entails considerable short- and long-term costs for the mainstream party. The established party is not only faced with the standard expenses of researching and promoting a new issue, but its pursuit of these active, salience-heightening strategies also increases the costs of competing on that new issue dimension. Voters will be more aware of and sensitive to the parties' positions on this issue than on other, less-salient issues. Thus, any change in party position either toward (accommodative) or away from (adversarial) the niche party will involve more potential costs as well as benefits than if issue salience had not been heightened (i.e., than if a dismissive strategy had been pursued). Because of the lock-in effect described in Chapter 2, active strategies also entail higher commitment costs than their dismissive counterparts.[4]

So far the discussion has revealed the relative costs and benefits of these three strategic options. Yet, to determine which tactics a mainstream party pursues in any given situation, it is also necessary to understand the party's motivations. Central to this and most strategic theories of political behavior is the assumption that parties are rational. Parties choose tactics that will maximize their benefits while minimizing their costs.[5] In other words, these actors seek to maximize their utility.

But how do parties define utility? Strategic models typically assume that parties are power maximizers; whether their goals are measured in terms of votes or office, parties are thought to adopt strategies that will strengthen their position within the political or electoral arenas (e.g., Downs 1957; Müller and Strøm 1999). When presented with a direct threat to that power, a party will respond in order to maintain its current level of power or to at least minimize its losses.

While this goal is consistent with a party's pursuit of vote-reducing dismissive and accommodative tactics, this standard Downsian assumption cannot account for why some actors employ strategies that do not directly increase their electoral support. The adversarial response of the British Labour Party to the National Front cannot be understood in terms of a preference for power maximization alone. Instead of dismissing this common mainstream party behavior as irrational, I argue that party actors in competition between unequals are pursuing a slightly different goal, that of *relative* power, or margin, maximization.[6]

---

[4] As discussed in Chapter 2, switching between accommodative and adversarial tactics undermines the effectiveness of these tactics. On the contrary, movement between dismissive and these active strategies – assuming no significant hesitation in the adoption of accommodative tactics – does not alter the effectiveness of the individual tactics.

[5] All else being equal, it follows that parties prefer less-costly forms of strategy to more-costly ones.

[6] This goal of margin maximization is critical to Adams, Merrill, and Grofman's (2005) analysis of party competition in Norway. It is also the logic behind Adams and Merrill's (2006) predictions of "policy divergence" and a "reverse shift effect" behavior in models of three-party competition. Evidence of this assumption of party margin-maximization is clear from their claim that the right party's electoral prospects are increased by the center party "siphoning away support from party L [the left party] among center-left voters" (2006: 406).

With this objective, parties are driven to maximize the size of the electoral gap – in terms of votes or seats – between themselves and their main opponents. This goal can be achieved by maximizing a party's own power, behavior consistent with the standard Downsian vote-maximization assumption. However, in situations where vote gain is not possible, a party can also maximize its *relative* power by minimizing a competitor's power.[7] Such conditions arise in a three-party system when a party is not threatened by a new competitor, but its mainstream party opponent is. Although the unscathed party may not be able to directly improve its own electoral position, it can undermine the strength of its main opponent by boosting the threat of the new challenger. In the zero-sum environment of the electoral arena, it makes sense that a party would not only aim to be as strong as possible, but also to be *stronger* than its opponents.

UNDER WHAT CONDITIONS DO PARTIES CHOOSE PARTICULAR STRATEGIES? A MODEL OF STRATEGIC CHOICE

Driven to maximize their relative power, how do mainstream parties respond to their single-issue party challengers? The regression results of Chapter 3 confirm that mainstream parties have access to a set of weapons that allow them to decrease and increase the electoral strength of their niche party challengers. Yet, it is not clear from the statistical analysis under which conditions a rational party will adopt one strategy over another. When does a party try to reduce niche party threat with less-potent dismissive tactics as opposed to the stronger accommodative strategies? When are potentially costly adversarial tactics employed?

To answer these questions, we need to model the interaction of mainstream and niche parties and see how the mainstream actors respond under varying electoral conditions. In its simplest form, the construction of such a model requires knowledge of the political actors, their goals and strategic options, and the motivations and policy preferences of the voters; where the direction and intensity of party behavior is dictated by a cost-benefit analysis, precise estimates of party policy responses can be derived only when these parameters are specified.[8]

The configuration of the game of competition between unequals was largely spelled out in the previous section. To reiterate, the political space is occupied by mainstream parties, niche parties, and voters. Competition is confined to interaction on the one, new issue dimension. Both the niche party and the voters exhibit fixed preferences on the new issue dimension.[9] The specific distribution of voters varies by case.[10] It follows from the discussion in Chapter 2 that voters

---

[7] According to traditional Downsian models of party interaction, such situations cannot exist. In those models, a party does not have the tools to decrease an opponent's vote without simultaneously increasing its own. My proposed mechanism for indirectly increasing a party's relative power assumes that parties can alter the strength of nonproximal opponents.

[8] As the case of cycling in multidimensional policy space demonstrates, even when these parameters are specified, there is no guarantee that precise estimates of behavior can be produced.

[9] The niche party does not have a position on any other issue.

[10] Whereas standard spatial models routinely assume that voters are normally distributed either along one or multiple dimensions (e.g., Adams 2001; Downs 1957; Enelow and Hinich 1984),

vote sincerely for the party that maximizes their utility, where voter utility is a product of the perceived attractiveness (proximity) and issue credibility (ownership) of parties on *salient* issue dimensions. I assume that mainstream parties are vote seekers with margin-maximizing motivations.[11] The mainstream parties must decide whether to enter and compete with a niche party on its new issue dimension.[12]

Niche Party Threat

In this game of competition between unequals, I argue that a mainstream party's choice of strategies depends critically on a niche party's degree of threat, where threat is a function of the electoral strength of the new party and the spatial location of the votes it captures. A niche party is a danger to a mainstream party if it takes (a significant number of) votes from it. Conversely, the niche party is not a direct threat if it does not take any (or many) of a party's votes.[13] In this analysis, therefore, we are not following the conventional conception of a party's importance as measured by a party's total vote percentage (e.g., Lijphart 1990; Rae 1971; Sartori 1976; Taagepera and Shugart 1989). Rather, the focus of this model of strategic choice is on how many votes a niche party wins and from whom.

When assessing niche party threat, the level of a given party's vote loss to the neophyte is therefore important. Mainstream party responses turn on whether a challenger steals many or few of its votes. However, where parties are relative-vote maximizers, level is not the only component of party threat. For parties that aim to increase their power relative to others, the degree to which one mainstream party is menaced is also a function of how many votes its opponent loses to that same niche party. With this in mind, measures of niche party threat should also include the ratio of the number of voters defecting to the niche party from one mainstream party to the number of voters defecting to the niche party from a second mainstream party.

---

voter preferences on a niche party's polarizing issue dimension rarely are normally configured and, more importantly, vary across issues, countries, and even over time. Consequently, I make no *a priori* assumption about the shape of the voter distribution.

[11] Although I treat the party as a vote seeker for the purpose of the discussion of the theory and its implications, this model also applies to office-seeking parties. The reader should note that this presentational choice has ramifications for my model's predictions of strategic behavior under PR electoral rules (Müller and Strøm 1999).

[12] Before the mainstream party makes its initial move, it is assumed to have *no* position on the niche party's new issue dimension.

[13] In this section, I present niche parties as taking votes from either mainstream party, both, or none. In the last case, mainstream parties are predicted to implement dismissive strategies. However, in political systems with sizeable electoral abstention rates, it is possible for a niche party to gain significant percentages of the vote from those who previously abstained, even if the mainstream parties do not lose any votes to it. Under these circumstances, mainstream parties might engage in either accommodative or adversarial tactics – the choice depends on the spatial location and "natural party affiliation" of the disaffected voters. The rarity of this case leads to its exclusion from the general discussion of the model.

I argue in general that a party will employ dismissive tactics when neither mainstream party is significantly affected by the niche party. A mainstream party faced with a weak and relatively unthreatening niche party challenger will not take a potentially costly position on the neophyte's new issue dimension. If, however, the niche party threatens the vote share of one or both established parties, the strategizing mainstream party will turn to more active tactics. Given significant vote loss, a mainstream party that loses more votes to the niche party than its opponent will adopt accommodative tactics; the threatened party moves from having no position on the niche party's issue to adopting a stance similar to that of the niche party in order to recover lost voters. Conversely, an established party losing fewer votes than its mainstream opponent will generally engage in an adversarial strategy; the less-threatened party will take a position on the new issue dimension opposite to that championed by the niche party. Rather than remain passive, as most standard spatial models would expect in this scenario, this relatively unscathed mainstream party seeks to increase its relative electoral power, as reflected in the vote margin, by exacerbating the niche party's threat to its mainstream party opponent.[14]

Contextualizing Strategic Choice: The Role of Electoral Systems

Predictions of individual party behavior and, ultimately, niche party electoral success depend on the relative electoral threat of the neophyte challenger. Yet, party interaction does not take place in a vacuum. Strategic choices are sensitive to the setting in which they are made. I have already alluded to the role of voter distribution in shaping the costs and benefits of party behavior and, thus, a party's rational course of action. But voter distribution is not the only variable conditioning the strategic choices a party makes. The incidence and form (issue-based, organizational, or institutional) of specific tactical choices are also dependent on the structure of the electoral system.

Given that party behavior is predicated on a niche party's degree of threat, how does the electoral environment influence a party's strategic choice? It is widely recognized that the rules by which votes are counted and seats are allocated alter the perceived significance of electoral threats. Under one set of electoral institutions, a niche party capturing 5 percent of votes from an electorally secure mainstream party may be considered a danger, whereas under a different set of institutions, that neophyte may be seen as little more than a nuisance. What differs between electoral systems is the relative significance of each vote cast and, thus, the parties' sensitivity to that level of vote loss. Where parties react to threats, any factor that alters the perceived significance of those threats naturally affects party behavior.

Before examining how a party's tolerance for vote loss affects its choice of strategy, it is important to understand the mechanisms by which electoral

---

[14] In the process of publicly opposing the niche party's issue position, the adversarial party also will attract like-minded voters.

institutions alter that tolerance. The electoral threshold is typically held up as the key electoral structure mitigating party threat. Where the electoral threshold is low to nonexistent, the literature argues, even slight vote loss can result in seat dispossession and a decrease in a party's governmental strength (Taagepera and Shugart 1989). Party sensitivity to threat in this system is therefore particularly high. Conversely, in systems with high thresholds to office attainment, parties are more resilient to vote loss. Electoral thresholds, therefore, change the level of vote loss at which the mainstream party feels menaced.

The proportionality of the electoral rules has a similar, if overlooked, influence on the perceived strength of a niche party threat. When seats are allocated in direct proportion to the vote obtained, parties are relatively indifferent between the loss of their vote in one district or another; a niche party gaining 5 percent of the vote poses the same threat regardless of the district in which that niche party competes. However, as the vote-seat disproportionality index increases, that is, as the electoral system becomes less proportional, a niche party's threat to a mainstream party begins to depend on *where* those votes are won. Under these conditions, not all votes are equally important to a party; the geographic distribution of the niche party's vote matters. A mainstream party in a restrictive electoral system with plurality rules will react differently if the opponent gains votes in a district the mainstream party controls with a strong majority versus one in which its hold is more precarious (Ellis 1998). In these latter, "marginal," districts, a slight shift of the balance of votes could result in the loss of the seat.[15] Consequently, a party may be more susceptible to seat loss in a marginal district where a competing party gains 4 percent of the vote than in a "safe" seat where the niche party captures 8 percent (Cornford and Dorling 1997).

Changes in the Incidence of Party Strategies. As these discussions have revealed, the institutional setting shapes a party's vulnerability to electoral threat. Electoral systems alter the *specific level* of niche party threat necessary to prompt mainstream party strategies. In electoral systems where the barrier to legislative representation through seat attainment is low, extreme party sensitivity to vote loss means that dismissive strategies will be less common; mainstream parties will need to be more certain of the negligible future prospects of the niche party before employing a strategy that ignores its presence and the importance of its new issue.[16] Thus, all other things being equal, the level of niche party threat at which parties trade dismissive for active strategies is lower in systems with low to nonexistent electoral thresholds.

Likewise, the proportionality of an electoral system, and specifically the location of vote loss, alters the level of niche party threat that prompts active strategies.

---

[15] A marginal district is defined as an electoral district in which the difference between the first- and second-place parties' or candidates' vote shares is 10 percentage points or less.

[16] Conversely, accommodative tactics will be less commonly employed against niche party threats in systems with higher electoral thresholds.

In systems where the vote-seat disproportionality index is high, mainstream parties losing votes in marginal districts are more likely to resort to accommodative tactics than parties losing votes in secure seats. The precarious hold that the established party has in these districts makes any loss of support in these seats damaging to the party's electoral security. Thus, the level of niche party threat prompting accommodative behavior will be lower where that vote loss is concentrated in marginally held districts. The British Conservatives' accommodative response to the threatening but fairly weak National Front, described in this chapter's introduction, illustrates this phenomenon.

Changes in the Form of Party Strategies. Just as the characteristics of the electoral environment alter the incidence of mainstream party strategies, they also affect the form that those tactics take. Organizational strategies, for instance, are more likely to be adopted the more proportional the electoral system. The prevalence of coalitions in permissive electoral systems decreases the novelty of such tactics (Laver and Schofield 1998: 26, 195–215). Moreover, the high level of party fragmentation common in systems with proportional representation (Duverger 1954: 217; Powell 2000: 29) means that programmatic strategies become relatively costly. With more parties crammed into the policy space, voters have many close political alternatives from which to choose; too great a policy shift by a strategizing party may render it unattractive to its former electorate, who can vote for a closer political actor. Organizational strategies, which allow a mainstream party to alter a niche party's issue ownership without having to move on that issue, become the less-costly choice.

Contextualizing Strategic Choice: The Interaction of Mainstream Parties

In exploring the strategic preferences of mainstream parties under various levels of niche party threat in different institutional settings, the analysis so far has assumed that the positions of all other political actors are fixed. The strategizing party is the only actor to react to the niche party; no other mainstream party takes a position on the new issue dimension. However, this simplifying assumption is unrealistic. Where mainstream parties from across the political spectrum can shape the electoral fate of a niche party, multiple parties can and commonly will react to the niche party. The impact of one mainstream party's tactics – on both the niche party's vote share and its own electoral strength – depends, therefore, on the behavior of other mainstream party actors.[17]

Determining the optimal strategy of one party in light of other parties' actions has proven a difficult enterprise for political scientists and economists.

---

[17] In choosing a strategy, a party must therefore take into account how an opponent's actions will alter its own payoffs, or vote share. For the mainstream party reacting to a niche party, its concerns also extend to how an opponent's strategies will affect the *niche party's* vote.

Theoretical and analytical work by spatial modelers suggests the rarity of stable, optimal policy stances, or policy equilibria, in two-party competition over multiple issue dimensions (Adams 2001; Eaton and Lipsey 1975; Enelow and Hinich 1984; Hermsen and Verbeek 1992; Mueller 1989; Shaked 1975).[18] Yet, although precise estimates of equilibrium strategic combinations either cannot be derived or exist only in extremely unusual or contrived scenarios, we can determine the relative direction of party movement on a given issue dimension. In other words, we can predict whether parties adopt no position (act dismissively), generally agree with the niche party on the issue (act accommodatively), or generally disagree with the niche party (act adversarially).

To calculate the optimal margin-maximizing strategic combinations of multiple mainstream parties, we once again look to the degree of niche party threat. This time, our focus is on a mainstream party's *relative* degree of vote loss. Whereas this measure was previously used to describe niche party threat to one strategizing party, this ratio of vote loss also characterizes the extent of the neophyte's threat to the entire party system.[19] Three different scenarios of mainstream party–niche party competition derive from the range of possible values of this relative measure: the niche party threatens neither mainstream party (vote loss ratio is undefined), it threatens one more than the other (vote loss ratio is > or < 1), or it threatens both equally (vote loss ratio = 1). Because niche parties hold noncentrist stances on the new issues that they introduce, as demonstrated by the expert survey data (Benoit and Laver 2006; Laver and Hunt 1992) discussed in Chapter 3, it follows that each of these three scenarios corresponds to a different voter distribution. In the next pages, I examine each of these categories of mainstream party–niche party competition, spelling out the implications of their configurations of voters for mainstream party strategic combinations.

Scenario 1: Absent Niche Party Threat. The most common scenario of competition between political unequals is the one in which a niche party threatens neither mainstream party. In other words, the vote loss ratio is undefined. In this case, a niche party emerges but does not attract any or many votes from the mainstream parties.[20] Given that a niche party competes only on its new issue,[21] this situation occurs when voters do not have preferences on the niche party's issue.[22] The

---

[18] The theoretical literature predicts that party policy positions will be highly unstable in this multiparty, multidimensional environment. Although empirical analyses reveal slightly more stability in the observed behavior of parties, the empirical literature also notes that "party equilibria among vote-maximizing parties will exist only under extremely unusual or contrived conditions" (Adams 2001: 192n10).

[19] Assuming a three-party system, with two mainstream parties and one niche party.

[20] The level of threat deemed insignificant depends, as discussed previously, on the electoral system.

[21] Based on the single-issue nature of these parties as established in Chapter 3, niche parties are assumed to have no position on other policy dimensions. Consistent with the directional model of party competition (e.g., Rabinowitz and Macdonald 1989), this could be represented as a position of zero on those policy axes.

[22] Alternatively, a niche party will not be a threat if voters with preferences on the new issue dimension find the issue to be irrelevant.

voters may have positions along the economically defined Left-Right dimension, but they do not move off that axis into the niche party's issue space.

Under these circumstances, both mainstream parties are expected to pursue dismissive strategies, and a DIDI strategic combination results. Faced with voters who have no policy preferences on a particular issue, neither mainstream party has an incentive to adopt a position on that issue. Moreover, because there is little to no voter demand for the niche party's policy stance (or even demand for attention to its issue *dimension*), mainstream parties' accommodative and adversarial strategies would have minimal effect on the support of the unpopular niche party, and such tactics would be costly for the strategizing mainstream parties. For example, the established parties would be encouraging the flight of their own voters, by prioritizing an issue effectively deemed irrelevant by the voters to the exclusion of other, more vote-drawing campaign themes. Conversely, by pursuing joint dismissive tactics, the mainstream parties would be echoing the views of the majority of their voters and using a low-cost and noncontroversial means of (further) reducing niche party support.

Scenario 2: Unequal Niche Party Threat. If it was not rational for mainstream parties to respond to a weak niche party challenger, how does the expected behavior of the mainstream parties change if the niche party threatens their electoral support and legislative hold? Consider first the case of unequal niche party threat. In this scenario, the niche party emerges and proposes a popular policy position on a new dimension. On the basis of that single issue, the niche party attracts a significant number of voters, with more voters coming from one mainstream party than from another.[23]

Faced with such a niche party threat, the mainstream parties adopt different strategies. The established party that is losing more votes, Party A, is driven to recover those lost voters. It therefore pursues an accommodative strategy, entering the new issue space and moving toward the threatening niche party. If effective, this tactic will allow it to boost its own support while undermining that of the single-issue party.

The less-affected mainstream party, Party B, does not remain passive. Although it cannot recover voters lost to the niche party without losing additional support, Party B can increase its *relative* electoral strength by undermining the electoral support of its mainstream party opponent. Given that Party A has a dominant accommodative strategy, Party B will turn to an adversarial strategy.[24] As discussed in Chapter 2, Party B is expected to acknowledge the importance of the niche party's issue but take an opposite position to the niche party on that dimension. This offensive maneuver will reinforce the niche party's issue

---

[23] In general, this also means that more voters from the second mainstream party than the first oppose the niche party's position on the new issue dimension.

[24] An issue-salience-reducing dismissive strategy would not allow Party B to challenge the issue-ownership-transferring accommodative tactics of Party A and the resulting flow to Party A of niche party voters who still found the issue to be important. Thus, a dismissive strategy would be likely to decrease Party B's relative electoral strength.

ownership, thereby potentially frustrating Party A's efforts to co-opt the new party's issue and voters. The goal of the adversarial strategy is a stronger niche party and an indirectly stronger Party B.

One side note about the adversarial strategy is in order: an adversarial strategy could be a means of directly boosting a strategizing mainstream party's electoral support. Indeed, according to the voter distribution described in this scenario, Party B's movement away from the niche party could be understood as a vote-seeking move – a move consistent with standard spatial conceptions of party behavior. It would attract those voters who oppose the niche party's position.

However, as argued by the PSO theory, this is not the only, or even the primary, purpose of the adversarial tactic. Where the goal of the strategizing party is to weaken its mainstream party opponent, an adversarial strategy may be the best option even in the case in which few voters are located toward that opposite pole. Such was the situation confronting the British Labour Party in its competition with the National Front. Despite the low popularity of the pro-immigrant and pro-immigration position, the adoption of adversarial tactics toward the National Front was Labour's best chance to increase its relative electoral strength vis-à-vis the Conservatives.[25]

Under conditions of an unequal niche party threat, the mainstream parties are therefore expected to employ an accommodative-adversarial strategic combination. These tactics represent the best tactical response, *a priori*, for mainstream parties aiming to maintain or even improve their individual electoral prospects. The actual electoral effects of this "battle of opposing forces" will depend, as shown in the results of Chapter 3, on the relative intensity of the constituent tactics. If the accommodative tactics are stronger than the adversarial ones, Party A's vote will increase, and possibly increase relative to that of Party B. Conversely, if the adversarial tactics are stronger, Party B's vote will increase relative to Party A's, and possibly increase in absolute terms.[26] In the absence of information about the relative intensity of their strategies *ex ante*, mainstream parties facing an unequal niche party threat will still arrive at an accommodative-adversarial strategic combination.

Scenario 3: Niche Party as an Equal Threat. The previous scenario describes the standard view of mainstream party–niche party competition in the literature. However, while most environmental, radical right, and, to a lesser extent, ethnoterritorial parties are assumed to be "flank parties" drawing more votes from

[25] In a 1971 policy document, the Labour Party Immigration Study Group acknowledged the party's inability to gain votes using an accommodative strategy: "Since the Tories could always outvote Labour in a contest to win votes on a racialist basis, this retreat [i.e., accommodation] could not save Labour from defeat, and will not in the future" (LPA, S. S. Gill, *Race Relations and the Labour Party*, Labour Party Immigration Study Group, RD 74 [London: Labour Home Policies Committee, 1971]: 2).

[26] The support of the niche party would also change. It would decline in the first scenario and increase in the second (at the expense of A).

one mainstream party than another (e.g., Carter 2005; Kitschelt 1994, 1995; Rohrschneider 1993), there are examples of niche parties that equally threaten the established parties.[27] Such a case occurs when an equal and significant number of voters from each mainstream party express policy preferences similar to those of the niche party on the new issue.

In this scenario, the mainstream parties are expected to respond with joint accommodative tactics. Both established parties will recognize the importance of the new issue and move toward the niche party's popular issue position. When combined with the transfer of issue ownership that also characterizes accommodation, these tactics should halt and reverse voter defection. The niche party's vote will decline, with the mainstream parties capturing voters in proportion to the intensity and credibility of their co-optative tactics.[28]

Where the niche party is equally threatening to the mainstream parties, no other individual or joint strategy offers the mainstream parties the same promise of absolute vote gain and the possibility of relative vote gain. Joint dismissive or joint adversarial tactics will only serve to encourage the flight, from both parties, of voters who support the niche party's issue position. Similarly, a mainstream party's unilateral use of dismissive or adversarial strategies will further alienate its voters – driving them to the accommodating mainstream party or niche party, depending on the type and intensity of the employed tactics. The joint accommodative strategy therefore emerges as the optimal strategic combination.[29]

From these typical scenarios of mainstream party–niche party competition, we arrive at three distinct predictions of mainstream party strategic behavior. To summarize, when the niche party is not a threat, mainstream parties will adopt joint dismissive tactics. An accommodative-adversarial strategic combination will occur when the niche party threatens one party more than another. Mainstream parties will adopt joint accommodative tactics when the niche party threatens both established parties equally. Under these ideal conditions, we would therefore expect to observe only three of the six possible strategic combinations. Although the components of DIAC, DIAD, and ADAD strategies may prove to be individually rational under certain circumstances, relative-vote maximizing parties should not jointly arrive at these combinations.

[27] The literature has long assumed that because environmental and radical right parties draw disproportionately from mainstream parties, these parties are on the flanks of the Left-Right dimension. Although these parties may affect one mainstream party more than another (a possibility, but not a necessity, as the next section shows), it does not mean that these single-issue parties can be placed on the economically defined Left-Right dimension. This book maintains that niche parties compete only on the basis of their newly introduced issue.

[28] It is unlikely that both mainstream parties will be equally perceived to be the rightful owner of the new issue. As will be demonstrated in the discussion of the British Green Party in Chapter 5, the title of issue owner may shift from one accommodating party to another before becoming entrenched.

[29] Although the relative electoral strength of the mainstream parties is not expected to increase if both accommodative tactics are pursued with equal intensity, the relative electoral strength is also not expected to decrease with this strategic combination.

Constraints to the Implementation of Rational Strategies

Armed with an awareness of its level and degree of vote loss relative to that of an opponent, a mainstream party can determine its best response to a niche party in a given institutional and electoral environment. However, knowledge of the most rational strategy for improving a party's relative electoral strength and altering niche party support does not always ensure adoption of that tactic. Indeed, while 74 percent of the strategic combinations employed by Western European parties toward niche parties from 1970 to 1998 consisted of the three "optimal" strategies, mainstream parties pursued the "less-optimal" DIAC, DIAD, and ADAD in 26 percent of the cases.[30] Just as electoral institutions and the behavior of others shape a party's choice of tactics, we need to explore those factors that constrain a party's ability to implement the seemingly optimal tactics. In the following sections, I identify the two most critical barriers to mainstream party strategic implementation – organizational and reputational constraints. Though not exhaustive, these factors bring us closer to understanding why established parties arrive at strategies that, in a given electoral environment, do not maximize their probability of increasing their relative vote shares. I begin by considering a party's organizational characteristics.

Organizational Constraints. Like many theories of strategic choice, this one has, up until this point, assumed that a party is a unitary actor insofar as it makes and executes decisions. Moreover, I have maintained that a party and its decision makers are autonomous, being able to arrive at policy decisions without external interference. However, as Aldrich (1995) and others have shown, these simplifying assumptions obscure critical factors that help to explain why parties do not always follow the most optimal path, or any path at all. To understand why suboptimal tactics may prevail, we must open the black box of party organization. In doing so, our attention is directed to those organizational characteristics that are central to the policy-making process and whose absence would alter a party's likelihood of pursuing specific tactics.

Among the likely suspects, a party's degree of elite ideological cohesiveness and leadership autonomy stand out. As noted by Tsebelis (1990) and others, the existence of policy differences, especially among elite decision makers, slows down the creation of a political consensus and, in situations of extreme factionalism, prevents it completely.[31] Even if a strategy is arrived at without significant

---

[30] These percentages are calculated from the incidence of strategic combinations toward green, radical right, and ethnoterritorial parties recorded in Tables 3.3 and 3.10. While largely consistent with the predictions, these findings are not, in themselves, conclusive evidence of the validity of the strategic choice hypotheses. Because these percentages are calculated without assessing the rationality of the individual strategies, more rigorous testing is necessary and will be carried out on the case studies in the remaining chapters of the book.

[31] Here.factions are understood as intraparty groups whose members "share a common identity and common purpose and are organized to act collectively – as a distinct bloc within the party – to achieve their goals" (Zariski 1960: 33). In this analysis of faction effects on strategic choice, I am specifically focusing on elite-level groups organized around issue-based disagreements. In

delay, it may not be the optimal strategic choice. To quote Müller and Strøm (1999: 294–5):

> Either a factionalized party adopts a strategy that satisfies all factions, and thus is the party's lowest common denominator (Müller and Steininger 1994), or it faces difficulties in implementing its strategies. Both scenarios represent severe constraints on party leaders.

The absence of leadership autonomy similarly constrains a party's ability to respond to a threat. Unlike its counterpart in a highly centralized and insulated party organization, the leadership in a decentralized party is not protected from the opinions and interventions of activists and rank-and-file party members. Faced with more veto points through which nonelite groups can interject competing policy and strategic proposals, policy makers in decentralized parties cannot react to electoral challenges as quickly or decisively as centralized elite (Kitschelt 1994: 253).[32] In addition to decreasing the timeliness of decision making, a decentralized party structure may also affect the content of that decision. Researchers of parties in advanced industrial democracies (see Aldrich 1995; Converse 1975; Inglehart 1984; Iversen 1994a, 1994b) have noted the heterogeneity of policy preferences across elites, activists, and voters. The need for leaders of decentralized parties to gain policy approval from multiple political actors with different preferences thus increases the likelihood that no consensus will be reached or that only uncontroversial strategies will be adopted.[33]

As these discussions imply, elite factionalism and low levels of leadership autonomy constrain a party's strategic behavior. Specifically, the presence of these organizational traits reduces a party's ability to choose electorally costly or resource-intensive strategies. During periods of policy indecisiveness caused by elite disagreements or a decentralized decision-making process, low-cost dismissive tactics become the default strategy. But even when policy consensuses can be reached, parties plagued by elite factions or a decentralized policy-making structure gravitate toward lower-cost, uncontroversial strategies. Where the goal is to reduce niche party support, dismissive strategies may be actively chosen over accommodative ones. Because adversarial tactics are not designed to reduce the immediate threat of vote loss to an opponent and their payoffs are thus concentrated mostly in the future, divided or decentralized parties will hesitate before adopting them; this predominantly offensive – as opposed to defensive – measure will be among the first behaviors to be eliminated in the drive to reduce unnecessary internal party opposition. At the same time, the strategies that are employed

the language of Janda's (1980) typology of party incoherence, I am examining the effects of issue factionalism, as opposed to the more general ideological factionalism or particularistic leadership factionalism.

[32] A similar argument has been made about the legislative efficiency of centralized versus decentralized states. See Immergut (1992) and Huber, Ragin, and Stephens (1993).

[33] That decentralized parties would tend toward less-controversial or less-extreme strategies is consistent with the findings from across a variety of Western European countries and parties that, contrary to May's law of curvilinear disparity, activists tend to be less extreme than party leaders (e.g., Iversen 1994a; Kitschelt 1994: 208; Narud and Skare 1999; Norris 1995).

will be in their least controversial forms: extreme positions in favor of or opposed to the niche party and its new issue will be more costly under conditions of elite factionalism and decentralized decision making. Although this constraint most commonly alters the intensity of programmatic positions, it also limits the use of organizational tactics, such as coalition building, that require an outward-looking organization not plagued by questions of party loyalty or division.

In addition to encouraging the adoption of less-controversial and typically less-effective tactics, compromised leadership autonomy and internal party factionalism may also be responsible for reducing the effectiveness of those tactics that are implemented. Elite divisions and decentralized decision-making structures hinder the timely adoption of strategies. Recall from Chapter 2 that accommodative strategies are expected to be particularly sensitive to delays in implementation. This hypothesis received some support from the regression results in Chapter 3, but a more detailed analysis is needed, and will be provided in the case studies, to see whether, when parties hesitate – because of elite factions, a lack of leadership autonomy, or even electoral miscalculations – the effectiveness of subsequent active tactics is reduced.

Reputational Constraints. Just as the organizational characteristics of a political party can inhibit its adoption of the most rational or effective strategy, there are constraints external to the party that encourage the pursuit of less-than-optimal tactics. As mentioned in Chapter 2, the effectiveness of a strategy depends on the credibility of the party that implements it. A party that pursues consistent policy objectives will be considered more responsible and trustworthy than one that vacillates between opposing policy positions. A lack of policy "responsibility," to use Downs's (1957) term for policy consistency, undermines the intended effects of strategies.[34] One implication of this need to be responsible is that parties may enact suboptimal strategies in order to maintain policy consistency between electoral periods.

An example illustrates how party behavior is constrained by past policy positions. Consider a party that implements an accommodative strategy against a threatening niche party in a situation of unequal niche party threat. If, in a second electoral period, that party no longer loses more votes than its mainstream party opponent to the niche party, it finds itself in a different predicament. As suggested by the second scenario of competition between unequals discussed previously, the optimal tactic for the less-threatened mainstream party may be an adversarial one. Yet, in this situation, the price of adopting the "rational" tactic is preclusive; by switching from supporting to opposing the niche party's issue position, the mainstream party will lose credibility and thus votes. Consequently, this party's best strategy for the second period may be a dismissive one. This strategy of disregard allows the party to maintain its electoral hold without actively calling attention to its reduced efforts to court niche party voters. Dismissive tactics

---

[34] As discussed in Chapter 2, the same can be said for policies that run counter to a party's ideology.

serve as the best "second-stage strategy" for any party that would ideally move between adversarial and accommodative tactics.[35]

CONCLUSION

The model of strategic choice constructed in this chapter rests on the observation that parties are not necessarily motivated to maximize their vote share by eliminating the niche party competitor. Instead, mainstream parties view their response to niche parties as a means to increase their electoral strength relative to that of mainstream party opponents. A party's choice of strategies, therefore, does not depend solely on the magnitude of the niche party's threat to the mainstream party. A strategizing party also takes into consideration the threat posed by the neophyte to other party actors. The *relative* level of niche party threat helps to determine whether an established party will try to improve its relative electoral position by reducing its own rate of vote loss to the niche party or by facilitating an opponent's vote loss to the neophyte. The predictions for an individual party, *ceteris paribus*, are summarized in hypotheses H4.1a-c in Table 4.1.

But competition does not take place in a vacuum, as hypotheses H4.2 to H4.5 remind us. First, the permissiveness of the electoral system determines the importance of the votes lost to the niche party, thereby influencing the incidence and form of tactics used by the mainstream parties against it. Second, the actions of other parties change the expected effects of a particular strategy on niche party fortune and on the relative electoral strength of the strategizing party. Consequently, a party can identify its best strategy only in light of the behavior of its mainstream party opponents; predictions of these optimal strategic combinations are summarized in hypotheses H4.3a to H4.3c. And third, even if the optimal tactic is recognized, there may be organizational and reputational constraints to the pursuit of that tactic. Elite factionalism and decentralized policy-making powers hinder a party's ability to adopt the rational strategy or, in extreme cases, any policy at all. The need for policy consistency across time, likewise, can inhibit the pursuit of the strategy considered optimal for the current electoral and institutional conditions.

These constraints to optimal strategic choice and, thus, to strategies' impact on niche party success are not trivial. But to what extent were these restrictive conditions prevalent across Western Europe? Were the observed effects of mainstream party strategies the product of ideal party behavior or, rather, the outcome of strategizing under restrictions? Although the aggregate analysis of niche party success in Chapter 3 confirmed that strategies matter, we have yet to ascertain why specific tactics were adopted by these Western European mainstream parties. Did parties adopt the optimal tactics, as dictated by their relative vote loss

---

[35] Movement between dismissive and active strategies does not pose the same costs as movement between accommodative and adversarial tactics because, in the former, parties are shifting between having no position and having a position on a given issue dimension. That said, active strategies adopted after years of dismissive tactics are often less effective, as shown by the regression results of Chapter 3.

TABLE 4.1. *Hypotheses of the PSO Theory of Strategic Choice*

H4.1: Mainstream party behavior depends on the absolute and relative levels of niche party threat, as measured by vote loss.

> H4.1a: A mainstream party employs a *dismissive strategy* when the niche party poses little to no threat to *any* mainstream party.
> H4.1b: A mainstream party employs an *accommodative strategy* when the niche party threatens it more than its mainstream party opponent.
> H4.1c: A mainstream party employs an *adversarial strategy* when the niche party threatens its mainstream party opponent more than itself.

H4.2: The electoral system alters the perceived threat of a given niche party and, therefore, influences the incidence and form of mainstream party strategies.

> H4.2a: Active (accommodative and adversarial) strategies will be used more frequently in systems with low electoral thresholds.
> H4.2b: In systems with high vote-seat disproportionality indices, accommodative and adversarial tactics will be employed more frequently against low-threat niche parties in marginally held seats than in safe seats.
> H4.2c: Under systems of proportional representation, organizational strategies are more common.

H4.3: The behavior of one mainstream party is dependent on the behavior of others. Based on the three configurations of party competition discussed in this chapter, we arrive at the following predictions of strategic behavior:

> H4.3a: Where neither party loses significant votes to the niche party, a joint dismissive strategy is optimal.
> H4.3b: Where one mainstream party loses more votes than another, an accommodative-adversarial combination is optimal.
> H4.3c: Where both mainstream parties lose an equal number of votes to the niche party, a joint accommodative strategy is optimal.

H4.4: Elite factionalism and low levels of leadership autonomy reduce a party's ability to adopt costly tactics (e.g., active strategies and organizational forms of strategy).
H4.5: The need for policy consistency constrains a party's strategic options in future electoral periods, making dismissive tactics more likely.

---

under particular institutional conditions? If not, what constraints did they face, and how did those factors influence their adoption of strategies?

A lack of quantifiable data across multiple cases reduces the utility of large-N statistical analyses for answering these questions. In-depth case studies of party interaction, on the other hand, allow us to test the validity of the propositions of the strategic choice theory and their underlying logic. Supplementing information about the objective conditions of niche party threat with archival evidence of the mainstream parties' strategic motivations, the following chapters piece together the rationale behind mainstream party behavior toward niche parties and demonstrate the effects of those tactics on niche party electoral support. This detailed exploration of mainstream party strategic response begins in Chapter 5 with an analysis of the struggle of the Labour and Conservative parties with the

Green Party in Great Britain. Although these center-left and center-right parties succeeded in undermining the electoral support of that environmental party, niche party containment is not always the goal of mainstream parties, and it is not the only outcome of competition between unequals. In Chapter 6, we turn to the country of France and examine how the behavior of the French Socialist and Gaullist parties led to strong voter support for the radical right party, the Front National. Chapter 7 returns to the British context to explore how the strategies of the British Labour and Conservative parties ensured the electoral success of the ethnoterritorial Scottish National Party.

5

Stealing the Environmental Title

British Mainstream Party Strategies and the Containment of the Green Party

In 1989, the British Green Party surprised the political establishment by capturing 14.9 percent of the vote in the European Parliament (EP) elections. Green Party candidates attracted more support than Labour candidates in six constituencies and challenged the Conservatives' hold of two of its safe seats. With its phenomenal electoral score, the Green Party surpassed the Liberal Party to become the number three party in the country.

While some scholars have downplayed the importance of the 1989 victory, this election was seen by the British mainstream parties as a warning. Concern about the environment – and, with it, the membership of the Green Party – had grown in recent years. The level of postmaterialism in Great Britain had increased by 75 percent since the Green Party, at that time named the People's Party, first contested Westminster elections in 1974. By 1989, the environment had surpassed unemployment, the perennial favorite, as the most important problem facing the United Kingdom according to MORI survey respondents (MORI polls).

More importantly for the mainstream parties, this growing public interest in the issues of pollution and nuclear power was influencing voting decisions. Even before the June 1989 EP elections, Green Party candidates were capturing an average vote of 8 percent and peak votes of 14 percent in the May 1989 local county elections (O'Neill 1997: 288). Although supporters of environmental parties are often first-time voters, the British Green Party was stealing voters from the established parties. Analysis of the voting patterns from the 1989 EP elections shows that 27 percent of Green voters had voted for the Conservatives and 17 percent for the Labour Party in the 1987 General Election.[1] Furthermore, despite claims that the defection of the voters from the Conservative Party was merely a sign of midterm malaise and backlash against the governing party, a NOP/Independent postelection survey found that 74 percent of the 1989 Green supporters voted "positively in favor of the Greens," with only 16 percent having

[1] Calculations from van der Eijk et al. 1994.

voted negatively to show disfavor toward another party (Rüdig et al. 1996: 18n21). Not only were the mainstream parties losing voters because of dissatisfaction with their environmental policies, but it also appeared that they would continue to lose them. Fifty-eight percent of those surveyed said that they were highly likely to vote for the Green Party in future *national* elections, and 42 percent expressed their intention to cast ballots for the Greens in the next British General Election.

Eight years later, the Green Party had largely disappeared from the radar screens of the British electorate. Support for environmental organizations and concern for the environmental health of the society had not diminished, but this interest was not matched by votes for the niche party. Indeed, in the 1997 Westminster elections, the party received a national vote of 0.2 percent, or an average of 1.4 percent per candidate. Its vote levels in the more permissive EP elections were equally down, to a record low of 3.1 percent. Given sustained public support for the environmental party's issue, how do we account for the decline in the Green Party's vote? Why did an electorate that was willing to forgo tax cuts for more environmental protection abandon this environmental issue promoter?[2]

The answer, this chapter argues, lies with the strategic behavior of the British mainstream parties. Although cross-national research on green parties has generally chalked up the relative failure of the British Green Party to the restrictiveness of Britain's electoral institutions (see Kitschelt 1994; Müller-Rommel 1996), that approach underappreciates the Green Party's threat to its mainstream party opponents and the importance of those parties' responses to the niche party's support. As the next pages will demonstrate, behavior, not just institutions, shaped niche party fortune. In spite of an electoral climate inhospitable to third parties, the British mainstream parties pursued costly accommodative tactics to highlight the environmental issue and wrest ownership of it away from the Green Party. This case also demonstrates that mainstream party strategic responses – and co-optative ones in particular – are not limited to the "traditional" green party rivals of the center-left. Both Labour and the Conservatives adopted accommodative strategies to recapture issue voters from the Green Party.

This chapter begins by situating the Green Party's emergence and electoral contestation in a British political and electoral environment characterized by growing instability. It then explores the nature of the Green Party's threat to the mainstream political actors and how and why those dominant parties responded to the niche party. Supplementing the findings of the statistical analysis of Chapter 3 with individual-level data on British voters, I examine how the accommodative and dismissive strategies of the Conservative and Labour parties changed voters' issue priorities and their perceptions of environmental issue ownership – the microlevel mechanism behind modified spatial tactics – to alter their vote choice.

---

[2] To quote Bill Jones (1989/1990: 50), "In November 1988 a poll revealed that three-quarters of all voters were so concerned about pollution that they would accept higher prices for goods in exchange for a cleaner and healthier environment."

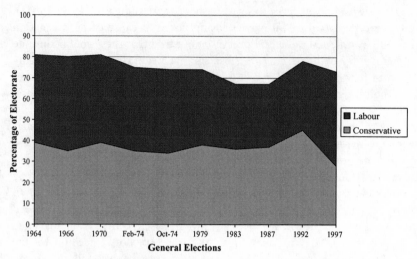

FIGURE 5.1. British Party Identification, 1964–97. *Sources:* Denver 1994: 30–3; British General Election Studies 1979, 1983, 1987, 1992, 1997.

THE POLITICAL AND ELECTORAL ENVIRONMENT OF POST–WORLD WAR II BRITAIN: THE DESTABILIZATION OF BRITISH POLITICS

In 1974, when the People's Party first contested national elections, the British political and electoral climate was in a state of flux. For almost three decades after World War II, British mainstream parties had enjoyed a period of stable electoral cleavages, strong partisan loyalties, and an almost guaranteed monopoly of the electoral and governmental arenas. The two major parties, Conservative and Labour, received an average of over 90 percent of the electorate's votes in the national parliamentary elections (Butler and Butler 2000), and 80 percent of voters identified themselves as Conservative or Labour partisans (Denver 1994: 33). Yet, by the 1970s, British voters were no longer according their loyalties or their votes to the mainstream parties in such large numbers. Whether prompted by decreasing social class cohesion or disaffection with increasingly unresponsive political parties, the electorate's attachment to the Conservative and Labour parties declined. As shown in Figure 5.1, for the first time in the postwar period, fewer than 80 percent of the electorate identified with these two main parties. Among those who did, there was an even more dramatic drop in the perceived strength of their affiliation (see Figure 5.2). With an increase in the number of unattached voters, voter volatility was on the rise; between 1960 and 1979, the average net shift in party vote increased from 5.2 percent to 8.3 percent (Bartolini and Mair 1990: Appendix). Likewise, the parties' combined number of votes per election fell to levels not seen since the first post–World War II election.[3] It is

---

[3] The average total number of votes received by the Labour and Conservative parties for an election in the 1970s was 23,996,086. To put this in perspective, the average electoral total for these parties

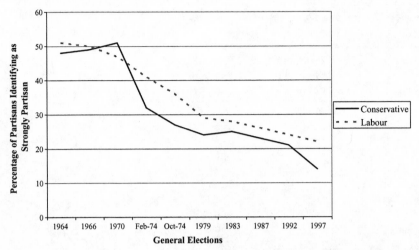

FIGURE 5.2. Decline of Strong Party Identification among British Partisans. *Sources:* Denver 1994: 30–3; British General Election Studies 1979, 1983, 1987, 1992, 1997.

generally agreed that Britain was entering a period of dealignment (Alt 1984: 301; Denver 1994: Chapters 2 and 3; Särlvik and Crewe 1983).

Partisan dealignment and loss of party voters did not, by themselves, constitute a major crisis for the dominant British mainstream parties. If dealignment resulted only in the flight of voters from the electoral arena, then partisan decline would translate into a decrease in the overall turnout level of registered voters; it would not cause a decline in the percentage of cast votes received by any party. However, the situation was further destabilized by an explosion in the number of new political parties and new political issues in Britain. More than forty-eight new parties contested their first national elections between 1960 and 1998.[4] These actors, which included variants of the established, economically oriented parties as well as niche parties, increased the electoral options at a time when voters were growing dissatisfied with the existing political parties.

The direct result of new party presence was a weakening of the electoral strength of the mainstream parties. Although the Conservative and Labour parties managed to maintain their control of the parliament and prime ministership throughout this period, their hold of individual seats was rendered more tenuous. According to Denver (1994: 80), by 1983, 56 percent of the top two candidates in British electoral districts were representatives of parties other than Labour and the Conservatives; only twenty-eight years earlier, that number was a mere

---

for the post–World War II period up until this point was 25,109,466. Calculations from Butler and Butler 2000.

[4] These new parties made up 46 percent of the parties contesting elections between 1960 and 1998. They include both newly formed organizations and those resulting from splits and mergers of existing parties. Calculations from Craig 1977, 1980, and 1984.

TABLE 5.1. *Electoral Strength of British Mainstream Parties,*
1955–97

Election	Turnout of Registered Voters (%)	Percentage of Votes for the Mainstream Parties
1955	76.7	96.1
1959	78.8	93.2
1964	77.1	87.5
1966	75.8	89.8
1970	72.0	89.4
February 1974	78.7	75.0
October 1974	72.8	75.0
1979	76.0	80.8
1983	72.7	70.0
1987	75.3	73.1
1992	77.7	76.3
1997	71.5	73.9

Source: Butler and Butler 2000.

4 percent.[5] Three of these new parties repeatedly obtained seats in the West-minster parliament, quite a success in a country characterized as the archetypal two-party system (Lijphart 1999).

Even when the new parties could not credibly compete with the mainstream parties for seats, their presence increased the crowdedness and boosted the competitiveness of the British political arena. The average combined mainstream party vote share fell dramatically with the emergence of these political alternatives, from an average of more than 90 percent pre-1970 to an average of less than 77 percent since (see Table 5.1). In addition to decreasing the general electoral security of the mainstream parties, in many cases, voter defection to the new parties directly cost mainstream party candidates their seats. During the four General Elections held during the 1970s, 187 Conservative- and Labour-held seats turned over. In twenty-four of those districts, the number of votes received by a single new party exceeded the margin by which the former MP, or Member of Parliament, lost his or her seat.[6] While the individual-level data needed to analyze the origins of the new party's voters in each of these districts are not available, the voting patterns that emerge from national-level surveys suggest that defection to these new parties was responsible for at least some of these seat losses. New parties – in particular, niche parties – directly threatened British mainstream party strength.

[5] This percentage of new parties coming in first or second place includes the not-so-new Liberal Party. However, even if we exclude that party from the calculation, the increase in the number of electorally prominent new parties between 1955 and 1983 is still significant. Butler 1995: 80.

[6] It is important to note that the new parties described in this statistic are niche parties, specifically the Scottish National Party, the Plaid Cymru, and the National Front, not the economically based and not-yet-formed Social Democratic and Liberal Democrat parties.

Adding to the new parties' direct electoral threat was their indirect challenge to the content of the British political debate. The niche parties that figured prominently in the wave of new political actors voiced their rejection of the economic orientation of the political system. In its place, parties like the National Front, the Green Party, the Plaid Cymru, and the Scottish National Party advocated new issue dimensions that often cross-cut traditional partisan coalitions. Coming at a time when social class voting was in decline, the noneconomic appeals of the niche parties found a receptive public. Indeed, survey data suggest the centrality of the niche parties' single issues to the decisions of their voters. In the case of the Green Party, for instance, not only were voters and nonvoters alike unsure of where the Green Party stood on the economically defined Left-Right spectrum – making it hard to claim that they were voting on the basis of that dimension – but the only issue preference that the Green Party voters had in common was their position on the environment.[7] Themes, like the environment, that had been inadequately addressed or purposefully ignored by the Conservative and Labour parties were motivating and mobilizing the voters.

THE ELECTORAL TRAJECTORY OF THE GREEN PARTY

It was onto this scene that the British Green Party emerged. Begun as the People's Party in 1974 and renamed the Ecology Party in 1975 and the Green Party in 1985, the environmental party first presented a handful of candidates – five and four – in the February and October 1974 Westminster parliamentary elections, receiving average votes of 1.8 percent and 0.7 percent per candidate, respectively.[8] The party would assemble a larger and nationally more successful slate of candidates for the 1979 Westminster General Election. It also participated in the 1979 European Parliament election. In these campaigns and the ones that followed, the party urged voters to think about the ecological effects of Britain's industrial development. Through industrialization, a party document (Ecology Party 1979) claimed,

man has found out . . . how to poison and pollute our environment; how to destroy complex ecosystems on whose stability we depend for survival; how to use up energy resources and minerals in a few generations.

Rather than being the key to Britain's economic health and stability as implied by the Conservative and Labour parties' platforms, perpetuation of the industrial society would "bring catastrophe on ourselves" (Ecology Party 1979). The Ecology Party's solution – movement toward a "postindustrial age" – could be

---

[7] Of the respondents to the 1994 European Election Study, 48 percent answered "don't know" to the Left-Right placement of the Green Party. Calculations from Schmitt et al. 2001.

[8] After 1985, two separate but affiliated Green parties emerged, one for England and Wales and one for Scotland. To facilitate cross-time comparisons for this party and niche parties in general and in keeping with the trend in the literature (see Butler and Butler 2000; Frankland 1990; O'Neill 1997; Rüdig et al. 1996), all references to the Green Party's vote share, number of candidates, and voter opinions include both parties.

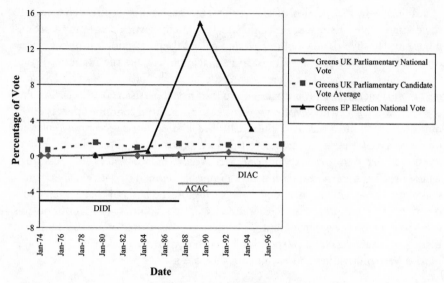

FIGURE 5.3. British Green Party Support in Nationwide Elections. *Sources:* Butler and Butler 2000; Frankland 1990; O'Neill 1997; www.europeangreens.org.

achieved by eliminating industrial waste, prioritizing clean sources of power, and promoting an environmentally sustainable economy based on natural resource conservation and recycling.

In the late 1970s and early 1980s, when both the Conservative and Labour parties were campaigning on industrial solutions to Britain's economic woes, the Ecology Party's environmental focus set it apart. However, in its first electoral contests, these programmatic differences resulted in little electoral support for the niche party. As shown in Figure 5.3, the party captured averages of just over 1 percent of the vote in the 53 and 108 constituencies it contested in the 1979 and 1983 Westminster elections, respectively, for a mere 0.1 percent of the vote nationwide in each election.[9] The Green Party fared better nationwide in the elections to the EP but still gained an average of less than 4 percent of the vote per candidate in the 1979 elections and only 2.6 percent per candidate in the 1984 EP elections (these numbers not shown in Figure 5.3).

By the end of the 1980s, however, the Green Party's electoral fortunes were changing. Its distinctive emphasis on environmental problems finally began to pay dividends. British voters – the majority of whom had professed strong concern about pollution and environmental damage – were recognizing the Green Party as the rightful owner of the environmental issue (MORI polls). This association translated into votes for the niche party. The Green Party's support began to increase as early as 1987; in the 1987 General Election, it surpassed its previous vote share to win an average of 1.4 percent for each of the 133 candidates

---

[9] Prior to the renaming of the party into explicitly Scottish and English/Welsh parties, the Ecology Party ran candidates across the United Kingdom. Following the convention established for this case study, the one Scottish candidate contesting the 1979 election and the eleven Scottish and one Northern Irish candidate in the 1983 election are included in these numbers.

competing, or 0.2 percent of the vote nationwide. Its support jumped more significantly two years later. In the May 1989 local English and Welsh elections, the Green Party gained 8 percent of the vote (Oakley 1990), and several months later, in the 1989 EP elections, the Green Party captured 14.9 percent of the vote to become the third most popular British party. As mentioned previously, the vast majority of these votes were cast in positive support of the environmental party and its policy stances.

Buoyed by this achievement and the subsequent dramatic growth in public involvement in and contributions to nongovernmental environmental organizations,[10] the Green Party nearly doubled the number of candidates it presented in the next General Election. However, although the party netted its best national vote average to date (0.5 percent), its 1992 support levels were a far cry from those received in the 1989 local and EP elections, or even the anticipated levels of 5 to 8 percent reported in opinion polls taken in 1990 (MORI polls cited in Oakley 1990). And if we judge the party on the basis of votes per candidate, a figure unaffected by the dramatic increase in the number of seats contested, we find that the Green Party performed slightly worse than in 1987, scoring only 1.3 percent. As shown in Figure 5.3, the downward slide in popularity continued in the next two elections – the EP election in 1994 and the General Election in 1997. In the latter contest, the Green Party's nationwide support fell to 1987 levels, with the party winning only 0.2 percent, albeit 1.4 percent per candidate. Sustained public concern about the environment was not translating into votes for the niche party.

UNDERSTANDING THE GREEN PARTY'S ELECTORAL TRAJECTORY

The growth and decline of the Green Party's electoral support begs the question of why. Why did an electorate that became and remained highly concerned about the environment fail to deliver its votes to the environmental proponent during the 1990s? Why did the Green Party lose votes both in national and supranational elections? Where did its voters go?

Traditional explanations of party success offer incomplete answers to these questions. Institutional theories (see discussions in Kitschelt 1994; Müller-Rommel 1996) cite Great Britain's restrictive governmental and electoral institutions as the cause of the relatively poor showings of the Green Party in national parliamentary elections; the unitary state structure and the single-member, simple-plurality electoral system used for the General Elections are generally thought to disadvantage nongeographically concentrated minor parties. Institutionalists would expect only slightly better results for such a party in the EP elections. Even though many scholars have touted these supranational

---

[10] MORI surveys reveal that membership in environmental groups, like the World Wide Fund for Nature, doubled between 1989 and 1990. Similarly, the number of people contributing to environmental charities also doubled between those years, to total more than half of the country's population. And four out of ten people in 1990 as opposed to only two out of ten in 1988 said that they would choose a product because of its environmentally friendly packaging (Oakley 1990).

contests as "second-order elections" where individuals express their sincere preferences and thus are more likely to vote for minor parties, British MEPs during this period were chosen by the same restrictive plurality rules that were used for the General Elections.[11]

While predictive of the low levels of Green Party vote relative to greens in other countries, these theories have a hard time explaining the observed swell and retreat of the British niche party's support in national and, especially, in EP elections. Britain's electoral rules and governmental structure remained constant during these two decades. In other words, with no new institutional incentives to promote and then undermine voter support for and candidate affiliation with the Green Party, these theories cannot account for any variation in the environmental vote in Britain.

Although better at predicting changes in party electoral support over time, sociological theories also fail to explain fully the shape of the Green Party's electoral trajectory. Turning first to the Inglehart value orientation hypothesis, Britain's low level of postmaterialism relative to other European Community members leads to predictions that its environmental party should likewise fare relatively poorly. This expectation is borne out. Yet, if we consider the level of postmaterialism over time, the theory's predictions are not corroborated; although postmaterialism in Britain increased monotonically from 1970 to 1992 (the last election year for which data were available), the Green Party's support at the national or European parliamentary levels did not.[12]

An examination of the economic factors hypothesized to cause green party success also demonstrates the poor fit of these approaches. Contrary to the expectations of sociological theories, British Green Party vote is not negatively correlated with unemployment rates. In fact, support for the Green Party rose as unemployment rates jumped into the double digits and fell as the unemployment rate dropped.[13] The predictions of the sociological theories do seem to hold, however, when comparing GDP per capita and Green Party vote. Consistent with the findings of the cross-section time-series analyses in Chapter 3, GDP per capita is positively and significantly correlated with British Green Party vote. Yet, closer examination of these variables calls into question the explanatory force of this finding. Although both the Green Party's national vote share and GDP per capita increased up to 1992, support for the niche party fell after this point despite the continued upward trend in GDP per capita. Thus, at most, the evidence suggests that GDP per capita might have influenced the *rise* in Green Party support. It cannot account, however, for the Green Party's subsequent decline.[14]

---

[11] Electoral rules for the election of Members of the European Parliament (MEPs) were changed to PR starting only in 1999.

[12] The correlation between Green Party vote share and postmaterialism proves insignificant at $p < .1$ in a one-tailed test.

[13] These two variables have a correlation of 0.65, significant at $p = .12$ in a two-tailed test.

[14] The explanatory power of the sociological approach is further challenged by Rüdig et al.'s (1996: 17n12) finding of little relationship between the electorate's subjective assessment of the economy and support for the Greens.

Strategic Responses to the Green Party Competitor

Stronger and more consistent clues to the Green Party's success and failure begin to emerge if one looks instead at the behavior of the political actors. As depicted in Figure 5.3, dismissive strategies characterized the mainstream parties' response to the Green Party from the 1970s to 1987. Both the Labour and Conservative parties downplayed the environmental issue and publicly ignored its niche party proponent. No major bill on the environment was proposed and passed during this period.[15] And the parties devoted an average of only 3 percent of their election manifestos to environmental issues between 1979 and 1987. Moreover, there is evidence that both parties postponed policy statements or decisions on the environment during this period of time. For example, in the 1983–84 parliamentary session, the Thatcher government pushed off recommendations by the House of Commons Environmental Committee for the reduction of sulfur compounds from power stations, citing the "need to assess the costs of such measures against the scientific evidence of the likely benefits."[16] Regardless of the legitimacy of the excuse, the effect was the same: the environment had been banished from the political discussion.

Labour's Dismissal of a Costly Issue. The mainstream parties' dismissive strategies did not emanate from ignorance. Internal Labour and Conservative Party documents demonstrate that these parties and their officials were conscious of the growing public concern with the environment and the emergence of the Green Party when they adopted dismissive stances. As early as 1977, a confidential report from Labour's Environment Study Group acknowledged the party's neglect of the issue:

Despite the growing world wide concern with these problems, our broad policy statements continue to devote no more than a couple of short paragraphs to them, usually in the form of 'we are in favour of the environment and against pollution.' Such declarations have, of course, the same worth as those in respect to virtue and sin. . . . So far, apart from the efforts of groups such as SERA and the odd article in the *New Statesman*, the Grand Debate has been conspicuous by its absence.[17]

The lack of a serious Labour Party discussion on the environment in the late 1970s was met with warnings by its own MPs that "if people who are concerned about environment and world ecology are made to feel that no political party is bothered about their anxieties, then there will be separate ecology parties standing at the

---

[15] The exception was the passage of the Wildlife and Countryside Act of 1981. Yet, as will be argued later in this section, this bill "safeguarding wildlife and landscapes of primary importance and provid(ing) specific protection to listed species of flora and fauna" (Conservative Party 1986/87: 2) was neither well advertised to the public nor focused on the type of environmentalism advocated by the Green Party and demanded by the electorate.

[16] Response in Cmnd. 9397 cited in the Conservative Party's *Campaign Guide*, 1987: 363.

[17] LPA, Labour Party, Environment Study Group, "Chapter 1: Environment and Our General Philosophy." RE 1393/December 1977: 1.

next election."[18] The party's strategy did not change following the fulfillment of that prophecy with the Green Party's increased participation in the 1979 General Election. Labour Research Department briefings and speeches simply discussed the party's dismissive stance in the same breath as the Green Party's electoral presence.

Labour's decision to publicly ignore the environmental party for the first thirteen years of the Green Party's participation in the electoral arena reflected both the electoral weakness of the Green Party and the Labour Party's own stakes in entering the environmental debate. The few Green candidates that contested the parliamentary elections stood mostly in Labour or Conservative safe seats.[19] In the 1979 and 1983 General Elections, some Green MP candidates did manage to gain enough votes to exceed the margin between the mainstream party winner and mainstream party loser. But this happened in only two Labour-retained marginal seats in 1979 and only one Labour-retained marginal seat and two Conservative-gained marginal seats in 1983.

Labour's reluctance to launch an active campaign against the Green Party was motivated even more by the costly nature of the endeavor. In contrast to the view of Rohrschneider (1993) and others, a pro-environmental policy was not necessarily a natural extension of the Labour Party's economically leftist program. A popular belief held as late as the 1980s was that socialism was incompatible with environmental protection. A 1977 report of the Labour Study Group on the Environment reads "'the environment' is seen, at best, as a luxury that we might be able to afford again once North Sea oil makes its impact on the economy, or, at worst, as a consideration that only lengthens the dole queues."[20] Protection of the environment was not a policy of the working class. Rather, the cause was "coming to have ... a trendy, middle-class aspect."[21] The costs that this reputation entailed for the Labour Party were highlighted by a member of the Joint PLP-NEC Environmental Group in an early 1970s report:

When we talk about plans for the environment we must ensure that traditional Labour supporters feel involved. At present there is a clear impression that the environment is the exclusive property of the middle class and that their interest is merely that of preserving their way of life.[22]

[18] This quote comes from a confidential letter from MP Lena Jeger to Labour General Secretary Ron Hayward sent in April 1978 after the People's Party had contested a mere handful of seats in the 1974 elections and before the Ecology Party contested national-level elections. LPA, Home Policy Committee, Study Group on the Environment, Document RE 1604, Lena Jeger, MP, "Letter to Ron Hayward, April 1978."

[19] The Green Party presented candidates in 8 percent of seats in 1979, 17 percent in 1983, and 20 percent in 1987. Calculations from Butler and Butler 2000: 173.

[20] LPA, Labour Party, Environment Study Group, "Chapter 1: Environment and Our General Philosophy." RE 1393/December 1977: 1.

[21] This observation was made in a confidential Labour Party note dated December 1972 from Lena Jeger, MP – member of Labour's Study Group on the Environment – to the National Executive Committee (NEC). LPA, Terry Pitt Papers, Document RD 499, "Implementation of Composite Resolutions 29 and 30: A Note by Lena Jeger," December 1972.

[22] LPA, Report, by an unnamed PLP Member of the Joint PLP–NEC (Parliamentary Labour Party–National Executive Committee) Environmental Group, Labour Party, from between 1970 and 1974: 1. This document was possibly written by David George Clark, MP.

The working man's concerns with price stability were seen as clashing with expensive policies to restrict industrial development and prevent pollution.

Attempts to reconcile Labour's working-class interests and working-class reputation with the increasingly popular issue of environmental protection were made by the party over the course of the 1970s and 1980s. According to internal party documents, Labour Party elite advocated the reframing of environmental issues such as air and noise pollution, refuse disposal, and pesticides in terms of their effect on urban regions and industrial workers.[23] By 1986, these efforts to highlight the socialist worker's natural concern for environmentalism had moved from being confidential talking points to being expressed by individual Labour Party members at the annual Labour Party conference. However, these views were still not championed in the official party platform nor prioritized by Labour Party leadership. The electoral threat of the Green Party remained too low and the risk of alienating Labour voters too great.

Downplaying the Importance of Conservation. As established in a previous section, the Conservatives and the Conservative Thatcher government also pursued a dismissive strategy during this period. And, like the Labour Party, this strategy was deliberate; the Tories adopted this tactic despite their awareness of the growing popularity of the environmental issue. Documents published by the Conservative Research Department and the Conservative Political Centre, a branch of the Conservative Party, confirm that MPs and MEPs were conscious of the environment as an issue by the early 1980s.[24] In a 1984 pamphlet, MP Kenneth Carlisle not only recognized the significance of environmental issues and environmental pressure groups but also, like many of his fellow Tory pamphlet writers, warned of the possible effects of Conservative Party dismissive strategies:

The political party which ignored these growing movements (National Trust and the Royal Society for the Protection of Birds) would be foolish indeed. The great popularity of the nature documentaries on television, for example, suggests that the pressure will increase (Carlisle 1984: 6).

MP Kenneth Carlisle's caution about the Conservatives' neglect of the Green Party and its environmental issue might seem surprising, especially given the literature's view that environmental parties are the natural challengers of left parties. Whereas the Conservative Party acted rationally in dismissing an electorally weak niche competitor that was not threatening its hold of marginal or safe districts, the adoption of a dismissive stance was not an easy decision for the Tories. The Conservatives in the United Kingdom had long been associated with the rural dimension of the urban-rural cleavage and, as a result, perceived themselves to be the party of the countryside. To quote a 1981 Conservative

[23] Such targeting of the working-class electorate was seen in both confidential and published Labour Party documents. One example is LPA, Labour Environment Working Party, Document RE 965, "Introductory Notes on the Scope of an Environmental Programme Prepared by the Secretary," February 1977.

[24] *Caring for the Environment, Conserving the Countryside: A Tory View, Greening the Tories,* and *Conserving Our Environment* were published in 1981, 1984, 1985, and 1986, respectively.

Party pamphlet (Johnson 1981: 7), "There is more than an etymological similarity between the words 'conservation' and 'conservatism'."[25] A similar claim was made in a 1986 brochure: "The Conservatives are the natural Party of conservation. Conservatives care about conservation. That, after all, is what Conservatism is about."[26]

While caring for the environment meant more to the average voter by the 1980s than just stewardship of the countryside and protection of nature, the Conservatives did not sever their ties to conservation and adopt a more inclusive understanding of environmental problems. Thus, it comes as little surprise that the Conservative perspective on environmentalism was not recognized as such by the electorate. To quote MP Kenneth Carlisle's pamphlet again:

[T]he Conservative Party has always felt that it understood and protected the countryside better than any other party. Yet we deceive ourselves if we believe that this is the perception of the general public. In the public mind we are too often seen as not really caring for the future of the countryside, and of only taking action when it is forced upon us (1984: 6).

And because the electoral threat of the Green party was so low, no elite-level effort was made to reconcile Conservatism with the new framing of the environmental issue.

1987–92: The Rise of the Green Party Threat

All of this changed in the years between 1987 and 1992. In the 1987 General Election, the Green Party fielded a larger number of candidates who each, on average, captured a greater percentage of support than in the 1983 election; as noted in Figure 5.3, the average vote share for each of the 133 candidates was 1.4 percent, raising the niche party's national vote share to 0.2 percent. Even though the Green Party was not capturing seats in the Westminster parliament, it did pose a threat to the mainstream parties' electoral strength. Support for the Green Party helped weaken the mainstream parties' hold of seats and, in some cases, led to their turnover. The Green Party's presence contributed to the transformation of seven Conservative-held and two Labour-held districts from safe seats in 1983 to marginal seats in 1987. In two marginal districts retained by the Conservatives, the Green candidate's vote share exceeded the Tory margin of victory over Labour, suggesting that the Green Party voters could have made the difference between a Conservative-held and a Labour-gained seat. Support for the niche party also played a role in the turnover of five Conservative districts to the Labour Party and one Labour district to the Conservative Party.[27]

---

[25] Johnson (1981: 7) elaborated on this connection: "Historically, of course, the Conservatives are a party with strong roots in the countryside. The love of nature and wildlife is often most highly developed in those who are closest to them. . . . The sense that we hold land on trust for posterity and that we should not therefore permit random destruction and degradation is much a part of the Conservative spirit."

[26] CPA, *Conserving our Environment*, (London: Conservative Research Department, 1986): 2.

[27] The Green Party's presence also contributed to the turnover of one Conservative district to the Liberal Party. As indicated previously, the numbers quoted in the text include English, Welsh, and Scottish districts.

The niche party's threat to the mainstream parties' electoral success became even more apparent two years later.[28] In the May 1989 local English and Welsh county elections, the Green Party more than doubled its previous local election per-candidate vote from 3.4 percent in 1985 to more than 8 percent (Frankland 1990: 17). Although this showing only resulted in one Green Party county council seat, the Greens unsettled the existing balance of party power; Green candidates outperformed Labour candidates in 11 percent of their confrontations, and the Green Party surpassed the Social Democratic Party to earn the title of Britain's fourth party (Matthissen and Rose 1989: 1–2; cited in Frankland 1990: 17).

These successes in the local elections foreshadowed the strong performance that the Green Party would have in the European Parliament election several months later. As indicated in the introduction of this chapter, the Green Party surprised its rivals, capturing 14.9 percent of the vote to become the third most popular party in the United Kingdom. Admittedly, the turnout for this election, 36.2 percent, was much lower than that for any General Election.[29] But as this turnout level surpassed that of any previous EP election, the Green Party's vote represented real gain. Moreover, although supporters of niche parties, and in particular environmental parties, are often first-time voters, the Green Party's support was not drawn entirely from these new members of the electorate. Rather, 27 percent of Green Party voters in 1989 had formerly supported the Conservatives and 17 percent had previously voted for Labour.[30] The Green Party's gain translated directly into the mainstream parties' loss.

The defection of mainstream party voters in EP elections is often dismissed as a low-cost, antigovernment gesture in unimportant, low-turnout "second-order" elections.[31] However, scholars are also quick to emphasize that these elections encourage sincere voting (Reif and Schmitt 1980).[32] The electorate is more likely to demonstrate their true feelings in these electoral circumstances. Consequently, even if the results of an EP election are not expected to be replicated in the votes for national parliamentary candidates, they do capture the issue interests of the voters.

This implies, therefore, that a vote for the Green Party in 1989 was indicative of a voter's increased concern for the party's issue – the environment. Evidence to this effect is found in the various surveys administered around this time. According

---

[28] Between the 1987 General Election and the 1989 EP elections, Green candidates contested seven parliamentary by-elections in which they captured an average of almost 3 percent of the vote (Frankland 1990: 16). Their levels of support increased from the 1988 to the 1989 by-elections, consistent with the party's rising popularity.

[29] The turnout for the previous General Election was 75.3 percent (Butler and Butler 2000: 239).

[30] These two mainstream parties were not the only victims of the Green Party's relative electoral success. The established parties of the economic center – the Liberals and the Social Democrats – were the source of the largest percentage of Green voters in the 1989 EP elections. However, as will be explained later in this chapter, these centrist parties were not responsible, independent of the Labour and Conservative parties, for the subsequent weakening of the Green Party.

[31] The term "second-order election" was introduced by Reif and Schmitt (1980) to capture the difference between national parliamentary and presidential, or "first-order," elections and less-important, subnational and supranational elections.

[32] Reif and Schmitt (1980) refer to votes in second-order elections as "votes with the heart."

to the 1989 European Election Study, those who voted for the Greens were more likely than those who supported other parties to view the environment as a "very important issue."[33] This pattern holds regardless of the party the respondent voted for in the previous national election. Confidence in the issue-based nature of the 1989 Green Party voting is further reinforced by the finding of the NOP/Independent survey that 74 percent of 1989 EP Green voters claimed that their vote was a positive one in favor of the Green party and its platform.[34] The Green vote in 1989 was not a mere protest vote.[35] Add to that the findings that more than three-quarters of 1989 European Election survey respondents supported "preventing pollution" over "keeping prices down" and that 83 percent of 1989 Green Party voters believed that drastic measures were needed if the environment was to be saved (NOP/Independent survey cited in Kellner 1989), and it is clear that the single-issue party was becoming a significant threat to the environmentally dismissive mainstream parties. As Peter Kellner reported in *The Independent* newspaper in July 1989, "The potential for further Green advances is considerable, if the other parties continue failing to persuade voters that they have workable answers."

The Conservative Volte Face. The Conservative Party responded to the increased popularity of the Green Party and the environmental issue by trading its dismissive strategy for an active accommodative one. Despite having been returned to government with a fifty-one-seat majority, the Conservatives were losing a significant number of voters to the Greens. In the 1989 EP elections, Green Party support almost cost the Tories victories in two of their safe seats (O'Neill 1997: 289). More important, my model suggests, was the fact that the Greens were drawing disproportionately from the Conservatives' electorate.[36] This would have been particularly troubling for a margin-maximizing party, especially one that saw itself as the protector of flora and fauna. Under these circumstances, the Conservative Party could not adopt an adversarial strategy without hurting itself more than its mainstream party competitor. An accommodative strategy, on the other hand, would allow the Tories to halt further voter defection and reclaim former supporters while challenging the Greens for the title of environmental issue owner. Given that the opposition Labour Party was also expected to react accommodatively – as will be discussed in the next section – the Conservatives'

---

[33] Of the 1989 Green Party electorate, 88 percent deemed the environment a "very important issue," as opposed to 77 percent of those who voted Conservative, 75 percent who voted Labour, and 84 percent who voted Social Democratic Liberal. In contrast to supporters of all the other parties, no Green voter responded that the environment was of "little importance" or "not important." Calculations from van der Eijk et al. 1994.

[34] These statistics also undermine the popular claim that the Green Party vote reflected "centre-right voters wishing to register a mid-term protest against the government while not going so far as to vote Labour" (Rüdig et al. 1996: 9).

[35] Only 16 percent of respondents to a 1989 NOP/Independent postelection survey voted negatively to show disfavor with another party (Ibid.: 18n21).

[36] Analyses of the 1989 EP elections show that "the Greens largely drew votes away from disgruntled Conservatives and former centrist voters in a low-turnout election" (Frankland 1990: 19).

strategy would, at the minimum, serve to inhibit the transfer of issue ownership and environmental voters to Labour.

Starting from a position of having neglected the environmental issue, the Conservatives fought to demonstrate their devotion to this cause. To quote Bill Jones (1989/90: 50) on Tory leader and Prime Minister Margaret Thatcher: "her former indifference towards environmental issues was replaced by a ringing public endorsement." This green campaign was launched with a noteworthy speech by Thatcher before the Royal Society in 1988. It was her first speech on the environment in over nine years as prime minister. As if overnight, Thatcher went from describing the environment as "a humdrum issue" to calling it "one of the greatest challenges of the late twentieth century."[37] This momentum continued at the annual Conservative Party conference that October when Thatcher reiterated her party's dedication to conservation (Frankland 1990: 13). The Conservative Party's preoccupation with this issue surged in the following two years with the organization of an international conference on the ozone layer; outspoken support for a European environmental agency, which the Conservatives had previously opposed; and proposals for a new Environmental Protection Bill.[38] Environmental issues gained a newfound prominence in party documents and in motions and speeches made at the annual Conservative Party conferences.[39]

An examination of the Conservative Party's "volte face" points to strategic considerations.[40] First, the party only embraced its concern for the environment *after* the increase in popularity of the Green Party. According to Virginia Bottomley, Parliamentary Under Secretary of State in the Department of the Environment at the time, the Conservatives recognized the Green Party as "a barometer of mounting concern" for the environment.[41] Although other policy advisors close to Thatcher have stressed the unprompted origins of her Royal Society speech – crediting Thatcher's chemist background and her awareness of the transnational

---

[37] Thatcher made the first statement about the environment during an address to the annual conference of the Scottish Conservative Party in May 1982 (McCormick 1991: 58). The second comes from the body of her Royal Society speech (http://www.margaretthatcher.org/speeches/displaydocument.asp?docid=107346).

[38] This proposal was formalized as the white paper, *This Common Inheritance*, in 1990 (United Kingdom, Department of the Environment 1990).

[39] In the 1987 *Conservative Campaign Guide*, the party platform on "the environment and conservation" was listed nineteenth out of thirty-one issues. In the 1989 *Campaign Guide*, that issue had jumped to eighth place out of twenty-four. Moreover, the threat posed by the Green Party was so significant that discussion of Tory Party policy on the Green Party merited its own separate section. In terms of speeches, O'Neill (1997: 290) describes how in 1989, "Michael Howard, the Minister of State for the Environment, followed up what was a blatant appeal to win back former Conservatives who had switched to the Greens, by outlining the Government's current list of environmental schemes – from encouraging household waste recycling to examining the idea of marketable permits for emissions."

[40] Term employed in Jones 1989/90: 50.

[41] Interview with the Right Honorable Mrs. Virginia Bottomley, MP, former Parliamentary Under Secretary of State, Department of Environment and Conservative MP, London: May 18, 1999.

problems[42] – its timing and the timing of the Conservatives' sudden and unprece-
dented prioritization of environmental issues during the height of Conservative
voter defection to the Greens are telling. Indeed, it should not be forgotten that
the "humdrum" comment was Thatcher's only notable public statement about
the environment prior to 1988.

Even if one entertains the idea that the Conservatives might have constructed
an environmental policy prior to this electoral period – evidence cited in the
previous section shows that the problems of the countryside and the greenhouse
effect were at least discussed among party members – it only became publicized
after 1987. Given that strategies are only effective at altering a party's electoral
prospects if the electorate is aware of them, from the voters' perspective, the
Conservative Party was not pro-environment before this time.[43]

Although the timing of the Conservatives' accommodative tactics suggests that
they were strategically aimed at the Green Party, timing alone is not sufficient to
prove that they were tactical maneuvers. Indeed, external environmental crises,
such as the Chernobyl nuclear accident and the Exxon Valdez oil spill, captured
headlines during this period. These events changed public opinion about the
importance of the environment and could have influenced the Conservatives'
agenda. But a second piece of evidence allows us to have more confidence in the
classification of the Tories' actions as reactions to the Greens' threat: the Conservatives' accommodative campaign explicitly acknowledged and targeted the
Green Party and its voters. For the first time in 1989, the *Conservative Campaign
Guide* included a detailed section on the Green Party's policies and its electoral
threat next to the standard sections on the Labour Party, the Social and Liberal
Democrats, and the Social Democratic Party. In speeches and interviews, Conservative Party elite, including the prime minister, paired positive discussions
of their environmental proposals with specific attacks against the Green Party's
competence on environmental matters (for examples, see O'Neill 1997: 290 and
Young 1990). Consistent with an effort to win issue ownership and, thus, lure back
former voters who had switched to the Greens, the Conservatives were arguing
that they would do a better job of protecting the environment than the Green
Party.

---

[42] Interview with Sir Crispin Tickell, Former U.K. Ambassador to the UN and informal advisor
to Margaret Thatcher on environmental issues, London: July 6, 1999; Interview with the Right
Honorable Mrs. Virginia Bottomley, MP, May 18, 1999.

[43] In a policy paper, Secretary of State for the Department of the Environment Nicholas Ridley wrote,
"The Government's programme for environmental protection seems to have come as something
of a shock to some of the less well informed commentators. Because they suddenly 'discovered'
the issue following the Prime Minister's speech to the Royal Society on 27 September 1988, they
assumed that no policy existed before, rather like the philosopher who claimed that things did not
exist until he looked at them!" (CPA, Nicholas Ridley, *Policies Against Pollution: The Conservative
Record and Principles*, Policy Study 107 [London: CPS, 1989]: 5). However, what Minister Ridley
did not acknowledge is that the existence of a party position on a specific set of issues is irrelevant
to electoral behavior if the public is not aware of it. Thus, if Prime Minister Thatcher and the
Conservative Party were not seen by the voters as being environmentally friendly, then for the
purpose of making the Green Party superfluous, the Conservative Party was not pro-green.

The most blatant attempt to undermine Green Party support and recover defected voters came in an unusual publication by the Conservative Research Department in 1989 entitled *The Green Party and the Environment*. Not just another policy document, this was a multipage attack against the Green Party's credibility as an environmental supporter and potential governing party. The Green Party's plans to protect the environment were decried as "totally misguided and unrealistic" (p. 3). The pamphlet further claimed that the implementation of the niche party's proposals would serve to damage the environment, rather than preserve it. The Greens, according to the Conservative document, were merely "superficial environmentalists" (p. 1).[44]

With the first two sections designed to raise doubts about the environmental credentials and competence (environmental and governmental) of the niche party,[45] the third part of the pamphlet reinforced the Conservative Party's claim to the environmental title. It described the Conservatives' environmental proposals and enumerated the Tory government's achievements in improving environmental protection. It painted a picture of a Conservative Party eager to and capable of being an environmental advocate and the owner of the environmental issue. Thus, in this one document, the Conservative Party addressed all three facets of an accommodative strategy: it highlighted the importance of the environmental issue, demonstrated its commitment to the pro-environment position, and tried to wrest issue ownership away from the Green Party.

Although there are numerous examples of Conservative co-optative tactics, the publication of this pamphlet best reveals the intense nature of the Conservative strategy against the Green Party. First, it was a particularly costly exercise for the party. Upon the release of the document, the Green Party formally charged the Conservative Research Department with slander, resulting eventually in the dismissal of one of the pamphlet's authors.[46] Second, and more telling, the British Conservative Party had never before written or publicly distributed such a document about any other national niche party.[47] The legal suit and bad press of the slander case may have deterred future endeavors. It is surprising, however, that such a violent reaction was not directed toward other more harmful new party challengers, like the radical right National Front in the 1970s.

---

44 In addition to questioning the "greenness" of the environmental party, the document highlights the governing advantage inherent to mainstream parties in competition between unequals by calling into question the ability of the Green Party – perceived by voters to be a single-issue party and chosen on that basis – to govern (and the desirability of its governing) on a variety of political issues.

45 Interview with Richard Marsh, one of the authors of the document and a former member of the Conservative Research Department, London: May 24, 1999. With this same objective in mind, the term "lunacy" was peppered throughout analyses of the niche party in the *Conservative Campaign Guides*. Clearly, the Tories thought that this criticism would influence the electorate's perception of the Greens.

46 Information about the firing of Charles Villers comes from an interview with Richard Marsh, May 24, 1999.

47 I have yet to find any other official document or mention of any official document issued by the Conservative Party on a nonregional niche party from the period of 1970 to 1997.

Although one can only guess at the reasons for this discrepancy, the exclusivity and costliness of this accommodative strategy signaled the intensity of the Conservatives' campaign against the perceived Green threat.

The Conservative Party manifesto published for the 1992 General Election reflected this increased concern for and mobilization around the environment. As data from the Comparative Manifestos Project (Budge et al. 2001) reveal, the percentage of sentences devoted to environmental issues increased from 3.5 percent in the Conservatives' 1987 platform, *The Next Moves Forward*, to 5.8 percent in the 1992 document, *The Best Future for Britain*. Coming at the end of the electoral period when Green Party support was already on the decline, Conservative programmatic attention to the environment was probably lower in 1992 than it would have been mid-term.[48] Even so, the Conservative prioritization of green issues still represented a sizeable increase over that seen in 1987.

The Labour Party's Accommodation. Faced with the possibility of continually losing to the Conservatives, the Labour Party also paid "the Greens the compliment of stealing their clothes" (Jones 1989/90: 50). Although the Labour Party was losing fewer of its voters to the Green Party than its mainstream party opponent, Green Party support in the 1987 election was showing a marked increase in twelve of Labour's marginal seats, seats that Labour held or gained by 10 percentage points or less.[49] With 73 percent of Labour partisans prioritizing the prevention of pollution over the reduction of prices,[50] Labour voters were becoming potential supporters of the Green Party's policies. As even a small transfer of votes in these marginal districts could lead to seat loss – something a Labour Party in opposition for almost a decade could ill-afford – my model would expect the Labour Party to try to halt further defection and reclaim former (and other green) voters. Given the interdependence of mainstream party electoral strength, and thus strategic choice, Labour's accommodative strategy would also have been motivated by the Conservative Party's own attempt to steal away the environmental issue and like-minded voters from the Green Party. Because electoral success is relative, the losing Labour Party could not ignore the erosion of its support or the potential bolstering of its mainstream party opponent's.

The accommodative strategy employed by Labour between 1987 and 1992 was much less aggressive than that of the Conservative Party. No equivalent of the Conservatives' name-calling pamphlet, *The Green Party and the Environment*, emerged from the Labour camp. Instead, the Labour Party used positive measures to try to beat the Greens at their own game. Recognizing the popularity and value of the environment as an electoral issue, the party established a new campaign unit for environmental policy (McCormick 1991: 42). Topics such as air pollution,

---

[48] As this statement reveals, reliance on manifesto data that is produced at four- to five-year intervals leads to difficulties in the assessment of issue emphasis in the intermediate years.

[49] Calculations from Outlaw 2005.

[50] Calculations from Heath 1989.

nuclear waste, and the greenhouse effect were prioritized in public addresses in policy forums and in Parliament after 1987.[51]

But professing support for the environment was not sufficient for trying to gain issue ownership. Whereas the Conservatives could justify their pro-environmental position as an extension of their pro-flora-and-fauna image, the Labour Party needed to actively establish that its pro-environmental claims were consistent with its existing reputation as a working-class party. Thus, in these policy pronouncements, the Labour Party and its members repeatedly reinforced the connection between environmental problems and the plight of their working-class electorate. This perspective stands out in comments by Dani Ahrens, member of the Brighton Pavilion Constituency Labour Party, at the 1988 annual Labour Party conference:

Basically, comrades, this is an economic issue. It is an issue for socialists and it is a class issue. It is a class issue because we have to look at whose interests are at stake. It is working class people who suffer most.[52]

Although surveys show that support for environmental protection actually cut across class barriers and was widespread by the end of the 1980s, Labour tried to convince voters of the symbiotic relationship between the environment and the economy as a means of attracting green voters without alienating its traditional electorate.

Continuing with its accommodative strategy, the Labour Party issued *An Earthly Chance* in 1990. This document, not unlike the Conservative government's 1990 white paper *This Common Inheritance*, presented a comprehensive discussion and set of policy recommendations for more than fifty-six environmental issues. Although the Conservative Party appeared as the target of choice in that policy statement,[53] debate within Labour Party conferences from 1987 onward explicitly identified the Green Party as the focus of this latest environmental campaign. A trade union representative to the 1991 Labour conference stated this goal unambiguously when he proclaimed:

There is one major point that I should like to make, colleagues. To argue against the arrogance and patronisation of the Green Party...we must be seen to be pushing the environment to the top of the agenda. We want our leaders raising environmental issues and speaking on them at regular intervals.[54]

---

[51] Party Leader Neil Kinnock devoted twenty minutes of his 1988 Labour Party Conference address to the environment.

[52] Quoted in Labour Party, *Report of the Annual Conference of the Labour Party 1988*, 1988: 144.

[53] Where two mainstream parties are fighting for control of a niche party's issue, it seems reasonable to expect the focus of their strategies to be their mainstream party opponent as much as the original niche party issue promoter. Thus, once Labour convinced issue-based voters that they needed to support a credible governmental party, its next task was to persuade them that it, not the Tories, was the most dedicated environmental mainstream party. However, one would not expect to see an accommodative party emphasize its mainstream opponent when an ACAD strategy is being implemented.

[54] Ivan Monckton, representative of the Agricultural and Allied Workers, Transport and General Workers Union, quoted in Labour Party, *The Report of the Annual Conference of the Labour Party 1991*, 1991: 250.

Further evidence of this ideological attack can be seen in Labour's increased attention to environmental issues in its 1992 campaign manifesto. As in the Conservatives' party platform, the percentage of sentences on the environment in the Labour manifesto increased between 1987 and 1992, from 4.8 percent to 6.6 percent (Budge et al. 2001).[55] In addition to this programmatic attack, the Labour Party did attempt organizational tactics, such as employment offers to popular ex–Green Party figurehead Jonathan Porritt and even an electoral pact with the Greens, presumably with an eye toward the 1992 General Election (O'Neill 1997: 299). Due to the nationwide decline in the popularity of the Green Party after 1991, however, these organizational forms of accommodation were never realized.

1992–97: Green Party Electoral Decline

By the start of the 1992 General Election campaign, the popularity of the Green Party was falling. Despite the fact that a larger percentage of people favored protecting the countryside over creating new jobs than had five years before,[56] less than 2 percent of those surveyed in national opinion polls intended to vote for the niche party (McCormick 1993: 281).[57] And even this estimate far exceeded the actual level of support received by the Greens. Driven by a doubling of the number of candidates run, the Green Party's national vote share rose to 0.5 percent. Its vote percentage per candidate, however, was slightly down, falling to 1.3 percent. While stronger than in the General Election, the Green Party's performance in the 1994 EP elections was likewise lower than its 1989 level. The niche party candidates captured only 3.1 percent in the 1994 contest.[58]

These numbers tell the story of a decline in Green Party performance relative to the 1987 General Election and, most noticeably, relative to the 1989 elections to the European Parliament. But a closer examination of the contests reveals that the Green Party threat had not completely disappeared, at least not for one party. In their analysis of the 1992 General Election results, Curtice and Steed (1992: 343) point out that the niche party's support base had shifted from the Southwest of England to urban areas. The Greens were no longer poaching voters in traditional Conservative territory; their support was coming from Labour seats and, as will be shown later, from Labour voters. The loss of voters was particularly worrisome in the Labour Party's less-secure seats. Even though Green Party vote

---

[55] This evidence is consistent with the claim that the Labour Party was trying to distinguish itself as the more-sincere mainstream environmental actor. The party hoped that those issue voters who were already disenchanted with the Green Party's lack of governing power would be encouraged to support the Labour Party over the also-accommodative Conservative Party. Although Labour's co-optative campaign between 1987 and 1992, on the whole, was less intense than that led by the Conservatives, its emphasis on the environment in its 1992 manifesto was marginally higher than that of the Conservative Party.

[56] In 1987, 58 percent of respondents preferred protecting the countryside from development over creating new jobs. In 1992, that percentage was 68 percent. Calculations from Heath 1989 and Heath et al. 1996.

[57] This was down from the 3 percent recorded by an April 1991 Guardian poll (Atkins 1991: 6).

[58] This decline in support occurred despite comparable levels of voter turnout in the two EP elections.

per district was slightly down on the whole, its support levels increased in all eight of the seats it contested in which the Labour Party was re-elected by a margin of 10 percentage points or less.[59]

In the 1994 EP elections as well, Labour stood out as the more threatened mainstream party. Of those who supported the Greens in 1994, 20.4 percent had voted Labour in the previous General Election.[60] Although still losing some voters to the Green Party in this election, former Conservatives made up only 9.7 percent of the niche party's electorate – a sharp reduction from the 27 percent in the last European election.

Remaining in opposition, albeit by a much reduced margin, the Labour Party would be expected by my model to continue with its accommodative tactics toward the threatening Green Party. For the Conservatives, on the other hand, the incentives to continue a costly accommodative effort were lacking. The party was returned to government, and the Greens had gained few votes in Conservative marginal seats. Moreover, the tide of Conservative defections to the Green Party had turned; many of those who supported the Greens in 1989 had returned to the Tories, and few new defections took place in 1992. The fact that the Conservatives were losing fewer voters than Labour to the Green Party might suggest that an adversarial strategy would be optimal. However, the Conservative Party was constrained by its past behavior. Following their intense accommodative strategy of 1987 to 1992, the Tories' pursuit of adversarial tactics would undermine the party's reliability and responsibility, leading to costly voter retaliation in the form of defection in the future, if not the short term. In this situation, therefore, we would expect the Conservatives to employ a dismissive strategy. Even though the Conservatives would not be able to directly foil the effects of Labour's accommodative tactics, the party could lessen the electoral benefits of Labour's environment-based mobilization by downplaying the importance of the issue.

Labour's Quest for the Environmental Title. Consistent with the model's predictions, the Labour Party intensified its co-optative tactics toward the still-menacing Green Party during this period. In 1994, the party produced its most powerful form of issue accommodation to date with the publication of *In Trust for Tomorrow*. Developed by Labour's Policy Commission on the Environment, it was an expansive document placing the environment at the center of every policy area. This publication also encouraged the Greens to work together with the Labour Party, a continuation of the organizational strategies considered immediately following the Green Party's 1989 EP success. The third element of this strategy was publicity; recognizing that issue co-optation is effective only if the electorate is aware (and convinced) of the party's position, the Labour Party increased the promotion of its pro-environmental proposals.

---

[59] The Green Party's support levels also increased nontrivially in twelve of the sixteen seats that Labour captured from another party in 1992 by a margin of 10 percentage points or less. Calculations from Outlaw 2005.

[60] Calculations from Schmitt et al. 2001.

The rationale behind Labour's accommodative strategy was clearly articulated. As stated by a party member during the 1993 annual Labour Party conference debate on the environmental policy, "[we should] support these composites [i.e., proposals] which will be good for our environment and for the people of Britain and which, at the same time, will be good for the popularity of Labour."[61] Labour voters, it was understood, were concerned about the effects of environmental damage.[62] And the political target of the strategy was equally evident: "In 1989, the Green Party polled millions of votes. The environmental concern represented by those votes has not gone away. We must make sure that those votes go to us."[63]

By the time of the 1997 General Election campaign, however, the expected support for the Green Party was negligible. Consequently, although the Labour Party had actively prioritized environmental issues during the first half of the electoral period, its attention to these concerns during the 1997 campaign was dramatically reduced; the percentage of manifesto sentences on green issues was almost halved from 6.6 percent in 1992 to 3.4 percent in 1997. This shift can be interpreted as a cost-cutting move and also as a strategic tactic to downplay an issue that, because of Labour's earlier accommodative efforts, no longer threatened its support.

The Conservatives' Dismissive Stance. In the five years after the 1992 General Election, the Conservative Party de-emphasized their pro-environmental stance. The Tories did not release any new major documents or environmental programs to follow up on their 1990 white paper. What pro-environmental action John Major's government did take – specifically, attending the UN Rio Summit in June 1992 and passing legislation consolidating various authorities into a new Environmental Agency – reflected commitments established when the Green Party was still seen as an electoral threat *prior* to its dismal electoral results in 1992.[64] The marginalization of the environment and its niche party proponent is reflected in the documents circulated to party faithful; the Conservatives' *Campaign Guide* of 1994 (Conservative Party 1994) only passively lauded past Tory

---

[61] Statement by Meg Russell of the Constituency Labour Party in Islington South and Finsbury, at the 1993 Labour Party Conference. Labour Party, *Report of the Annual Conference of the Labour Party 1993*, 1993: 65.

[62] As noted by Meg Russell, "Major polls taken before the last election confirm the popularity of the issue. They show that 54 per cent of people are concerned about the effect that environmental problems have on their health, and a huge 82 per cent are concerned about what the effects will be on their children and grandchildren.... Many of these people are Labour's traditional supporters, who after all suffer the worst effects of environmental degradation." Labour Party, *Report of the Annual Conference of the Labour Party 1993*, 1993: 65.

[63] Statement by Shaun Spiers, Ex Officio, Prospective European Parliament Candidate for London South-East at the 1993 Labour Party Conference. Labour Party, *Report of the Annual Conference of the Labour Party 1993*, 1993: 66.

[64] Indeed, the creation of the Environmental Agency was not even mentioned to this author by John Gummer, Secretary of State for the Environment from 1993 to 1997, in an interview about the Conservatives' environmental policy under John Major. Interview with Gummer, London, May 1999.

environmental efforts, while dismissing the Green Party. Given that the issue was downplayed to party members, it comes as little surprise that a Conservative environmental stance was not emphasized to voters. By the run-up to the 1997 General Election, the attention paid to the environment had further declined. The 1997 *Campaign Guide* did not make any mention of the Greens (Conservative Party 1997). And only 2 percent of the Conservative Party manifesto was dedicated to the topic, down from 5.8 percent in 1992 (Budge et al. 2001). The environment received less coverage than in any Conservative manifesto since 1979, years before Thatcher even acknowledged the topic as a humdrum issue.

INTERACTIVE EFFECTS OF MAINSTREAM STRATEGIES:
QUELLING THE GREEN BEAST

The 1997 General Election served as further confirmation of the Green Party's electoral decline. From a nationwide score of 0.5 percent in 1992, the niche party's national support level dropped to 0.2 percent. This was partly a function of the party's fielding candidates in only 95 districts, as opposed to 254 in the previous election – itself a sign of the fading political presence of the Greens. However, the low vote total also reflected decreases in the Green Party's vote share in those districts it did contest. In the sixty-five districts in which the Green Party competed in both 1992 and 1997, the average vote share per candidate declined slightly from 1.51 percent in 1992 to 1.46 percent in 1997.[65] When we combine this information with the fact that the Green Party's average vote share per candidate nationwide increased from 1.3 percent to 1.4 percent across these two elections, we can conclude that the niche party by 1997 was losing voters from some of its more successful districts and not contesting less-promising ones.

Such poor overall election results prompted the British media and political analysts to write the Green Party's obituary. Following a period of ten years of accommodative strategies from at least one of the mainstream parties, it is not surprising that the Green Party and its electoral threat would be subdued; this is consistent with the PSO theory's predictions. But did these tactical combinations decrease or reverse voter defection and do so by altering the salience and ownership of the issue as expected? In other words, was niche party failure actually caused by the deliberate actions of the Labour and Conservative parties – strategies that followed the modified spatial logic of the PSO theory?

1987–92: The Battle to Be "Green"

A review of the strategies employed by each mainstream party reveals the effects that we would expect to see if the modified spatial strategic explanation holds. Recall that, between 1987 and 1992, both mainstream parties engaged

---

[65] District lines were redrawn between the 1992 and 1997 General Elections. These calculations are based on the sixty-five districts whose names were identical in the 1992 and 1997 elections and in which Green Party candidates ran in both elections. Calculations from Outlaw 2005.

in accommodative strategies. According to my model, the effect of joint pro-environmental campaigns, or ACAC, in a given period should be an increase in the salience of the Green Party's issue and a loosening of its reputation as environmental issue owner, *ceteris paribus*.

The fact that these accommodative strategies were not employed until thirteen years after the niche party fielded a handful of candidates, and eight years after it presented a significant slate of prospective MPs in national elections, raises the possibility that these effects will be mitigated; as discussed in Chapter 2, the ability of mainstream parties to undermine niche party vote depends on their implementation of active strategies prior to the reputational entrenchment of the niche party as the sole issue owner. In this case, however, several factors combined to increase the length of time that the window of ownership transfer opportunity was open.[66] First, because Green Party candidates competed in only 8 percent of the General Election seats in 1979 and 17 percent in 1983, many members of the national electorate were not aware of the Green Party or familiar with its policy proposals, let alone convinced of its issue credibility. The fact that major surveys, like the Gallup Poll, did not ask about the popularity of the Green Party or its ownership of the environmental issue prior to late 1988/early 1989 reflects the low political visibility of the niche party.[67] Second, the restrictiveness of the British electoral system exacerbated that limited visibility by reducing the likelihood that the Green Party's candidates would gain office. As demonstrated by the Green Party's German counterpart in 1983, niche party ascension to office hastens the entrenchment of issue ownership and the closing of the window of ownership transfer opportunity (Meguid 2001). With the British Green Party being relatively unknown and not a credible challenger for office, it comes as little surprise that its reputation as "the environmental owner" was not yet solidified by 1987, even after more than ten years on the national scene. Indeed, as late as October 1988, only 11 percent of those surveyed thought that the Green Party would be the best party to protect the environment.[68] The window of opportunity had not yet closed.

Thus, the mainstream parties' hesitation is expected to have limited effects on the potency of their joint accommodative strategies from 1987 to 1992. Consistent with the findings of the green-party-specific regression analysis in

---

[66] This suggests that predictions about the effects of hesitation on accommodative strategies are contingent on factors other than just the number of prior periods of dismissive tactics. The coding of the hesitation variables for inclusion in the statistical analysis in Chapter 3 was simplified for cross-national application; it could not fully capture the mechanism dictating the opening and closing of the window of ownership opportunity. This may explain why, in the green-party-specific model, even the delayed versions of the DIAC and ACAC strategies reduced green party vote.

[67] In May of 1987, the Gallup Political Index included, for the first time since its inception in 1937, a question about the ownership of the environmental issue. It did not, however, include a response category for the Green Party. It is telling that between 33 percent and 43 percent of respondents in May and June of that year answered "don't know" or "none" (meaning not the Conservatives, Labour, or the Liberal–Social Democratic Party Alliance) to the question. *Gallup Political Index*, *1987–88*; King 2001.

[68] Harris Poll cited in *The Observer*, October 23, 1988; cited in Frankland 1990: 15.

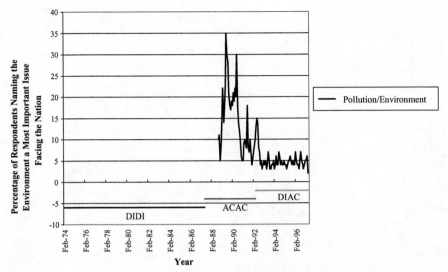

FIGURE 5.4. Salience of the Environmental Issue in Britain. *Source:* MORI Polls.

Chapter 3,[69] these joint accommodative tactics – even with some delay – are expected to result in a decrease in voter defection to the Green Party and even a return of issue-based voters to the credible mainstream party issue owner.

Evidence in support of these predictions comes in three different forms: an increase in the perceived salience of the environmental issue, a transfer of issue ownership to the mainstream parties, and the return of 1989 EP Green voters to the mainstream parties from which they defected. As Figure 5.4 shows, the relative salience of the environmental issue did shift during this period of ACAC tactics. When asked to identify the most important issues facing the country, 10 percent of MORI poll respondents in October 1988 named the environment.[70] By July 1989, that number had risen to 35 percent, signifying the peak of environmental importance. The environment even surpassed the perennial favorite of unemployment to earn the distinction of the number one problem facing Britain. Despite some perturbations, the salience of this issue remained relatively high until the end of 1990, when it dropped to 5 percent. By July of 1991, salience had climbed again to 18 percent and, over the next year through the 1992 General Election campaign, would establish a new average, with 10 percent of the survey respondents prioritizing the environmental issue. Although this level of issue importance did not rival that recorded in 1989, it still indicated the centrality of the environment in the minds of British voters (MORI Polls).

[69] Although there are few incidents of delayed strategy across the entire data set examined in Chapter 3, the significant negative effect of delayed ACAC tactics found in the green-party-specific model is not dependent on the inclusion of this British observation.

[70] These percentages represent the combined responses of those surveyed to two open-ended questions. The first is "what would you say is the most important issue facing Britain today?" The second is "what do you see as other important issues facing Britain today?" MORI Polls.

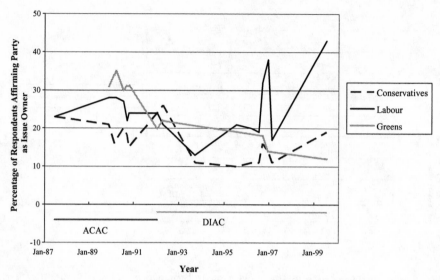

FIGURE 5.5. Environmental Issue Ownership in Britain. *Source:* Gallup Political and Economic Index.

During this period, we also witnessed the relative "greening" of the mainstream parties' reputations. According to British respondents to the Gallup Political and Economic Index, the British Green Party was judged the best party to handle environmental problems as of 1990, given that title by more than 30 percent of those surveyed (see Figure 5.5).[71] Labour placed second, and the Conservatives trailed in third. This last assessment is echoed in the findings of a February 1990 MORI poll which shows that 61 percent of those surveyed thought that the Thatcher government was doing a poor job protecting the environment (Oakley 1990).

But the Green Party's environmental issue ownership did not go unchallenged over this electoral period. By the 1992 General Election, its claim to be the British environmental hegemon had expired. Only 22 percent of those surveyed viewed the Green Party as most able to handle environmental problems, as opposed to 26 percent naming the Conservatives and 21 percent Labour.[72] The co-optative strategies of the mainstream parties were clearly muddying the waters of environmental issue ownership. And as expected during this electoral period, the Conservatives, with their intense accommodative campaign, were slightly ahead of the also-accommodating Labour Party.

With the voters primed to think about the environment and ownership of the issue being wrested away from the Green Party, we would expect to see the

[71] The wording of the Gallup question was as follows: "I am going to read out to you a host of problems facing the country. Could you tell me for each of them which political party you personally think would handle the problem best? The environment." *Gallup Political Index, 1989–90*, 1989–90. This publication was continued from 1991 onward under the title, *Gallup Political and Economic Index*.
[72] *Gallup Political and Economic Index, 1992*, 1992.

defection of Green Party voters to the mainstream parties as well as an overall decline in niche party support levels. We see some evidence of this second point: the Green Party's score of 14.9 percent in the 1989 EP elections represented the all-time high for the party. The party's average vote per candidate in the 1992 General Election was also lower (albeit marginally) than in 1987.

While some caution is necessary in drawing conclusions based on small sample sizes, individual-level evidence of voter response to the changing issue ownership can be found in the movement of voters to and from the Green Party, as recorded in national and European election surveys during this period. According to the 1992 British Election Study (BES), the Greens suffered a net loss of voters to the mainstream parties between 1987 and 1992. And, of those who supported the Green Party in 1987, 20 percent left to vote for the Conservatives and 27 percent for the Labour Party in the 1992 election.[73]

What happened to the significant number of voters who supported the Green Party in the 1989 EP elections? Based on the respondents to the third wave of the 1989 European Election Study, we know where they came from: Conservative voters made up about 27 percent and Labour voters constituted 17 percent of the Green 1989 EP vote. However, no survey asks how those who supported the Greens in 1989 actually voted in the 1992 General Election. From the 1989 European Election Study, we get some clues as to their *intended* future behavior. Seventeen percent of 1989 Green voters voiced their intention to support the Conservatives in the next national election, and 22 percent stated that they were likely to support Labour. That said, not all who voted Green in 1989 anticipated their subsequent defection; 42 percent of the 1989 Green voters were planning to vote for the Greens again in the next national election, and 58 percent reported a high likelihood of supporting the Greens in a national election in the future.[74] Given that only 171,927 individuals actually voted Green in 1992 – a figure representing a mere 7.3 percent of the number who voted Green in 1989 – we know that some of these "confidently Green" voters must have defected, most likely to the pro-environmental mainstream parties.[75]

1992–97: The Crowning of a New "Environmental" Party

The interaction of a dismissive Conservative strategy and an accommodative Labour strategy between 1992 and 1997 yields different predictions. Unlike in the previous period, the mainstream parties were no longer both promoting the environment. With the Conservatives downplaying the issue while Labour

---

73 The Conservatives only lost 0.2 percent and the Labour Party only 0.3 percent of their 1987 voters to the Greens in 1992. Even with the mainstream parties' electorates being much larger than that of the Green Party, more voters defected to each mainstream party from the Green Party than switched from each to the Greens. Calculations from Heath et al. 1996.

74 To the question, "how probable is it that you will ever vote for this party in general elections?" 58 percent reported scores of 8, 9, or 10 out of a scale of 0 to 10, where 0 was equal to "not at all" and 10 was labeled "very probable." Calculations from wave three of van der Eijk et al. 1994.

75 Calculations from Butler and Butler 2000: 514; Mackie and Rose 1997.

continued to prioritize it, the PSO theory predicts a decrease in the importance of the environment relative to the prior electoral period. The Conservatives, moreover, abandoned the race for environmental party title. Given the Labour Party's persistent implementation of co-optative tactics, we would expect issue ownership to be captured by Labour. Along with this title, the Labour Party is expected to gain support from former Green voters.

Survey data corroborate these expectations. The Labour Party gained the overwhelming majority of Green Party defectors in both the 1994 EP and 1997 General elections. According to the 1994 European Election Study, 39 percent of 1992 Green Party supporters, or 61 percent of the 1992 Green Party voters who did not vote Green in 1994, voted Labour in the European election.[76] The Tories, conversely, were not successful in wooing former Green voters in the 1994 contest. The Green Party did not stop attracting mainstream party voters in the 1994 EP elections; indeed, it experienced a net gain.[77] But, consistent with the Tories' assessment, the Green Party was more of a threat to Labour than to the Conservatives.[78]

By the 1997 General Election, however, the accommodative Labour Party was both luring Green voters and retaining its own. Sixty-five percent of 1992 Green voters switched to support the Labour Party in the 1997 General Election while an insignificant percentage supported the Conservatives.[79] The BES results further suggest that voter defection from the mainstream parties to the Greens in 1997 was trivial – a conclusion consistent with Conservative and Labour judgments of the niche party's low threat.

But were these trends in voter support caused by the dismissive-accommodative strategic combination of the Conservative and Labour parties? Evidence of the predicted changes in issue salience and ownership is highly supportive of that conclusion. In the aftermath of the 1992 General Election, the perceived importance of the environmental issue declined (see Figure 5.4). According to a MORI poll conducted only eight months after that election, a scant 3 percent of those surveyed believed the environment to be the most important issue facing the nation. Over the next four years, issue salience hovered around 5 percent, an immobility recorded even during the 1994 EP election campaign. This low level of prioritization, consistent with a dismissive-accommodative strategy, was a far cry from the 35 percent high enjoyed by the environmental issue.

---

[76] Thirty-six percent of 1992 Green Party voters supported the Green Party in the 1994 EP elections, according to the 1994 European Election Study. That many former Green Party voters supported a mainstream party in the 1994 EP elections and that the Green Party's 1994 vote share declined serve as further evidence that these supranational elections are not simply opportunities for voters to cast protest votes for minor parties.

[77] This is consistent with the fact that the Green Party was viewed as the environmental issue owner at the time of the 1994 EP elections. See Figure 5.5.

[78] Those who voted Labour in 1992 comprised 20 percent of the Green Party voters whereas 1992 Conservative supporters made up less than 10 percent. Calculations from Schmitt et al. 2001.

[79] Calculations from Heath et al. 2000.

Trends in issue ownership also reinforce my claims about the co-optation of the environmental issue. During this electoral period, as shown in Figure 5.5, the Green Party was no longer consistently viewed as the greenest British political party. After perceiving the Conservative and Labour parties to be equally responsive to environmental matters throughout 1992, a plurality of survey respondents awarded the environmental title to the Labour Party by late 1993. This outcome coincides with the publication of Labour's environmental paper *In Trust for Tomorrow* and the Conservatives' noticeably absent dialogue on green issues. This distinction between the greenness of the parties only grew over time, with more and more survey respondents choosing the Labour Party over the Conservative Party. As expected, the number of people perceiving the Green Party to be the environmental hegemon continuously declined. These survey results show that the Labour Party was able to co-opt the environmentalist image along with the Green Party's voters.

AN ALTERNATIVE EXPLANATION: THE ROLE OF THE LIBERAL DEMOCRATS

This chapter has argued that the Green Party's electoral decline can be attributed to the strategic behavior of the mainstream parties, specifically the mainstream parties of the center-left and center-right. Yet, while the most prominent, the Conservative and Labour parties were not the only economically focused mainstream parties to compete and employ strategies in the British political scene. Since the birth of the Green Party, the Liberal Democrats have emerged to become a non-negligible electoral player of the political center. Moreover, an examination of the centrist party's manifestos, publications, and pronouncements during the late 1980s and early 1990s shows that the Liberal Democrats did adopt strategies, specifically accommodative ones, targeting the Green Party. If we take the prioritization of the environmental protection issue in its election manifestos as an indication of strategic intensity, the strength of the Liberal Democrats' accommodative strategy surpassed that of both Labour and the Conservatives between 1987 and 1997 (Budge et al. 2001). When this information is paired with the claim by Rüdig et al. (1996) that the vote share of the Liberal Democrats and the Greens are negatively correlated, it seems plausible, as some scholars suggest, that the tactical maneuvers of the Liberal Democrats may have shaped the electoral trajectory of the Green Party.[80]

---

[80] Rüdig et al. (1996) also claim that the interchangeability of the Liberal Democrat and Green votes might be based on their role as protest votes. According to Rüdig et al. (1996: 9), Green Party vote reflected "centre-right voters wishing to register a mid-term protest against the government while not going so far as to vote Labour. In that context, the poor performance of the Liberal Democrats becomes particularly significant as they should have been the 'natural' beneficiaries of Tory protest votes." This interpretation is less plausible in light of the fact that almost three-quarters of 1989 Green Party voters said they were motivated by issue concerns. It is further undermined by the fact that Green Party voters cannot simply be described as center-right voters; as confirmed by the

To corroborate this claim, we would need evidence that Green Party voters defected to the centrist party. Moreover, if this strategic explanation follows a modified spatial logic, we would need to see additional indications that the Liberal Democrats won over these voters by altering the salience of the environmental issue and transferring its ownership to themselves. As the next pages demonstrate, however, this evidence is not forthcoming.

The British and European Election Studies reveal that former Liberal Democrat voters made up a significant percentage of the Green Party electorate, especially in the 1989 EP elections. However, the centrist party was not consistently or overwhelmingly the destination of the return flow of environmental voters. Of the 27 percent of the 1989 Green Party supporters who voted Social Liberal Democrats in the 1987 General Election, only 17.2 percent intended to support the centrist party in the 1992 General Election.[81] Moreover, across the 1989 Green voters in general, few indicated their likelihood of voting for the Liberal Democrats at *any* point in the future.[82] Recall that future support for the Labour Party – both in the next General Election and in the unspecified future – was significantly higher. Similarly, in the 1994 EP elections, the Liberal Democrats were overshadowed by the Labour Party as the party of choice for former Green Party voters: 39 percent voted Labour in 1994 as opposed to 12 percent who voted Liberal Democrat.[83] Given that a vote for an MEP is more likely to reflect sincere preferences than strategic considerations, the fact that the plurality of General Election Green Party voters supported Labour in the EP elections can be seen as an indication of the relative strength of Labour's environmental reputation over that of the centrist party.

Analysis of party vote switching between General Elections, on the other hand, reveals a somewhat weaker pattern. Consistent with the information described in the previous paragraph, the results of the 1997 British General Election Study show that Labour received a larger percentage of former Green voters than the Liberal Democrats. Whereas 65 percent of 1992 Green voters switched to support Labour in 1997, less than 12 percent of 1992 Green voters defected to the Liberals.[84] But Green Party voter defection between the previous two General Elections seems to have more greatly benefited the Liberal Democrats. According to the 1992 BES, five out of fourteen respondents who voted for the Greens in 1987 voted for the Liberal Democrats in 1992, as opposed to four who voted for Labour and three who voted for the Conservatives. However,

1989 and 1994 European Election Studies, the policy preferences of Green voters are distributed across both sides of the economic Left-Right dimension. Calculations from van der Eijk et al. 1994; Schmitt et al. 2001.

[81] Thirty-six percent said that they would vote for the Greens, 28.4 percent would vote Labour, and 7.7 percent would vote Conservative. Calculations from wave three of van der Eijk et al. 1994.

[82] To the question, "how probable is it that you will ever vote for the Social Liberal Democrats in general elections?" only 10 percent reported scores of 8, 9, or 10 out of a scale of 0 to 10, where 0 was equal to "not at all" and 10 was labeled "very probable." Calculations from ibid.

[83] Calculations from Schmitt et al. 2001.

[84] Calculations from Heath et al. 2000.

given that the differences in the number of respondents are not significant in such small samples, these results should not be viewed as strong support for the Liberal-Democrats-as-issue-owner hypothesis.

Even more striking than the fact that former Green voters were generally less likely to switch to the Liberal Democrats is the finding that the centrist party was considered one of the *least* green British actors (Gallup Political and Economic Index). Despite its highly intense accommodative strategy, the party consistently placed last, or fourth, behind both mainstream parties and the Greens between 1987 and 1992. At the 1992 General Election – the halfway point of its strong co-optative efforts – the Liberal Democrats were seen as competent owner of the environmental issue by only 14 percent of survey respondents. Its score averaged in the teens across the next electoral period, and although it tried to creep up in the rankings, the Liberal Democrats had fallen to last place again when Labour emerged from its competition with the Conservatives to become the clear owner of the green issue. Given such an "ungreen" image, it is not surprising that the environmental issue–based voters who composed the Green Party's electorate would not have defected to the Liberal Democrats. This discussion reveals, counter to the claims of Rüdig et al. (1996), that although the centrist party may have reinforced the accommodative efforts of the other mainstream parties, the Liberal Democrats were not the driving force behind the electoral marginalization of the Green Party.[85]

CONCLUSION

The electoral decline of a niche party in a first-past-the-post system has typically been explained by institutional and sociological factors. This chapter, however, paints a more complex picture of party failure as the result of the deliberate and costly strategies employed by multiple threatened mainstream party actors. Faced with an electorate that supported environmental protection over job creation and a like-minded Green Party that was gaining support in key marginal districts, both the Conservative and Labour parties were driven to adopt active and often controversial accommodative strategies to ward off the new competitor. Thus, rather than being immune to the Green Party, as many institutionalists might expect, the mainstream parties – both the economically left Labour Party and the economically right Conservative Party – struggled to be as "green" as possible so as to retain control of their electorates.[86]

In unraveling the strategic decisions of the Conservative and Labour parties over the life-span of the Green Party, this chapter has called into question the conception of strategies and strategic interaction espoused by the standard spatial model; the tactics of the British mainstream parties have not been restricted to

---

[85] Indeed, in a 2000 paper, Rüdig and Franklin conclude that the connection between the electoral performance of the Liberal Democrats and the Green Party is spurious.

[86] The evidence presented here directly contradicts the claim by Kitschelt (1994: 143) that the British Greens "have been too insignificant . . . to affect Labour strategy."

the manipulation of the relative positions of the parties on a given environmental dimension. As the survey evidence shows, the strategies of the Labour and Conservative parties toward the Greens coincide with changes in the salience and ownership of the environmental issue. Mainstream party accommodative tactics called attention to an issue that the parties had previously ignored and allowed Labour and the Tories to undermine the Green Party's control of the environmental issue. Only with the transfer of issue ownership away from the niche party did we witness the loosening of the Green Party's hold on issue-based voters and these voters' return to the mainstream parties.

Although the outcome of this competition between unequals – the electoral decline of the Green Party – is consistent with the mainstream parties' wishes, this discussion also shows that a mainstream party's ability to undermine the competitiveness of a niche party is not unconstrained. The Conservative and Labour parties' past strategic behavior restricted their future tactical choices. Consistent with the hypothesis presented in Chapter 4, the costs involved with wild shifts in strategy tend to discourage parties from making them. Thus after 1992, we saw the Conservatives follow their second-best strategy of dismissive behavior, rather than switch to adversarial tactics to try to sabotage the Labour Party's efforts to win issue ownership.

The story of mainstream party manipulation of niche party success continues in Chapter 6 with an analysis of the electoral fortune of the French radical right party, the Front National. Instead of being characterized by the efforts of both center-left and center-right parties to weaken a single-issue party, the French mainstream party competition with the Front National is best described as a battle of opposing forces. The utility of the typically ignored adversarial strategy becomes apparent in this case, as we see how the Socialists used the radical right party as a weapon against the Gaullists, and how the fortune of the Front National became a by-product of the larger competition between mainstream party equals.

6

"The Enemy of My Enemy Is My Friend"

French Mainstream Party Strategies and the Success of the French Front National

Rallying to the cry of "France for the French"[1] and "One million unemployed, one million immigrants too many,"[2] the Front National burst into the French political limelight in the 1980s. Despite the fact that there had been a moratorium on immigration to France for almost a decade, this single-issue, anti-immigration party captured almost 10 percent of the vote and thirty-five seats in the 1986 legislative elections. Its support did not flag over the next decade, with the radical right party gaining increasingly larger shares of the vote. By 1997, the Front National had surpassed all expectations of its success; in that election, it earned 14.9 percent of the vote and the title of the third most popular party in the French political system.

The electoral success of the Front National was made all the more threatening – especially to the dominant Socialist (PS) and Gaullist (RPR) parties – by its cross-party appeal. A 1981 SOFRES poll reveals that 70 percent of all respondents were opposed to the arrival of further immigrants to France and that between 15 and 22 percent of survey respondents favored the expulsion of all immigrants, policy positions espoused by the Front National.[3] Seven years later, and several years after the start of the Socialists' pro-immigrant campaign, the percentage of survey respondents still preferring the repatriation of immigrants was over 20 percent.[4] A close analysis of niche party support shows that issue voters from

---

[1] This articulation of the FN's demand for "national preference" is a hallmark phrase of the party's leader, Jean-Marie Le Pen (Givens 2005: 36).

[2] This was the Front National slogan in 1978 (quoted in RPR 1997: 1). By 1985, this appeal had changed to "three million unemployed = three million immigrants." It was uttered by Jean-Marie Le Pen at *Dîner-Débat de Bron*, February 25, 1985 quoted in Archives de l'OURS, *Lutter contre l'extrême droite: des outils pour l'action*, 1990: 28. Unless otherwise noted, all translations from French are my own.

[3] Archives du CEVIPOF, Sondages, "Les Français et les travailleurs immigrés," (Montrouge: SOFRES, 1981).

[4] More than 22 percent of the survey respondents to the 1988 French Presidential Election Survey located themselves at a 1 or 2 out of a scale of 1 to 7, where 1 was agreement with the statement "It is necessary that immigrants return to their country of origin," and 7 was agreement with the

across the political spectrum were drawn to the FN on the basis of these tough positions on immigration.[5] Although the electoral base of the RPR was hardest hit by the rise of this xenophobic party, no mainstream party was immune to the Front National threat.

What is puzzling from the perspective of the parties literature is exactly how the resonance of this single-issue party's message translated into consistent and growing support for a third party in an electorally unfavorable environment. Institutional theories explain why rational voters under these conditions should *not* waste their votes supporting a nonregionally based third party. Sociological explanations likewise predict a decline, not the observed increase, in the perceived salience of the Front National's anti-immigration platform and its vote during the late 1980s and early 1990s – a period of growing GDP per capita, falling immigration levels, and steadying and then declining percentages of foreigners in the country. Taking a very different approach, standard spatial theories similarly are perplexed by the electoral success of this radical right party given the accommodative tactics of the niche party's ideological neighbor, the RPR.

This chapter answers the question of Front National success with a modified spatial strategic explanation. I argue that the entrenchment of the Front National in the French political system is a result of the behavior of both of its mainstream political actors. The Socialists' timely implementation of a range of adversarial tactics facilitated the legitimization of the niche party in the electoral sphere; voters favoring immigration restrictions and repatriation were encouraged to support the issue's "true owner" – the FN. By the time the RPR was able to overcome internal factionalism to adopt an accommodative response after the 1986 election, the issue credibility of the Front National had already been established. The subsequent policy inconsistency of the center-right party only further reinforced the FN's ownership of the anti-immigration position. Persuaded by the early adversarial strategies of the PS and not dissuaded by the ineffective co-optative efforts of the RPR, issue voters flocked to the Front National.

This chapter begins its explanation of the astronomical rise of the French radical right party with an examination of the electoral and political environment that characterized France from 1970 to 2000. In an era of declining partisan attachment, the Front National and its newly politicized issue of immigration threatened the established party system and, in particular, the electoral and governmental hegemony of the mainstream parties. Following a discussion of the challenges posed by the FN, this chapter will explore the "what" and "why" of the strategies pursued by the PS and the Gaullists. An analysis of how the adversarial and accommodative tactics of the mainstream parties affected the salience and ownership of the FN's anti-immigration issue offers support for the modified

---

statement "It is necessary to integrate immigrants who currently live in France into French society." Calculations from Pierce 1996.

[5] Interview with Jean-Pierre Delalande, RPR Député of Val d'Oise, former Secretary in Charge of Relations with Other Parties (1981–83) and member of the High Council on Integration, Paris, France, November 12, 1998; RPR 1997: 4.

spatial logic of the PSO theory of competition between unequals and reveals the mechanism behind the Front National's unusual electoral success.

FRENCH ELECTORAL AND POLITICAL ENVIRONMENT OF THE FIFTH REPUBLIC

The creation of the French Fifth Republic brought stability to a previously tumultuous and highly fragmented political environment. Despite the brief period of intense electoral volatility at the end of the 1950s as the party lines were being redrawn,[6] the French political system was organized along clear lines of division.[7] In 1962, three-quarters of French survey respondents identified themselves as partisans of a particular party (Lewis-Beck 1984: 432). Close to 50 percent of all French voters gave their electoral support to parties of the center-left and center-right.[8] Moreover, interest and involvement in politics were high, with the average voter turnout in the first decade of the Fifth Republic above the 75 percent mark.[9]

However, by the time that the Front National first started contesting elections in the 1970s and 1980s, French voters were no longer as active or as partisan. The percentage of survey respondents feeling close to a particular party fell to 59 percent by 1975; eighteen years later, this number had dropped by an additional twelve points (Dalton 2000: 25).[10] Of those who remained partisans, the strength of their attachment also weakened (ibid.). Diminishing partisanship was followed by a decline in voter turnout. Although turnout did not continuously drop throughout the 1970s and 1980s, the percentage of registered voters participating in legislative elections fell to an average of less than 68 percent starting in 1988, the year that Wattenberg (2000) identifies as the start of the low participation trend in France.

During this period, the electorate was also relatively mobile. Although the degree of electoral volatility decreased from its high level in the 1950s and 1960s, the net electoral shift in party vote in the mid-1990s was still 19.15 percent (Anderson 1998).[11] Given the drop in the number of loyal partisans during a period of significant voter movement, it is not surprising that average voter support levels for the mainstream parties declined. By the 1990s, the combined vote of

---

[6] According to Bartolini and Mair (1990: Appendix 2), the electoral volatility of the French political system in 1958 was 26.5 percent. A similar, although slightly lower, figure of 20 percent is reported by Wattenberg (2000: 41) for the 1950s.

[7] Although French voter volatility was certainly higher than that in the United Kingdom, France still enjoyed a relatively stable political system.

[8] Those mainstream parties were the Gaullists and the Section française de l'internationale ouvrière (SFIO), the predecessor of the PS.

[9] This number represents the average turnout of registered voters from the first four legislative elections: 1958, 1962, 1967, and 1968. Mackie and Rose 1991: 148, 152.

[10] Dalton cites measures from the Eurobarometer surveys because of the stability of the surveys' question wording over time. Similar conclusions of the general decline in French partisanship between the 1970s and 1990s also emerge from the French National Election Studies, surveys in which the wording of the relevant question changes over time.

[11] This calculation is based on an average of data from 1993 and 1995.

TABLE 6.1. *Electoral Strength of French Mainstream Parties in the Fifth Republic, 1958–97*

Election	Turnout of Registered Voters (%)	Percentage of Votes for the Mainstream Parties (PS and RPR)[12]
1958	77.2	36.1
1962	68.7	46.1
1967	81.1	51.9
1968	80	54.5
1973	81.3	45.1
1978	83.2	45.6
1981	70.9	57.8
1986	78.5	73.9[13]
1988	66.2	55.7
1993	69.3	38.7
1997	67.9	39.2

Note: Following convention, percentages refer to the first round of the French legislative elections.

Sources: Mackie and Rose 1991, 1997; http://www.electionworld.org/france.htm; and author's files.

the dominant PS and RPR parties had fallen below 40 percent in the first round of legislative elections (see Table 6.1). Voters were no longer automatically according their support to these mainstream parties. France, albeit to a lesser extent than Britain, was experiencing a period of electoral instability.

Although troubling for existing parties, increases in voter exit and decreases in voter loyalty are not sufficient in themselves to alter the relative balance of power between political parties. A third factor is necessary: an increase in the available political options. Unfortunately for the French mainstream parties, dealigned voters did have access to a burgeoning population of new parties during this period. Mair (1999: 211) lists as twelve the number of new political parties to emerge in France between 1960 and 1998. Half of those parties can be classified as niche parties. Given that the official French electoral results do not individually name the smaller parties, but group them under the general rubrics of "other Right," "other Left," and "regionalist," the actual number of newly created parties, including niche parties, could be much higher.[14]

The impact of these new parties has not been limited to their crowding of the political space. Many of these parties posed direct and formidable electoral

---

[12] This column includes vote shares for the PS, RPR, and their predecessors, the SFIO and the variously named Gaullist parties, respectively. The PS replaced the SFIO in 1969.

[13] This value represents the result of a UDF-RPR electoral pact. As a result, there are no separate counts of their individual vote shares for the 1986 election. If this noncomparable value is excluded from the analysis, we see even more clearly a downward trend in mainstream party support from the 1980s to the 1990s.

[14] This way of presenting election data, which has been emulated by the main secondary data sources (e.g., BDSP data; Lancelot 1983, 1998; Mackie and Rose 1991, 1997), prevents scholars from counting the number of less-successful and often newly emerged parties.

challenges to the existing parties. Nine of the twelve new parties gained at least one seat in the National Assembly, and four of the twelve captured an average vote of more than 5 percent. Indeed, as a result of their strong electoral appeal, the effective number of parties in France increased from 5.8 in the 1950s to 7.9 in the 1990s (Wattenberg 2000: 43).[15] With the magnitude of this change in France's party fragmentation index equal to the *absolute level* of party fragmentation found in some countries,[16] it is clear that the new political opponents represented a substantial addition to the French political system.

An underexamined, but important, effect of these new competitors has also been their ability to indirectly rob the mainstream parties of office. As seen in Britain, but to a lesser extent, the increase in the number of new parties was accompanied by a rise in the competitiveness of individual district races. This manifested itself in France in several ways. First, fewer candidates won seats on the first ballot of the legislative elections. In 1981, 154 seats were won in the first legislative round. This number dropped consistently over the next four elections to a mere seven seats in the 1997 election.[17] Second, in those seats in which a second ballot was held, there was an increase in the number of three-way races. Whereas the majority of French second-ballot races are runoffs between two parties, any candidate (up to three) capturing more than 12.5 percent of the number of registered voters in the first ballot is eligible to contest the second. Even though the 12.5 percent threshold level has not changed since 1978, the number of three-way races in the second round jumped from 1 out of 417 in 1978 to 79 out of 548 in 1997.[18]

Niche parties were participants in the vast majority of those three-way races, often capturing vote percentages that exceeded the gap between the winning and losing mainstream party candidates. To get a sense of the omnipresence and competitiveness of niche parties in these races, let us examine the 1997 legislative election. In the second round of that election, only 2 of the 79 three-way races *did not* involve at least one niche party.[19] And in 73 of the 79 three-way races, the

---

[15] These figures were calculated according to the Laakso/Taagepera formula, which takes into account the electoral and legislative significance of parties.

[16] For example, the effective number of parties in Britain in 1951 was 2.1. The addition of forty-eight parties between 1960 and 1998 only served to increase its party fragmentation index to 2.26 – an *absolute value* just slightly higher than the *change* in the effective number of parties experienced by France. Anderson 1998: 577–9.

[17] The number of seats won in the first round is as follows: 115 in 1988; 72 in 1993; and 7 in 1997. The 1986 legislative election is excluded because it employed only one round of PR rules. Calculations from Banque de Données Socio-Politiques (BDSP), legislative results. I thank the BDSP for making the constituency-level electoral data available to me.

[18] The requirement for second-ballot participation has been changed twice during the Fifth Republic. For the 1962 legislative elections, a candidate was only required to get 5 percent of the valid (*exprimé*) votes. For the 1967, 1968, and 1973 elections, the requirement was increased to 10 percent of the registered voters (*électeurs inscrits*). As indicated in the text, the requirement was made even more onerous for elections starting in 1978. Schlesinger and Schlesinger 1990: 1098.

[19] The overwhelming majority of the second-round niche party candidates were from the Front National. That there were few Green Party candidates is not surprising given that the Green Party and the PS had an electoral pact in 1997 and shared (mostly PS) candidates in the second round. Calculations from BDSP.

vote share of a third-place niche party – the Front National in every case – was larger than the winner's margin of victory.[20] Thus, whereas the niche parties were typically not capturing seats in the French legislative elections, their presence was contributing to the failure or success of the mainstream parties.

The electoral threat of the niche parties was further exacerbated by their role as promoters of new or previously ignored political issues. Unlike the new parties of Lutte ouvrière (LO) and Mouvement des radicaux de gauche (MRG), who tried to challenge the PS and RPR on issues that the mainstream parties already owned, the green, ethnoterritorial, and radical right parties popularized topics that the mainstream parties had previously ignored or depoliticized. For example, the Union Démocratique Bretonne asked workers and employers to replace class-based alliances with regional ones. The green parties, les Verts and la Génération Écologie, called for the prioritization of environmental protection over industrial advancement. The Front National tried to unite those of the Left and Right on the issue of immigration control. As these examples demonstrate, the niche parties were both discounting the centrality of the economically focused political space and advocating topics and policy positions that would appeal to voters across traditional partisan lines. Faced with potential ideological challenges to their support bases, the PS and RPR had no choice but to respond to these competitors.

THE RISE OF THE FRONT NATIONAL (1972–97)

The Front National was to become one of the major political challenges, if not *the* major political challenge, facing the French mainstream parties at the end of the twentieth century. Founded in 1972, the Front National campaigned for the reinforcement of what it feared was an eroding French national identity.[21] Not only did the party call for the protection of the patriarchal family structure, but it also railed against the introduction of new customs, new languages, and new religions into the conception of "Frenchness." These objectives required, it argued, an end to further immigration to France and the forced return of immigrants, especially the "unassimilatable" population of Northern Africans.

The Front National and its anti-immigration (and anti-immigrant) message received little electoral support during the 1970s. It contested its first national-level legislative elections in 1973, and only one year later, the FN's leader, Jean-Marie Le Pen, gathered enough signatures to appear on the ballot in the presidential election. In neither election, however, did the niche party make a mark on the French political scene. The Front National in combination with other extreme right parties received a mere 0.6 percent in 1973, and Le Pen managed to win only 0.74 percent in the 1974 presidential election. As shown in Figure 6.1, these levels of support would not improve significantly over the next

---

[20] Ibid.
[21] Archives de la FNSP, Fonds Mayer, 3NA29, Dr 5, Elections 1974, 1974 Presidential Campaign Document of Le Pen; Front National 1993.

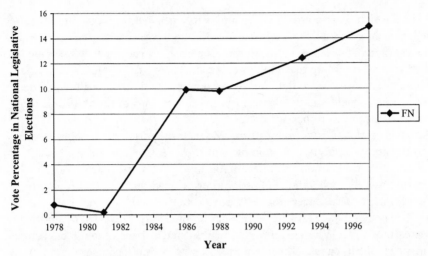

FIGURE 6.1. Electoral Support of the French Front National. *Sources:* Mackie and Rose 1991, 1997.

two legislative elections. The Front National captured 0.8 percent in 1978, but only 0.2 percent in the 1981 legislative elections.[22]

Low popular support for an anti-immigration party was not a surprise in the 1970s. Large-scale immigration officially ended in France in 1974, so the inflow of new immigrants was already curtailed.[23] Moreover, any concern that there was among political parties about this issue focused on the integration or assimilation of *existing* immigrants or the deterrence of illegal immigration; the expulsion of legal immigrants was not considered or discussed as a political option (Keeler and Schain 1996: 14). It should also be emphasized that the topics of immigration and immigrants were viewed as administrative matters, not political ones. Thus, while anti-immigrant rhetoric was not absent from the headquarters and conference rooms of French political parties during the 1970s, these sentiments did not translate into the promotion of anti-immigrant platforms by either the center-left or center-right French parties or widespread interest in this issue by the French electorate during this time.

By 1983, however, support for the Front National began to swell. Within a year, the FN had a deputy mayor elected in the town of Dreux and captured over 11 percent of the vote and ten seats in the 1984 EP elections. In the 1986 legislative election conducted under proportional representation, the FN won 9.9 percent of the vote to win thirty-five seats in the National Assembly. Although the subsequent reinstatement of the more restrictive two-ballot plurality system

[22] According to the BDSP records, 0.8 percent of the valid votes went to extreme right parties in the first round of the 1978 legislative elections. Although the FN was the most prominent radical right party, this vote share could include votes for other extreme right parties. By 1981, the Front National was distinguished from other extreme right parties in the BDSP election returns.

[23] As a result, the percentage of foreigners in France was stabilizing.

reduced the niche party's chances of retaining its parliamentary seats, the FN surprised many by essentially maintaining its vote at 9.8 percent. Its vote share grew over the next two legislative elections to 12.4 percent in 1993 and 14.9 percent in 1997.[24] It is worth noting that support for the FN in legislative elections was also matched by support for Le Pen in the presidential elections. The FN candidate received 14.4 percent and 15.0 percent in the first rounds of the 1988 and 1995 presidential elections, respectively.

Although scholars have found little evidence supporting the radical right's claim that immigrants cause unemployment (e.g., Golder 2003b), the FN's slogan "one million unemployed, one million immigrants too many" was clearly resonating with French voters. Those who prioritized the issue of immigration in their voting decisions were more likely to vote for the FN than for any other party. The issue salience rankings of Front National voters revealed this distinction as early as 1984. Whereas immigration was listed fifth out of five issues across the majority of survey respondents in 1984, it was ranked second among radical right voters, just behind the related topic of law and order.[25] By 1986, the issue moved to first place among FN voters. The supporters of no other party ranked the issue nearly as high; voters for the RPR and the Union pour la démocratie française (UDF) were the next most likely groups to rank immigration first, and only 3 percent and 16 percent, respectively, did so.

A decade later, even after the FN increased the number of issues it discussed in its manifestos, concern over immigration still distinguished voters of the FN from those of other parties. In 1993, three-quarters of FN partisans named immigration as the most important social problem affecting France, as opposed to only 41 percent of RPR and 28 percent of UDF partisans.[26] The single-issue distinctiveness of FN voters is also seen in survey results from the 1995 presidential election; these indicate that Le Pen voters were motivated much more by the issues of immigration (75 percent) and security of citizens (53 percent) than Chirac voters (30 percent and 36 percent) or Balladur voters (25 percent and 36 percent).[27]

An anti-immigration stance is also one of the few points of policy commonality between FN voters. Despite the association between the economic right and anti-immigrant parties conveyed by the names "radical right" and "extreme

---

[24] The FN won no parliamentary seats in 1993 and only one seat in 1997.

[25] The five issues were law and order, immigration, unemployment, the economy, and social inequality. Exit poll, SOFRES/TF1 June 17, 1984, cited in Schain 1994: 265. According to an IFOP/RTL-Le Point poll, immigration was the number one issue among FN voters in the 1984 EP elections (Archives de la FNSP, Dossiers de Presse, Richard, 1984).

[26] The differences in immigration prioritization were even starker between those respondents who expected to vote for these parties in the 1993 legislative elections; 71 percent of those who expected to vote for the FN named immigration as the number one social problem, as opposed to 36 percent of expected RPR voters and 26 percent of expected UDF voters. For comparison purposes, only 22 percent of PS partisans and 18 percent of expected PS voters ranked immigration as the top social problem. Calculations from Chrique 1997.

[27] These were the issues on which there was the greatest difference between the FN, RPR, and UDF voters (Ysmal 1995: 4).

right," voters supporting the FN are not single-minded in their economic policy preferences. In an analysis of the motivations of blue-collar workers and small business owners – two groups overrepresented in the FN – Ivarsflaten (2005) finds divergence, rather than convergence, in their views on the economy. The issue on which these supporters of the FN agree is the topic of "exclusion," which includes attitudes toward immigrants, asylum seekers, and minority groups. This is the issue that holds the FN electorate together.

That voters were motivated to cast their ballots for the FN on the basis of the immigration issue is further confirmed by negative findings about other voting explanations. First, votes for radical right parties cannot be dismissed as protest votes (McGann and Kitschelt 2005; van der Brug et al. 2000). Research by van der Brug et al. (2000: 82) demonstrates that FN supporters are motivated by policy, more than the desire "to demonstrate rejection of all other parties." Second, French radical right voters are not attracted primarily by the charismatic leadership of Jean-Marie Le Pen or other features of the party organization. To quote Lewis-Beck (1993: 9):

As Haegel shows, National Front (NF) supporters have weak commitment to the party itself, but strong commitment to the party's ideas. Other data confirm this observation. In an April 24, 1988, exit poll by Bull and BVA, 76 percent of the Le Pen voters said they were motivated by "ideas" rather than "personality" or "party," a percentage far exceeding that for the supporters of other right-wing candidates (respectively, 46 percent for Chirac, 57 percent for Barre [*Le Monde* 1988: 42]).

In other words, issues – and more specifically, the issue of immigration – were driving voter support for the FN. The French political system was under threat from what can be described as a single-issue party and its single-issue voters.

STANDARD EXPLANATIONS FOR RADICAL RIGHT PARTY SUCCESS

Given that most niche parties do not displace established parties to become the third most popular party in a given country, the electoral success of the Front National stands out as exceptional. The case turns from a merely interesting exception to a fascinating puzzle when one considers that the Front National was competing in an electorally restrictive environment designed to discourage support for third parties. How did this radical right party succeed when its anti-immigration counterpart in another plurality-based system, the British National Front, failed to capture more than 0.6 percent nationwide? What explains the Front National's success?

Institutional Explanations Prove Insufficient

A review of the French institutional environment suggests the limitations of these approaches for understanding the FN's electoral success. The French employ a two-ballot plurality system in which the top candidates compete in a second round of elections if no candidate wins a majority of the votes in the first. Although this system is more permissive than the simple plurality system used in the United Kingdom, it shares some of the former's attributes. It is biased against nongeo-graphically concentrated parties. It also presents a high threshold for a candidate to attain office or even to advance to the second round of legislative competition. With regard to the latter, the threshold level has varied during the Fifth Republic. At the time of the FN's first widespread electoral participation in 1978, a candidate needed to win at least 12.5 percent of the registered voters to compete in the second round.[28] It remained at that level through the end of the 1990s.

This combination of majority runoff-style elections and a high second-round threshold is thought to discourage voter support for third parties and, especially, for anti-establishment parties. While many, including Duverger (1954), have long claimed that dual-ballot systems encourage sincere, rather than strategic, voting in the first round of French-style elections, Cox argues that strategic voting, although less common than in one-ballot plurality systems, is not absent.[29] He (1997: 137) states:

In top-two majority runoff elections with three or more candidates, voters *always* face incentives to vote strategically. And when there are four or more candidates, these incentives (in a frictionless model) destroy candidacies not in the running for a runoff spot, just as in plurality elections they destroy candidacies not in the running for a seat.

Since the overwhelming majority of the second-round ballots in French legislative elections have involved two candidates, Cox's claim about the prevalence of strategic voting in a top-two majority runoff system suggests that niche parties in France will receive low levels of support on the first ballot. Because of its perceived extremist stances, a radical right party, like the Front National, would be additionally disadvantaged under runoff rules; lacking coalition potential, it would be "poorly positioned in the bargaining that goes on between first and second rounds" (Sartori summarized in Cox 1997: 138). With support for niche parties, and the FN in particular, discouraged on the first and second ballots, institutional theories would not expect such parties to be created or strongly supported.

Consideration of the other institutional features of the French political environment leads to similarly pessimistic conclusions about the likelihood of third party formation and success. According to Willey (1998) and Harmel and Robertson (1985), a unitary state, like that which characterized France until 1986 and to some extent afterward, is inimical to third party success. While not as inhospitable as a pure presidential system, France's semipresidentialism also provides voters with incentives to vote only for parties that can credibly field presidential

---

[28] When the FN contested select districts in the 1973 legislative election, the percentage needed for second-round participation was only 10 percent of the registered voters. Schlesinger and Schlesinger 1990: 1098.

[29] Cox (1997: ch. 6) explains that strategic voting is less common in dual-ballot than in single-ballot plurality systems because the informational requirements for the voter are more onerous, and the calculations necessary to vote strategically are more complicated.

candidates.[30] In other words, parties like the Front National should have been disadvantaged.

And yet, the facts run counter to these predictions. The Front National did emerge and compete successfully in French legislative elections. Moreover, *contra* the expectations of Cox (1997), empirical analyses of voting behavior in the 1980s have found little evidence of strategic voting in France (Boy and Dupoirier 1993: 164).

The power of the institutional explanations increases somewhat if one takes into consideration the changes to the electoral rules that occurred in France during the time period under analysis. A system of proportional representation replaced the two-ballot plurality rules for the 1986 national legislative elections, and the unitary structure of the state loosened after 1986 when regional parliaments were first directly elected. A quick glance at the vote level of the radical right niche party shows dramatic electoral changes around this date. The support of the Front National jumped from 0.2 percent in 1981 to 9.9 percent in 1986, a vote level significant enough to net the party thirty-five seats in the Assemblée Nationale. The party likewise benefited from PR rules in the subnational elections held that year, multiplying its number of officeholders and gaining exposure. It would not be controversial to attribute much of the Front National's electoral success in this election – consistent with the theories of Duverger (1954) and Harmel and Robertson (1985) – to a reduction in the disproportionality of the electoral system and the development of subnational offices.

Yet, even these relationships highlight the limitations of the explanatory power of institutional arguments. For instance, if electoral institutions shaped the incentives and behavior of voters in 1986, why did they not encourage voters to avoid wasting their votes on the FN once plurality rules were reinstated in 1988? It is unclear how the same institutional theories can account for the continued increase in FN voter support when the next three legislative elections were conducted under restrictive electoral rules. And returning to the case of the 1986 elections, the fact that institutions seemed to affect FN support does not necessarily establish the independent causal influence of these factors. Rather, as the rest of this chapter will argue, institutions are not exogenous to the political arena. They are adopted, often strategically, by political parties.

Findings Run Counter to Sociological Expectations

The explanatory power of the sociological theories likewise seems to be limited. Recall that these theories expect radical right party support to increase as the economy weakens. The logic is that economic insecurity encourages voter support for anti-immigration parties. Although the results of the cross-national time-series analyses in Chapter 3 find no systematic relationships between economic factors and radical right party vote, bivariate correlations reveal statistically

---

[30] With the introduction of *cohabitation* by François Mitterrand, the disincentives for voting for a third party that could not capture the presidency declined somewhat.

significant, but inconsistent, relationships in the case of the French FN. The Front National's vote is strongly and positively correlated with the unemployment rate in France. But it is also strongly and positively correlated with GDP per capita.[31] The first positive relationship is predicted by sociological theories, but the second relationship runs counter to expectations.

Consideration of other sociological measures touted by this literature does not improve the theories' predictive power. In contrast to Golder's (2003b: 455) findings for populist parties – the category in which he places the FN – voter support for the French radical right party is not positively correlated with the percentage of immigrants in France.[32] Instead, FN vote share increased across the 1980s and 1990s as the percentage of immigrants in the country leveled off and then decreased.[33] A bivariate correlation confirms a strong negative and statistically significant relationship between these variables.[34]

The statistical significance of the correlations between FN vote and sociological indicators means that these factors cannot be dismissed as easily from this analysis of niche party vote as they could from the British case in Chapter 5. However, the counterintuitive direction of some of these relationships raises doubts about the explanatory force of these sociological theories. Since correlation does not equal causation, perhaps the unexpected positive correlation between FN vote and GDP per capita (or the unexpected negative correlation between FN vote and immigrant percentage) can be explained away as the coincidence of two positively trending lines. Of course, this "solution" also introduces the possibility that the *anticipated* positive relationship between FN vote and unemployment could be similarly explained away.[35]

If a causal relationship does hold between vote and unemployment, it is not clear how this connection is maintained, as implied by sociological theories, without human intervention. As I argued in Chapter 1, the salience of an issue, and thus the resulting behavior of voters, does not respond automatically to changes in socio-economic variables; these factors are not pegged like exchange rates. Rather, political actors must play a role in this sociological story. Consider the fact that, since the 1970s, immigration levels to France have fallen sharply and the number of foreigners in the country has leveled off and then declined as

---

[31] Recall that the relationship between GDP per capita and radical right party support was not found to be statistically significant in any of the models in Chapter 3.

[32] Golder (2003b: 455) finds that populist parties gain support as the percentage of immigrants increases, regardless of the level of unemployment.

[33] The explanatory power of the immigrant hypothesis does not improve if one considers other measures. Indeed, the puzzle of increasing FN support is even more intractable if one considers the sharply falling rate of immigration to France during this time period.

[34] It is statistically significant at $p = .02$ in a two-tailed test. The negative finding is tempered somewhat by the conditional relationship between unemployment and immigrant percentage. Consistent with the findings of the radical-right-party-specific model presented in Chapter 3, there is a positive and statistically significant relationship between the interaction term and FN support. This means that, whereas FN vote decreases as the percentage of immigrants rises, it decreases by less as the unemployment rate increases.

[35] These possibilities are strengthened by the fact that neither the GDP per capita variable nor the unemployment rate variable is a significant predictor of radical right party vote in any of the pooled or niche-party-specific models of Chapter 3.

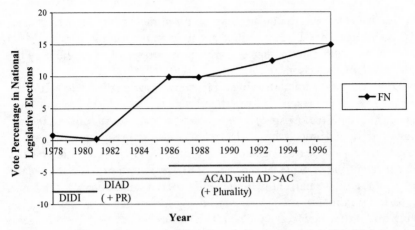

FIGURE 6.2. Electoral Support of the French Front National with Mainstream Party Strategies. *Sources:* Mackie and Rose 1991, 1997.

unemployment has risen. Given that fewer foreigners are around to compete with Frenchmen for the scarcer jobs, why should an increase in unemployment "naturally" lead to an increase in the perceived salience of the immigration issue and increased voter support for a party promising the repatriation of immigrants? The answer lies with the role of political parties as interpreters and conduits of information. As I will argue, the success of the Front National can only be understood when we consider how the most powerful actors, the mainstream parties of the left and right, fostered or manipulated the FN's message.

A STRATEGIC EXPLANATION OF THE FRONT NATIONAL'S SUCCESS

The limitations of the institutional and sociological theories drive us to consider an actor-based theory of niche party support. Analysis of party competition in France will demonstrate that the electoral success of the Front National was the product of the tactical behaviors – both freely chosen and constrained – of the Socialist and Gaullist parties. A preview of what those strategies were and how they shaped the FN's vote was provided in Chapter 3. These strategic combinations are summarized again in Figure 6.2. The rest of the chapter will explore the rationale behind the strategic decisions of the mainstream parties and the parties' abilities to alter the salience and ownership of the FN's immigration issue. As will be shown, the strategic out-maneuvering by one mainstream party of another hampered by factionalism ensured the reputational entrenchment of the Front National as the immigration issue owner and, as a result, the FN's electoral success.

1972–81: The Emergence (and Isolation) of the Front National

The future success of the Front National could not be anticipated from its unimpressive electoral performance during its first decade of political life. In its first three legislative elections, the niche party captured meager vote shares of less than 1 percent. Its leader, Le Pen, gained a mere 0.74 percent in the 1974 presidential election and did not gather enough support to qualify for candidacy in the 1981 presidential election.

Given these dismal electoral showings, it is no surprise that the Front National was met with dismissive reactions from the Socialist and Gaullist parties during this period. The mainstream parties ignored the niche party and its policy suggestions. Issues of law and order – the CMP category I use as a proxy for immigration (Budge et al. 2001) – were missing altogether from the Socialists' election manifestos from 1973 to 1981, whereas the topic of multiculturalism was discussed in an average of less than 3 percent of each manifesto. Law and order was similarly de-emphasized in the Gaullists' manifestos, being mentioned on average in less than 2 percent of the sentences in the manifesto for each of these three elections. Praise for either traditional morality or multiculturalism across these elections was also scarce.

The significance of the Front National as an organization was similarly downplayed by the French political establishment. On several occasions from 1979 to 1983, Le Pen complained of his party's marginalization and isolation by the other political parties. As recorded in reports by the Ministry of the Interior, Le Pen accused the mainstream political parties of "refusing voice to all who do not belong to their system by preventing access to radio and television stations."[36] While Le Pen's complaint was no doubt a means of attracting attention, it was true that the French government, and thus the party in power, had control over media content and, as will be shown in the next section, had the power to regulate the FN's coverage.

Although the issue of immigration and its niche party proponent were not publicly discussed or prioritized by the Socialists and Gaullists during the 1970s, it was not out of ignorance. Socialist Party documents of the time reveal that the party engaged in internal discussions about immigration and immigrants and was aware of the policy stances of the more vocal political parties. By February 1981, the PS had established a national commission on immigrants, and that body had deliberated over possible policy positions on immigration and immigrant rights.[37] Much like the British parties when they first faced the Green Party and its newly introduced issue, the PS repeatedly emphasized the need to research the topic before rushing to enact any policy decisions.[38] Such hesitation continued

---

[36] Confidential report on a press conference by Le Pen on May 30, 1979, recorded in Archives du Ministère de l'Intérieur, Archives Nationales, Dossiers autour des élections présidentielles, 940421/9.

[37] Archives de l'OURS, "Les Socialistes et l'Immigration," *Documentation socialiste*, special issue #2, (Paris: Club Socialiste du Livre, 1980); Archives de la FNSP, Parti Socialiste, Commission Nationale Immigrés, "Collectivités locales et immigration: Document du travail issue des journées nationales 'Collectivités locales et immigration' du 6 décembre 1980 et 8 février 1981, organisées conjointement par le Secrétariat aux Collectivités locales et par le Secrétariat international (secteur immigration)."

[38] Archives de la FNSP, Parti Socialiste, Commission Nationale Immigrés, "Collectivités locales et immigration: Document du travail issue des journées nationales 'Collectivités locales et

despite awareness both that racism and racist attacks were on the rise and that "this situation is used by the Right to strengthen its power while exacerbating, in particular, feelings of concern and insecurity."[39]

The RPR also consciously downplayed the topic of immigration during the 1970s. Under the Chirac government of 1974–76, for example, attempts made by Secrétaire d'Etat aux Immigrés André Postel-Vinay to address the living conditions of immigrants were blocked. According to the resignation letter sent by Postel-Vinay to Chirac, the prime minister had expressed his total disinterest in pursuing this topic.[40] Even out of office, the RPR maintained its dismissive stance, citing a need to maintain the Gaullist status quo – i.e., no stance on immigration – when faced with a UDF government proposal on immigrant repatriation.

It is interesting to note that, although the RPR and PS remained largely silent in public on the issue of immigration and immigrants during the 1970s, these topics were prioritized by the Communist Party (PCF) and, to a lesser extent, the UDF.[41] Indeed, since the late 1960s, the PCF had been a vocal opponent of continued legal and illegal immigration to France, specifically the arrival of foreign workers. Motivated by a desire to protect the wage level of French workers against an influx of cheap foreign labor, the PCF and its affiliated union (the CGT) campaigned for an end to immigration and, toward the end of the 1970s, the repatriation of those foreigners already living in France.[42] Although the PCF's repeated efforts to popularize this issue were noted by the other mainstream parties, the Communist Party was unsuccessful at forcing the issue into the political and public debate.

1981–86: The Growing Front National Threat and the Asymmetrical Response of the Mainstream Party Actors

With the awakening of the Front National's electorate in the early 1980s, mainstream party attention to the immigration issue began to grow. Although the Front National got off to a slow start with Le Pen's failure to appear on the presidential ballot in 1981 and the party's poor score of 0.2 percent in the 1981 legislative elections, its electoral potential became evident beginning in 1983. In the municipal elections of that year, lists presented by the Front National had some success in isolated districts. The list led by Jean-Marie Le Pen in

immigration' du 6 décembre 1980 et 8 février 1981, organisées conjointement par le Secrétariat aux Collectivités locales et par le Secrétariat international (secteur immigration)," pp. 1, 6.

[39] Ibid., 4.

[40] Postel-Vinay writes, "You said at the 'Comité restreint' on the 12th of July that 'the question of social housing had no importance in your eyes'" (Weil 1991: 366).

[41] As noted in a report to the Ministry of the Interior dated October 1967, "Except for the PCF, the French political parties are not interested in any direct manner in foreign workers." Archives du Ministère de l'Intérieur, Renseignements Généraux, "L'Immigration: Situation-Problèmes Actuels." 900353 art 11 liasse 3.

[42] CGT stands for Confédération général du travail, or the General Confederation of Labor. Archives du Ministère de l'Intérieur, Renseignements Généraux, "Notes de Police sur les problèmes liés à l'immigration, 1960–1981." 900353 art 11, liasse 3.

the twentieth *arrondisement* of Paris, for example, received 11.3 percent of the vote.[43] Only a few months later in the municipal by-election in the Socialist town of Dreux, the list led by FN candidate Jean-Pierre Stirbois shocked the community, and the country, by capturing a record 16.7 percent of the votes in the first round (RPR 1997: 1). This was followed by the 1984 EP elections in which the Front National gained 2.2 million votes, or 12.1 percent. Although it was claimed that the exemplary performance of the Front National was either the result of idiosyncratic circumstances or a function of the second-order elections in which it participated,[44] the popularity of the niche party at the national level and in the 1985 cantonal elections demonstrated its staying power.

The repeatedly high electoral scores of the Front National should have caused the mainstream parties to sit up and take notice. Not only had the niche party indirectly caused mainstream party candidates to be eliminated from the second round of the vote in some local elections, but the Front National was also stealing the mainstream parties' voters in the supranational and subnational elections. Analyses of the 1984 EP elections demonstrate that the xenophobic party drew voters from all major political parties. However, it was the electorate of the Right and specifically the RPR that was most affected; a SOFRES poll finds that 25 percent of those who voted for the FN came from the RPR camp, with an additional 34 percent characterizing their political partisanship as that of the extreme right.[45] On the contrary, only 11 percent of the FN's vote came from supporters of the Left or Ecologists. Moreover, the survey data suggest that RPR votes for the Front National cannot be dismissed as mere protest votes: consistent with the possibility of sincere, issue-based voting, almost half of RPR partisans approved of Le Pen's stances on immigration, and security and justice in 1984.[46]

According to the PSO theory, when faced with a significant defection of its voters, the opposition RPR party is expected to act defensively and employ an accommodative strategy. The FN was not only jeopardizing the RPR's electoral standing in the short term; its ideological attractiveness to Gaullist voters also threatened to eviscerate the Gaullist Party in the long run. Continuation of the RPR's dismissive strategy would likely fail to stem the flow of motivated issue voters to the radical right party. Although it might reduce the salience of the immigration issue for some voters, dismissive behavior would not challenge the FN's ownership of the anti-immigration position.

---

[43] The FN won only 211 out of a possible 501,278 seats in the municipal councils across France. However, the contestation of these local elections increased the public's familiarity with the Front National and its policies (Perrineau 1996: 42).

[44] Perrineau verbalized a thought that many political scientists and journalists entertained. He stated (1996: 45): "One could imagine that this success, received in a European election without clear and mobilizing stakes (only 56.8 percent voter turnout), would know no future and that the FN's electorate would redistribute itself in the cantonal elections of March 1985 among the candidates of the traditional Right. That was not the case."

[45] This breakdown roughly mirrored that seen in the municipal elections. Archives de la FNSP, Dossiers de Presse, "M. Jean-Marie Le Pen: un activiste," *Le Monde*, June 20, 1984.

[46] Of the RPR partisans, 44 percent somewhat or strongly agreed with "the campaign led by Jean-Marie Le Pen on the theme of immigration" (Ysmal 1984: 11); "L'Extrême Droite" 1985: 180.

By contrast, the Socialists are expected to pursue an adversarial strategy. This approach would undermine the co-optative efforts of the Gaullists as well as play to the PS's own electoral base – voters who were less attracted to the xenophobic positions of the FN than their RPR counterparts. That said, the adoption of adversarial strategies would not be costless for the PS. Immigration was a cross-cutting issue drawing supporters from the Left as well as the traditional Right. Working-class and unemployed voters in the traditional Socialist electorate in particular were susceptible to the appeals of the niche party (Hainsworth 2000: 21; RPR 1997: 3).

The Enemy of the Socialist Party's Enemy Is Its Friend. Yet, as the behavior of these two parties during the 1981–86 electoral period showed, the predicted strategies were not equally pursued by the French mainstream parties. The Socialist Party, for its part, waged a consistent and intensive adversarial campaign against the xenophobic niche party. This campaign emerged out of multiple internal party meetings, party summer conferences (*stage d'été*), and reams of reports on the Front National and the mainstream parties of the Right.[47] The assault extended along three lines: (1) the adoption of policy positions opposite to those of the Front National, (2) a formal condemnation of the niche party including a refusal to participate in any electoral pacts or coalitions with it, and (3) perhaps its most powerful and unusual weapon, the institutional facilitation of the Front National's electoral entrenchment.

In terms of policy, the Mauroy government relaxed some of the harsh anti-immigrant laws adopted by the UDF government; it eliminated the restriction on the formation of immigrant associations and strengthened the previously lax "formal protection of immigrant families against arbitrary administrative action" (Schain 1994: 260). In addition, the party elucidated its own policy on immigration. What emerged was a dual policy of control and integration. As if accepting the FN's claim that immigration was linked to problems of unemployment, the PS upheld the 1974 ban on immigration to France and strengthened its stance against illegal immigration.[48] This action no doubt helped to legitimize the radical right party's framing of the immigration issue. At the same time, however, the Socialists came out firmly against the FN's anti-immigrant policy position. Taking cues from its voters, the PS affirmed its commitment to the integration of existing immigrants into the French political and economic arenas.[49] This commitment

---

[47] See, for example, Archives de l'OURS, Archives Christophe Prochasson, 48APO5, PS, "Stage d'été sur 'le PS face à la droite et à l'extrême droite'," July 13–19, 1986: 2; Archives de la FNSP, Fonds Weil, WE 56: Associations pour les immigrés et prises de positions des partis face aux immigrés, Georgina Dufoix, "Grandes lignes de votre politique," August 14, 1984.

[48] Although its control measures were in some respects stronger than those put in place by the previous UDF government, the PS's reputation was colored more by its integrationist, "pro-immigrant" approach (Silverman 1992: 60–2). Surveys have shown that the public perceived the immigration policy of the PS to be much more liberal than that of the RPR. Calculations from Pierce 1996.

[49] Archives de la FNSP, Fonds Weil, WE 56: Associations pour les immigrés et prises de positions des partis face aux immigrés, Dufoix, August 14, 1984; Archives de l'OURS, Archives Christophe Prochasson, 48APO5, PS, July 13–19, 1986: 2.

extended to ideological and financial support by the PS and Socialist government for pro-immigrant organizations such as SOS-Racisme (Faux et al. 1994:
29). Finally, the PS created a new ministerial post focusing on immigration and
immigrants – aptly named the Minister of National Solidarity – thereby emphasizing its role as the natural ally of immigrants and the natural foe of the Front
National.[50] The PS was the only mainstream party at the time to clearly oppose
the FN.

Beyond these legislative and organizational measures, the PS sought to keep
the Front National in the public eye. Members of the Socialist Party regularly
vilified the niche party and its demagogue leader in the national press. At the
March 1984 meeting of the Comité directeur, the PS officials decided to "wage
an offensive ideological battle against the Right and its extremists. As well as
protests, the party also agreed to host a conference on 'the extreme right and its
complicity.'"[51] This was one of several such conferences on the extreme right
that the PS held in the early 1980s. This constant demonization of the niche
party was designed both to solidify the FN's reputation as the owner of the
anti-immigration and anti-immigrant position and to reinforce the niche party's
credibility as a main actor within the French political system. Indeed, in response
to the claims by some members of the Right that ignoring the FN would lead
to its disappearance, the head of the Socialist Party justified his party's actions as
follows:

Each time that a movement of the extreme right develops which fosters racism, antipar-
liamentarism, and brutality, one finds good souls who say that the evil will be calmed if it
is not discussed. For me, that sets off alarms. One can never be too vigilant.[52]

Although Poperen's remarks seem to make sense logically, they nevertheless
reflect a much more devious and instrumental use of the xenophobic niche
party.

That view of the Front National as a tactical instrument emerges from the
organizational strategies that the Socialists used against the niche party. As part
of their adversarial strategy, the PS refused to appear on the same stage with Le
Pen or any other FN official during a debate. Just as the British Labour Party
officials had done in the 1970s when confronted with their radical right party –
the National Front – PS National Secretary Poperen left a television interview
program in 1984 when he heard that Le Pen had arrived.[53] Avoiding discussions
with the Front National might seem to contradict Poperen's previous emphasis
on confronting "the evil." But, this injunction against appearing on stage with the

---

[50] This ministry was renamed Ministère des Affaires sociales et de la Solidarité nationale during the
third Mauroy government of March 1983 to July 1984. It was in this ministry that the Secrétaire
d'Etat aux Immigrés was located.

[51] Archives de la FNSP, Dossiers de Presse, Gilles Bresson, "Le PS aux anti-Le Pen: Du calme!"
Libération, May 26–7, 1984.

[52] Archives de la FNSP, Dossiers de Presse, Jean Poperen, secrétaire national du PS, interviewed in
"'La bande des 4' juge Le Pen," *Le Point*, February 13, 1984.

[53] Archives de la FNSP, Dossiers de Presse, Françoise Berger, "Faut-il parler avec Le Pen?" *Libération*,
June 19, 1984.

FN had less to do with silencing the radical right candidate and more to do with increasing public awareness of the FN and of the PS's opposition to its policies. In fact, the Socialist Party actively worked to ensure that the Front National was present at these events. Mitterrand's letters and interviews show that Le Pen only got invited to appear on such shows in the first place because of the Socialist President's intervention with the television and radio stations![54]

As if publicly chastising the FN's issue positions and boosting the party into the media spotlight only to demonize it were not sufficient, the PS employed a third form of the adversarial strategy. In 1985, the Socialists pushed through legislation that reformed the electoral rules for the 1986 legislative election: proportional representation rules would replace the two-ballot plurality system. The rationale behind this reform was twofold. Despite the fact that Mitterrand, "in principle, preferred majority voting to proportional representation" (Tiersky 1994: 123–4), he was a pragmatist. He recognized that PR would lessen the PS's expected seat loss in the forthcoming election.[55] In an interview, Mitterrand explained "[the reforms to education] have cost us a government. Next, it is necessary for me to salvage the situation with proportional representation" (Giesbert 1990: 235).

But this was not the most important reason for the institutional reform. As Minister Rocard noted during the April 1985 Council of Ministers meeting in which the decision to adopt PR was made, "this electoral system will not, under any circumstance, be able to provide us with the victory" (quoted in Giesbert 1990: 237). Rather, the evidence suggests that proportional representation was chosen because it would eliminate the "wasted vote logic," allowing the Front National to gain seats at the expense of the RPR.[56] As Tiersky (1994: 135–7) explains:

PR meant National Front votes would be "useful," would not be wasted as in a majority system where the FN would lose almost everywhere because it had no allies with whom to seek majorities. . . . Mitterrand hoped that the PR law, by maximizing the National Front's success, would split the right-wing vote enough to prevent an RPR-UDF victory.

---

[54] In response to a complaint by Le Pen about the lack of media coverage for his party, François Mitterrand wrote to the FN leader on June 22, 1982: "The incident to which you called my attention should not happen again. From now on, I will ask the Minister of Communication to alert the heads of the radio and television companies of the omission of which you spoke" (Faux et al. 1994: 21). And Mitterrand followed through on this promise. As he informed the authors of *Plumes de l'ombre* (Faux, Legrand, and Perez 1991: xx), "I told the television stations to make him (Le Pen) come." According to Faux et al. (1994: 21), "As of the following day, June 29, the guest on the 11 o'clock news program on TF1 was Jean-Marie Le Pen!"

[55] Interview with Gérard Grunberg, political scientist, Paris, June 2004.

[56] This understanding of the Socialists' institutional reform is shared by Pascal Perrineau, as shown in this excerpt of an interview between him and the authors of *La main droite de Dieu*: "For Pascal Perrineau, the change in the electoral law was part of the President's strategy: [Perrineau quoted] 'With these elections, one sees well the management of the Le Pen phenomenon. One waits for 1985, after the cantonal elections, to give a political opening to the Front. It is, at this moment, the use of PR.'" To the interviewers' retort that this "was part of the 110 propositions of candidate Mitterrand in 1981," Perrineau responded, "'Yes, but why wait until 1985 to put it into place?'" Interview of Pascal Perrineau, March 17, 1994 quoted in Faux et al. 1994: 29.

This rationale for adopting PR was alluded to by both adversaries and advocates of the reform inside and outside of the PS. Members of the RPR regularly accused the PS of using the electoral change to boost the Front National (and undermine the RPR).[57] In a 1998 RPR document entitled *Socialist Party, Front National: Dangerous Liaisons*, the author, RPR Député Nicole Catala charged (RPR 1998: 3):

It was again François Mitterrand who shortly thereafter [after the 1985 cantonal elections] caused the Front National to enter Parliament. The adoption of PR rules was decided for the 1986 legislative elections as a quasi-acknowledged plan for dividing the votes of the Right and causing FN deputies to be elected to the Assemblée Nationale.

According to the document (1998: 1), "weakening the republican Right by diverting a part of its electorate to the extreme right" was a "persistent political objective of François Mitterrand."

These claims might be dismissed as the "cheap talk" of embittered losers, but a similar logic was expressed by those within the PS.[58] Mitterrand acknowledged that "Proportional representation is an electoral system against the RPR" (Giesbert 1990: 236). Rocard, a Socialist opposed to institutional change, alluded to the mechanism by which this would be achieved in the April 1985 Council of Ministers meeting:

You [the other PS Ministers] have chosen the most defeatist solution. The most dangerous, also, because you are going to encourage the entry of the extreme right into the Palais Bourbon.[59]

Fostering the electoral and legislative prospects of the FN was consistent with a larger Socialist strategy already articulated by 1984. According to then-Minister of Social Affairs, Pierre Bérégovoy:

We have every interest in pushing the FN. It will render the Right ineffective. The more the FN is strong, the more we will be undefeatable. It is a historic opportunity for the Socialists.[60]

The FN was viewed by the PS as a weapon to be wielded against the Gaullists.

Although the Socialists' actions were driven by electoral concerns, it should be noted that their manipulation of the immigration issue, the electoral rules, and the anti-immigrant party's success was not necessarily at odds with a desire to ensure the passage of pro-immigrant policies; there was no strict tradeoff between

---

[57] Similar charges are levied by Alain Juppé during his interview on "Elections 92: Le grand débat." Archives de l'OURS, Transcript of "Elections 92: Le grand débat," March 5, 1992 at 20h50.

[58] Unlike the RPR, internal opponents of the Socialists' adversarial tactics did not attempt to publicly undermine the strategy.

[59] The Palais Bourbon is the building that holds the Assemblée Nationale. Rocard quoted in Giesbert 1990: 237. Due to his opposition to what he saw as the manipulation of the electoral rules to aid the FN, Michel Rocard resigned from the Fabius government. Interview with Michel Rocard, Former PS Prime Minister, Minister, and Député, Cambridge, MA, February 21, 2002. Interview with Gérard Grunberg, Paris, France, June 2004.

[60] Bérégovoy interview with Giesbert, June 21, 1984 quoted in Giesbert 1990: 15.

the Socialists' electoral objectives and any policy objectives that they had.[61] As the preceding evidence indicates, the PS's adversarial strategy was designed to use the FN to reduce the RPR's vote by enough to minimize the likelihood of Gaullist parliamentary victory. But dividing the Right's electorate and keeping the RPR from government would also reduce the possibility that anti-immigrant policies – policies that the PS opposed and policies that the RPR would come to adopt – would be enacted.[62] Convincing voters that the Front National was the true anti-immigrant party was, therefore, also a means of dooming anti-immigrant policy.

A Dismissive Strategy by a Divided Gaullist Party. As the more threatened mainstream party, the RPR is expected, according to the strategic choice model, to have responded promptly and accommodatively to the Front National.[63] A strong co-optative reaction was even more critical given the all-out adversarial battle waged simultaneously by the Socialist Party. However, the behavior of the Gaullists did not follow this prediction. Rather, between 1981 and 1986, the RPR vacillated between dismissive and accommodative behavior. This contradictory approach was a result of party factionalism both within the national-level elite as well as between national- and local-level politicians.[64] These conflicts not only slowed the reaction time of the national RPR party, but also decreased the effectiveness of the strategies that were eventually enacted.

The RPR's official national party strategy toward the Front National for much of the electoral period can best be described as dismissive. According to RPR General Secretary Bernard Pons:

The only "Le Pen phenomenon" is to discover that it is a phenomenon. Rather it is a constant of the French political life. . . . [I]t is not the time to dramatize; that would be a political mistake.[65]

By not validating the niche party, the RPR hoped to make voters forget the FN, as voters had forgotten countless other new parties that emerged on the legislative and European parliamentary ballots in France at each election. To this end, the RPR downplayed immigration and security issues in its public addresses following

---

[61] It is true that the Socialists' initial adoption of an adversarial strategy would encourage the RPR to adopt an accommodative strategy, in which the RPR would push through anti-immigrant legislation. It is thus tempting to claim that the PS pursued a strategy that ran counter to its policy interests. However, given the degree of RPR voter defection to the FN, accommodation was the rational strategy for the RPR *regardless* of the behavior of the Socialists. And as noted in the text, the PS's adversarial strategy was ultimately designed to keep the RPR out of power and, thus, keep it from passing anti-immigrant laws.

[62] The assumption – not unreasonable – was that control of the government would continue to alternate between the left and right party blocs, and specifically between the RPR and PS.

[63] This prediction is made by both the standard spatial model and my PSO theory.

[64] Three different factions were identified within the RPR during this time. Archives de la FNSP, Dossiers de Presse, "Le ralliement de certains militants du RPR et de l'UDF aide le Front national à étendre son implantation," *Le Monde*, January 11, 1984: 9.

[65] Archives de la FNSP, Dossiers de Presse, Bernard Pons, secrétaire général du RPR, interviewed in "'La bande des 4' juge Le Pen," *Le Point*, February 13, 1984.

the 1981 elections. No RPR document was released on these subjects. Similarly, the leader of the RPR, Jacques Chirac, ignored requests by Le Pen to form a national-level RPR-FN alliance.[66]

While the national party leaders maintained a policy of disregarding the Front National, division grew within the RPR. High-ranked national-level party elite began to express concern over the future loss of Gaullist voters to the niche party. Given that the RPR provided the largest number of supporters to the new party, this was not an unfounded fear. Ignoring the official dismissive stance of the party, these well-placed elite, whose ranks included Charles Pasqua and Jean-Pierre Soisson, advocated an accommodative strategy; they expressed their affinity for the ideological and organizational convergence of the mainstream and niche parties (Gaspard 1995: 130). Pasqua made a direct appeal to former, issue-oriented RPR voters when he declared that he shared "common values" with the FN.[67] This was followed by support from him and others for local-level coalitions between the RPR and the FN – coalitions that were expressly rejected and even forbidden by Chirac (Gaspard 1995: 128–9).

As this last point suggests, this factionalism was not restricted to the national level. The occasion of the 1983 municipal elections emphasized how pervasive the internal party division over strategy was. In the town of Dreux, the local RPR elite entered into a coalition with the Front National for the first and second rounds of the 1983 elections. This alliance was repeated in an election rematch held six months later, an election which led to the victory of the combined RPR-UDF-FN ticket and the installation of FN Jean-Pierre Stirbois as the deputy mayor of the town. This maneuver revealed the desire of local RPR officials to consolidate their power and benefit, if not from a programmatic position similar to the FN, then at least from an organizational arrangement. Comparable alliances were formed for local elections in Aulnay and Valhomme.[68]

But in using FN support to assure RPR officials local-level offices, these alliances only intensified the bitter battle within the RPR over strategy. Jacques Chirac was joined by prominent Gaullist elite such as former Prime Minister Jacques Chaban-Delmas and Olivier Stirn in his condemnation of the local-level coalitions. However, the fragmentation of the RPR – both at the national and local levels – meant that little could be done to ensure the discipline of defectors. Consequently, not only did supporters of these alliances go unpunished,[69] but their accommodative message competed with the dismissive behavior of their

---

[66] Archives de la FNSP, Dossiers de Presse, "M. Jean-Marie Le Pen," *Le Monde*, May 20, 1981; Archives de la FNSP, Dossiers de Presse, "Le Front national appelle les classes moyennes à politiser leurs actions revendicatives," *Le Monde*, September 21, 1982.

[67] Reference from Archives de l'OURS, *Lutter contre l'extrême droite: des outils pour l'action*, 1990: 9. As cited in Lagrange and Perrineau (1989: 228n1), Pasqua stated: "On the whole, the Front National is interested in the same preoccupations, the same values as the majority."

[68] Archives de l'OURS, *Lutter contre l'extrême droite: des outils pour l'action*, 1990: 10.

[69] Supporters of the alliances included Jean Lecanuet, Alain Carrignon, and Jean-Pierre Soisson. Gaspard 1995: 130.

RPR colleagues. Internal policy debate resulted in a contradictory strategy. The presence of accommodative actions, therefore, reduced the effectiveness of the official dismissive stance.

1986–88: The Entrenchment of the Front National

It was clear by the 1985 cantonal elections and certainly by the run-up to the 1986 legislative elections that the Front National would become a more important and electorally successful party challenger. In 1985, the 1,521 FN candidates garnered an average of 10.44 percent of the vote in the districts they contested, or 8.8 percent of all ballots cast nationally (Bréchon 1995: 50). Expectations for the 1986 legislative and regional elections were almost as high. With these elections to be conducted under the more permissive rules of proportional representation, polls were reporting that the niche party would gain not only one but many seats in the National Assembly. The election results bore out these predictions: the Front National list captured 9.9 percent of the vote and thirty-five seats. In the regional elections, the FN's score was similar at 9.5 percent of the vote.[70] The radical right party was being pronounced equally attractive at local, regional, and national levels of governance.

Of the two mainstream parties, the RPR continued to be harder hit by the FN threat. Although a third of the FN's 1984 electorate returned to their parties of origin in 1986 – many of them to the RPR – the Front National continued to steal voters from the Gaullists. According to a SOFRES survey (SOFRES 1988), 20 percent of the 1986 Front National voters claimed to be partisans of either the RPR or UDF. This number does not include those former RPR partisans who, by 1986, already professed an allegiance to the Front National.[71] By contrast, only 8 percent of FN voters claimed to be partisans of the Left, down from 10 percent in the 1984 EP elections (SOFRES 1988: 139).

In this electoral climate of continued Gaullist vote loss, the PSO theory's expectations for the mainstream parties' strategies remain unchanged. Despite the fact that the RPR almost doubled its representation in the National Assembly and formed a government under the leadership of Jacques Chirac, the Gaullist Party could not afford to ignore (through dismissive tactics) or encourage (through adversarial ones) the defection of its anti-immigrant voters to the Front National; the RPR's lead was not secure, with the RPR owing much of its success to its electoral pact with the UDF. Moreover, even though the RPR pledged to reinstate the two-ballot plurality rules for the next legislative election, the party could not count on this institutional change to automatically return its defected voters from the FN. Under these conditions, the RPR's best option was to pursue accommodative tactics in order to halt voter loss and facilitate voter recovery. Although

---

[70] This resulted in the election of 137 FN officials. Hainsworth 2000: 20.
[71] The SOFRES poll finds that 57 percent of 1986 FN voters self-identified as FN partisans, of which many were former Gaullist partisans (SOFRES 1988).

weakened by the legislative election, the PS was not sufficiently threatened by the FN for accommodative tactics to be productive. Rather, adversarial tactics remained the Socialists' best means to boost their relative electoral standing.

The Gaullists' (Divided) Accommodation. The new electoral period ushered in a changed Gaullist strategy. No longer were Le Pen and his xenophobic party dismissed as a *feu de paille*, a straw fire that was more smoke than substance. The electoral success of the Front National in the 1986 legislative and regional elections had largely erased that image. The RPR was ready to use programmatic tactics to recover and retain its voters. Co-optation was the strategy of choice.

Following an electoral campaign in which it had downplayed the immigration issue, the RPR government reacted swiftly to the perceived Front National threat. Within six months of the legislative election, the government had submitted to the National Assembly two laws restricting the rights of immigrants in France and access to French nationality. The first bill, known as the Pasqua Law after the right-leaning minister of the interior, became infamous for easing governmental restrictions on the expulsion of immigrants.[72] Like its companion bill, which sought to remove the automatic conferral of citizenship on those born in France,[73] the Pasqua law was an explicit measure to "woo the extreme right electorate" (Blatt 1996: 333).

Not only did the content of these laws parallel the demands voiced by the Front National,[74] but the RPR officials also promoted these reforms by adopting the language of their xenophobic competitors. Indeed, as recounted by Silverman (1992: 65), "In May 1987 [Charles Pasqua] showed himself capable of sinking to the same rhetorical depths as Le Pen when he promised to deport illegal immigrants in train-loads." Pasqua's use of Nazi images represented one extreme, but even the more moderate members of the RPR were not opposed to invoking FN-style imagery of a France losing its culture, language, values, and identity to a population of rapidly multiplying immigrants.[75]

Although the party mobilized around programmatic forms of FN co-optation,[76] the internal divisions that had previously sabotaged the timely and

---

[72] In addition, the bill increased the financial requirements for entering France.

[73] This reform of the French Nationality Code was eventually rescinded due to wide-scale protests. Instead, the government established a nonpartisan advisory body known as the Nationality Commission. In the end, the commission recommended the implementation of the controversial nationality reforms originally sought by the government. Blatt 1996: 349.

[74] FN official Jean-Pierre Stirbois is famous for urging "immigrants from beyond the Mediterranean" to "go back to [their] huts." From a speech by Stirbois in Nice in 1982, quoted in Hainsworth 2000: 24.

[75] For a typical example, see the 1988 presidential manifesto of Jacques Chirac. Service de Presse du RPR, "La décennie du renouveau," (Paris: RPR, 1988).

[76] In addition, the RPR instituted an institutional form of accommodation. It changed the electoral rules for the legislative elections back to the previously used two-ballot plurality format. According to institutional theories, this change was expected to reduce the number of votes and seats obtained by the FN.

consistent tactics of the RPR had not been fully quelled. During the Chirac government, factionalism emerged once again, and the intraparty quarrels of the RPR were forced into the public spotlight. At issue were the extremism of the party's programmatic accommodation, as embodied in the Pasqua law and the reform of the Code of Nationality, and the RPR's decision to enter alliances with the Front National.[77] The party's policy, largely formed by hard-liners such as Minister of the Interior Charles Pasqua and Minister of Security Robert Pandraud, was considered by liberals to be both electorally and morally dangerous. These more moderate ministers, including Philippe Séguin, Claude Malhuret, and Michel Noir, worried that pandering so clearly to Front National demands would cause the RPR to cede the political center (and its voters) to their UDF political opponents (Blatt 1996: 332–3). Although none of these disgruntled RPR members directly jeopardized the passage of these bills – the Pasqua bill passed and the Code of Nationality Reform was withdrawn in response to Leftist and popular protest[78] – they undermined the unitary image of the party by expressing their opposition in the media and by voting with the Leftist parties for amendments to their own government's bills.[79]

Internal party divisions over the issue of alliances with the FN had an even greater impact on the RPR's image and the effectiveness of its strategy. Recall that alliances are organizational forms of accommodation. Electoral pacts and coalitions between the RPR and the FN had been concluded at both the local and regional levels during this electoral period and the preceding one.[80] Whereas the RPR leadership had previously ignored all discussions of a national-level coalition between the parties, support for such an idea among high-ranking cabinet members now forced the issue onto the agenda.[81] Despite Chirac's prior opposition to such an alliance (Gaspard 1995: 128–9), the position of electoral pragmatism advocated by the RPR hard-liners was given priority in 1987.[82]

However, this shift in policy was neither easily nor quietly accepted by the liberals within the party. Sparking what would come to be called the "Noir scandal," Minister of Foreign Commerce Michel Noir announced to the press that "it is better to lose a Presidential election than to lose one's soul by colluding with Le Pen and his ideas" (Joffrin 1987: 9); this was a clear rejection of the RPR's

---

77 In 1987, seventy RPR députés representing the party hard-liners joined with the FN députés to vote for Pierre Arrighi (FN) for vice president of the National Assembly.

78 The Pasqua bill was passed with unanimous support from the RPR députés. *L'Année politique, économique et sociale en France 1986*, 1987: 128.

79 Six members of the RPR voted in favor of an amendment to the Pasqua law that "would have protected youth under 18 from expulsion under any circumstance." Article from *Le Monde*, July 18, 1986 cited in Blatt 1996: 336.

80 Perrineau 1996: 48; Archives de l'OURS, *Lutter contre l'extrême droite: des outils pour l'action*, 1990: 10; Bréchon 1995: 50–1.

81 Archives de la FNSP, Dossiers de Presse, Catherine Pégard, "Front national: la tactique Pasqua," *Le Point*, October 19, 1987.

82 Archives de la FNSP, Dossiers de Presse, Marie Guilloux and Jean-Michel Thenard, "Chirac siffle Noir hors jeu," *Libération*, May 20, 1987.

co-optative tactics. While, as presidential candidate, Chirac would eventually refuse a second-round alliance with the FN in the 1988 presidential election,[83] Noir's policy statement was not welcomed by the then-prime minister.[84] The intraparty debate that ensued split the party.[85] The RPR emerged as a divided party unable to pursue a consistent accommodative strategy. The voters were sent the mixed message that the RPR both *was* and *was not* the credible owner of the Front National's ideas.

The Continuation of the Socialists' Adversarial Strategy. Once out of office, the Socialists did not let up in their battle to demonize the Front National and thus reinforce its electoral strength. The PS maintained its strategy of keeping the niche party in the center of public debate. The Socialists directly criticized the restrictive and discriminatory policy stances of the niche party in party documents, annual congresses, and the popular press. They focused in particular on the exclusionary immigration and citizenship conceptions put forward by the FN and its affiliated Club de l'Horloge.[86] By presenting the French electorate with the actual proposals of the FN juxtaposed against its own pro-immigrant policies,[87] the PS hoped to "show that the Front National was not a party like the others."[88]

The same message was sent about the FN's leader, Jean-Marie Le Pen. The PS publicized every inappropriate and offensive statement made by Le Pen. For instance, the Socialists repeatedly recounted the FN leader's 1987 dismissal of the Nazi gas chambers as a "small historical detail" (Bréchon 1995: 52). This personalization of the niche party as the vehicle of Le Pen continued into the run-up to the 1988 presidential election. Despite the fact that French campaign documents rarely mention the name of competing candidates, Mitterrand's campaign literature explicitly named and rebuked Le Pen for being "racist and hateful" and for "using immigrants as scapegoats."[89]

The ultimate goal behind these strong adversarial attacks against the Front National was the strengthening of the Socialists' own electoral position. Vilifying the FN and its leader was a means of reinforcing the PS's opposition to the FN's position, while at the same time discouraging the defection of any Socialists to the

---

[83] Chirac did this knowing that he would not win the presidency without Le Pen's support. Interview with Yvan Blot, FN, 3rd in command, Paris, February 16, 1999.

[84] Archives de la FNSP, Dossiers de Presse, Guilloux and Thenard, 1987.

[85] Archives de la FNSP, Dossiers de Presse, Sylviane Stein, "RPR: la fronde des rénovateurs," *L'Express*, May 19, 1988; Archives de la FNSP, Dossiers de Presse, Claude Weill, "Extrême-droite: pas d'ennemis pour Toubon," *Le Nouvel Observateur*, August 27, 1987.

[86] Archives de la FNSP, Fonds Weil, WE 56 Dr 1, Le Guen, de la Gontrie, Storah, and Terquem, "Rapport sur l'immigration," (Paris: PS, 1986).

[87] The PS considered itself to be the natural party of immigrants. During this period, it even put forward a proposal to extend local voting rights to noncitizens. While this policy was never enacted due to both internal party pressure and external party opposition, it was emphasized by the PS as a sign of its concern for this population. Ibid., 8.

[88] Archives de l'OURS, *Lutter contre l'extrême droite: des outils pour l'action*, 1990: 8.

[89] Archives du CEVIPOF, Professions de foi, 1988 presidential election campaign flyer for Mitterrand.

niche party. But, perhaps more importantly, this strategy was a means for the PS to increase its *relative* electoral strength. Reinforcing the FN's anti-immigration issue ownership while tainting that very policy stance that the Gaullists were attempting to co-opt was a way for the Socialists to weaken their mainstream opponent.

That the public would draw a connection between the xenophobic positions of the Front National and the Gaullists was not left to chance. During this period of RPR accommodation, the PS's adversarial strategy involved speaking out not only against the Front National but also against the Gaullists. And the RPR government's series of new bills on immigration and nationality provided ample fodder for the Socialists. As mentioned earlier, the Socialists rallied against what they called the overly restrictive nature of both the Pasqua and Nationality laws. President Mitterrand – typically a silent president in this period of cohabitation – even voiced his disagreement with the Nationality law.[90] Consistent with their efforts to strengthen the Front National's issue ownership and vote, Socialist parliamentarians accused the Gaullist government of pandering to the demands of the FN.[91] A clear message was being sent: the Front National is the original anti-immigration and anti-immigrant party, and the RPR is merely its xenophobic copy (Brubaker 1992: 154).

1988–93: The Strengthening of the Niche Party

Following campaigns dominated by discussions of immigration, nationality, and security, the 1988 presidential and legislative electoral results were naturally seen as indicators of the credibility of mainstream party policies in these areas. Unfortunately for the RPR, the message revealed in the vote percentages was not one it wanted to hear. In the presidential election, Le Pen emerged with 14.4 percent of the vote on the first ballot. Furthermore, despite the reinstatement of the two-ballot plurality system with its "wasted vote" effect in the legislative elections, the niche party essentially maintained its support level with 9.8 percent of the vote.[92] Even though the Front National only captured one seat in the National Assembly, these electoral scores signaled that the radical right party was not a transitory actor.[93] This perception was further reinforced by the FN's results in the 1989 elections to the European Parliament: with more than 11 percent of the vote, the party gained ten seats.

The Front National's electoral threat was very much alive, especially for the RPR. In the first round of the presidential election, more than 12 percent of

---

[90] According to a Mitterrand spokesperson, the law "was inspired by a philosophy that he [Mitterrand] did not share." Quoted in Brubaker 1992: 154.

[91] During the Senate's discussion of the Pasqua law, Socialist Senator Jean-Pierre Bayle accused the government of giving into vote-seeking tendencies "by equating immigration with the issue of insecurity." Quoted in *L'Année politique, économique et sociale en France 1986*, 1987: 135.

[92] This percentage represents a slight decline from the last election in the actual number of votes received: from 2.7 million in 1986 to 2.4 million in 1988. RPR 1997: 5.

[93] Yann Piat was elected FN député in a by-election in December of 1988.

RPR partisans voted for Le Pen according to the 1988 CEVIPOF survey.[94] By contrast, a negligible number of FN partisans voted for Chirac, the RPR candidate in the first round.[95] And this trend did not change in the second round of the election by as much as the RPR hoped. Due to the refusal of Chirac to enter into any second-round alliances with Le Pen – another sign of the conflicted Gaullist accommodative strategy – Chirac gained only 65 percent of the FN votes (Platone 1994: 69). Almost 20 percent went to Mitterrand. With Mitterrand winning by less than 10 percentage points, it has been argued that Chirac's failure to fully co-opt the FN voters cost him the presidency (Platone 1994: 66).

In the legislative elections that followed, the RPR continued to lose voters to the niche party. According to the 1988 CEVIPOF study, which was conducted before the legislative elections, 5.8 percent of the RPR's 1986 voters and 3.8 percent of its partisans expected to defect to the FN.[96] Although, in this election, the RPR regained many of the seats previously held by Front National deputies, this legislative recovery was due more to its formation of electoral pacts with UDF candidates than to its popularity relative to the FN.[97] Bréchon (1995: 53) calculates that had the RPR and UDF not presented joint candidates in almost every district, the FN would have been the leading party in more than 120 districts, rather than in just the eight districts.[98] The lasting threat of the niche party to the RPR was even more obvious in the 1989 municipal elections, where the Front National's refusal to withdraw from the second ballot cost the Right victory in eight cities (Blatt 1996: 388).

The Socialists emerged relatively unscathed by the FN vote. In the 1988 CEVIPOF survey conducted after the presidential election, 4 percent of PS partisans reported voting for Le Pen in the first round.[99] According to that same survey, only 1.1 percent of those who voted for the PS in 1986 and 1 percent of PS partisans planned to support the FN in the legislative elections.[100] The party's losses to the Front National in both the 1989 municipal and EP elections were likewise negligible (Duhamel and Jaffré 1990: 240). That said, research has shown

---

[94] This figure was a bit higher – at 17.5 percent – according to Pierce's 1988 French Presidential Election Study. Regardless of the survey, the RPR emerged as the mainstream party losing the largest number of partisans to the FN. According to the Pierce survey, there were as many FN partisans as RPR partisans supporting Le Pen in 1988. Calculations from CEVIPOF 1995 and Pierce 1996.

[95] According to the 1988 survey, 2.2 percent of the 137 FN partisans surveyed voted for Chirac. Calculations from CEVIPOF 1995.

[96] Ibid.

[97] There were also a handful of districts in which the RPR negotiated electoral pacts with FN candidates. The RPR-UDF coalition "owed victory in some twenty districts at least in part to the withdrawal of FN candidates eligible to remain on the second ballot." Article in *Le Monde Dossiers et Documents* of 1988 quoted in Blatt 1996: 388.

[98] The RPR's ability to steal seats from the FN was due to its manipulation of the number of parties competing in each district, not to its credibility as an anti-immigrant party.

[99] Calculations from CEVIPOF 1995.

[100] Ibid.

that the Front National did manage to draw support from the *potential* electorate of the Socialist Party; in the 1988 legislative elections, the niche party attracted 20 percent of working-class voters – traditional supporters of the PS and PCF.[101] However, such a threat was small relative to that faced by the Gaullists.

With the FN remaining a strong, but unequal threat to the French main-stream parties, my theory of strategic choice predicts a continuation of the accommodative-adversarial strategy. Hoping to regain lost voters and their lead over the Socialists, the Gaullists are expected to maintain their accommodative tactics. Although the Socialists entered government short of a majority, their net electoral position could not be improved by appeasing FN voters. A strategic about-face to stem the trickle of potential Le Pen supporters would not be cred-ible given the PS's consistent and intense adversarial tactics to date and would result in the defection of its pro-immigrant voters to other parties. The PS is thus expected to engage in an adversarial strategy.

Another (Divided) Attempt to Quiet the Front National Enemy. Relegated to the opposition, the RPR seemed more determined than ever to solve the electoral problem posed by the vote-stealing Front National.[102] During this period, the Gaullists joined with the UDF to push a strong, unrelenting strategy of issue co-optation. According to a report by Philippe Lamy of the Ministry of the Interior, by 1989, there was a "radicalization of the discourse of the right which borrowed the extreme right's argumentation on immigration and insecurity."[103] In a 1990 joint meeting of the RPR and UDF on the "state of the opposition," the question of immigration was prioritized.[104] The parties maintained their support for the controversial reform of the Code of Nationality as well as their fight against illegal immigration.[105] Where the parties intensified their pursuit of Front National voters was in the area of social rights for immigrants. Adopting the FN's issue position, the RPR and some members of the UDF[106] declared: "A foreigner in France does not have automatically and intrinsically all the rights linked to French

---

[101] This trend would continue in the 1990s. Hainsworth 2000: 21.

[102] According to Ysmal and Cayrol (1996: 132), "it was from the success registered at European elections (confirmed at other elections but without any seats being won) that the FN became a strong force in the conservative camp, presenting the parties of the moderate right with a dilemma: either deal with the FN (join forces with the devil) or risk never gaining a majority."

[103] Archives du Premier Ministre, Fonds de Michel Rocard, "Notes de Guy Carcassonne sur le FN, 1989–91," Box 920622, art. 2, Philippe Lamy, "Le FN et les municipales."

[104] Service de Presse du RPR, Etats Généraux de l'opposition, "Propositions pour une politique de l'immigration," Les débats de la convention à Villepinte, March 31–April 1, 1990.

[105] The Rightist parties also criticized the leniency of the Socialists' policy. In the joint UDF-RPR manifesto prepared for the 1993 legislative elections, the parties vowed to abolish Socialist laws on expulsions (*Lois Joxe*), which they felt were not strict enough. Service de Presse du RPR, "Le projet de l'Union pour la France," (Paris: UDF-RPR, 1993): 11.

[106] The Centre des démocrates sociaux (CDS), which together with the Parti republicain and the Parti radical made up the UDF, disagreed with this statement. Instead, it claimed to support the equal treatment of immigrants and French-born in the area of social protection. Service de Presse du RPR, Etats Généraux de l'opposition, 1990: 7.

citizenship."[107] This exclusionary attitude was clearly demonstrated in the RPR's campaign against the PS's proposal to extend voting rights in local elections to noncitizen residents.[108]

Reinforcing the credibility of this issue co-optation was the FN-inspired language employed by the RPR and its leadership. Raymond Barre spoke of the French being "crippled by the immigration phenomenon."[109] The RPR-UDF's *Propositions for an Immigration Policy* opened with the same dire warning that pervaded the Front National's policy document, *300 Measures for the Rebirth of France*. Alluding to a supposed imbalance caused by the presence of immigrants in a country with significant unemployment and an overstretched welfare state, the RPR-UDF document cautioned: "If measures are not taken to remedy the disequilibria and tensions that are observed in the country, the risk of seeing grave fractures emerge in the heart of the national community inevitably will grow."[110]

In reaction to polling data showing that support for the FN was on the rise, Chirac too played the anti-immigrant card. Fostering the FN's image of immigrants as welfare grubbers, Chirac told an audience in Orléans in 1991:

[There is a] worker who lives in Goutte d'Or, who works along with his wife to earn about 15,000 francs per month. He sees, on the same floor in the HLM,[111] a family consisting of a father, three or four wives, and some twenty kids, who draw 50,000 francs per month in social allowances, of course without working. If you add to this the noise and the smell, the French worker on the same floor goes crazy (quoted in Perrineau 1997: 71).

As if this language were not enough to convince the voter of its anti-immigrant credibility, the RPR released an official statement in 1991 that aimed to reinforce the perceived programmatic proximity between it and the FN. The document claimed that many of the FN's policy positions, including the strengthening of border control, the reform of the asylum laws, and the suppression of the automatic conferral of citizenship, were stolen from the RPR and UDF![112]

Complementing these programmatic tactics, the RPR engaged in an informal pursuit of disgruntled Front National elite. In the months that followed the 1988 legislative elections, three former niche party officials, including the only

[107] Ibid.
[108] In late 1989/early 1990, Jacques Chirac "used a televised address to launch a national petition campaign against granting immigrants the vote and later called for a referendum on the subject" (Blatt 1996: 400).
[109] Archives de la FNSP, Dossiers de Presse, "Mme Danielle Mitterrand ne dit pas non à la proposition de M. Pasqua," *Le Monde*, March 15, 1990.
[110] Service de Presse du RPR, Etats Généraux de l'opposition, "Les débats de la Convention: Immigration," March 31–April 1, 1990: 5.
[111] HLM stands for Habitation à Loyer Modéré. This term refers to state-subsidized, low-income housing.
[112] Service de Presse du RPR, "Communication de la Commission Executive du Rassemblement," November 20, 1991.

FN député, left the niche party for the RPR. While these defections were a direct reaction to Le Pen's offensive behavior,[113] the Gaullists had provided an ideological and organizational environment enticing enough to woo the departed FN leaders.

Yet, as in previous electoral periods, there was a limit to the intensity of the RPR's accommodative campaign. First, although the RPR managed to attract former FN officials to its party, it also lost some of its own leadership to the radical right party. In a particularly harsh blow to the RPR's claim to immigration issue ownership, Yvan Blot, former cabinet director of the General Secretary of the RPR from 1978 to 1983 and member of the central committee of the RPR in 1979, defected to the Front National in 1989 becoming the *third in command* (Mouvement des Jeunes Socialistes 2001: 197).

The issue of coalitions with the FN proved a second source of problems for the coherence of the RPR's accommodative strategy. Although the party approved of RPR-FN alliances in the mid-1980s and even in 1987 – a year before the legislative elections – the balance of forces within the RPR shifted during the second round of the 1988 presidential election, and the anti-alliance camp became dominant. In 1989, the party reaffirmed the decision to reject any local- or national-level coalition with the Front National (Bréchon 1995: 54; Schain 1994: 266). The policy was not fully respected at the local level, where in some smaller cities, FN officials were placed on RPR lists.[114] However, the addition of an adversarial coalition policy, even a weak one, to the RPR's accommodative programmatic and organizational tactics undercut the RPR's attempts to secure anti-immigration and anti-immigrant issue ownership.[115]

Continued Use of the Front National to Divide and Conquer the French Right.

At the same time as the RPR was struggling to maintain a unified but limited co-optative position vis-à-vis the Front National, the Socialists were entering their third straight electoral period of intense adversarial behavior. As in the past, this strategy took several forms, most notably a promotion of issue positions at odds with the niche party and a more direct attack on the FN's proposals. Following a lull in the discussion of the immigration issue after the 1988 elections, the

---

[113] FN Député Yann Piat and former Députés Pascal Arrighi and François Bachelot resigned in 1988 over Le Pen's inappropriate play on words using Michel Durafour's name; Le Pen referred to him as "Durafour-crématoire," or Durafour-crematorium, based on the word "oven" which is found in Durafour's name. Bréchon 1995: 53; Mayer and Perrineau 1996: 385.

[114] Archives du Premier Ministre, Fonds de Michel Rocard, "Notes de Guy Carcassonne sur le FN, 1989–91," Box 920622, art. 2, Philippe Lamy, "Note de Philippe Lamy à l'attention de Ministre de la Défense, Object: Elections partielles du 26 novembre et 3 décembre 1989."

[115] When discussing the RPR's strategy during the by-elections of November/December 1989, Philippe Lamy of the Ministry of the Interior noted that such a strategy was not only para-doxical but would be met with electoral sanction. Archives du Premier Ministre, Fonds de Michel Rocard, "Notes de Guy Carcassonne sur le FN, 1989–91," Box 920622, art. 2, Philippe Lamy, "Note de Philippe Lamy à l'attention de Ministre de la Défense, Object: Elections partielles du 26 novembre et 3 décembre 1989."

Socialists re-emphasized their position as the natural party of the immigrant in 1989.[116] In his annual New Year's Eve speech of that year:

Mitterrand formally launched a new effort on behalf of immigrants – the excluded and rejected – which was immediately followed by several circulars from the Minister of the Interior that would limit the application of the Pasqua law (Schain 1994: 259).

Cobbling together an electoral majority, the Rocard government was able to put such a revision into effect. As part of this same initiative, the PS created a new cabinet position and a bipartisan council concerned with the integration of immigrants into French society.[117]

These positive measures were combined with aggressive and highly publicized responses to the Front National. In 1990, the Secrétariat de la Formation of the Socialist Party released a series of pamphlets that both detailed the policy positions held by the Front National and described ways to combat them. The first of the three pamphlets, *Tools for Action: How to Battle against the Extreme Right*, clearly conveyed the PS's stance on the niche party:

Because the Front National represents absolute evil, it must be combated absolutely. Because the Socialists have placed liberty, democracy and the rights of man at the center of their mission, they must be on the watch to fight against the Extreme Right. That is why the attack against the influence of the FN should be one of our highest political priorities.[118]

Similar sentiments were expressed by PS officials throughout the electoral period.[119] For example, Socialist Prime Minister Bérégovoy denounced the niche party as "a moral leper" and "a poison" in a 1992 speech before the National Assembly.[120] These statements were part of the PS strategy to, again, "make it understood that the Front National is not a party like the others."[121]

These incendiary statements helped to differentiate the Socialists' position from that of the niche party. But they were also designed to reinforce the issue ownership of the FN. According to many politicians of the Right and Left, the PS was deliberately keeping the FN's name in the headlines in order to strengthen the

---

[116] The "affaire du foulard," in which the principal of a French junior high school expelled three Muslim girls for refusing to remove their headscarves, explains the timing of the PS's pro-immigrant pronouncement. However, the implementation of that specific adversarial strategy reflected the larger, persistent threat of the FN and its ability to further politicize the issues of national identity raised by the headscarf case.

[117] Claude Evin, Ministre de la Solidarité, de la Santé et de la Protection sociale, quoted in Archives du Premier Ministre, Fonds de Michel Rocard, "Notes de Guy Carcassonne sur le FN, 1989–91," Box 920622, art. 2. "Les orientations gouvernementaux concernant l'immigration," 1989.

[118] Archives de l'OURS, Gérard Lindeperg, "Introduction," *Lutter contre l'extrême droite: des outils pour l'action*, (Paris: PS Secrétariat national de la Formation, 1990): 3.

[119] In 1992, Socialist Party leaders pledged to lead a "nonstop battle" against the Front National and the Rightist parties that adopted its policies. According to a party document, "No compromise will be made with the Extreme Right, nor with the Right that collaborates with it." Archives de la FNSP, Box 3NA31, Unnamed Socialist Party Document, 1992: 7–8.

[120] Archives de l'OURS, "Les Prioritaires du gouvernement Bérégovoy," *PS Info*, April 11, 1992.

[121] Archives de l'OURS, Gérard Lindeperg, "Introduction," *Lutter contre l'extrême droite: des outils pour l'action*, 1990: 10.

niche party's support. The PS's complicity in the electoral success of the FN, both in the 1980s and the 1990s, was the main message of the RPR's 1998 document *Socialist Party, Front National: Dangerous Liaisons.* Similar claims also came from the PS's opponents on the Left. In a televised interview in 1992, Communist leader Jean-Claude Gayssot observed that the Socialists "were trying to make the Front National stronger in order to try to divide the Right."[122] Although these statements were made by opponents of the PS – people who had incentives to defame the PS – there is truth to the claim by Alain Juppé and the others that the PS was "the main producer of propaganda for the Front National."[123] As discussed already, this was part of the Socialists' self-avowed plan.

1993–97: Front National: A Permanent Member of the Party System?

And the Socialists' plan appeared to be working. The Front National's support continued to grow between 1988 and 1993. In the National Assembly elections of 1993, the niche party scored its highest legislative score to date – 12.4 percent. Although this vote share did not result in any seats for the Front National, the party did advance to the second round in approximately 100 districts, often taking votes away from parties of the left and right (Bréchon 1995: 58). Following a set of regional elections in which the Front National list gained 13.9 percent and increased its regional representation from 137 to 239 seats, the national legislative showing made it clear that the electoral threat of the niche party was not abating. Indeed, in the EP elections one year later, the FN increased its number of MEPs from ten to eleven.[124]

By 1993, the Front National was drawing most of its electoral support from a growing party faithful: 71 percent of those who voted for the niche party on the first ballot of the 1993 legislative elections professed FN partisanship.[125] To the extent that the FN continued to steal voters from the mainstream parties, the RPR remained its primary victim. Thirteen percent of those who voted for the niche party on the first ballot of the 1993 elections claimed RPR partisanship.[126] While the Gaullist loss was less significant than it had been in 1988, the RPR

---

[122] Gayssot interviewed on "Elections 92: Le grand débat." Archives de l'OURS, Transcript of "Elections 92: Le grand débat," March 5, 1992 at 20h50, 42.

[123] Juppé interviewed on "Elections 92: Le grand débat," Ibid., 36. RPR Député Alain Juppé made this accusation on several different occasions. In a different interview, Juppé said: "I find that the PS begins to dishonor itself. What is the only thing that they talk about? Le Pen. I have never heard Mr. Joxe speak about the region, the only thing of which he speaks is Le Pen. Because if Le Pen gained support, that would mean that the UPF [alliance between RPR and UDF] would be weakened and therefore, that is the Socialists' game. I accuse the Socialists of having mounted a series of protests in order to validate Le Pen. They are objectively in collusion with Le Pen." Service de Presse du RPR, "Presse Audiovisuelle, 11.03.1992, Le préparation des élections régionales."

[124] The FN's net gain of one MEP occurred despite a slight decline in its vote percentage relative to 1989.

[125] Calculations from Chrique 1997.

[126] Ibid.

was still experiencing a net defection of voters to the niche party.[127] Moreover, the presence of the FN in second-round battles often ensured the loss of UDF and RPR seats to the Socialists.[128] The failure of Front National voters to rally behind the parties of the classic Right to defeat the Left revealed the electorate's dedication to the niche party and the FN's persistent threat to the Gaullists.

Continuing the trend, the PS did not lose many of its former supporters to the FN; only 2.4 percent of PS partisans voted for the FN in 1993.[129] But research demonstrates that the PS was not unthreatened by the niche party in the 1990s. Perrineau notes that the mid-1990s saw the emergence of *gaucho-lepénists* – first-time voters who, apart from their support of the FN's anti-immigration position, would have allied themselves with the Left.[130] Strong evidence for the single-issue nature of FN voters, these otherwise traditional Leftist voters were casting their ballots for the anti-immigration niche party.

The relative danger of the FN was tempered somewhat by the mainstream parties' positions following the 1993 legislative elections. Running a joint platform, the RPR and UDF captured almost 40 percent of the votes, which translated into 256 seats for the RPR. With a plurality of the votes (and tacit support from the UDF's 214 deputies), the Gaullists took control of the government. The PS, on the other hand, left the election with a mere fifty-four seats.

Yet, despite the newfound electoral strength of the RPR and the weakening of the PS, the parties were still locked into the same accommodative-adversarial battle against the radical right foe. For the PS, a change of course to accommodative tactics would prove ineffective at increasing its overall vote and seat level. Even with the loss of *gaucho-lepénists*, the balance of pro-immigrant and anti-immigrant voters within the Socialist electorate indicated that an adversarial strategy would be more electorally advantageous. For the Gaullists, maintaining an accommodative strategy was the best option. The adoption of adversarial tactics would have been both costly and not credible, and the embrace of a dismissive strategy in this competitive climate would have only increased the RPR's vote loss to the Front National.

Another Period of Accommodation Muddied by Internal Party Division. Consistent with the predictions of my strategic choice theory, the RPR continued its co-optive stance, enacting its most intensive accommodative tactics to date. In its campaign materials, the party prioritized, to a degree not seen before, issues thought to be related to the Front National, such as illegal immigration and

---

[127] According to the study by Chrique (1997), 5.4 percent of RPR partisans voted for the FN in the first round of the 1993 legislative elections as opposed to 8 percent of FN partisans who voted for the RPR or UDF. Due to the smaller number of FN partisans, these defections resulted in a net loss of RPR voters to the FN.

[128] In the fourteen incidents of triangular second-round races between the Right, FN, and the Socialists, the FN candidate managed to retain, on average, his or her vote percentage from the previous round. Bréchon 1995: 58.

[129] This group constituted 6 percent of the 1993 FN electorate. Calculations from Chrique 1997.

[130] Perrineau discussed in Hainsworth 2000: 21.

Islamic religious extremism.[131] It created a one-man taskforce to research and reflect on the party's strategy against the FN, with the resulting recommendations on how to demonstrate the RPR's greater competence on FN issue positions released to all party members.[132]

Beyond these tactics designed mainly for the party faithful, the Gaullist Party pursued a public programmatic and organizational strategy aimed directly at recovering many of the voters it had lost to the Front National over the previous decade. Prioritized within this approach was its proposal of revisions – often demanded by the niche party – to the French nationality code and laws on immigration control and internal security. The resulting Pasqua law of 1993 indeed reflected the policy preferences of the Front National for "zero immigration" and stronger surveillance of immigrants within the country.[133] Four years later, the RPR proposed a second bill, the Debré law, which also increased the measures available to track foreigners in France.[134] Both bills were denounced by the PS and other social organizations as promoting racist activity. Ironically, such comments might have played into the hands of a Gaullist Party courting FN voters.

Beyond these direct attempts to win over issue-based voters, the RPR sought to disarm the Front National from the inside out. In this organizational strategy, the Gaullist Party actively tried to recruit FN elected officials. Jacques Peyrat, the mayor of Nice during the 1990s, was one of those niche party members whom the RPR co-opted.[135] In areas of the country in which FN support was pervasive, such as Provence-Alpes-Côte d'Azur, organizational appropriation of local Front National leaders was seen as the only way to achieve large-scale voter defection. The RPR had already co-opted the niche party's policies; all that remained to convince voters were the familiar faces of the extreme right.

That said, the intensity, and thus effectiveness, of the RPR's accommodative strategy was limited yet again by the relative strength of its Socialist opponent's tactics and by the continued contradictions within the RPR's behavior. Although

---

[131] In the joint RPR-UDF manifesto for the 1997 legislative elections, the first policy pledge listed was to strengthen the state's control over a series of issues, including illegal immigration and Islamic religious extremism. Service de Presse du RPR, "Un nouvel élan pour la France," 1997: 1.

[132] This assignment was given to RPR Député Jean-Pierre Delalande. Interview with Delalande 1999.

[133] As explicated by Virginie Guiraudon (2001), "The 'Pasqua law' of 1993, named after French interior minister Charles Pasqua, sought to stem the remaining legal flows in a variety of ways: by prohibiting foreign graduate students from accepting job offers by French employers and denying them a stable residence status, by increasing the waiting period for family reunification from one to two years, and by denying residency permits to foreign spouses who had been illegally in the country prior to marrying."

[134] In essence, the Debré law required that each resident report the arrival and departure of his or her guests to the mayor. The bill gave mayors discretion over whether visitors could or could not stay. In addition, it sought to create a database of foreigners' fingerprints.

[135] Archives de la FNSP, Dossiers de Presse, Michel Noblecourt, "M. Jospin dénonce les 'connivances' entre droite extrême et extrême droite," *Le Monde*, April 20, 1996; Archives de la FNSP, Dossiers de Presse, "Jospin s'en prend au Front national," *Le Figaro*, April 19, 1996.

the Gaullist Party employed extensive legislative means to convince the voters
of the credibility of its anti-immigrant policy, it undermined these efforts by
demonizing the niche party, the policy position it was trying to imitate, and, by
association, the voters it was trying to co-opt. The RPR expressed its hatred for
the Front National regularly and vociferously. According to Philippe Séguin, the
FN is "a shameful French exception" (Parti socialiste 1998: 1). Such sentiments
were also extended to the niche party's leader. RPR Prime Minister Alain Juppé
characterized Le Pen as "profoundly, almost viscerally, racist, anti-Semitic and
xenophobic."[136] And there is evidence that this strategy – one also practiced by
an adversarial PS – was effective. In a November 1995 letter to *Le Monde*, Le Pen
complained that the use of the term *extrême droite* to describe the Front National
served to place it in a category separate from the other political parties, a category
whose members were characterized by "a rejection of democracy and elections,
an appeal to violence, racism and the desire to establish a one-party state."[137]

Viewing the Front National as a party unlike others, an evil that must be
ostracized, the RPR also refused all alliances with the FN during this period. As
affirmed by the RPR Secretary General, Jean-François Mancel, it was "out of
the question that there would be the least accord, the least discussion, the least
cohabitation with the representatives of the Front National."[138] In contrast to
previous electoral periods, this policy was fairly consistently practiced between
1993 and 1997, even though it often led to FN victory in second-round district
elections. The RPR and Chirac eschewed second-round electoral pacts with the
FN in the 1995 presidential and 1997 legislative elections;[139] this behavior was
also seen in the 1995 municipal elections.

Yet, although consistently applied, the RPR's anti-alliance policy and demonization strategy belonged in an adversarial campaign, not an accommodative
one. This strategy proved problematic for a party that was trying to co-opt FN
policy positions and to use the "credibility" of former FN politicians to win back
voters. From the perspective of the voter, if the RPR deemed the FN's policies racist, why would the mainstream right party want to champion them? If
the Front National was tantamount to a neo-Nazi group, why would the RPR
want to welcome former FN officials into its ranks? These contradictory actions
undermined the credibility of the RPR's accommodative behavior.

---

[136] *Le Monde*, September 21, 1996 quoted in Fysh and Wolfreys 1998: 200.
[137] Translation by Rydgren 2004: 216 from a quote found in Mayer 1996: 14.
[138] *Le Monde*, June 4–5, 1995 quoted in Ivaldi 1998: 11.
[139] Because the RPR actively rejected the FN during the 1995 presidential election, Le Pen refused
to direct his first-round voters to vote for the natural second choice (Chirac) in the second round.
Instead, Le Pen encouraged his voters to "vote blank." The FN reacted more strongly to the
RPR's rebuff in the second round of the 1997 legislative elections. In districts in which FN
candidates were not standing, FN voters were directed to vote *against* specific Gaullist politicians.
Consequently, the results of that election show that FN voters were more likely either to spoil their
ballots or to vote for the PS candidate in the second round than they were in past presidential or
legislative elections. Given this behavior, it is not surprising that the RPR's strategy of no alliances
cost them potential support. Shields 1997: 34n6.

Moreover, a rejection of alliances with the FN – especially those that would have ensured the RPR legislative office – sent a harsh message that the voters of the anti-immigrant party were not welcome in the ranks of the mainstream party. As verbalized by RPR Député Delalande in 1997 in his review of past RPR strategy toward the FN, demonization does not encourage the return of defected voters.[140] Not surprisingly, those voters who leave the mainstream parties to support a niche party cannot be expected to return to a party that has stigmatized them.[141] One would predict this reaction to be particularly strong in the case of FN voters because significant numbers of them were not recent defectors. Of those who voted for the FN in 1997, 42 percent had also voted for the Front National in the 1993 elections.[142] With the RPR treating these voters' party as a pariah, even the Gaullists' strong accommodative efforts would have been insufficient to lure (back) FN voters.[143]

Repeating the Formula for Boosting the Front National's Vote. Meanwhile, the Socialist Party conducted a multiprong adversarial attack against the Front National. This strategy consisted of attacking the FN, attacking its allies, and proposing pro-immigrant measures, such as the extension of voting rights to noncitizens in local-level elections.[144] Returning to a tactic employed successfully in 1986 to increase FN support and divide the Right, the PS even reintroduced the idea of adopting proportional representation for the legislative elections.[145] However, most of the PS's attention during this period in opposition was focused on discrediting its adversaries.

[140] In his brief comments to the press about his 1997 "Fiches argumentaires sur le Front National," Delalande noted that the Gaullist Party should "clearly mark the boundaries (between the FN and the RPR), but by overly demonizing the FN, one risks reinforcing its hard core, making its electorate close in on itself" (Barjon 1997).

[141] This dilemma of "how to condemn the FN but not its voters" (Rydgren 2004: 219) was recognized by both politicians and scholars.

[142] Similarly, 43 percent of 1997 FN voters had cast their ballots for Le Pen in the 1995 presidential election. Calculations from CEVIPOF 2001.

[143] The inability of the RPR to reduce FN support in the 1997 legislative elections led many Gaullist members to suggest abandoning the tactic of demonizing the FN for one of "regularizing" FN voters. Among the most prominent supporters of this AC tactic were Alain Peyrefitte, Robert Pandraud, and Jean-Pierre Soisson. Shields 1997: 32.

[144] The fact that the PS lacked any real legislative power during this period did not prevent it from proposing measures to encourage the integration of immigrants into French society and to grant them additional rights. For example, Socialist parliamentarians resurrected Mitterrand's 1981 pledge to accord local-level voting rights to "noncitizens," understood to refer to immigrants. While this proposal engendered some disagreement within the party, a compromise was eventually reached; the party would actively campaign for local-election voting rights for immigrants when electoral and parliamentary conditions allowed. Archives de la FNSP, Dossiers de Presse, Michel Noblecourt, "Les rocardians et la Gauche socialiste relancent le débat sur le vote des étrangers," *Le Monde*, May 14, 1996: 8; Archives de la FNSP, Dossiers de Presse, Michel Noblecourt, "Compromis au Parti socialiste sur le droit de vote des étrangers," *Le Monde*, May 26, 1996.

[145] The party's campaign platform for the 1995 presidential election also included the goal of "modifying the electoral law so that 20% of the deputies would be elected by PR" (Carton 1995).

As ever, the primary target in the Socialists' battle remained the Front National. Internal policy documents written by PS immigration specialists during this period begin with the recommendation to criticize the niche party.[146] Socialist politicians were urged to emphasize the extremist nature of the party – both its historical connection to Fascism and Nazism and its place outside the realm of normal, democratic French politics.[147] Jospin's statement in 1996 to the citizens of the FN-governed town of Toulon clearly demonstrates this tactic:

It is necessary to firmly denounce the ideas of the FN and the FN for what it is: an extreme right, xenophobic and even racist party, a party whose leaders carry out anti-Semitic discourse, cultivate Petainist nostalgia, a party which claims to be populist but whose program is reactionary and anti-social.[148]

In addition to antagonizing the niche party and its leaders, the Socialists stressed the importance of discussing and discrediting the fallacious claims made by the Front National.[149] Lest we begin to think that the PS was sincerely appalled by the FN and was attempting to undermine its support, we should note that, by 1997, the party emphasized *démontrer* over *dénoncer* in its tactics toward the FN.[150] The PS's goal was to publicize but not denounce its radical right adversary while establishing its own credibility as a pro-immigrant party. The formation of an anti–Le Pen organization by PS shadow minister Jean-Christophe Cambadélis was one example of this tactic.[151]

The Socialists also launched an aggressive ideological and personal attack against the co-opters of the FN's message, the RPR. Both in the National Assembly and in the streets, the PS vehemently protested against the Gaullists' racist and exclusionary reforms of the nationality code that were contained in the Pasqua laws.[152] Similar criticisms were raised against the Debré laws. Even parliamentary reports written by RPR-led committees were the subject of condemnation. PS leader Jospin criticized a report issued by the Commission of Parliamentary Study on Illegal Immigration for exaggerating the degree of the immigration

---

[146] Archives de l'OURS, Gérard Le Gall, *Rapport d'Orientation pour un combat efficace du Parti Socialiste contre le Front National: analyses, recommendations, propositions*, (Paris: PS Documentation, 1997): 39.

[147] One such recommendation from this report states "Le Pen demands that one not use the term 'extreme right,' an excellent reason to use it." Ibid., 41.

[148] Archives de la FNSP, Dossiers de Presse, Jospin quoted in "Jospin: 'Ne pas diaboliser le FN'," *Le Figaro*, March 8, 1996.

[149] The PS report by Le Gall called for the construction of "detailed argumentation against the policy proposals of the FN." Archives de l'OURS, Le Gall, 1997: 48.

[150] Démontrer means to display, whereas dénoncer means to denounce. François Hollande quoted in "Les dirigeants politiques et le FN," 1998: 72.

[151] Cambadélis is the president of the Mouvement le Manifeste contre le FN. Interview with Jean-Christophe Cambadélis, Socialist National Secretary Responsible for Relations with Other Parties and Groups and Socialist Député, Paris, December 4, 1998.

[152] Archives de l'OURS, "Appel à la manifestation contre les lois Pasqua," (Paris: PS Secrétariat National, 1994).

problem in order to increase the popularity of the xenophobic policy positions of the Right (and Extreme Right).[153]

Although this approach inevitably enhanced the RPR's reputation as an advocate of repressive immigration practices, Socialist documents tried to emphasize the FN origins of these ideas. For example, in his public criticism of the RPR report on illegal immigration, Jospin stated that "the report is directly inspired by the theses of the Front National."[154] The French electorate was repeatedly told of the RPR's status as a lesser copy of the niche party original. Moreover, the Socialists did not hesitate to remind voters that the RPR's issue co-optation was motivated by electoral concerns.[155] To give one example, a PS flyer calling for protests against the Pasqua laws stated that the RPR was advocating discriminatory acts in the hope of flattering the FN's electorate.[156]

1997 AND BEYOND: THE IMPLANTATION OF THE FRONT NATIONAL AND ITS STRATEGIC CAUSES

"It is clear that the Front National is durably implanted in the French political life," reported French political scientist Pierre Bréchon in 1995. The electoral results of the niche party after this date only reinforce his statement. In the first round of the 1995 presidential election, Le Pen gained a record 15.15 percent of the vote, almost doubling the Communist candidate's vote and earning Le Pen fourth place.[157] Later that year in the municipal elections, the niche party gained control of the mayoralties in three cities, two of which had more than thirty thousand inhabitants.[158] The 1997 legislative elections brought the Front National its strongest legislative showing to date. In the first round of the elections, the party captured 14.9 percent of the vote. Despite winning only one seat, this niche party had once again surpassed the Communists to become the fourth most popular party in the French political system.

The FN was building a loyal following: about 90 percent of FN voters in the 1993 and 1995 elections supported the radical right party again in 1997 (Shields 1997: 25), and 80 percent of those who voted for Le Pen in 1988 did so again in 1995 (RPR 1997: 4). But the radical right party's electoral *growth* in the 1990s continued to be built on the votes of former RPR supporters. In the 1995 presidential election, 14.6 percent of those who voted RPR in 1993 supported Le Pen in the first round. A mere 4 percent of former FN supporters,

---

153 Archives de la FNSP, Dossiers de Presse, "Jospin s'en prend au Front national," *Le Figaro*, April 19, 1996; Archives de la FNSP, Dossiers de Presse, Michel Noblecourt, "M. Jospin dénonce les 'connivances' entre droite extrême et extrême droite," *Le Monde*, April 20, 1996.

154 Archives de la FNSP, Dossiers de Presse, "Jospin s'en prend au Front national," 1996.

155 Archives de l'OURS, Le Gall, 1997: 42.

156 Archives de l'OURS, "Appel à la manifestation contre les lois Pasqua," 1994; Archives de la FNSP, Dossiers de Presse, Noblecourt, 1996.

157 Le Pen finished behind Socialist Lionel Jospin (23.3 percent), Gaullist Jacques Chirac (20.8 percent), and Gaullist Edouard Balladur (18.6 percent). Keeler and Schain 1996: 7.

158 These cities were Toulon, Orange, and the smaller Marignane.

on the other hand, cast their ballots for Chirac in the presidential election.[159]
Vote transfers also occurred in the first round of the 1997 legislative elections.
The RPR lost 6 percent of Chirac's 1995 first ballot vote to the niche party,
while a mere 2.8 percent of the much smaller 1995 Le Pen electorate returned
to the Gaullist fold.[160] With 14.9 percent of the 1997 legislative vote, the Front
National was not losing steam, and the RPR was continuing to provide the largest
group of defectors.[161]

How did this single-issue party transform from a minor political character into
the main challenger to the supremacy of the mainstream political actors? Why
was its success not stymied like that of other niche party actors in France or even
its radical right counterpart, the National Front, in Britain? In this chapter, I
have argued that the strategic behavior of the Socialist and Gaullist parties was
the key to the electoral fortune of the xenophobic party. Although the RPR tried
to reduce the popularity of the Front National, its efforts were limited by two
factors: the inconsistency of its accommodative efforts and the pre-emptive and
more intense adversarial response of the Socialists. Indeed, I argue, the latter was
more critical to the FN's success. The early programmatic, organizational, and
institutional tactics of the PS helped to establish the Front National as a credible
political option and the owner of the anti-immigration position. By the time
the RPR responded, its actions were insufficient to undermine the niche party's
reputation and its electoral base; the window of issue ownership opportunity had
closed.

The story told so far seems to support this interpretation, but more specific
evidence is necessary to test my strategic explanation and its hypotheses. Did the
mainstream parties' strategies result in the electoral changes anticipated by the
PSO theory? Or does a standard spatial interpretation of party competition hold?
Moreover, is there evidence of the proposed salience- and ownership-altering
mechanism at work? These questions are the subject of the next section.

A Modified Spatial Account of Front National Electoral Support

A comparison of the predictions of the standard spatial theory and my PSO
theory with the observed trajectory of the French Front National suggests the
greater predictive power of my modified spatial approach. Recall that, according
to the standard spatial model, only the behavior of the proximal mainstream
party should affect the strength of the niche party actor. If we follow this logic
and consider only the RPR and its strategy of accommodation, we would expect
the popularity of the FN to fall, not rise as observed. The standard spatial model's
prediction does not change, and thus its explanatory power does not improve,

---

[159] Calculations from Lewis-Beck et al. 1996.
[160] Calculations from CEVIPOF et al. 2001.
[161] After former FN voters, former RPR voters constituted the largest group to vote for the FN.
RPR party identifiers also were the largest group of partisans, after those of the Front National,
to vote for the niche party. Calculations from CEVIPOF et al. 2001.

even if we recognize the RPR's hesitation in first responding to the radical right party.

A story consistent with the FN's observed success emerges when we consider instead the predictions of the modified spatial theory of party interaction. Positing that the behavior of both proximal and distant mainstream parties will influence the electoral outcome of a niche party, the PSO theory predicts the general strengthening of the Front National over the period of 1981 to 1997. Ignored by the standard spatial theory, the Socialists' adversarial tactics overpowered the RPR's dismissive behavior to boost the radical right party's support between 1981 and 1986. According to my theory, the net effect of the mainstream parties' accommodative-adversarial tactics pursued since 1986 depends on their relative intensity. As this chapter has shown, the Socialists prioritized and publicized their stance on immigration more than their Gaullist counterparts.[162] The PS's programmatic tactics were part of a multiprong strategy in which the PS also "attacked" the Front National with organizational and institutional tactics. Moreover, the Socialists employed their tactics in a timely and consistent manner, unmarred by the kind of internal party divisions and dissent that plagued the RPR. This evidence suggests therefore that the PS's adversarial strategy was more intense than the RPR's accommodative one. Consequently, we expect the electoral strength of the Front National to rise throughout the 1986–97 period.

A glance back at Figure 6.2 reveals an electoral trajectory consistent with these predictions and the cross-national findings of Chapter 3 for DIAD and ACAD (where AD > AC) strategic combinations. Between the 1981 and 1986 legislative elections, the Front National gained 9.7 percentage points. And as expected, the majority of the new radical right voters came from the French mainstream right.[163] Front National gains at the expense of the RPR had also taken place during the earlier 1984 EP elections. Although not a national election and therefore not directly comparable, the 1984 supranational election provides another example of the increasing power of the radical right party at the hands of Socialists.

In contrast to the claims of the standard spatial model, the electoral strength of the Front National did not fall after the implementation of the RPR's accommodative strategy in 1986. Rather, the radical right party continued to gain support over the course of the next three elections. A closer look at the behavior of individual voters confirms the predictions of my modified spatial theory: more RPR voters were defecting to the FN than FN voters were returning to the RPR. For example, in the first round of the 1988 presidential election, 17.5 percent of RPR partisans voted for the FN candidate, Le Pen, whereas only 6 percent of

---

[162] Additional examples of this prioritization include the fact that François Mitterrand's 1988 presidential campaign literature devoted a third more space to the issues of immigration and citizenship than that of RPR candidate, Jacques Chirac. Moreover, as mentioned earlier, the Socialists took the unusual step of clearly identifying and slandering their political opponents – the Front National – in their campaign documents. Mitterrand 1988; Chirac 1988.

[163] Of the FN's vote in the 1986 legislative elections, 20 percent came from RPR or UDF partisans. SOFRES 1988: 139.

the much smaller group of FN partisans voted for the RPR candidate, Jacques Chirac.[164] The situation was repeated in the 1988 and 1993 legislative elections, when a greater number of RPR partisans defected to the radical right party than FN partisans returned to the RPR.[165] A comparison of the defection of voters across these parties between 1995 and 1997 shows a similar trend; only 2.8 percent of those who voted for Le Pen in the 1995 presidential election switched to the RPR in 1997, as opposed to 6 percent of the larger group of 1995 Chirac voters who cast their ballots for FN candidates in the 1997 elections.[166] Thus, despite its accommodative tactics, the RPR was not gaining significant numbers of former radical right party voters. It was not even stopping the flow of its own voters to the new party.

From this analysis, the PSO theory appears better able to predict the shape and timing of the Front National's electoral trajectory. Consideration of the strategies of merely the proximal party leads to incorrect predictions about the electoral withering of the radical right party. Only when the adversarial tactics of the ideologically distant Socialists are included in the analysis can we account for the phenomenal and early and lasting success of the Front National.

Testing the Mechanism: Shifts in Issue Salience and Ownership. This chapter has revealed a strong similarity between the FN's electoral trajectory and the PSO model's expectations, but has it also demonstrated that the mechanism behind my theory's new conception of strategies was at work? In other words, did the strategies produce the expected results because they altered the salience and ownership of the radical right party's issue dimension and issue position?

According to the PSO theory of party competition, the strategic combinations pursued by the two mainstream parties from 1981 until 1997 should have boosted the perceived salience of the FN's immigration issue. Between 1981 and 1986, the RPR was trying to play down an issue on which its party could find little agreement. Unfortunately for the Gaullists, their Socialist counterparts were, during this time, initiating a pro-immigrant campaign, an active tactic that should effectively overwhelm the impact of the dismissive one. The resulting rise in issue salience is expected to continue during the period of accommodative-adversarial strategies, when both parties were trying to encourage the electorate to vote on the basis of the immigration issue.

[164] Calculations from Pierce 1996. Given that only a very small percentage of voters self-identified as FN partisans in 1988, a better assessment of voter flow involves examining those voters who supported the FN in 1986. Of those voters, only 4 percent cast their ballots for the RPR candidate in the first round of the 1988 presidential election. Conversely, almost 16 percent of 1986 RPR voters supported Le Pen in the 1988 presidential election. Calculations from CEVIPOF et al. 1995.

[165] The percentage of RPR partisans planning to cast their ballots for FN candidates in the 1988 legislative elections was more than five times the percentage of FN partisans intending to support RPR candidates (ibid.). In 1993, 5.4 percent of RPR partisans defected to the FN, and 8 percent of FN partisans voted for the RPR. Because of the smaller size of the radical right party's partisan base, the RPR experienced a net loss of voters to the FN. Calculations from Chrique 1997.

[166] Calculations from CEVIPOF et al. 2001.

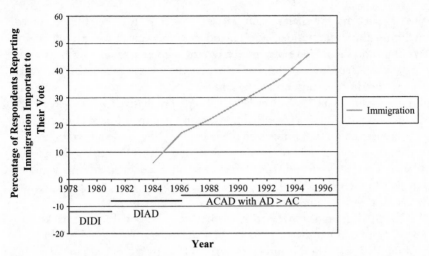

FIGURE 6.3. Salience of the Immigration Issue in France. *Sources*: Chrique 1997; Lewis-Beck et al. 1996; Perrineau 1996; Schain 1994.

Survey data presented in Figure 6.3 confirm these predictions. Whereas only 6 percent of survey respondents noted the importance of the immigration issue in 1984, the number jumped to 17 percent by 1986.[167] At that time, immigration even surpassed the issues of social equality and the economy to be ranked the third most important issue in determining voting decisions. In the following years, despite the fact that the observed level of immigration to France fell and the percentage of foreigners was leveling off and then declining, the salience of the topic continued to rise. In 1988, 22 percent of respondents to a CSA poll deemed the issue important to their vote.[168] By 1993, that number was up to 36.9 percent; according to the study by Chrique, immigration was considered the top social issue facing France. In addition, when all economic, social, and political issues were considered, immigration ranked second after the perennial favorite of unemployment.[169] In a 1995 poll, the most recent survey in our period of analysis to pose the question, 45.8 percent of respondents said that immigration was a critical issue influencing their vote.[170] Thus, even as the number of immigrants arriving decreased and the percentage of immigrants in France declined, the behavior of the mainstream parties ensured that the salience of the radical right's issue was high.

[167] SOFRES/TF1 1984 poll and SOFRES 1986 poll reported in Schain 1994: 265.
[168] CSA poll "Sortie des urnes," from April 24, 1988 reported in Perrineau 1996: 62.
[169] In this survey, unlike the others, an explicit connection was not made between issue importance and vote choice. The questionnaires were administered, however, near the 1993 legislative elections, and thus the respondents' answers can reasonably be interpreted to reflect the importance of the immigration issue for that election. Calculations from Chrique 1997.
[170] This number represents the percentage of respondents giving immigration a score of 8, 9, or 10 on a scale of 0 (least important) to 10 (most important). Calculations from Lewis-Beck et al. 1996.

What impact did the mainstream parties' strategies have on the perceived ownership of the immigration issue? In other words, given the prevalence of issue voting, who should have benefited from the increased salience of the immigration issue? According to the PSO theory, the tactics pursued from 1981 until 1997 should have reinforced the Front National's ownership of the anti-immigration issue. The PS's adversarial strategy emphasized to the electorate that the Front National was its polar opposite on the dimension of immigration, thereby strengthening the connection made between the anti-immigration issue position and the radical right party. The failure of the RPR to actively respond to the new party and its issue until 1986 left the Socialists' claim unchallenged. Even after the RPR officially adopted accommodative tactics in 1986, the inconsistency of the Gaullist message undermined its efforts to acquire issue ownership. Given the RPR's initial hesitancy in reacting to the Front National, it is unclear that even a coherent and consistent accommodative strategy after 1986 would have allowed the RPR to steal the anti-immigration title away from the niche party; once entrenched, issue ownership is sticky (Petrocik 1996) and thus not quick to respond to changes in party tactics.

The lack of survey questions on issue ownership hinders the conclusive testing of this dimension of the modified spatial theory. However, it is possible to get some sense of the perceived credibility of the various parties on the immigration issue from the available data. In 1988, more than 80 percent of respondents to the French Presidential Election Study considered the Front National to have a strong anti-immigration stance.[171] A mere 7 percent of respondents claimed that the RPR, the main challenger to the FN's issue ownership, had the same reputation. It is interesting to note that this perceived weakness in the RPR's anti-immigration stance was noted shortly after the party had enacted the Pasqua law, one of its toughest bills restricting entry into France and limiting immigrant rights!

Moreover, there was less ambiguity about the anti-immigration policy position of the FN than that of the RPR. Not only was the variance around the mean survey response for the FN much smaller than that for the RPR, but also fewer respondents were unable to identify the issue stance of the niche party than that of its rightist mainstream party competitor. Less than 6 percent of survey respondents did not know the FN's position on immigration, as opposed to nearly 17 percent who were unclear about the RPR's policy stance.[172] While finding that a party holds a particular issue position is not the same as proving that it is the most credible owner of that issue, the former is a necessary condition of the latter. As these numbers show, the FN stands out as the strongest and most obvious advocate of the anti-immigration position – two indicators of issue ownership.

---

[171] The PS was recognized by the vast majority of those surveyed as the proponent of a less-restrictive policy toward immigration, an issue position reflective of its adversarial stance. Calculations from Pierce 1996.
[172] Ibid.

This reputation was maintained over time. The 1995 French Presidential Election Study reveals that Le Pen stood out as the "best presidential candidate on immigration." Of those respondents with an opinion, 39 percent chose the leader of the Front National versus 18 percent who named Chirac.[173] And this was not an ambiguous response; the number of "don't know" and "none of them" responses was lower for this issue than for most (Chiche and Mayer 1997: 226). Although a respondent's answer to this question depends on his or her preferred policy position, the similarity between the espoused policies of the FN and RPR at that time allows us to draw a conclusion about the outcome of the ownership battle between these two parties; the FN was retaining its title as issue owner.

Our confidence in these findings of FN issue ownership is reinforced by the fact that this reputation was recognized by respondents from across political parties, most importantly by partisans of the accommodative RPR. A breakdown of perceived issue ownership by the 1993 legislative vote of those surveyed reveals that a plurality of RPR voters, not to mention almost all FN voters, agreed that Le Pen was the most credible (anti)immigration candidate.[174] As expected, the weak accommodative efforts of the Gaullists had been unable to undermine the Socialist-reinforced issue ownership of the Front National. The niche party remained the most credible issue owner.

This analysis confirms the expectations of my modified spatial theory of party competition. As predicted, shifts in the salience of the immigration issue correspond with the timing of the implementation of the mainstream parties' strategies toward the Front National. The stability of immigration ownership in the face of RPR accommodation seems best explained by the adversarial tactics of the PS. In other words, the mechanism behind my expanded conception of strategies seems to be at work. In turn, the timing and direction of these effects on salience and ownership match the shifts in the electoral support of the radical right party. The strategies of the PS and RPR, we can therefore conclude, were driving the spectacular success of the Front National. Informed by the salience-, ownership-, and position-altering tactics of the PS and RPR, anti-immigration voters – mainly from the ineffectively accommodative RPR – were casting their ballots for the more credible issue proponent, the Front National.

THE ROLE OF A DIVIDED AND NONCREDIBLE GAULLIST PARTY:
A SPATIALLY BASED ALTERNATIVE EXPLANATION

This chapter has argued that the observed success of the radical right party can be explained by the PSO theory of party competition. Yet, while the trends in issue salience and ownership support the presence of a modified spatial mechanism, it is possible that the spectacular FN support levels could have arisen for other

---

[173] Calculations from Lewis-Beck et al. 1996.
[174] Of the 1993 RPR voters with an opinion, 43.5 percent said that Le Pen was the most credible candidate. Ibid.

reasons consistent with the standard spatial model. Turning to the most credible alternative hypothesis, one could perhaps argue that the inability of the RPR's accommodative strategy to suppress the FN's vote was a result of the Gaullists' internal party division, rather than the PS's adversarial strategy.

Though internal party disagreement has not been advanced as a cause of the electoral success of the Front National by other scholars, this argument appears plausible. In any model of party competition, the effectiveness of party strategies depends on their credibility. If the RPR's accommodative efforts were not perceived to be credible by the electorate, then anti-immigration voters would not be expected to cast their ballots for the RPR. In this situation, the Front National's electoral support should continue to rise. Voters should return to the RPR only when its internal party divisions are erased and the party pursues a unified accommodative strategy.

There is support for the claim that the French public was aware of the internal divisions plaguing the RPR. Analysis of data from the 1988 French Presidential Election Study suggests that the electorate did not have a precise idea about where the RPR stood on the issue of immigration. Indeed, as mentioned previously, the variance around the mean survey response was larger for the Gaullist Party than for any other political party, except the Communists.[175] If, in fact, the RPR was seen as having an ambiguous position, it would be reasonable for issue voters to withhold their support from the party. Perhaps, therefore, voters continued to cast ballots for the Front National because they were unsure of the RPR's anti-immigration stance.

However, closer examination of the survey data discounts the force of this finding and the plausibility of the alternative explanation. Although perceptions of the RPR's policy position on immigration were widely distributed across the group of survey respondents, individual RPR partisans saw the RPR's stance as approximating their own personal policy position; 47 percent of all RPR partisans believed the party to be sharing their policy preference, and an additional 34 percent perceived the party position to be within one unit of theirs.[176] Thus, a shift to individual-level analysis reveals that the Gaullist Party was not seen as holding an ambiguous policy position by each of its voters. Rather, each partisan had his or her own conception of party policy, and most thought that policy corresponded with his or her own viewpoint.

Given the perceived ideological affinity between the RPR and its partisans, the standard spatial model cannot account for the fact that many of these RPR affiliates chose to cast their ballots for the candidate of the single-issue radical right party. According to survey data from the 1988 presidential election, those voters who shared immigration policy positions with the Gaullist Party made

---

[175] Calculations from Pierce 1996.

[176] The survey asked respondents to locate the immigration policy preferences of themselves and the French parties on a scale from 1 to 7, where 1 represents agreement with the statement "immigrants should return to their country of origin" and 7 represents agreement with the statement "immigrants living in France should be integrated into French society." Ibid.

up 28 percent of Le Pen's electorate in that election.[177] Combine this with the finding that the RPR was perceived to be the closest political option to most RPR partisans, and it becomes clear that these voting decisions were not being determined simply by spatial proximity. Some other factor was in play.

Evidence from other elections suggests that this factor was issue ownership. According to the 1995 Presidential Election Study, 83 percent of former RPR voters who supported Le Pen in the first round of the election named the FN leader as the most credible proponent of the immigration issue.[178] In contrast, only 32 percent of those RPR voters who remained loyal to their party leaders (Chirac or Balladur) named Le Pen as the issue owner. Moreover, former RPR voters who thought that Le Pen was the most credible immigration candidate were more likely to defect and vote for the FN leader in 1995 than to vote for Chirac. Those Gaullist voters who deemed Chirac to be the issue owner were less likely to defect. The electoral behavior of former FN voters similarly depended on their views of the rightful owner of the immigration issue; those few 1993 FN voters who voted for the RPR in 1995 were more likely to consider Chirac the issue owner than radical right partisans who continued to support Le Pen. Voting decisions were clearly turning on issue reputations more than programmatic positions.

In sum, the disunity of the RPR's stance on immigration cannot account for the nonproximal voting of RPR partisans and the resulting electoral success of the Front National. Rather, this examination of the alternative explanation suggests that other, nonpositional aspects of voter and party behavior are critical to understanding the fortunes of target parties – a finding consistent with the predictions of the PSO theory of party competition.

CONCLUSION

Why has the Front National flourished in a country founded on the idea of immigration? The answer to this question does not lie in an electoral and institutional environment generally considered hostile to new parties. Nor can a clear, consistent, and simple answer be found in the economic and demographic pressures facing France at the time. Immigration had been halted for more than a decade before the electoral explosion of the radical right party, and the percentage of foreigners in the country stabilized and then even began to decline during this period. GDP per capita was continuously rising. A steadily increasing unemployment rate should not be ignored and, indeed, was often linked by politicians, including those of the Front National, to the FN's electoral appeal. However, to

---

[177] Ibid.
[178] Former RPR voters consist of those who voted RPR in the first round of the 1993 legislative elections. The percentages are very similar if one compares issue ownership as perceived by RPR partisans instead: of the RPR partisans who supported Le Pen, 81 percent named Le Pen as the issue owner as opposed to 12 percent who named Chirac. Conversely, 48 percent of RPR partisans who voted for Chirac in 1995 identified him as issue owner, and 29 percent identified Le Pen as the most credible on the immigration issue. Calculations from Lewis-Beck et al. 1996.

understand this connection between unemployment and the electoral fate of an anti-immigration party, one needs to look at the actors that promulgated (and manipulated) its anti-immigration and anti-immigrant message.

As this chapter has argued, the success of the Front National sprang from the strategic behavior of the dominant French political parties. The Socialists' timely and decisive adversarial tactics kept the immigration issue in the limelight and reinforced the niche party's claim to issue ownership, thereby encouraging the further defection of (mostly RPR) anti-immigrant voters to the Front National. After an initial delay in reacting to the radical right party, the RPR attempted to recover lost voters by mirroring the FN's xenophobic platform. The effectiveness of the RPR's strategy was undermined, however, by intraparty factionalism, an inherently contradictory policy, and, perhaps most importantly, the pre-emptive ownership-reinforcing behavior of the Socialists. The outcome was a strong radical right party, firmly entrenched in the French political system.

In the course of unraveling the strategic decisions of the Socialist and Gaullist parties in their fight against the Front National, this chapter has called into question the traditional spatial conception of party interaction. Not only has this discussion demonstrated that strategies manipulate the salience and ownership of issues as well as party issue positions, but the chapter has also highlighted the critical, but typically overlooked, role of nonproximal parties in party competition. Largely unthreatened by the Front National, the Socialist Party nonetheless had a stake in the electoral fortune of the radical right party. Through adversarial tactics, the PS made the FN into a weapon in its larger competition with its mainstream opponent, the RPR. Boosting awareness of and support for the FN by publicizing its issue position and lowering the electoral threshold, the PS was using the "enemy of its enemy" to divide the Right and thus enhance its own electoral security. The electoral success of the Front National was a secondary effect.

In revealing how the Socialists were able to successfully manipulate their niche party competitor, this chapter emphasizes that the effectiveness of mainstream party strategies is not without constraint. In this case of competition between unequals, the potency of the RPR's tactics was constrained from within and without. Consistent with the discussion in Chapter 4, internal factionalism decreased the Gaullists' ability to respond in a timely manner and, even when action was taken, to present a coherent message. But the timely and intense adversarial strategy of the PS also presented barriers to RPR tactical success. Socialist demonization of the Front National prevented the RPR from being able to co-opt the FN's policy position without also inheriting the racist label that by then accompanied it. The presence of this stigma raised the costs of accommodation and indirectly contributed to the already brewing policy disagreements within the RPR. In addition, the Socialists' actions – including the adoption of PR – facilitated the entrenchment of the FN's reputation as anti-immigration issue owner. By the time that the RPR began to react, the window of ownership opportunity had already begun to close. RPR tactics were rendered relatively powerless.

Chapter 7, on the electoral support of the Scottish National Party, continues this emphasis on the constrained effectiveness of mainstream party tactics in competition between unequals. As in the case of the FN, the mainstream parties of Britain pursued opposite strategies toward the ethnoterritorial party with unequal intensity. The SNP's early success, however, speaks more to the deep internal divisions within the accommodative Labour Party, than to any preemptive adversarial tactics by its mainstream opponent. As the next chapter will again highlight, where strategies work by altering the salience and ownership of niche party issues, mainstream party indecision translates into niche party success.

7

An Unequal Battle of Opposing Forces

Mainstream Party Strategies and the Success of the Scottish National Party

There is a changing mood in Scotland. Every Liberal, Socialist, of which ever variety of Socialist you mean, every Conservative has changed over the last few years, and we must accept that those changes are in part a response to some of the things that the Scottish National Party have been saying.... If we do not recognise it and we do not do something about it, the Scottish National Party is sitting there, vulture-like, hairy kneed vulture-like, waiting to pounce.[1]

And pounce it did. By the time Alistair Smith issued this warning to his fellow members of the Conservative Party in 1976, the Scottish National Party had already emerged as an unexpected and almost unstoppable force. Although it never gained a national vote of more than 3 percent, its true menace is revealed in the vote percentages it obtained in Scottish seats – the seats in which it competed. Between 1970 and 1997, the SNP consistently captured more than 11 percent of the vote in Scotland, with an average vote of 18.8 percent. In the October 1974 General Election, it achieved its peak vote of 30.4 percent, just 6 percentage points shy of Labour's electoral plurality.[2] In this same election, the ethnoterritorial party surpassed the Conservatives to become the second most popular party in Scotland. Although support for the SNP would decline somewhat in the 1980s, the party reasserted its strength on the Scottish electoral scene in the 1990s. The SNP captured more than 20 percent of the vote in each of the 1992 and 1997 elections, and, in 1997, it once again replaced the Conservatives as a main, although not mainstream, party in Scotland.

The strong, swift, and long-lasting success of this niche party in Britain has puzzled scholars, journalists, and politicians since the 1970s. As was highlighted in Chapter 5, Britain is Sartori's quintessential two-party system. Even though plurality systems can sustain regional parties, the Scottish political scene, like the English, was clearly dominated by Labour and the Conservatives even as late as

---

[1] Dr. Alistair Smith, Member of the Scottish Conservative and Unionist Association, quoted in Conservative Party, *Verbatim Report of the 93rd Annual Conservative Party Conference* 1976: 106.
[2] In that general election, the SNP's U.K. vote share was 2.9 percent.

the 1960s. Moreover, self-government – the substance of the SNP's message – also seemed unlikely to appeal to Scottish voters. Scotland was not characterized by racial, linguistic, or cultural distinctiveness – factors thought to be associated with a strong ethnoterritorial identity and support for ethnoterritorial movements (Fearon and van Houten 2002; Jolly 2006).

Economic conditions in Scotland do not lead to strong expectations of the SNP's electoral ascendancy either. The region does not seem poor enough, given its middling levels of GDP per capita relative to the rest of the United Kingdom and the discovery of "Scottish oil" in the North Sea, to foster a nationalism built on regional deprivation, or prosperous enough, with its high levels of unemployment relative to the country as a whole, to develop a strong ethnoterritorial identity and party support centered around ideas of economic superiority (*Eurostat Statistics* 2003).

What then accounts for the phenomenal electoral success of the SNP? The answer lies in the behavior of the British Labour and Conservative parties. As this chapter will show, both mainstream parties initially tried to stem the flow of their voters to the threatening ethnoterritorial party with promises of regional self-rule. Scottish devolution, however, was not universally supported by the elite of either party. The replacement of pro-devolution Conservative Party Leader Edward Heath with anti-devolution Margaret Thatcher just as the Tories were recognizing their inability to beat Labour in the race for devolution issue ownership created an opportunity for a change in Tory strategy. The Conservatives consequently abandoned their accommodative tactics for an unrelenting adversarial strategy. Although this tactical about-face limited the effectiveness of the Tories' subsequent efforts to reinforce SNP issue ownership, the SNP's competitiveness was ensured by the inconsistency of the Labour Party's co-optative efforts. By the time Labour Party discipline was finally imposed in the mid-1990s, Labour's proposals to create a Scottish Parliament could not undermine the issue reputation of the SNP and, thus, its attraction of issue-based voters. The SNP had become a lasting fixture on the Scottish and British political scenes.

This chapter begins with an analysis of the electoral and political conditions under which the SNP emerged, focusing specifically on the situation in Scotland. The role of the SNP as a regional single-issue party is explored. Following the structure of the previous case study chapters, the discussion then turns to explanations of the niche party's electoral ups and downs. The rest of the chapter is devoted to the testing of the theories presented in Chapters 2 and 4: it examines the decisions behind the Labour and Conservative parties' strategies and their effects on the salience and ownership of the devolution issue and on voter support for the SNP.

THE SCOTTISH POLITICAL AND ELECTORAL ENVIRONMENT

When the SNP won the Hamilton by-election of 1967, marking its re-entry into the Westminster parliament and its post–World War II electoral reawakening, forces of political and electoral change had already begun to transform Great

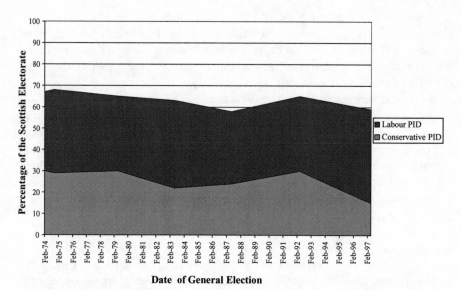

Date of General Election

FIGURE 7.1. Scottish Partisan Identification, 1974–97. *Sources:* British Election Studies, 1974 (February and October), 1979, 1983, 1987, 1992, 1997.

Britain.[3] Recall from Chapter 5 that the country was witnessing a decline in the number of partisan identifiers and a decrease in voter turnout in general. Voter volatility was on the rise, and the percentage of votes for the two mainstream parties was falling.

Scotland was not spared this process of dealignment. As Figure 7.1 reveals, the percentage of people identifying with the mainstream Labour and Conservative parties was decreasing, albeit slowly. More significantly, the percentage of people who professed no attachment to any political party was rising. Based on survey data from the British Election Studies, the percentage of unattached voters in Scotland increased from an average of 8 percent in the 1970s to an average of 14 percent just a decade later.[4] Among those people who maintained their loyalty to one of the two mainstream parties, the strength of their attachments was weakening. As shown in Figure 7.2, the percentage of "very strong" Labour partisans was almost halved over a twenty-five-year period. Even though Conservatives were more weakly attached to their party to begin with, the strength of Conservative partisanship in Scotland also exhibited a downward trend, despite an uptick at the end of the 1980s.

With voters either less likely to identify with the two mainstream parties or likely to identify less strongly, it is not surprising to find corresponding changes in voter electoral behavior. Voter volatility increased markedly in Scotland starting in the 1970s. Scotland's Pedersen Index score – measuring the net change in party support between elections – averaged almost 11 for the period of 1970 to 1997,

---

[3] The SNP won a by-election in 1945, giving the party its first seat in the Westminster parliament.
[4] Calculations from various *British Election Studies*.

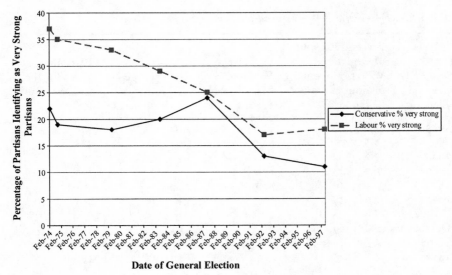

FIGURE 7.2. Decline in Strength of Party Identification among Scottish Partisans. *Sources:* British Election Studies, 1974 (February and October), 1979, 1983, 1987, 1992, 1997.

after averaging 4 for the elections of 1951 to 1966.[5] Recall from Chapter 5 that the comparable change in Britain as a whole was more muted, from 4.9 between 1951 and 1966 to 7.6 afterward (until 1992) (Denver 1994: 151).

Not only were voters switching parties, but they were also considering non-mainstream party options in record numbers. The post–World War II period witnessed a steady drop in voter support for the Conservative and Labour parties. As shown in Table 7.1, mainstream party support fell from 96.8 percent in 1955 to 87.6 percent in 1966. This downward trend picked up speed in the 1970s. By the end of the 1990s, the Labour and Conservative parties had clearly lost their monopoly on Scottish politics; only 63.1 percent of Scottish voters were casting their ballots for these two parties.

Although similar processes of partisan dealignment were affecting these mainstream parties across all of Britain, the threat to Labour's fortune was exacerbated in Scotland. The Labour Party was the dominant party in Scotland, capturing the majority of the region's parliamentary seats in every election since 1959. But it was also the case that Labour's national electoral support and parliamentary standing were disproportionately dependent on Scottish votes and seats. Keating and Bleiman (1979: 147) report: "In every election since 1950, Labour has gained a larger proportion of Scottish seats than English seats. After 1959, Labour also secured a larger proportion of the Scottish than the English vote."

A ramification of this regional dominance is that Labour's hold on Scottish seats directly determined its ability to control the British government. According to Brand (1979: 4):

---

[5] Calculations from Butler et al. *The British General Election*, various years; Lynch 2002.

TABLE 7.1. *Post–World War II General Election Results for Scotland*

General Election	Percent Turnout of Registered Voters (percent turnout in United Kingdom)	Percentage of Votes for the Mainstream Parties	Percentage of Votes for the Labour Party	Percentage of Votes for the Conservative Party
1955	75.1 (76.7)	96.8	46.7	50.1
1959	78.1 (78.8)	93.9	46.7	47.2
1964	77.6 (77.1)	89.3	48.7	40.6
1966	76.0 (75.8)	87.6	49.9	37.7
1970	74.1 (72.0)	82.5	44.5	38.0
February 1974	79.0 (78.7)	69.5	36.6	32.9
October 1974	74.8 (72.8)	61.0	36.3	24.7
1979	76.8 (76.0)	72.9	41.5	31.4
1983	72.7 (72.7)	63.5	35.1	28.4
1987	75.1 (75.3)	66.4	42.4	24.0
1992	75.5 (77.7)	64.6	39.0	25.6
1997	71.3 (71.5)	63.1	45.6	17.5

Sources: http://www.alba.org.uk/westminster/turnout.html; Brown et al. 1999: 7; Butler and Butler 2000; Lynch 2002; Newell 1998.

Only in the elections of 1945 and 1966 was the Labour Party able to command a majority of the seats in England and Wales alone. In other words, Labour won the elections of 1950, 1964 and the two elections of 1974 by depending on Scottish seats.

Although written in the late 1970s, this observation was nonetheless true of the entire post–World War II period: on all but a few occasions, the difference between a Labour Party electoral majority (and prime ministership) and a Labour Party in opposition was the control of Scottish seats. Consequently, a threat to Labour's hold in Scotland would jeopardize its *national* standing.[6]

The Conservatives, on the other hand, were less threatened than Labour by the dealignment process taking place in Scotland. In contrast to Labour, the Conservatives' control of the House of Commons in the post–World War II period depended more on the party's popularity in England than in Scotland or Wales. For example, the 1959 Conservative government would have been established even in the absence of *any* support from Scottish voters. This phenomenon repeated itself in the 1983, 1987, and 1992 Conservative victories![7] The fortune of the national Conservative Party seemed immune to the failures of its Scottish comrades.

---

[6] To quote Brand (1979: 4): "If the SNP replaced Labour as the majority party in Scotland, the probability of Labour forming a British government would be seriously diminished."

[7] Calculations from Butler and Butler 2000: ch. 4.

NATIONALISM IN ASCENDANCY: THE SCOTTISH NATIONAL PARTY (1966–97)

In an environment characterized by partisan dealignment, the Scottish National Party stood out as a potential threat to British mainstream party dominance. Formed in 1934, the SNP challenged the centralized British government by calling for Scottish self-government. This goal was expressed at different times as either devolution of political and financial powers to the regional level or as Scottish regional independence (Paterson 1998: 15; Scottish National Party 1966a). The rationale behind these goals was the same, however: "Scottish control of Scottish affairs" was seen as necessary to protect Scottish interests against the often contradictory interests (and, thus, policies) of Britain (Scottish National Party 1974: 5). Unlike other pro-devolution ethnoterritorial movements in Western Europe, the SNP was worried less about the preservation of a historical cultural identity and more about the relative economic health of the region.[8]

Despite its emergence in the interwar period, the SNP was not a regular participant in national parliamentary elections until after World War II. And even then, in the first five Westminster elections after the end of the war, the SNP contested an average of only four seats per election and captured a little more than 10 percent per contested seat. But by 1960, the number of SNP candidates standing in each election grew to double digits, and its platform for greater regional autonomy was publicized beyond a handful of districts scattered across Scotland.[9] Signs of the SNP's potential as an electoral spoiler and even a credible political competitor emerged in by-elections in the former Labour seats of Glasgow Pollok and Hamilton in 1967. SNP participation in Glasgow Pollok led to the transfer of the seat to the Conservatives, while SNP contestation of Hamilton yielded the niche party and its candidate, Winnie Ewing, a seat in the Westminster parliament.

Following this by-election win, support for the SNP began to rise dramatically, as shown in Table 7.2. Already doubling its vote in the 1970 General Election, the niche party would capture a record high 30.4 percent of voter support in the October 1974 election. Not only did this score earn the niche party eleven seats in the House of Commons, but it also allowed the SNP to surpass the Conservatives to become the second party of Scotland.

During a period of political disenchantment, when the mainstream parties focused on English problems, the SNP's demands for Scottish self-rule resonated with Scottish voters. The devolution issue proved popular across the political spectrum. A 1975 Opinion Research Centre poll showed that nearly

---

[8] The economic rationale for the SNP's decentralization demands was evident in its campaign materials from 1966 and 1974. SNP 1966a, 1966b, 1974.

[9] Changes in another measure of the SNP's reach, the number of local party branches, also demonstrate the party's dramatic development in the 1960s. In 1960, the party had twenty-three branches. By the end of 1966, that number had increased to 205. Two years later, the number of branches was 484. Lynch 2002: 108.

TABLE 7.2. *SNP Performance in Westminster Parliamentary Elections*

General Election	Percentage of Vote in Scotland	Number of Seats Won
1966	5.0	0
1970	11.4	1
February 1974	21.9	7
October 1974	30.4	11
1979	17.3	2
1983	11.8	2
1987	14.0	3
1992	21.5	3
1997	22.1	6

Source: Lynch 2002.

three-quarters of Scottish survey respondents wanted more devolution for Scotland (Mackintosh 1975: 12).

And, more threatening to the Labour and Conservative parties, voters were flocking to the SNP on the basis of that issue position. As early as June 1968, a Conservative Research Department memorandum noted that the SNP was largely a one-issue party, with its voters motivated only by the topic of self-government.[10] This perception was consistent with the niche party's refusal to "place itself on the conventional left-right spectrum" (Bennie, Brand, and Mitchell 1997: 82).

The single-issue orientation of the SNP is also suggested by the findings of British Election Study surveys from the 1970s to the 1990s. Those who voted for the SNP were more likely than other voters to prioritize the issue of devolution. For instance, 53 percent of SNP voters who responded to the February 1974 British Election Study stated that devolution was the most important issue facing Britain as opposed to only 18 percent of Labour voters and 3 percent of Conservative voters in Scotland.[11] In the 1979 General Election, the issue of a Scottish government played an equally critical role in shaping the voting decisions of SNP voters. According to the 1979 Scottish Election Study, 50 percent of SNP voters ranked it "extremely important" versus 14 percent of Labour voters and 10 percent of Conservative voters.[12]

In addition to prioritizing the issue more, SNP supporters were more likely than any other group of voters to support political and financial decentralization. Of the October 1974 SNP voters, 88.5 percent voiced their support for

[10] According to the author of that document, the SNP's membership would "fragment, once again, into Left and Right if its one policy was ever achieved." CPA, CRD, Keith Raffan, "Memorandum to Mr. Sewill on the Scottish National Party 34th Annual National Conference," (London: CRD, June 10, 1968): 4.

[11] Unless otherwise noted, all survey percentages in this chapter are for Scotland only. Calculations from Crewe et al. 1975a.

[12] Calculations from Miller and Brand 1981.

devolution, as opposed to 57 percent of Labour voters and 55 percent of Conservative voters.[13] In 1997, 94 percent of SNP voters supported various plans for greater regional autonomy versus 82 percent of Labour voters and 38 percent of Conservative voters.[14] On other issues, however, SNP sympathizers did not exhibit common policy preferences. Diversity of opinion characterized SNP voters' views on a range of controversial and otherwise polarizing economic and social issues, from wage control and social services to the death penalty. Analyses of survey data from the 1974 and 1979 elections reveal that the distribution of preferences of SNP voters on these issues is similar to the spread of preferences across the Scottish electorate as a whole.[15] Although the diversity of SNP supporters' preferences on other issues did decline to some extent in the 1990s, devolution still stood out as the issue on which they were most unified.[16] It seems that, just like the voters of the French FN, SNP voters were coming from across the economic and social spectrum to vote on the basis of one issue – in the Scottish case, devolution.

Dependent on the popularity and exclusivity of its devolution position, the SNP had a difficult time increasing its vote share above its October 1974 score of 30.4 percent. Support for the niche party fell over the next two elections to a low of 11.8 percent in 1983. But even then, the party maintained a presence in the Westminster parliament with two MPs. Refusing to retract its calls for Scottish self-government, the SNP would battle back in the 1980s and 1990s to regain a voter base of more than 20 percent, control of up to six seats, and, by 1997, a place as (once again) the second most popular party in Scotland.

STANDARD APPROACHES TO UNDERSTANDING ETHNOTERRITORIAL PARTY SUCCESS

In a time period when the dominance of the mainstream parties was challenged but rarely undermined, the SNP's replacement of the British Conservative Party as the second player in Scottish politics is noteworthy. How did this single-issue party manage to capture an average of almost 20 percent of the vote across twenty-seven years? And what explains the fluctuations in the SNP's electoral fortune

---

[13] In the October 1974 Scottish Election Study, this policy preference was represented by the sum of two choices: "more decisions made in Scotland" and "run its own affairs." These calculations are based on the October 1974 SES data included as part of a panel in the 1979 Scottish Election Study. All subsequent references to the October 1974 SES will refer to this data and be noted as coming from Miller and Brand 1981.

[14] Calculations from McCrone et al. 1999. These percentages include support for all the nonstatus quo, pro-devolution options for governing Scotland included in the 1997 Scottish Election Survey. Unlike previous election studies, the 1997 SES options distinguished between types of independence (within or outside of the EU) as well as types of an elected Scottish Assembly (with or without taxation powers). The difference between the percentages of SNP voters and other parties' voters who support independence are even greater than reported in the preceding text. However, as this chapter will show, the SNP's support for independence plays less of a role than some might think in the mainstream parties' (in)abilities to quell the SNP threat.

[15] Calculations from Miller and Brand 1981.

[16] Calculations from McCrone et al. 1999.

over time? Why was there wide support for it in the 1970s and 1990s, but a drop-off in its popularity during the decade in between?

Institutional Explanations Fall Short

Institutional variables offer some explanation for the relative electoral success of the Scottish ethnoterritorial party. Recall that while the British electoral and political environment is considered hostile to minor parties in general, its plurality electoral rules are seen as providing some advantages to ethnoterritorial niche parties. Because of their geographic concentration of support, ethnoterritorial parties have a greater likelihood of winning a seat under plurality rules than a niche party with an equal number of voters spread across the country (Rae 1971; Sartori 1986). The regression results from Chapter 3 support this claim with evidence that ethnoterritorial party support across Western Europe is higher in systems with low district magnitudes than systems with higher ones.

It has similarly been argued that the state structure in Britain has advantaged ethnoterritorial parties over their green and radical right counterparts. Scholars of regionalist parties (De Winter and Türsan 1998; Levi and Hechter 1985) typically have claimed that these parties perform better in unitary states.[17] Although all niche parties in a unitary state are hurt by the lack of patronage opportunities associated with federalism, these scholars argue that ethnoterritorial parties are more likely to draw voter support when their main demand of greater regional autonomy has not been met.[18] Approaching the question from an interest in national versus regional party system formation, Chhibber and Kollman (2004) likewise predict strong regionalist party support in Britain and specifically for the SNP, but for opposite reasons. They describe Britain after 1970 as being in a state of "increasing regionalism" (2004: 163). Decentralization – or, in this case, credible promises thereof – they argue, increase (future) resources at the regional level and increase the likelihood of voters supporting regional as opposed to national parties (2004: 80).

Consistent with the general predictions of these institutional theories, a comparison of vote shares across Britain reveals that the SNP fared better electorally than other, nonregional niche parties. The SNP's average vote of 18.8 percent from 1970 to 1997 and its peak vote of more than 30 percent vastly exceed the electoral average and peak vote received by the Greens and National Front.

However, the institutional explanation falls short when trying to account for variation in ethnoterritorial party support over time or even across different ethnoterritorial parties within the same country. Regardless of whether the SNP's vote share is regionally or nationally calculated, the rise, fall, and subsequent rise in SNP support between 1970 and 1997 cannot be explained by fixed electoral

---

[17] Recall that Jolly (2006) posits the existence of a curvilinear relationship where support for ethnoterritorial parties is also strong at high levels of decentralization.

[18] The relationship between ethnoterritorial party vote and state structure was found to be statistically insignificant in the cross-national time-series analysis in Chapter 3.

rules. Other institutions, such as the British parliamentary system and the unitary state structure, likewise remained stable during this period of SNP vote variation.

The capacity of these approaches to account for ethnoterritorial vote change appears to increase if one considers the Chhibber and Kollman argument that credible steps toward institutional change are sufficient to cause vote shifts. But as will be described at length later in this chapter, the actual timing of serious party and government commitments to devolution is not consistent with their claims (2004: 197); concrete and credible discussions about devolution and attempts by the government to pass devolution legislation only came *after* the SNP's dramatic vote increase in the 1974 elections. Moreover, although their model might be able to account for the drop in SNP support in the 1980s when devolution plans were downplayed by the mainstream parties, it would have a hard time also explaining why SNP vote declined after 1974 when the mainstream parties were articulating concrete devolution proposals.

Turning from explaining variation in support over time to variation in support across multiple ethnoterritorial parties in Britain, we find similar limitations to the explanatory power of institutional theories. Given that these parties were facing the same electoral and governmental institutions, these electoral rules or state structure cannot explain why the SNP got over 30 percent of the regional vote when its ethnoterritorial counterpart in Wales, the Plaid Cymru, achieved a peak vote of only 11.5 percent. Chhibber and Kollman's emphasis on the credibility of decentralizing proposals holds more promise, as Wales was the object of weaker and less-committed promises of decentralization than Scotland, but questions remain about the timing of regionalist party vote increases relative to the regionalization process.

Sociological Theories: Conflicting Expectations and Insignificant Answers

The explanatory power of sociological theories of SNP support is also limited. Recall from Chapter 1 that the literature on ethnoterritorial parties has proposed contradictory theories of party vote. While this should allow researchers to find support for at least one set of hypotheses, few significant relationships in fact emerge between economic or social factors and SNP vote.

The case of Scotland and the SNP has been held up, on separate occasions, as evidence of both Hechter's internal colonialism argument and the opposing theory of overtaxed development. Hechter (1975) includes a discussion of Scotland in his analysis of how economic deprivation caused by a cultural division of labor has led to strong feelings of regional identity in this part of the Celtic fringe. In this theory, nationalism, which is built on these feelings of economic resentment, feeds ethnoterritorial parties. Conversely, Nairn (1977) and Zariski (1989) name Scotland as a key example of how a wealthier region's desire to cut ties with a core that is stealing its resources results in stronger support for an ethnoterritorial party, such as the SNP.

Both sets of arguments have been employed by the SNP in its campaigns to drum up electoral support. Indeed, the ethnoterritorial party has often argued simultaneously that Scotland has been purposefully kept poor by London (internal colonialism) and that Scotland is subsidizing England (overtaxed development). Yet despite the use of this rhetoric, analyses of the relationships between various objective indicators of economic prosperity and the SNP's regional vote share fail to confirm the validity of these claims. The results from the large-N statistical analysis in Chapter 3 suggest the explanatory primacy of the overtaxed development argument, and, at first glance, there seems to be some evidence that this hypothesis holds in the case of the SNP. Bivariate correlations reveal that the regional unemployment rate is strongly and negatively correlated with SNP vote.[19] However, bivariate correlations of SNP vote with each of the other economic measures – regional GDP per capita, relative regional unemployment, and relative regional GDP per capita – prove statistically insignificant. Given that both the internal colonialism and overtaxed development arguments focus on a region's level of economic prosperity *relative* to the core, the lack of significant relationships, especially with the relative economic measures, means we cannot conclude that either sociological theory is supported in this case.[20]

Similarly, there is no evidence of the relevance of social factors for explaining SNP vote. Notwithstanding recent cross-national research findings that linguistic distinctiveness is central to ethnoterritorial party emergence and success (see Fearon and van Houten 2002; Jolly 2006), the SNP has flourished in a region lacking this characteristic. The indigenous language of Gaelic is spoken by less than 1.5 percent of the population.[21] Fluency is even rarer; as of 1991, only 0.6 percent of the population was able to read, write, and speak the language. Thus, although Fearon and van Houten classify Gaelic as being of "maximum difference from that of the predominant language of the country," the success of the Scottish National Party cannot be linked to a linguisitic factor that is associated with such a small number of people, let alone voters.[22] Indeed, there is a consensus among scholars of Scottish politics and of the SNP (e.g., Lynch 2002; Mackintosh quoted in Paterson 1998; McCrone 1992) that the SNP's support

---

[19] There is a correlation of -0.93, which is statistically significant at $p = .07$.

[20] It should be noted that proponents of the overtaxed development argument, including many within the SNP, typically employ measures of how much Scotland is subsidizing the United Kingdom rather than the relative regional GDP per capita or relative regional unemployment measures used in my cross-national analyses. However, contradictory evidence about the true level of this subsidization challenges any claims that it validates the overtaxed development theory. See Niall U'Aislainn ("The Big Lie – Scottish Revenue Taxes," http://www.alba.org.uk) as an example of the claim that Scotland subsidizes England and "The Economic Impact of a Welsh Assembly" cited in Gow (1997: 9) as a source indicating that Scotland is prospering more from the relationship than England.

[21] According to John Mackintosh (quoted in Paterson 1998: 66), that percentage was 1.2 percent in 1974. In 1991, the census listed the percentage as 1.4 percent (United Kingdom 1996: 251).

[22] See Chandra (2001) and Posner (2004) for forceful arguments about how the salience of cultural differences is neither a given nor a constant across contexts.

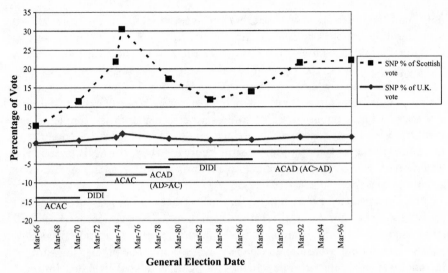

FIGURE 7.3. Scottish National Party Electoral Support. *Sources:* Butler and Butler 2000; Lynch 2002.

does not emanate from a traditional, ethnolinguistically defined conception of nationalism.[23] The SNP is popular *despite* the absence of this factor.

A STRATEGIC EXPLANATION OF THE SCOTTISH NATIONAL PARTY'S SUCCESS

The rest of the chapter considers a party-centered strategic explanation of how the SNP's fortune developed over the past thirty years (see Figure 7.3). Analysis of the behavior of the Labour and Conservative parties sheds light on how the SNP's internal colonialism and overtaxed development rationales for self-government came to resonate with the Scottish electorate, despite the insignificance of any independent relationship between the relative economic factors and SNP vote. As will be shown, mainstream party validation of the devolution issue and reinforcement of the SNP's issue ownership – although not always deliberate – drove pro-devolution voters to support the single-issue party and led to its electoral success.

1967–70: Mainstream Parties Respond to an Emerging Scottish Threat

The victory of SNP MP candidate Winnie Ewing in the November 2, 1967 by-election in Hamilton, Scotland marked the beginning of a thirty-year battle for control of Scottish voters and Westminster parliamentary seats. In that election, as in the Glasgow Pollok by-election eight months prior, the SNP candidates emerged from the sidelines to win an average of 37 percent of the vote. More

---

[23] As long ago as September 1974, John P. Mackintosh (quoted in Paterson 1998: 66) made the following observation about Scottish nationalism and support for the SNP: "Language, for example, is not a factor as only some 60,000 out of five million speak Gaelic."

important than the vote shares that they received, the SNP candidates managed to undermine Labour's control of these seats. In the marginal Labour seat of Glasgow Pollok, defection to the SNP was largely responsible for Labour's loss of 21.2 percent of its 1966 General Election vote in that constituency, ensuring a Conservative victory (Lynch 2002: 115). In Hamilton, Winnie Ewing captured the plurality of votes (46 percent), removing Labour from one of its long-standing safe seats.[24] These phenomenal Westminster performances were supplemented with strong SNP showings in the local elections of 1967 and 1968. SNP popularity was equally reflected in opinion polls; in February 1967, the SNP became the leading party in Scotland, securing 37 percent of Scottish respondents' support according to a *Scottish Daily Express* poll.[25]

This rapid growth in voter support for the SNP between 1967 and 1968 elicited active responses from the British mainstream parties. In what was clearly a small step designed to test the waters of SNP support and the dedication of its new voters, the Labour government created a Royal Commission on the Constitution in 1969 to examine the possible schemes for Scottish (and Welsh) devolution.[26] Though it was no more than a commitment to *consider* constitutional changes, this commission represented a significant move for a party that, at the time, advocated an international view of socialism opposed to regional particularisms. It is also important to note that this policy reversal was not the result of widespread pressure from within the party. According to Scottish Labour MP Tam Dalyell, this initial accommodative tactic was the decision of the home secretary with the assent of the prime minister, but without the consideration of the government's cabinet, let alone the party conference.[27] Coming after the SNP's trouncing of Labour support in two by-elections and in local elections, the establishment of the Kilbrandon Commission (as the Royal Commission would come to be called) was acknowledged by Labour members to be electorally motivated.[28] It was Labour's first bow to the power of the devolution voter.

---

[24] The Labour Party's vote share in Hamilton dropped from 71.2 percent in 1966 to 41.5 percent in the 1967 by-election. Lynch 2002: 115.

[25] A BBC poll conducted in May of 1968 found that the level of SNP support was even higher, at 43 percent. Cited in ibid., 118.

[26] The establishment of the Royal Commission was followed up with a discussion of devolution in the Labour Party's 1970 General Election manifesto. Mirroring the rhetoric used by the SNP, the manifesto appealed to SNP voters with the promise that Labour "would apply Scottish solutions to Scottish problems." Labour Party 1970: 20.

[27] To quote Tam Dalyell (1977: 81): "Mr. James Callaghan, then Home Secretary, took it upon himself, with Mr. Wilson's consent, but certainly without a Cabinet decision, or consultation with the Secretary of State for Scotland, Mr. William Ross, to set up a Commission on the Constitution under the chairmanship of Lord Crowther."

[28] At the 1968 Labour Party Conference, a proposal was submitted by the Edinburgh and Leith Constituency Labour Party calling on the government to recognize the Scottish people's desire for devolution. James Callaghan, then Home Secretary, responded to that resolution on behalf of the National Executive Committee. He said, "The Prime Minister has authorized me to say that the Government is at work on the problem as to how far and how best the facts of the alternatives can be established. There is every reason why we should examine our basic institutions once again." Several months later, the Royal Commission on the Constitution was created. Cited in LPA, Heffer Papers, Eric S. Heffer, MP, "The Devolution Crisis," undated draft of a manuscript: 2.

The Conservative Party was not as affected as Labour by the surge in SNP support in the late 1960s. Not only was it not the main source of the defecting voters, but Scottish support was also not critical to the electoral success of the Conservative Party. Driven by concern over its electoral strength relative to Labour, however, the Conservative Party did not remain silent on what would prove to be a controversial issue: devolution. Following the SNP's first by-election win in 1967, the Conservative Party commissioned a flurry of surveys and studies to examine the ramifications of heightened Scottish nationalism for the Tories' vote share.[29] In addition, a commission was established to review the machinery of the Scottish government. Spurred on by reports that "the [SNP] threat to Conservatives in Scotland is, if anything, more serious than was already known," not to mention the SNP's surprising successes in the 1968 municipal elections, Tory Leader Edward Heath announced his party's support for a directly elected Scottish Parliament.[30] His famous Declaration of Perth was later endorsed by a Conservative parliamentary committee,[31] and this policy became the centerpiece of the party's 1970 Scottish parliamentary campaign.

Much like the Labour Party's early accommodative strategy, however, this embrace of devolution was not natural for the Conservative Party. The party had long been opposed to Home Rule, a conceptual precursor to devolution associated with the fight to win greater independence for Ireland in the late 19th and early 20th centuries. Those within the Conservative Party who maintained this opposition voiced their disapproval of Heath's plan for Scotland. In the Conservative Leader's Consultative Committee meeting held less than two months after Heath's Perth Declaration, it was stated:

Within the Party in Scotland, there was now a certain amount of reaction against the proposal, mainly from what might be called the Right Wing, those in favour of Home Rule, and those of the opposite view who thought it was a "sell-out" to SNP (CPA, LCC(68) 247th Mtg., 1968: 1).

Although the degree to which the SNP actually threatened the Conservatives was questionable at this juncture, Conservatives, both for and against the strategy, identified their party's accommodative move as electorally motivated. According to Home Rule opponents, Edward Heath – being "excessively fearful of the threat posed by the SNP" (Mitchell 1990: 57) – was pandering to the Nationalists.

1970–73: Disappointing Results and the Downplaying of the Devolution Issue

Following the heady results of the SNP in local and by-elections of the late 1960s, the stage was set for a nationalist surge in the 1970 General Election in Scotland.

---

[29] Some examples include CPA, CCO, "ORC: A Survey on the Motivations behind Scottish Nationalism," March 1968; CPA, CRD, "Opinion Research – Nationalism," July 10, 1968; CPA, CRD, "Scottish Nationalism," November 15, 1967.

[30] CPA, CCO, "ORC: A Survey on the Motivations behind Scottish Nationalism," March 1968: 28.

[31] This Conservative Constitutional Committee, established in July 1968, was chaired by Sir Alec Douglas Home. It has subsequently been referred to as the Home Committee, with its 1970 report on devolution known as the Home Committee Report.

Opinion polls taken in January 1969 forecast an SNP General Election vote share of 20.9 percent.[32] While this number represented a significant decline from the 43 percent predicted only seven months earlier,[33] such a high level of support would still result in a monumental seat gain for the SNP.[34]

Yet the swell of nationalist sentiment did not translate into an explosion of SNP support in the 1970 General Election. SNP candidates contested more than three times the number of seats they had in 1966, but their average vote per seat contested dropped from 14.1 percent to 12.2 percent (Butler and Butler 2000: 181). The party did gain one seat – the Western Isles – but as they lost the Hamilton seat won in the 1967 by-election, their overall seat total remained the same. This was clearly a far cry from the thirty-one seats that they were expected to gain.

That said, the SNP did increase its overall support levels. In 1970, the party gained 306,802 votes, more than twice its 1966 total (Butler and Butler 2000: 237). And its percentage of the vote in Scotland increased from 5.0 percent in 1966 to 11.4 percent. However, with almost half of SNP support coming from first-time voters or abstainers who had not defected from a mainstream party,[35] the threat of the SNP to the mainstream parties seemed quite low.[36]

Based on these election results, how should the Conservative and Labour parties respond according to my PSO theory of strategic choice? The Conservative Party left the 1970 election with an electoral lead and control of the House of Commons (by 330 votes to Labour's 287). The SNP did gain support in four of the Conservatives' marginal Scottish seats, capturing enough votes in two of them to exceed the electoral difference between the top two candidates.[37] Yet, given the relative electoral security of the Tories and the fact that few Conservative voters were defecting to the SNP, this showing was not enough to warrant a costly accommodative campaign by the Tories.[38]

Although the Labour Party lost seats in the 1970 election, the SNP was not directly to blame. Of the votes that the ethnoterritorial party captured, the

---

[32] January 1969 poll taken by NOP cited in Butler and Pinto-Duschinsky 1971: 455.

[33] May 1968 BBC poll by Market Information Services cited in Butler and Pinto-Duschinsky 1971: 455.

[34] According to a Conservative Party analysis, the SNP would win thirty-one seats in the 1970 General Election if the following conditions held: "the SNP fought all the Scottish seats, and took away votes from Labour and Conservative in the same proportion as at Hamilton, and if there was also a swing from Labour to Conservative of 3.5 percent." CPA, untitled Conservative Party document, pre-1970: 3.

[35] This estimate is based on data from the February 1974 British Election Study. While the small sample size of Scottish respondents in the study raises concerns about its representativeness and, thus, the validity of our conclusion about a low SNP threat, our confidence is boosted by the similarly dismissive treatment of the SNP's vote share by secondary analyses. Calculations from Crewe et al. 1975a; Kellas 1971: 460.

[36] Many of the other voters who supported the SNP in 1970 defected from the Liberals. This was most notably the case in the north of Scotland, where the SNP returned its highest levels of support. Steed 1971: 402–4.

[37] Butler and Pinto-Duschinsky 1971: 376–9.

[38] Calculations from Butler and Stokes 1974.

majority did not come from former Labour supporters.[39] The SNP did run candidates in Labour-held safe seats, reducing Labour's electoral majority in them and even turning five of the safe seats into marginal districts. But, on the whole, the SNP's electoral presence did not threaten Labour's control of its seats or Labour's overall representation and strength in Scotland.[40]

Under these circumstances, both the Conservative and Labour parties are expected to ignore the low-level electoral threat. Assuming that voters take their cues from the mainstream parties, a joint dismissive strategy would decrease the perceived importance of the issue and, thus, the future draw of the SNP. Furthermore, this tactic would allow the mainstream parties to avoid the internal party debates over devolution that had already begun to surface after the announcement of Labour's and the Conservatives' lukewarm accommodative stances in the late 1960s.

The behavior of the Conservative Party in the period following the 1970 General Election conforms to these predictions. Initially a reluctant advocate of devolution, the Conservative Party took the electoral decline of the SNP as an opportunity to ignore the issue. Examination of the transcripts of the annual Conservative Party conference reveal that the topic was not mentioned in the meetings held from 1971 to 1973.[41] Moreover, despite promises to the contrary, the Heath government made no major speeches on the subject of devolution.[42] Indeed, this decision to postpone any discussion or action on the matter of Scottish devolution was clearly articulated in the agenda-setting Queen's Speech of 1970.[43] In response to a Labour MP's subsequent criticism about this delay, Heath stated, "The question of devolution, while clearly a related matter, has always seemed to us one which should be pursued separately, and later, in a United Kingdom context."[44]

While Heath would later contradict this statement by claiming that the Conservative Party's inactivity was due to the need to await the release of the Kilbrandon Commission Report (Mitchell 1990: 63), journalists and scholars have found ample evidence to the contrary.[45] The Conservatives' dismissive approach

---

[39] Ibid.; calculations from Crewe et al. 1975a.

[40] Calculations from Butler and King 1966: 323–4; Butler and Pinto-Duschinsky 1971: 376–9.

[41] Conservative Party, *Verbatim Report of the 89th Conservative Party Conference* 1971; Conservative Party, *Verbatim Report of the 90th Conservative Party Conference* 1972; Conservative Party, *Verbatim Report of the 91st Conservative Party Conference* 1973.

[42] Prior to the 1970 General Election, Heath pledged to follow through with the recommendations of the Home Committee Report. Yet, according to Drucker and Brown (1980: 85), "The Heath administration in fact did nothing about devolution."

[43] The Conservative Party chose to prioritize the reform of local government over the discussion of Scottish devolution. Mitchell 1990: 63.

[44] Quoted in John P. Mackintosh, "The Report of the Royal Commission on the Constitution, 1969–1973," *Political Quarterly* 1974. Cited in Mitchell 1990: 63.

[45] Geoffrey Smith, "The Conservative Commitment to Devolution," *The Spectator*, February 19, 1977; Geoffrey Smith, "Devolution and Not Saying What You Mean," *The Spectator*, February 26, 1977; Vernon Bogdanor, *Devolution*, (Oxford: Oxford University Press, 1979): 111. All cited in Mitchell 1990: 63.

to the SNP and the issue of devolution was deliberate. This strategy persisted throughout the electoral period. By 1973, the Conservative Party had, according to James Mitchell (1990: 63), "allowed devolution to slip away."

The Labour Party similarly downplayed the issue of devolution following the 1970 General Election. The topic was not raised at the Labour Party's annual conferences, where it was revealed instead that the party was preoccupied with the problems of the Common Market, education, and housing.[46] Although this claim was not explicitly expressed in any archival materials, it is likely that the Labour Party blamed its inactivity – to its electorate, members of the SNP, or even itself – on the slow workings of the Labour-created Kilbrandon Commission. Convened in 1970 before Labour left office, the commission did not report its findings until 1973. Whether the Labour Party justified its behavior in this manner or not, the decision to ignore the devolution issue and dismiss its nationalist party proponent was far from just a coincidence. As with the Conservatives' tactics, the timing of the adoption and later the abandonment of Labour's dismissive strategy depended on the electoral threat of the SNP.

1973–77: Mainstream Party Factionalism in the Face of a Rising Scottish National Party Challenge

By the end of 1973 and the beginning of 1974, the dismissive attitudes of the mainstream parties toward the SNP were largely supplanted by more co-optative stances. These changes in party strategy were sparked by the electoral resurgence of the ethnoterritorial party. The discovery of oil off the coast of Scotland a year earlier had provided further validation of the claim of regional economic self-sufficiency, evidence that the SNP did not fail to exploit. With "Scotland's oil," the Nationalists argued, the prospect of greater Scottish legislative autonomy or even national independence was less daunting. The resonance of the SNP's message was repeatedly demonstrated by the strong showing of the ethnoterritorial party in 1973 by-elections. Indeed, in November of that year, the SNP candidate, Margo MacDonald, won the Labour safe seat of Glasgow Govan. Following on the heels of the pro–Scottish Assembly recommendations of the Majority Report of the Kilbrandon Commission, this election served as a wake-up call to both mainstream parties.[47] The issue of devolution was salient again, and the niche party proponent of that issue stood to gain from its popularity – unless prevented by mainstream party strategies.

The urgency of responding to the SNP increased with the results of the February 1974 General Election. Although both the Labour and Conservative parties had increased their attention to and support of devolution during the run-up to

---

[46] Labour Party, *Report of the Seventieth Annual Conference of the Labour Party* 1971; Labour Party, *Report of the Seventy-first Annual Conference of the Labour Party* 1972.

[47] In addition to the Majority Report, which advocated the creation of legislative assemblies for Scotland and Wales, a Memorandum of Dissent was issued, which supported the formation of even more powerful assemblies for all regions in Britain (Peacock 1977: 57–8).

the February election,[48] their strategies seemed to be too little, too late to curtail the electoral success of the SNP. In the February election, the SNP contested seventy of the seventy-one districts, capturing 21.9 percent of the Scottish vote and seven seats.[49] Only eight months later, the minority Labour government called another general election. Once again, the election proved to the advantage of the SNP. The niche party contested all Scottish districts, winning 30.4 percent of the popular vote in the region and increasing its Westminster representation to eleven MPs.

The impact of these two elections on mainstream party strategy cannot be overestimated. The first 1974 election returned a minority Labour government, separated by only four votes from the Conservatives in opposition. Labour was therefore dependent on informal alliances with the Welsh and Scottish National-ist MPs. Ironically, it was those same informal coalition partners who had stolen Labour's support to get into Westminster. In Scotland, the SNP won support from as much as 10.5 percent of Labour's 1970 electorate.[50] The results of the British Election Study further suggest that the ethnoterritorial party gained as many votes from former Labour voters in the February General Election as it did from longtime SNP supporters.[51] The effect of the defection was the loss of two Labour seats to the niche party and the growing presence of the SNP in two of Labour's marginal districts.[52] Given the precarious nature of Labour's February 1974 lead, the SNP was a clear and immediate threat to the success of the Labour Party and Labour government.

The Conservatives were also directly affected by the rise of the SNP. If the BES sample is representative, almost 16 percent of the SNP's support in Febru-ary 1974 came from former Conservative Party supporters;[53] 9 percent of the

[48] In the final months of his government, Conservative Prime Minister Heath established a govern-mental committee to examine the recommendations of the (majority of the) Kilbrandon Commis-sion. The Conservative Party's commitment to devolution was also expressed in both the British and Scottish versions of its February 1974 General Election manifesto. In the Scottish program, the Tories vowed to "achieve the most effective and acceptable form of further devolution." Labour did not discuss the issue in its manifesto. However in 1973 and early 1974, several Labour Party officials, including Party Leader Harold Wilson, did mention the issue and even indicated grow-ing support for a Scottish devolution scheme. Conservative Party manifesto quoted in CPA, CRD 4/15/11, GW and SO'B, "Aide Memoir for Talks between Rt. Hon Margaret Thatcher, Rt. Hon Francis Pym and Rt. Hon James Callaghan, Rt. Hon Michael Foot on Devolution," March 2, 1977: 6; Labour Party behavior discussed in Keating and Bleiman 1979: 165.

[49] The SNP's average percentage of vote per candidate is thus even higher. Butler and Butler 2000: 237, 241.

[50] Our confidence in this finding from the 1974 cross-sectional British Election Study is boosted by the Labour Party's separate reporting of a 9.3 percent swing from Labour to the SNP between 1970 and February 1974. LPA, Home Policy Committee, "The Political and Economic Situation in Scotland," December 1975: 3.

[51] If the results of the British Election Studies are representative, 21 percent of the SNP's February 1974 vote came from those who voted Labour in 1970. Those who supported the SNP in 1970 also made up 21 percent of the SNP's 1974 vote. Calculations from Crewe et al. 1975a.

[52] The SNP won the seats of Dundee East and Clackmannan and Stirlingshire. Calculations from Craig 1977: 205–30.

[53] Calculations from Crewe et al. 1975a; Miller and Brand 1981.

Conservatives' 1970 Scottish electorate defected to the SNP. Although the Conservatives' loss to the ethnoterritorial party was slightly less than that of Labour, these vote transfers resulted in a greater loss of seats: the SNP won four formerly Conservative seats, three of which had been considered safe seats.

The outcome of the October election further reinforced the threat felt by the mainstream parties. The Labour Party remained in power, but with a slim majority of 319 seats out of 635. It increased its margin over the Conservatives, but only to seven percentage points and forty-two MPs United Kingdom–wide. In other words, Labour was still in a vulnerable electoral position.

And, in Scotland, the SNP was partially to blame. About 11 percent of the people who voted for the SNP in the October election had supported Labour eight months earlier.[54] And the niche party became the runner-up in all eleven of Labour's marginally held Scottish districts. Even though the SNP did not steal any new seats away from Labour, political analysts and politicians at the time concluded that the SNP posed a severe current and future danger to the Labour Party. As Labour MP John P. Mackintosh warned in 1975 (1975: 3):

If there was a 3% swing from Labour to the SNP, it would give the party a popular majority in Scotland and with each percentage point a number of the 36 seats held by Labour in which the SNP is now running second, would change hands.

The likelihood of this scenario was increased by the fact that the SNP was the second-choice party for the majority of Labour voters. The Labour Party, therefore, found itself hostage to the ethnoterritorial party.

The SNP threat to the Conservatives increased with the October election. For the first time, the SNP stole more voters from the Conservatives than from Labour; according to the October 1974 BES, 26.8 percent of SNP support in the second 1974 election came from those who voted for the Conservatives in the first 1974 General Election.[55] Based on this transfer of votes, the SNP gained four Conservative seats. In addition, the SNP scored a close second in four of the Conservatives' marginal seats.[56] In each of the other seven tenuously held Conservative districts, the ethnoterritorial party won enough votes to exceed the Tory candidate's margin of victory. With the Conservatives only winning a total of sixteen Scottish seats, the Tory position in Scotland was extremely precarious. And the SNP, which surpassed the Tories to become the number two party in Scotland, was the main culprit.[57]

On the basis of these electoral conditions, conditions that resemble scenario three in Chapter 4, both the Labour and Conservative parties would be expected

---

[54] Percentage based on calculations from Robertson 1977; Miller and Brand 1981.

[55] This number represents 22.7 percent of the Scottish voters who supported the Conservatives in February 1974. Calculations from Robertson 1977. Using data from the October 1974 wave reported in the 1979 Scottish Election Study, I arrive at the same conclusion that the former Conservative voters of the SNP outnumbered the former Labour supporters. However, these data indicate that the former composed only 16 percent of the SNP's October 1974 vote. Calculations from Miller and Brand 1981.

[56] Calculations from Butler and Kavanagh 1975: 321–3.

[57] This ranking is based on the parties' share of the popular vote in Scotland.

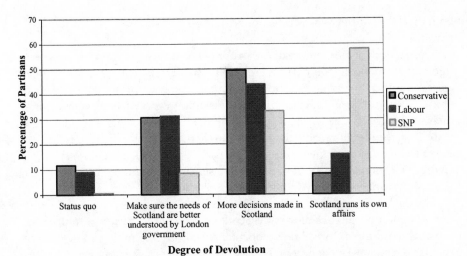

FIGURE 7.4. Partisan Preference Distribution on How to Govern Scotland, October 1974. *Source:* Scottish Election Study October 1974.

to implement accommodative tactics.[58] Only co-optative strategies would allow the mainstream parties to stave off further voter loss while trying to recover defectors; a continuation of dismissive tactics would probably be unsuccessful in burying the, by then primed, devolution issue or in encouraging the return of former voters. The pursuit of adversarial tactics would likewise be unwise. As shown in Figure 7.4, the majority of Scottish Conservative and Labour partisans were interested in some degree of decentralization for Scotland as indicated by the categories "more decisions made in Scotland" and "Scotland run its own affairs." The same degree of support for devolution was found among Scottish survey respondents in general (not shown). Consequently, adversarial tactics would further alienate defectors and promote additional vote loss.

Conservative Efforts to Be the "Party of Devolution." To a large extent, accommodation did become the official policy of the Labour and Conservative parties. Following the February election, the Conservatives began to emphasize their dedication to devolution. Signs of their support of devolution, or at least of its consideration, included the establishment of a committee on devolution led by Shadow Secretary Alick Buchanan-Smith, an increased number of party speeches on the topic, and the publication of Heath's *Charter for a New Scotland*, calling for the creation of an indirectly elected Scottish Assembly with tax-raising powers (Mitchell 1990: 70). The announcement of an October election brought increased Tory politicization of the issue. The Conservatives devoted several paragraphs in

---

[58] Conservative and Labour Party Archives reveal that the parties were aware immediately following the elections of the origins and destinations of these shifting voters. This information was considered by the parties when deciding on their strategies.

both their British and Scottish election manifestos to their proposals for Scottish devolution.[59]

The strength of the Conservative Party's accommodative stance would increase significantly following the loss of additional Tory voters to the SNP in the October election. Official party support for devolution was more prominent. Members of the Conservative Shadow Cabinet held several press conferences reaffirming their pledge to devolve legislative powers to Scotland. By 1976, Tory elite were embracing the idea of a relatively autonomous Scottish Assembly that was directly elected – a proposal that far exceeded the party's pledges from before the 1974 General Elections. The proliferation of Conservative committee proposals for a Scottish Assembly continued well into 1976.[60]

The Conservatives' move from a dismissive stance to advocacy of the devolution of significant political powers to Scotland was a direct response to the SNP threat. According to Tory elite, support for a Scottish Assembly was a means to appease the niche party and stem the flow of Tory voters to it.[61] In a private meeting with fifty Conservative MPs in 1976, Douglas Home "maintained that only legislating for an Assembly would prevent the return of a majority of SNP MPs at the following election" (Mitchell 1990: 78). A continuation of the Conservatives' dismissive strategy was rejected by the party as being too costly. This assessment was articulated by Conservative MP Alick Buchanan-Smith on the floor of the House of Commons. He stated:

The worst course of all is to do nothing. Opinion in Scotland cannot be ignored. This is something which will not just go away. If we in the House appear to frustrate the genuine aspirations of the Scottish people, this is the very thing which turns moderates into extremists. Scotland is not a country of extremists – Socialist, nationalist, or anything else. It is up to us in this debate to ensure that we do not turn moderates into extremists.[62]

Accommodation was seen as the answer.

Labour's Devolution Commitment. Just like their Tory counterparts, the Labour Party was trying desperately to satisfy the pro-devolution demands of Scottish voters. Within weeks of forming a government in early 1974, the Labour Party had already begun its co-optative campaign. In the March 1974 Queen's Speech,

---

[59] Manifestos quoted in CPA, CRD 4/15/10, "Parliamentary Briefing for Debate on January 13, 14, 15, 19, 1976 on the Government's White Paper, 'Our Changing Democracy,'" 1976: 20.

[60] By 1976, the Conservatives had created two additional committees to examine the issue of devolution in the United Kingdom. These were the Scottish Devolution Policy Group, led by Malcolm Rifkind, and the Study Group on Devolution, chaired by William Whitelaw.

[61] This goal was noted in many Conservative Party documents, including a February 1975 Conservative Research Department report that was circulated to the Conservative Study Group on Devolution. Its author, Nevil Johnson, wrote: "The real argument in favour of devolution is that if the UK Government does not grant it in some form or other, then the United Kingdom will break up. In other words, refusal to devolve equals Nationalist majorities in Scotland and Wales." CPA, CRD 4/15/8, Nevil Johnson, "Devolution Policy: Some Issues of Principle and Some Practical Problems," February 11, 1975: 6.

[62] Quote from a speech by Conservative MP Alick Buchanan-Smith on the second reading of the Scotland and Wales Bill, December 15, 1976. Cited in Paterson 1998: 104.

the Wilson government pledged to "initiate discussions in Scotland and Wales on the Report of the Commission on the Constitution, and bring forward proposals for consideration."[63] Within a few months of this statement, however, "policy consideration" had become "policy commitment." The Labour Party established a working group on devolution and released a white paper enumerating its proposals to create directly elected assemblies for Scotland and Wales.[64] In the run-up to the October 1974 General Election, the issue of devolution was forefront in Labour's electoral appeals in Scotland. A separate Scottish election manifesto was prepared for the first time in Labour history to emphasize the importance of decentralization and of the electoral support of the Scottish electorate to the Labour Party.[65]

Labour's shift from dismissive tactics to a strong accommodative strategy by the 1974 General Elections was motivated by the growing electoral threat of the SNP. As emphasized in Labour Research Department documents and in the writings of both pro- and anti-devolution Labourites, the party was preoccupied with the loss of votes – current and future – to the devolution-promoting niche party.[66] Labour MP John Mackintosh (1975: 3–4) summarized this rationale for Labour's surprisingly rapid embrace of devolution:

Some have accepted the need for this kind of devolution out of fear that unless action is taken along these lines, the SNP will gain even more than the 30% of the vote and the eleven (out of seventy-one) Scottish seats which it secured in the General Election of October, 1974. It is true that in large part it was this fear which pushed the Labour Party to include devolution in its election manifesto for the second general election of 1974.

In the wake of the October election, the need to retain and attract Scottish voters – three-quarters of whom favored devolution to Scotland[67] – drove the Labour Party to increase its commitment from issuing promises to legislating institutional change. The Labour Home Policy Committee concluded in 1975, "We must devolve. Both the Union [United Kingdom] and our own future as a major force in Scottish politics will stand or fall by the political strategy we now adopt in Scotland."[68] Thus, within a year of the 1974 General Election, the Labour government had turned its manifesto pledge for a Scottish Assembly into

---

[63] *The Scotsman*, October 26, 1975 quoted in Mitchell 1990: 75.

[64] The white paper was titled *Democracy and Devolution – Proposals for Scotland and Wales*. Cited in LPA, Heffer Papers, "The Devolution Crisis": 1.

[65] LPA, Labour Party Research Department Document Resolution 24, Alex Neil, "Memo on Labour's Strategy for Policies in Scotland," April 1974: 1.

[66] See, for example, ibid. For the justification of the accommodative strategy from the perspective of a vocal Labour Party opponent, see Dalyell 1977: 42–3.

[67] This number comes from a 1975 Opinion Research Centre poll cited in Mackintosh 1975: 12.

[68] LPA, Home Policy Committee, RE: 374, "The Political and Economic Situation in Scotland," (London: Labour Party Research Department, 1975): 5. A similar conclusion was reached by Alan Peacock (1977: 61–2), a member of the Kilbrandon Commission: "Its political survival, and, indeed, that of any alternative government is estimated to depend upon making some concession to the demand for political and economic decentralization."

a detailed proposal for a legislative body described in the 1975 white paper *Our Changing Democracy* (Cmnd. 6348). Just one year later, the Callaghan government made good on its promise, and the Scotland and Wales Bill was presented to Westminster.[69]

The bill proposed the creation of two directly elected regional assemblies within a sovereign United Kingdom. The Scottish Assembly would be endowed with legislative (law-making) and executive (law-implementing) powers, whereas the Welsh body would be limited to executive functions – the difference in the degree of devolution reflecting the relative threat levels of the Scottish and Welsh ethnoterritorial parties.[70] The proposal had undergone many revisions since its first formal articulation in Labour's 1974 manifestos: it was decided that the Scottish Assembly would not have tax-levying powers, and the U.K. government would retain some veto power over its actions.[71] Even so, the resulting bill seemed to many an effective way, and perhaps the only way, to appease the demands of Scottish, and especially SNP, voters. To quote one Labour MP:

The whole of the Labour Movement, both in Scotland and Wales, is convinced that devolution is necessary. It is a policy arrived at after years of study and argument. It will satisfy the national aspirations of both Scotland and Wales.[72]

Internal Party Factionalism: Plaguing Both Houses. However, at the same time as Conservative and Labour Party leaders were confirming their official support for a Scottish Assembly, voices of opposition within each party were growing louder. Devolution, as stated previously, had never been a universally accepted principle within either the Labour or Conservative parties. Their early commitments to a Scottish Assembly stemmed from the pronouncements of a few party elite, most notably Tory Leader Edward Heath and Labour Home Secretary James Callaghan.[73] Prior to being publicly announced, Labour's proposal for a Scottish Assembly was not discussed at its annual conference.[74] In addition, the British Labour Party organization affirmed its policy promises in 1973 despite the *explicit opposition* of the Scottish Labour Party Executive to home rule. It was only after being pressured by leading members of the party's NEC that the Scottish branch of the Labour Party agreed in a specially convened conference in 1974 to support legislative devolution (McLean 1992: 24). But by 1974 and 1975, with the drafting of Labour's white papers and the articulation of concrete devolution policies by the various Tory working groups, the costs to anti-devolutionists of

---

[69] The bill was introduced in November 1976.

[70] In the October 1974 election, the SNP won eleven seats whereas the Welsh Plaid Cymru won only three.

[71] These revisions were largely made in response to Conservative Party pressure. Veto power by the Westminster parliament would be maintained over "an Assembly bill or executive action if it adversely affected a matter outwith the Assembly's control." CPA, CRD 4/15/14, "Devolution," 1977–8: 1.

[72] Roy Hughes, MP (ex-officio, Newport) cited in Labour Party, *Report of the Seventy-fifth Annual Conference of the Labour Party* 1976: 199.

[73] On the isolated position of Tory Leader Edward Heath, see Mitchell 1990: 57.

[74] LPA, Eric S. Heffer, Labour MP, "The Devolution Crisis," undated draft of manuscript: 1.

remaining silent had become too high. From both Tory and Labour backbenches (and even cabinets), dissent could be heard.

Objections came from two distinct camps: those in both parties who were opposed to the specific formulation of the devolution schemes[75] and those who were opposed to devolution altogether. Members of the first group emphasized the conflict inherent in two executives,[76] the over-representation of Scottish MPs and Scottish interests in Westminster,[77] and the impotence of a legislative body without tax-raising powers.[78] English MPs in particular worried that the selective creation of subnational bodies was unfair to their own regions, prompting a debate between MPs as to which region was most hindered by its financial relationship with Westminster.[79]

Although members of the second group tried to couch their objections in the language of the disappointed devolutionists, their concerns were distinct and their opposition unyielding. Anti-devolutionists from both parties feared that devolution would undermine the unity of the United Kingdom; MPs throughout the United Kingdom saw the creation of a Scottish Assembly as the first step on a slippery slope toward Scottish separatism. In the words of one Labour Party member:

If anyone believes that the passing of the Devolution Bill will allay the attacks of the SNP he must be living in cloud cuckoo land....It will be the biggest stimulus to nationalism that there has ever been and I do not think anything can stop this nation from sliding into the disastrous separatism that will result.[80]

For these opponents, any devolution proposal by either the Labour Party or Conservative Party was dangerous.

The ability of the parties to address these objections differed. At this early stage in the drafting of the Scotland and Wales Bill, the Labour Party and Labour government tried to be responsive to the demands of their anti-devolutionists. Although the government was in no position to withdraw its pledge for a Scottish Assembly, it did bow to the requests of its backbenchers and even cabinet members

---

75 There were some strong pro-devolutionists who lamented the limited nature of the assembly offered by the Labour government. This was a position also taken by the SNP elite. However, unlike dissenters from within the Labour and Conservative parties, the SNP MPs, in general, would eventually support the government's proposals.

76 This concern with how devolution would affect the legitimacy and power of the Secretary of Scotland was largely expressed by Conservatives, including George Younger and Malcolm Rifkind. CPA, CRD 4/15/14, "Devolution," January–February 1978: 1.

77 The objection was made famous by Labour MP Tam Dalyell who referred to it as the "West Lothian Question." However, it was a common criticism raised by Conservative and Labour members who were, at least minimally, supporters of devolution. For discussion of this problem, see CPA, LCC/76/149, Francis Pym, "Number and Role of Scots and Welsh MPs," December 7, 1976.

78 This last concern was often articulated as the fear of an impotent talking-shop. Whale 1975: 4.

79 This game of regional one-upmanship was evident in the debate over devolution during the 1976 Labour Party Annual Conference. Labour Party, *Report of the Seventy-fifth Annual Conference of the Labour Party* 1976.

80 Frank Chapple, Leader of the Electrical, Electronic, Telecommunications, and Plumbing Union (EETPU) cited in ibid., 201.

to make the bill's passage subject to a popular referendum (McLean 1992: 26). Obviously, there were some staunch anti-devolutionists who were not satisfied by this mere modification of the assembly legislation. However, even though their angry voices began to filter into the press in 1975 and 1976,[81] the party (and its image) was still dominated by the stronger weight of its devolution policy commitment.

The Conservatives, conversely, were unable or unwilling to silence the growing internal party opposition to their position in favor of devolution. By 1976, a vocal set of anti-devolutionists led by Iain Sprout formed anti-Assembly organizations – first "Keep Britain United" and later "The Union Flag Group." These organizations publicized the debate over devolution that was raging in the heart of the Conservative Party.[82] At the same time, the Conservative Research Department began to consider the advantages and disadvantages of maintaining the Tory devolution policy.[83] Indeed, even though the internal party conflict had first erupted over the specific provisions of a devolution scheme – most notably whether the assembly was to be elected directly or indirectly (Mitchell 1990: 78) – by 1976, it was clear that the discussion had turned into a debate among the Tories over whether to actively support the idea of devolution at all.

1977–79: Conservative Hostility and Labour Division in the Face of a Sustained Scottish National Party Threat

The 1976–77 parliamentary debate on Labour's Scotland and Wales Bill marked a shift in strategy for the Conservative Party. Although there was no change in the relative electoral strength of the Conservatives in Scotland[84] and opinion polls indicated the continued appeal of devolution and, thus, the potential threat of the SNP,[85] the Tory Party deliberately moved away from accommodative tactics. This strategic move was most clearly indicated by the party's decision to implement a three-line whip against the Second Reading of Labour's Scotland and Wales Bill. By requiring that all their MPs vote against Labour's bill (i.e., the

---

[81] LPA, Heffer Papers, "The Devolution Crisis"; Whale 1975: 4.

[82] The British and Scottish Conservative Party conferences increasingly became fighting grounds for pro- and anti-devolution forces, the latter often led by the Union Flag Group. To minimize the perceived disunity of the party, the issue of devolution was basically omitted from the discussion during the 1976 Conservative conference in Brighton. However, even this formal exclusion of the topic from debate did not silence the discussion, as fringe meetings were dedicated to the question of a Scottish Assembly. Mitchell 1990: 80; Conservative Party, *Verbatim Report of the 93rd Conservative Party Conference* 1976.

[83] CPA, CRD, Graham Wynn, "Devolution: A Paper of Options Open to the Conservative Party," March 17, 1976.

[84] As of this point, no general elections or by-elections had occurred since the October 1974 General Election. Moreover, Scottish local elections did not take place until May of 1977.

[85] As reported in William Whitelaw's 1976 document to his party, "opinion polls suggest that only a very small minority even of Tory voters would vote against the (Labour) Government's plans." CPA, LCC/76/146, William Whitelaw, "Options for Voting by the Party in the Second Reading of the Devolution Bill," November 19, 1976.

three-line whip), the Conservative Party was, in effect, encouraging the electorate to see the party as being opposed to devolution. Indeed, in a Conservative Research Department document written before the vote, Deputy Party Leader and chief Opposition Spokesman on Devolution William Whitelaw warned the party of this likelihood.[86] The anti-devolutionist image of the Conservatives was intensified by the refusal of the Tory frontbench to explain its pro–Scottish Assembly alternatives,[87] despite the public urging of such prominent Tories as former Shadow Secretary for Scotland Alick Buchanan-Smith and former Party Leader Edward Heath.[88] Thus, the Conservatives entered the final debate of the Scotland and Wales Bill not with their customary "anti-this-Assembly" image, to use the language of William Whitelaw (CPA LCC/76/146: 2), but with an "anti-Assembly" one.

Unlike most strategic decisions I have discussed, this marked shift in party policy does not stem from an electoral change in mainstream or niche party fortunes; the last major election was in October 1974 and no local or MP by-elections had taken place since then. Rather, the Conservative Party's policy reversal was a reaction to the effectiveness of the Labour Party's strategies on an issue that was becoming increasingly divisive for the Tories. Thus, an adversarial strategy was not the Conservatives' first choice, as it was for the Socialists in France. It represented the Conservatives' best move under a highly constrained and not necessarily favorable environment.

The conditions that led the Tories to embrace an adversarial stance were many. First, the Conservatives had been losing the battle for the title of most credible devolutionist party. Even though the two parties officially condoned slightly different schemes for a Scottish Assembly, the nuances were lost on the electorate. The joint adoption of accommodative strategies by both the Labour and Conservative parties had naturally made them rivals in the competition to steal devolution issue ownership away from the SNP.

Yet, as the Conservatives recognized at the time, Labour was beating them at this game. A Conservative Party devolution survey report from the mid-1970s revealed that there were misperceptions among the public about the Conservatives' position on devolution; 20 percent of survey respondents thought that

[86] "As a result of the decision earlier in the year to adopt a low profile for the sake of Party unity, our alternative proposals have not been sold. Consequently such a vote is likely to be interpreted as anti-Assembly rather than anti this Assembly. If the Bill failed, or if there were a General Election before the Committee stage was completed, in a subsequent election the Tories would be labeled by all other Parties in Scotland as anti-Assembly." Ibid., 2.

[87] Mitchell (1990: 82) writes "Neither Thatcher nor Taylor mentioned Conservative support for an Assembly in their speeches."

[88] Buchanan-Smith and Malcolm Rifkind resigned from the frontbench to protest the enforcement of a three-line whip. However, after doing so and following the vote on the second reading, Buchanan-Smith gave an impassioned speech before the Parliament. In it he called on the Tory leadership to "speak of our party's commitment and belief in devolution and of an Assembly in Scotland." He went on to chastise his party: "I emphasize to my honourable Friends that simply to criticise the Government's proposals without spelling out any alternative will not do." Quoted in Paterson 1998: 103.

the Tories were opposed to Scottish devolution.[89] Tory elite confessed that even those pro-devolution voters aware of the Conservatives' pro–Scottish Assembly position were not likely to consider it a credible issue owner. Looking back on Conservative Party behavior in a February 1977 secret party document, then Shadow Scottish Secretary Teddy Taylor admitted:

I do not think that our devolution commitment carries any credibility in Scotland in any event. Voters point out that even when we were in Government between 1970 and 1974 with a clear commitment and with proposals pledged in the 1970 Queens Speech, we did nothing about devolution and "downgraded" the commitment to an indirectly elected Assembly in the 1974 election.[90]

Results from the October 1974 Scottish Election Study confirm this perception. The Labour Party, as the party in government and the sponsor of the only concrete assembly bill, was more widely recognized as a credible challenger to the SNP for issue ownership than were the Conservatives.[91]

Second, as discussed in a previous section, promotion of a pro–Scottish Assembly position was not costless for the Conservatives.[92] According to Conservative Party documents, the majority of the party's English and Welsh MPs and many of the Scottish MPs were opposed to devolution.[93] This opposition was also expressed by many Tory voters, most of whom lived in England and Wales. Trying to win over pro-devolution voters in Scotland was not only unlikely to be successful given Labour's stronger accommodative efforts, but it would also encourage the flight of anti-devolutionist Conservative elite and voters. And, the Conservatives were not willing to lose England to win Scottish seats. As early as February 1975, a Conservative Party Research Department document noted:

The strictly party interest of the Conservatives in Scotland and Wales is limited and probably declining. It is hard for a party to write off particular areas, but the Conservative party may, whatever happens on devolution, be compelled to do this in Scotland and Wales. Despite some weakness at present in Northern England, the party has a good prospect of remaining a dominant political force *in England*. (emphasis in original)[94]

While it would mean "writing off" pro-devolution voters, a Conservative adversarial strategy would also damage Labour's ability to win over SNP voters. Not only would the adversarial strategy reinforce the SNP's issue ownership, but it would also keep public attention on an issue that divided Labour Party elite. Thus, by embracing an anti-devolution policy, the Conservatives could use the

---

[89] CPA, "Draft Devolution Survey Report." Keith Britts is likely the author of this document written after the October 1974 General Election.

[90] CPA, LCC 1/3/13 (77) 156, Teddy Taylor, "Devolution – The Way Ahead: Some Arguments against the Party taking an Initiative to Propose an all-Party Convention," February 16, 1977: 2.

[91] Calculations from Miller and Brand 1981.

[92] This is not to suggest that it was costless for the Labour Party. However, the Labour leadership, unlike the Conservative leadership, remained firmly committed to the assembly.

[93] CPA, LCC/76/146, William Whitelaw, "Options for Voting by the Party in the Second Reading of the Devolution Bill," November 19, 1976: 5.

[94] CPA, CRD 4/15/8, Nevil Johnson, "Devolution Policy: Some Issues of Principle and Some Practical Problems," February 11, 1975: 7.

SNP and its devolution issue to both directly and indirectly undermine Labour's electoral support.

The calculus of Tory electoral gains and losses relative to Labour was the most critical variable convincing the party to abandon its accommodative tactics in favor of an adversarial strategy. But another factor reinforced this decision. During the mid-1970s, the Conservative Party was undergoing a change in leadership, and as a result, the prominence of those elite who supported devolution was in decline. The original supporter of devolution, Party Leader Edward Heath, was succeeded in 1975 by Margaret Thatcher, a woman whose lack of enthusiasm for devolution was widely known. Even while she reconfirmed her party's commitment to a "directly elected Scottish Assembly" as late as December 15, 1976,[95] she began to surround herself with other anti-devolution individuals, the most critical for the future of Conservative devolution policy being Teddy Taylor, the new Shadow Secretary for Scotland (Mitchell 1990: 82). With an ardent opponent of devolution leading Tory Scottish policy, a sympathetic anti-devolutionist in the position of party leader, and a multitude of like-minded MPs in Parliament, it is clear that the decision to stop appeasing the SNP had ideological as well as electoral motivations.

An Unequal Battle of Opposing Forces: Labour's Efforts Frustrated. Starting in 1977, therefore, the SNP was faced with a different mainstream party strategic combination: an accommodative-adversarial approach. The Labour Party maintained its official position of support for a Scottish Assembly. Having secured the passage of the Scotland and Wales Bill's second reading, albeit by a less than ideal margin,[96] the Labour Party pushed for its timely discussion before the entire House. When the time-tabling, or guillotine, motion failed, the government withdrew the bill, subsequently reintroducing it in the form of the new Scotland Bill in the next parliamentary session.[97] The Labour government hoped that this version of the bill – which focused only on Scotland and contained the original concessions made to anti-devolutionist Labourites – would be less controversial than the last.[98] Over the next two years, this bill and the popular referendum campaign it spawned dominated the agenda of the Callaghan government.[99] Indeed,

---

95 CPA, CRD 4/15/11, GW and SO'B, "Aide Memoir for Talks between Rt. Hon Margaret Thatcher, Rt. Hon Francis Pym and Rt. Hon James Callaghan, Rt. Hon Michael Foot on Devolution," March 2, 1977: 1.

96 The bill passed second reading by 292 votes to 247 on December 13, 1976.

97 The original bill proposed devolution schemes for both Scotland and Wales. Following the failure of the guillotine motion, the Labour government created two separate bills, one for Scotland and one for Wales.

98 Three notable changes from the original Scotland and Wales Bill were that "the UK override powers could only be used where a non-devolved matter . . . was affected; the implementation of EEC obligations was devolved; and the Scottish Assembly could devolve itself." To placate anti-devolutionists within and outside of the party, the implementation of the Scotland Bill was subject to a popular referendum. Quoted from CPA, CRD 4/15/14, "Devolution," January–February 1978: 2.

99 The Scotland Bill received Royal Assent on July 31, 1978.

by 1979, the Labour Party had staked the existence of its government on the creation of a Scottish Assembly.[100]

Once again, however, the effectiveness of Labour's co-optative tactics was undermined. Anti-devolutionists within the Labour Party maintained their opposition to the proposed Scottish Assembly; its new legislative packaging in the Scotland Bill did little to quell their hostility.[101] Within Parliament, these Labour MPs made motions to frustrate passage of the bill and render its popular acceptance by referendum more difficult (Norton 1980: 429–30). For example, with this goal in mind, Labour backbencher George Cunningham sponsored an amendment stipulating that the Labour government would repeal the Scotland Bill if a public referendum for a Scottish Assembly did not gain the support of at least 40 percent of the registered electorate (not just those casting ballots). The ramifications of the behavior of Cunningham and fellow Labour dissenters are summarized by Philip Norton (1980: 429–30):

Had a number of Labour Members not opposed the Government, the Scotland and Wales Bill would have been guillotined (and presumably passed), there would have been no referendums in Scotland and Wales with a requirement for a "Yes" vote by forty percent of eligible voters, and presumably there would now be Assemblies in Scotland and Wales. In effect, the Government failed to achieve the implementation of devolution, its most important constitutional proposal, because of opposition from the Conservatives and a number of its own back-benchers.

The anti-devolution Labour members also helped to sabotage their party's bill by appealing directly to the electorate. Media coverage of the debate within the Labour Party fostered an image of a party in turmoil and reduced the public's trust in the government. But more importantly, the Labour members opposed to devolution launched an active campaign against the Referendum for a Scottish Assembly. In 1978, the "Labour Vote No" group was formed by key Labour MPs such as Brian Wilson, Tam Dalyell, and Robin Cook (McLean 1992: 34). By influencing Scottish voters, the organization sought to "prevent the Labour Party from delivering the votes of its supporters for the Assembly, to create confusion over the 'real' Labour position, and to mobilize vested interests" (McLean 1992: 34).

---

[100] The Callaghan government survived one vote of confidence in 1977 with the help of the Liberals. The main stipulation behind the resulting Liberal-Labour alliance, also known as the "Lib-Lab pact," was that the Labour Party needed to introduce a second set of bills on devolution. By 1979, the Lib-Lab pact had been broken. In its place, a pact was formed between Labour and the Scottish and Welsh Nationalists (the SNP and PC). It should come as no surprise that implementation of a Scottish Assembly was a primary condition behind the maintenance of the SNP's parliamentary support for Labour.

[101] A Conservative Research Department report recorded the rates of participation by various MPs in the debate on the Scotland Bill. During the committee stage of the Scotland Bill, it was noted that "not only have few contributions come from the Labour benches, but of these over a third have come from committed anti-devolutionists." In addition, few Labour backbenchers even attended the debate. The degree of Labour MP commitment to the devolution bill appeared minimal. CPA, CRD 4/15/13, "The Committee Stage of the Scotland Bill – Days 1–6," 1977–78: 1.

An Unequal Battle of Opposing Forces: Conservatives United. Anti-devolutionists within the Labour Party were critical to ensuring the demise of the Scotland Bill, but they were not alone in their opposition. By 1977, the Conservative Party's adversarial strategy was in full swing. In addition to continuing to criticize Labour's specific devolution proposal during parliamentary debates on the original Scotland and Wales Bill, Tory anti-devolutionists were no longer restrained from attacking the desirability of *any* devolution scheme.[102] Their unanimous vote against Labour's guillotine motion was largely responsible for its failure and for the failure of the original Scotland and Wales Bill altogether. Although not every Tory MP, or even every member of the Tory Shadow Cabinet, switched his or her tactics after 1977,[103] the Conservative Party's dedication to undermining any future devolution proposal was overwhelming.[104]

The Tories' anti-devolution campaign intensified during the next session of Parliament with the debate over the Labour government's new Scotland Bill. Raising again the objections that made the original Scotland and Wales Bill intolerable to them,[105] the Tories dominated the discussion at the committee stage, making more than 50 percent of the speeches and 43 percent of the interventions.[106] Moreover, their support was critical to the approval of several "wrecking amendments" that undermined the scope and effectiveness of the Scotland Bill.[107] While their opposition to the bill did not stop its passage into law in July 1978, the actions of Tory MPs weakened the Labour Party's achievement.

Conservative Party opposition to Labour's bill and the larger project of devolution was not relegated to debates within the confines of Westminster. Like their anti-devolutionist Labour counterparts, the Conservatives launched a public

---

[102] CPA, CRD 4/15/13 "The Union Flag Group: Origins, Organization and Operation," 1977–78.

[103] In a speech before the House of Commons just before the vote on the second reading of the Scotland and Wales Bill, Conservative MP Alick Buchanan-Smith boldly stated his opposition to the Conservatives' strategic about-face. He said, "For nearly ten years I have campaigned within my party and in Scotland for what is embodied in the principle of the Bill – an Assembly for Scotland within the United Kingdom. I do not intend to change my position now." Buchanan-Smith quoted in Paterson 1998: 104.

[104] Following the withdrawal of the Scotland and Wales Bill, Devolution Spokesman Francis Pym suggested the establishment of an interparty constitutional convention to keep the issue of devolution on the table (see CPA, LCC 1/3/13 (77) 155, Francis Pym, "Devolution: Conservative Policy: A Proposal for an all Party Convention on Devolution," February 15, 1977). However, this proposal has been written off by Mitchell (1990: 85) as amounting to a "strategy of obfuscation and prevarication." Many Conservative officials, including Shadow Secretary for Scotland Teddy Taylor, opposed the idea, and no concrete action was ever taken (see CPA, LCC 1/3/13 (77) 156, Teddy Taylor, "Devolution – The Way Ahead: Some Arguments against the Party Taking an Initiative to Propose an all-Party Convention," February 16, 1977).

[105] According to a Conservative Research Department document, the changes to the Scotland Bill "did not seem to mitigate the criticisms, which were similar to those on the Scotland and Wales Bill." CPA, CRD 4/15/14, "Devolution," January–February 1978: 2.

[106] These figures represent the greatest number of speeches and interventions by any party. CPA, CRD 4/15/13, "The Committee Stage of the Scotland Bill — Days 1–6," 1977–78: 2.

[107] The most important of these amendments were the previously discussed Cunningham, or 40 percent rule, Amendment and the Grimond Amendment. This latter clause, proposed by a Liberal MP, allowed the Scottish islands of Orkney and Shetland to opt out of devolution.

assault against devolution and, indirectly, against Labour's co-optative campaign –
both during the debate on the Scotland Bill and, more noticeably, during the
period leading up to the referendum. Prominent Tories published pamphlets
expressing their opposition to a Scottish Assembly, warning the Scottish electorate again that it was a probable path to separatism. Consistent with an adversarial strategy, the SNP and its position on devolution were the targets of these
attacks. Once the Scotland Bill had received Royal Assent, Conservatives concentrated their efforts on campaigning for a "no" vote on the 1979 Referendum for
a Scottish Assembly. In fact, although cross-party and even Labour organizations
emerged to drum up opposition against the assembly,[108] the Conservative Party
was the only group to officially oppose a "yes" vote. Not every Tory MP was supportive of this position,[109] but the party managed to project a fairly strong and
consistent message to the Scottish electorate. The fact that even Lord Home, the
founder of the Conservatives' devolutionist policy, spoke out in favor of a "no"
vote demonstrated the seriousness of the Tories' stance and the intensity of their
adversarial strategy.[110]

While the efforts of the Conservatives in Parliament aimed to prevent Labour's
legislative co-optation of the SNP's issue, the public dimension of the Conservatives' strategy served to reinforce more directly the SNP's ownership of the
devolution issue. For instance, despite the fact that Conservative opposition was
directed against a Labour-proposed bill, the Conservative Party policy document on devolution, *Fighting for Scotland*, did not discuss the Labour position on
devolution.[111] Rather, the document juxtaposed Tory policies with those of the
SNP. Consistent with the PSO theory's definition of adversarial tactics, the Conservatives were encouraging those who favored their position to support them
and those who favored devolution (and its role as a possible stepping-stone to
regional independence) to support the SNP as opposed to Labour. The niche
party remained a central target in the Conservatives' "no" vote referendum campaign, with the "slippery slope to separatism" becoming a popular Conservative
refrain (Mitchell 1990: 93).

The concerted effort by the "Vote No" forces from the Labour and Conservative camps is largely seen as being responsible for the referendum's "failure";
with less than 40 percent of the registered electorate voting in favor of a Scottish
Assembly, the Labour government was obligated to propose a motion to repeal
the Scotland Act. It refused to do so and thus was subjected to a vote of no confidence. The Labour government lost this vote 311 to 310, and a new general
election was called.[112]

---

[108] "Scotland Says No" was one of those cross-party anti-devolution organizations.

[109] Alick Buchanan-Smith and Malcolm Rifkind remained committed to voting "yes" on the referendum.

[110] Mitchell (1990: 91) reports that Home's speech was "seen by some Conservative devolutionists
as the single most important event to aid the 'No' campaign."

[111] CPA, CRD 4/15/16, Teddy Taylor, George Younger, and Alex Fletcher, "Fighting for Scotland:
A Statement of the Conservative Approach for Scotland," 1978.

[112] In fact, it was the defection of the SNP MPs that actually led to the dissolution of the Labour
government. The SNP had tried to pressure Labour to uphold its commitment to "move the
repeal order" of the Scotland Act. Although encouraging the Labour government to eliminate

1979–87: Scottish National Party Retreat and the Downplaying of Devolution

Following on the heels of a bitter campaign for Scottish devolution that ended with a narrow defeat of the referendum, the 1979 General Election signaled a turning point in Scottish and, to some extent, in British party competition. The Conservatives swept into government on a postwar-record-high swing of 5.2 percent nationwide (Butler and Kavanagh 1980: 338), securing a majority in the House of Commons with a comfortable margin of seventy.[113] Against the Conservatives' national vote gain of 7 percent, Labour lost 2 percent of the vote and fifty seats and was relegated to the opposition benches – a location it would come to occupy for the next eighteen years.

The election also adversely affected the SNP vote. Despite introducing one of the major policy debates of the 1970s and being the focus of intense adversarial tactics, the SNP gained only 17.3 percent of the Scottish vote – down from 30.4 percent in the October 1974 election – and slipped from second to fourth place.[114] In the process, it lost seven seats to the Conservatives and two to Labour;[115] the SNP managed to keep only the two seats of Dundee East and Western Isles. Behind this seat transfer was a significant transfer of votes from the nationalists to the mainstream parties. Based on the sample in the 1979 Scottish Election Study, 12 percent of October 1974 SNP voters switched to support Labour in 1979, and 20 percent voted for the Conservatives.[116] Once a burgeoning political powerhouse, the SNP was losing its popularity and, with it, its electoral clout.

The reasons why the SNP lost support will be explored later in this chapter, but the mainstream parties saw the SNP's decline as a sign to switch from active tactics to dismissive ones. With the SNP failing to increase its electoral threat to the mainstream parties over the next two elections as well, joint dismissive tactics would characterize mainstream party responses to the SNP until after 1987.[117] Ignoring the niche party was rational for the Conservatives. The SNP was not a significant enough threat to make an expensive adversarial attack worthwhile. First, the Conservatives' dominance of English seats made them relatively immune to any direct SNP threat in Scottish seats and reduced the importance of protecting Scottish seats from Labour control. Second, the SNP's reputation

its law to create a Scottish Assembly may seem to contradict the SNP's central policy position, the SNP wanted to keep Labour in government at any cost; the SNP felt that only a Labour government would push through devolution plans. Little did the SNP know how right it was.

[113] The Conservatives had 339 seats to Labour's 269.

[114] Presented differently, the SNP captured 1.6 percent of the U.K. national vote while contesting all seventy-one Scottish seats. Data from Newell 1998; Butler and Butler 2000: 238.

[115] Two of the seven seats lost to the Conservatives had been safe seats – seats won by the SNP in the October 1974 election by more than a 10 percentage point margin. Calculations from Butler and Kavanagh 1975: 321–3.

[116] Calculations from Miller and Brand 1981.

[117] In the 1983 General Election, the SNP's support dropped to 11.8 percent, but it retained its two seats. At the same time, the Conservative Party increased its lead considerably, and Labour fell farther behind. The Labour Party did, however, recover some of the voters it had previously lost to the SNP. Butler and Butler 2000: 181.

as the credible issue proponent had already been established by the tactics of the Tories (and the wavering tactics of Labour) during the 1970s. Further bolstering of the SNP's image through adversarial tactics seemed unnecessary and unlikely to damage Labour's governmental prospects more than they had been hurt in general in the 1979 and again in the 1983 elections.

A dismissive strategy likewise appeared to be the best choice for the Labour Party. The SNP threat had diminished relative to what it was following the 1974 elections. Based on the results of the 1979 Scottish Election Study (SES), almost 6 percent of Labour's 1979 electorate was composed of former SNP voters. Although the Labour Party did lose 5 percent of its October 1974 Scottish voters to the niche party in 1979, these defections to the SNP did not jeopardize Labour's control of specific seats. In fact, Labour consolidated its hold of Scottish districts as a result of the 1979 election. It increased the number of its MPs from forty-one to forty-four and reduced the number of marginally held seats from eleven to five.[118] Whereas the SNP had been the runner-up party in each of Labour's eleven marginal districts in October 1974, by 1979 it was runner-up in only one of the five. Falling SNP vote shares in both safe and marginal Labour seats were further evidence of the low level of threat posed by the SNP.[119]

The Labour Party's electoral position became more precarious with the 1983 elections. In addition to performing poorly across England, Labour lost three seats in Scotland to drop its regional total once again to forty-one. However, a dismissive strategy remained rational for Labour because the specific threat posed by the SNP was even weaker than before. The ethnoterritorial party's vote share fell to 11.8 percent, and SNP candidates were not runners-up in any of Labour's ever-shrinking number of marginal seats.[120] Each of the three Scottish seats that Labour lost was won, not by the SNP, but by the Conservatives.

In addition, Labour's continuation of an accommodative strategy after 1979 would not have boosted Labour's electoral or governmental position relative to the Conservatives. As would have been evident in 1983 to party officials deciding strategy for the next electoral period, Labour would have taken only four seats away from the Conservatives (and one from the Social Democrats) in the 1983 election by winning over *every single* SNP voter.[121] And the addition of these five seats would not have been sufficient to ensure Labour's control of the British government. With Labour already winning more than a majority of Scottish seats in 1979 and 1983, Labour could not have become the governmental party even if the advocacy of devolution had handed Labour all remaining Scottish seats – an outcome we know to be impossible given the number of anti-devolution Conservative voters in Scotland.[122] Moreover, as seen in the intra–Labour Party

---

[118] Calculations from Outlaw 2005.

[119] The SNP's vote percentage fell between the October 1974 and 1979 elections in each Labour-won seat except one – the safe Labour seat of Caithness and Sutherland. Ibid.

[120] In 1983, three of Labour's districts were won by 10 percentage points or less.

[121] Calculations from Outlaw 2005.

[122] Even if Labour had captured the remaining thirty-one Scottish Westminster seats in 1983, its total number of seats would have only increased to 240, a number still short of the majority needed to control government. Butler and Butler 2000: 241.

debate over the Scotland Act, emphasizing the devolution issue could prove costly in terms of support lost from voters in the much-needed Labour stronghold of Northern England. A dismissive strategy, conversely, would be a low-cost means of reducing SNP support. And by simply downplaying the issue, the Labour Party would not be contradicting its previous position as a pro-devolution party.

To a large degree, the behavior of the two mainstream parties did not waver from this rational course of action. Following the 1979 General Election, both parties moved away from the active publicization of their devolution stances. The idea for an all-party constitutional convention on devolution – promoted by the Conservatives before the 1979 referendum – was quickly dismissed by both the Labour and Conservative parties. Initially hoping to uphold their pledge for a Scottish Assembly, the Labour Party leadership was confronted by much opposition from within the party. Indeed, many Labour MPs and party members blamed the devolution propositions for "sapping" the energy (and life) out of the last Labour government.[123] Members urged the party to forgo the devolution policy to ensure party unity – a condition considered necessary to oust the Conservative government in the next election. Labour leadership apparently listened, as few official statements on devolution were made during the 1980s.[124] Although the topic of devolution remained in Labour's 1983 and 1987 election manifestos, the issue was given less and less priority.[125] This de-emphasis of the issue was aided by the fact that many within Labour's Shadow Cabinet had been reluctant advocates of a Scottish Assembly. The man elected Labour Party Leader in 1983, Neil Kinnock, had even been a leading opponent of the Callaghan government's devolution plan!

The Conservatives more fully embraced their chance to ignore the SNP and downplay the devolution issue.[126] Their campaign promises to maintain a discussion on devolution were upheld in name only; the propositions the Conservatives discussed during this period had little in common with the concept of decentralization that had dominated the media and captured public interest in the 1970s.[127]

---

[123] I have paraphrased the statement made by T. Urwin, member of the Northern Labour Group, in a meeting held March 24, 1981. This opinion was shared by others, as is apparent from letters received by Party Leader Michael Foot and from transcripts of the meetings of numerous local branches of the Labour Party. LPA, Foot Papers, T. Urwin quoted in "Minutes of a Meeting of the Northern Labour Group," March 24, 1981: 2; LPA, Foot Papers, Letter from Ronald W. Brown, Chairman of the London Group of Labour MPs, to Michael Foot, MP, Leader of the Labour Party, July 16, 1981.

[124] According to the *Conservative Party Campaign Guide 1983* (Conservative Party 1983: 352), the Labour Party did release a pamphlet entitled *Scotland and Devolution*, in March 1983.

[125] The topic of Scottish devolution commanded less space and was placed farther back in the 1983 and 1987 documents than in the 1974 and 1979 manifestos. In addition, the policies articulated in the manifestos became less-detailed over time. Dale 2000: 277, 303.

[126] In a 1982 speech, Conservative George Younger articulated Conservative Party policy on devolution: "In spite of strenuous efforts by interested parties to re-start this debate I do not believe most people in Scotland are any longer interested in this subject as a practical proposition." Quoted in Conservative Party, *Conservative Party Campaign Guide 1983*, 1983: 352.

[127] All-party talks were still discussed. However, as correspondence between Labour and Conservative party officials reveals, the Conservatives were only willing to discuss the "management of Scottish Parliamentary business" in these talks. LPA, Michael Foot Papers, Letter from Russell Johnston

The issue was also purged from their more public statements. Devolution was not mentioned in the Conservative Party manifestos of 1983 and 1987 (Conservative Party 1983, 1987). To quote Mitchell (1990: 109): "The Conservative position between 1979 and 1987 was simply to deny that legislative devolution was an issue."

But a programmatic approach was not the only way of reducing the visibility of the issue. The party also removed Conservatives with devolutionist tendencies from top policy-making positions or relocated them to offices that did not deal with questions about Scotland and political decentralization.[128] For example, devolutionist Alick Buchanan-Smith was named a minister of state in the Department of Agriculture, Fisheries and Food, and former devolution spokesperson Francis Pym was made Secretary of State for Defence in 1979. The Thatcher-led party and government had tried to erase the issue of devolution from its radar screen.

1987–97: Return of Devolution and the Phoenix-like Rise of the Scottish National Party

But the slow demise of the devolution issue and its niche party proponent was not to be. In the 1987 General Election, the candidates of the SNP started to fight back, re-emphasizing their ownership of the devolution issue and reasserting its centrality to the economic and political recovery of Scotland.[129] And the public responded. Although far from its electoral heydays of the 1970s, the SNP increased its voter support slightly from 11.8 percent of the Scottish vote in 1983 to 14 percent in 1987.[130] After losing support in most seats in 1983, the party gained votes in sixty of the seventy-two seats four years later (Lynch 2002: 179, 181). And the SNP was once again feeding off the electoral bases of its opponents. Based on the results of the 1987 BES, 14 percent of the 1987 SNP voters had supported Labour in 1983, and 7 percent had voted for the Conservatives.[131] Because of the concentration of these vote gains, the SNP was able to capture three Conservative seats. Although it lost two seats to the Labour Party, the nationalist party saw a net increase in its representation at Westminster for the first time in eight years.

---

to Norman St. John Stevas, November 22, 1979, attached to a letter from Bruce Millan to Michael Foot, December 12, 1979.

[128] In what seems to be an exception to this trend, George Younger, a devolution sympathizer, was named Secretary of State for Scotland. However, as explained by Mitchell (1990: 98), "George Younger became Scottish Secretary because of the lack of an alternative as much as for any qualities he himself had." Although Younger was given a more prominent role than one might have expected and than Prime Minister Thatcher might have desired, he "was not a senior member of the Cabinet and sat on few major Cabinet committees" (ibid., 99).

[129] During an election that was dominated by the issue of the poll tax and its experimental implementation in Scotland before the rest of the United Kingdom, the SNP needed to do little to establish a connection between better economic treatment and the creation of a Scottish-run legislature.

[130] This represented a gain of approximately 84,500 voters. Butler and Butler 2000: 238–9.

[131] Calculations from Heath 1989.

Within a year of the general election, the SNP's electoral strength increased again. In a 1988 by-election in the Labour safe seat of Glasgow Govan, the unthinkable happened: the SNP captured the district by a landslide. While this increased the SNP's representation to only four MPs, it was the significance of this seat and the winning SNP candidate that caused Labour to take notice. First, Govan had been won by the SNP in the 1973 by-election that sparked the electoral success of the SNP in the 1970s. Second, adding insult to injury, the SNP candidate who won the 1988 by-election was a former Labour MP, the converted devolutionist Jim Sillars.[132] Labour had been beaten by its own on an issue it once hoped to control.

Given the vote loss of the mainstream parties to the SNP, what action were the Labour and Conservative parties expected to take? Even though the Conservative Party lost a handful of seats to the Scottish nationalists, one might easily conclude that the niche party posed little additional threat to the Tories. Thatcher's party still maintained a substantial lead over Labour, fueled primarily by Tory dominance in England. On their own, therefore, the Conservatives would have had no reason to prioritize the devolution issue.

However, the actions of their Labour counterparts constrained their strategy. Labour was confronted with a larger SNP threat and larger payoffs for co-opting the SNP vote. Facing another electoral term in opposition, but with a smaller seat margin between it and the governing Conservatives, the Labour Party found itself particularly sensitive to the increasing defection of its voters to the SNP. Poor Labour showings in the rest of England meant that electoral hegemony in Scotland was necessary if Labour was to have any reasonable chance of forming a national government in the future. Although Labour had gained seats in Scotland in the 1987 election, bringing its total to fifty out of a possible seventy-two, it could have won an additional five seats – four from the Conservatives and one from the Liberals – if it had co-opted the SNP's voters.[133] Being dismissive, in other words, had deprived Labour of these seats. Under these circumstances, my theory expects the Labour Party to implement an accommodative strategy and the Conservatives to adopt adversarial tactics in order to frustrate Labour's efforts.

The Conservatives' Embrace of Adversarial Tactics (Again). A revitalization of the Conservative and Labour Party campaigns on devolution occurred within a year of the 1987 General Election. The issue that many in both parties had tried to ignore or even bury was back on their political agendas, albeit to differing degrees. Despite the emergence of a new set of vocal pro-devolutionists within its ranks, the Conservative Party reaffirmed its opposition to any form of legislative devolution.[134] The Scottish Conservative Party Conference of 1988

---

[132] Interview with Jim Sillars, former MP for both Labour and the SNP, Edinburgh, Scotland, June 6, 2001.

[133] Calculations from Outlaw 2005.

[134] Local Scottish councilors Struan Stevenson and Brian Meek authored proposals for forms of decentralized governance. However, these individuals were neither central nor forceful players

almost unanimously approved a motion to oppose any degree of legislative devolution (Mitchell 1990: 111). Prime Minister Thatcher reinforced the decision of her Scottish counterparts when she stated clearly the policy of her government: "As long as I am Leader of this Party, we shall defend the Union and reject legislative devolution unequivocally."[135] Consistent with this attitude, the Conservatives refused to participate in the Scottish Constitutional Convention, a multiparty forum established in 1988 to examine possible constitutional alternatives for Scotland. Instead, the party continued its lone promotion of a centralized Great Britain.

The 1992 General Election signaled few changes in the SNP's threat to the Conservatives. However, with the SNP gaining a significant percentage of votes from Labour – 10 percent of Labour's 1987 electorate, according to the 1992 BES – the Tories maintained their adversarial strategy over the next electoral period.[136] The replacement of ardent anti-devolutionist Margaret Thatcher with the largely indifferent John Major as Conservative Party leader did not lessen the crusade against a Scottish Parliament – a fact that highlights the importance of electoral considerations over personality in the Conservatives' tactical decisions. On the contrary, the question of Scottish decentralization became a top Conservative priority for the first time in more than a decade.

Between 1992 and 1997, the Tories pursued a series of adversarial measures. For the first time since assuming control of the government in 1979, the Conservative Party published a white paper on devolution. Under the guise of proposing reforms to make the existing governmental structures in Scotland more accountable, the *Taking Stock* proposal of 1993 reiterated Conservative opposition to an elected Scottish Parliament. As conveyed by this document and the pronouncements of Conservative Party members in the years to follow, the major focus of the party's criticism of devolution had not changed much over the decades. The Scottish Parliament was still seen as a costly appeasement of the SNP that would (1) reduce the powers of the Scottish Secretary, (2) introduce an imbalance in the legislative powers of Scottish and English MPs (the West Lothian Question), and (3) increase the income tax of Scots (the Tartan Tax).[137] And, most critical for the ultra-Unionists who came to dominate the Conservative Party, an assembly for Scotland remained "a formula for eventual separatism."[138]

Although the Labour Party had by this time taken over the lead in the Scottish Constitutional Convention, Conservative speeches continued to juxtapose the

---

in the devolution debates. The high degree of party discipline enforced by Thatcher ensured that such dissenters were barely heard, especially outside the confines of internal party discussions. Mitchell 1990: 110.

[135] Speech by Margaret Thatcher to the Scottish Conservative Party Conference, Perth, Scotland, May 13, 1988, quoted in Conservative Party, *Conservative Campaign Guide 1989*, 1989: 456.

[136] Calculations from Heath 1993.

[137] Secretary of Scotland Michael Forsyth coined the term "Tartan Tax" to reflect the addition of tax-raising powers to the proposed Scottish Assembly. Paterson 1998: 225.

[138] Michael Forsyth, "The Governance of Scotland," The Richard Stewart Memorial Lecture, 1995, quoted in Paterson 1998: 248.

Tory anti-devolution position to that of the SNP. For example, in the speeches accompanying the *Taking Stock* "reforms," the SNP was identified as the credible proponent of the devolution position, with the Labour Party dismissed as a mere copy. To quote Ian Lang, the chief architect of the *Taking Stock* policy, at the 1994 Conservative Party Conference:

The SNP have a policy on Scotland and the Union that is at least clear-cut and consistent, but it is a policy of self-destruction. Labour's is a policy of appeasement and its ill-considered endorsement by this new leader [Tony Blair] says much about his sound bite philosophy (Lang quoted in Paterson 1998: 238).

Again the message was clear: advocates of devolution – who, by this time, were largely coming from Labour's camp – should support the issue owner, the SNP.

Another Attempt to Appease Scottish National Party Voters. As the Tories were re-cultivating their image as anti-devolutionists, not to mention anti-SNP, the Labour Party was hoping to claim devolution as its own. Within months of the 1987 General Election, the Labour Party had issued a white paper signaling its renewed and now unanimous commitment to a Scottish Assembly. This document spelled out in great detail the proposed features of the legislative body, its method of election, and even its proposed taxation powers.[139] In addition to offering policy pledges, the Labour Party helped initiate multiparty talks on the configuration of the Scottish Assembly.[140] While the Labour Party was not bound by the recommendations of the resulting Scottish Constitutional Convention, its participation in this forum helped to reinforce its reputation as the mainstream party dedicated to devolution.

In the aftermath of the 1992 General Election, the Labour Party's determination to oust the Conservative government grew even stronger. Not only had the Conservative Party beat out Labour for control of the Westminster government for the fourth time in thirteen years, but this election also saw Labour lose votes in Scotland, its heartland, while it gained votes in every other region.[141] Central to this decline was the defection of 10 percent of Labour's 1987 Scottish voters to the SNP.[142] The niche party was therefore threatening both Labour's hold of Scotland and its chance to beat the Conservatives. For Labour, accommodation of the niche party was, ultimately, the means to form the next U.K. government.

Facing pressure both from within its party and from its political ally, the Liberal Democrats, the Labour Party therefore increased the seriousness of its

---

[139] Conservative Party, *Conservative Campaign Guide 1989*, 1989: 456.

[140] The Scottish Constitutional Convention was formally created by the Campaign for a Scottish Assembly (CSA), a nonpartisan group that was founded in 1980 to foster widespread support for Scottish devolution. Although the Labour Party was initially hesitant to officially condone the plans of the CSA, many Labour members were intimately involved in the formation and workings of the Campaign. McLean 1992: 42.

[141] As shown in Table 7.1, Labour's vote share fell by 3.4 percentage points in Scotland.

[142] The SNP posed the largest political threat to Labour's Scottish electorate. Calculations from Heath 1993.

co-optative efforts.[143] Not only would legislative, executive, and tax-raising powers get devolved to the regional level, but the voters would get to elect the Scottish
Parliament (as the Assembly was now being called) by a system of proportional
representation. The Labour Party did back down from a prior pledge to eliminate
a referendum on the creation of this regional assembly.[144] Despite the objections
caused by this policy shift, the Labour Party presented a relatively unified stance
in favor of Scottish devolution.[145] It was this combination of an intense and persistent Labour campaign for a Scottish legislature and the discipline of the Labour
elite, MPs, and members that ensured that its accommodative strategy was both
understood by the electorate and perceived as credible.

WHY DEVOLUTION WAS NOT AN "ANTIDOTE TO NATIONALISM": THE EFFECTS OF THE MAINSTREAM PARTIES' STRATEGIES

According to many, including Scottish Labour Party Chairman George Robertson quoted in the preceding heading, the 1997 General Election should have
signaled the end of the SNP's electoral threat.[146] In the run-up to election day,
the Labour Party actively campaigned on the devolution issue. The majority of
Scottish voters were supportive of Labour's devolution proposal, and the electorate was primed to vote on the basis of this issue.[147] Yet, although Labour was
swept into government by winning 419 seats, fifty-six of which were in Scotland,
support for the SNP did not wither away. The nationalist party increased its
vote share slightly from 21.5 percent in 1992 to 22.1 percent and gained three
additional seats to bring its total to six. For the second time in history, the SNP
surpassed the Conservatives to become the number two party in Scotland.[148]

Mathematically, the SNP could not have earned this title without the effective elimination of the second-place Tories from the Scottish electoral scene.
But, the SNP's electoral success in the 1997 General Election had more to do

---

[143] Acknowledging that it would probably need support to get its devolution policy through the
House of Commons, the Labour Party agreed to the specific electoral system advocated by the
Liberal Democrats. Labour Party 1992: 23; Mitchell and Bradbury 2001: 258.

[144] Labour's decision to propose a two-question referendum reflected its need to balance Scottish
campaign promises with English promises to limit tax increases. By letting the Scottish people
vote for devolution, the party could claim that the building of an expensive Scottish Parliament
was not entirely its decision. At the same time, Labour hoped that the Scottish electorate would
still reward it for its implementation of devolution. Brown et al. 1999: 33.

[145] The number of Labour MPs who openly and vocally objected to the Scottish Parliament fell from
more than two dozen in the late 1970s to a mere handful in the late 1990s.

[146] George Robertson's statement, "devolution is the only antidote to nationalism," confirms the
rationale behind the Labour Party's devolution policy: to eliminate the SNP threat. George
Robertson quoted in *The Scotsman*, April 26, 1997.

[147] Of the respondents to the 1997 SES, 51.3 percent were in favor of the creation of a Scottish
Assembly – the position advocated by the Labour Party and the SNP. In addition, just over 50
percent of those who answered the survey indicated that the Scottish Parliament was an important,
if not extremely important, issue in their 1997 voting decision. Calculations from McCrone et al.
1999.

[148] Due to the electoral system, however, the SNP obtained only the third largest number of seats –
six – as opposed to Labour's fifty-six, the Liberals' ten, and the Tories' zero. Brown et al. 1999: 7.

with the strategic behavior of both mainstream parties over the past thirty years than the past five. In fact, as this chapter has demonstrated, the SNP benefited from the adversarial stance of the Conservatives and from a divided Labour Party with an inconsistent accommodative strategy. One may even conclude that the second factor was more critical; Labour's failure to present a unified policy stance in the 1970s hindered its ability to steal the devolution issue and issue-oriented voters away from the SNP. By the 1990s, Labour could promote and even ensure the creation of a Scottish Parliament, but it could not become *the* devolution party. The window of opportunity had closed.

Testing the PSO Theory: Shifts in Issue Salience, Issue Ownership, and Voters

How did the strategic behavior of the two mainstream parties lead to this outcome? Why was Scottish Labour Party Chairman George Robertson wrong when he claimed that "devolution is the only antidote to nationalism?"[149] An analysis of the effects of party tactics in each electoral period will both provide insights into this puzzle and test the explanatory power of my theory of strategic competition.

1970–73. Our investigation begins with the electoral period following the SNP's weaker-than-expected electoral results in the 1970 General Election. Between 1970 and 1973, the Conservative and Labour parties adopted dismissive strategies toward the SNP, downplaying the issue of devolution. According to my theory, the repercussions of this neglect of the question of Scottish devolution should be a decrease in the perceived salience of the issue, a decline in voter defection to the SNP, and even the return of issue voters to the mainstream parties. This strategy should have no effect on the ownership of the devolution issue.

Indeed, the years between 1970 and 1973 were rather disappointing ones for the SNP. The party started the decade on a low note, making less of an electoral dent in the support of the mainstream parties than it expected. Although there was no general election in this period with which to judge the electoral strength of the SNP, opinion polls show that support for the party was down (Miller 1981). This decline was accompanied by a drop in the membership of the SNP; according to the SNP's internal records, the party lost fifty thousand members between 1968 and 1971.[150] Indeed, many commentators dismissed the SNP as a fad and one whose "force was spent" (as noted by Kellas 1971: 446).

If a dismissive strategy works as stipulated by the PSO theory, then the observed drop in SNP support and membership should be preceded by a decrease in the prioritization of devolution in the public and political arenas. One measure of the

---

[149] Robertson quoted in *The Scotsman*, April 26, 1997.
[150] The SNP claimed that their membership fell from 120,000 in 1968 to 70,000 in 1971. Although it has been widely alleged that the first number is exaggerated, the relationship between them is still thought to hold: SNP membership declined significantly during this period. Kellas 1989: 142; Butler and Kavanagh 1974: 88.

relative unimportance of the decentralization issue can be found in the *absence* of the issue from public opinion polls. Between 1970 and 1973, the surveys regularly administered in Scotland and Britain by MORI and Gallup did not include devolution in the list of possible "important topics" for their questions on issue salience (or ownership). This omission by the leading polling firms in Britain suggests that Scottish decentralization was not yet considered a significant issue on the political agenda.

This conclusion is reinforced by the few opinion poll results that are available. Surveys administered by the Kilbrandon Commission prior to 1973 found that only 3 percent of Scottish respondents spontaneously mentioned devolution as a priority.[151] A similar percentage was recorded in a poll conducted around 1972 contained in the Conservative Party Archives.[152] Content analysis of the British/Scottish newspapers for 1970–72 also confirms that devolution was not a front-page story. When it was discussed, however, the SNP was the party most closely associated with the issue; ownership remained with the niche party, as expected.

1973–77. The fortune of the devolution issue and its niche party proponent changed dramatically over the next four years. In response to the repoliticization of the SNP's demand for decentralization[153] and the defection of significant percentages of Conservative and Labour Party voters to the Nationalist camp in the 1974 General Elections,[154] the mainstream parties abandoned their dismissive stance in favor of accommodative tactics. Based on the attempts by each party to co-opt the issue position of the SNP and, with it, the issue-based voters, the PSO theory forecasts an increase in the salience of the devolution issue.

Its predictions about the transfer of issue ownership and return of SNP voters to the accommodative mainstream parties are not as straightforward. Because the mainstream parties had been dismissive of the SNP from 1970 to 1973 – and dismissive strategies do not challenge the niche party's ownership of its issue – we would expect, at least initially, the SNP to retain its title as devolution issue owner. The SNP's issue ownership should weaken with the implementation of strong accommodative tactics, such as the mainstream parties' serious discussions of devolution and the Labour government's efforts to pass devolution measures, both occurring after the October 1974 election. In a situation of joint accommodative strategies, the recipient of the ownership title turns on the relative strength of the parties' tactics. As the previous analysis has shown, neither party presented a

---

[151] This number is cited in Drucker and Brown 1980: 67.

[152] CPA, undated survey, Table 3, 25–30.

[153] Recall that the SNP was able to reassert its political significance after the discovery of oil off the coast of Scotland in late 1972 and the release of the Kilbrandon Report in 1973. Mainstream parties' dismissive strategies prove relatively ineffective in the face of exogenous shocks that are exploited by the media and the niche party.

[154] Although the SNP did lose some of its former voters to the Conservatives during the February 1974 General Election, the Scottish party experienced a net gain of mainstream party voters. Calculations from Crewe et al. 1975a.

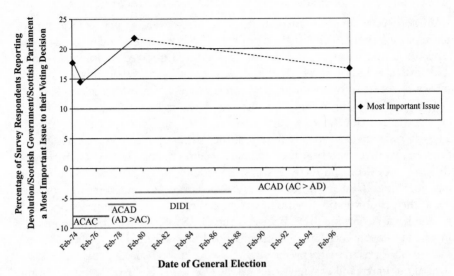

Date of General Election

FIGURE 7.5. Salience of the Devolution Issue to the Scottish Electorate. *Note:* For the 1979 and 1997 observations, the percentage deeming the issue "extremely important" is plotted. As there are no comparably measured data on issue salience in the 1983, 1987, and 1992 election studies, a dashed line is drawn connecting the 1979 and 1997 observations. *Sources:* British Election Study (February 1974) and Scottish Election Studies (October 1974, 1979, 1997).

unified policy of appeasement. Yet, while the Labour leadership tried to maintain a strong commitment to its official policy, the Conservative elite grew increasingly ambivalent about their devolution pledge. Given the imbalance in the intensity of their strategies, my theory would predict that Labour would benefit more from any loosening of the SNP's issue ownership and any recovery of pro-devolution voters during this time period.

From its position as an issue of little importance in the early 1970s, devolution surfaced as one of the more important issues to the Scottish electorate in the mid-1970s. In the British Election Study administered around the February 1974 General Election, 18 percent of the Scottish respondents deemed devolution a "most important issue" to their voting decisions (see Figure 7.5); 64 percent of those polled categorized it as at least fairly important.[155] The perceived importance of the issue was similar eight months later; 15 percent of respondents to the October 1974 Scottish Election Study reported that the issue was "the most important single thing" to their voting decision, and 59 percent said it was at least fairly important.[156] According to Miller (1981: 106), the true levels of devolution importance to vote choice across the electorate were probably higher because "those who reacted most strongly against it [i.e., devolution] tended to deny its importance."

[155] Ibid.
[156] Calculations from Miller and Brand 1981.

Although the sheer volume of mainstream party attention boosted the importance of the devolution issue, the recovery of SNP voters depended more on the consistent application, and thus credibility, of the parties' accommodative tactics. The critical question is whether the mainstream parties were able to transfer ownership of the pro-devolution position from the SNP to themselves.

The paucity of survey measures between 1974 and 1977 limits our ability to answer this question. Surveys conducted after the 1974 General Elections provide an early assessment of the credibility of the parties at a time when Labour and the Conservatives had begun to embrace accommodative tactics. Even though these surveys do not directly ask all respondents about the ownership of the pro-devolution (and anti-devolution) issue positions, we can derive information about the pro-devolution credibility of the political parties from pro-devolution respondents. According to the February 1974 BES, of those Scottish respondents in favor of devolution ("more decisions" or "run own affairs"), 35 percent said that the SNP was the party preferred on the devolution issue, 22.8 percent named the Labour Party, and 10 percent named the Conservative Party.[157] Eight months later, the survey questions had changed slightly, but the perceptions were similar. The SNP emerged as the owner of the "Scottish government issue," being named by 41 percent of those Scottish respondents who preferred devolution.[158] Labour was named by 18 percent and the Conservatives by 11 percent. Consistent with the PSO theory's expectations, it seems that the SNP was still benefiting from the mainstream parties' pre-1974 dismissive strategies to remain issue owner.

Although these data cannot reveal whether the SNP's hold on the devolution issue was weakened by the joint accommodative tactics over the next two years, they already suggest that Labour, not the Conservatives, would emerge as the stronger mainstream party competitor for the devolution title. Even with both mainstream parties pursuing similar strategies up to this point, the Conservatives were already perceived to be the least credible devolution proponent. And with party factionalism only increasing between 1974 and the end of 1976, the Tories' grasp of the devolution title was likely to grow ever weaker. Of course, party divisiveness also plagued the Labour Party during this time. It should not have been surprising, therefore, to see the SNP maintaining its ownership lead over even Labour.

But what of the impact of these strategies on the voting behavior of SNP supporters between 1973 and 1977? Because the mainstream parties' policy change was only formally adopted after the February 1974 General Election, and with more serious legislative efforts not conducted until the following year, we would not expect the accommodative strategies to have immediate effects on the electorate's behavior in the October 1974 election. This prediction is consistent with

---

[157] Calculations from Crewe et al. 1975a.

[158] These ownership reputations are robust to other measures of pro-devolutionists. Of those Scottish respondents favoring ("somewhat" or "very much") a Scottish Assembly, 36 percent said that the SNP was the preferred party on Scottish government, 22 percent said Labour, and 14 percent said the Conservative Party. These calculations are based on the responses to the October 1974 SES reported in the 1979 SES. Calculations from Miller and Brand 1981.

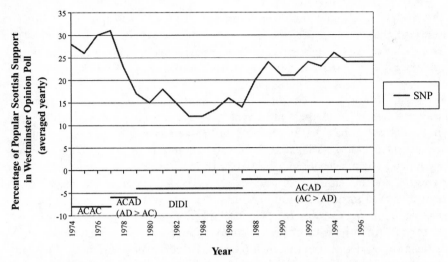

FIGURE 7.6. Public Support for the SNP in Scotland. *Source:* Herald System 3 Polls.

the high level of devolution issue salience and SNP issue ownership observed during this time.

These expectations are borne out. Whereas the Labour Party did regain some SNP voters by the October 1974 General Election,[159] this small recovery was off-set by a much more significant loss of both Conservative and Labour voters to the Scottish Nationalists. According to the British and Scottish Election Studies, 11 percent of the SNP's 839,617-member October electorate had voted Labour eight months earlier, and former Conservative supporters made up between 16 percent and 27 percent of the SNP's October voters.[160]

With the intensification of co-optative efforts by both parties, especially Labour, after 1974, the popularity of the SNP began to change. Using opinion poll data to capture voter preferences for the niche party between general elections, Figure 7.6 shows that support for the SNP fell from the end of 1974 through 1975.[161] This downward trend, not surprisingly, coincided with Labour's early consideration of concrete proposals for a Scottish Assembly. The mainstream parties seemed to be successfully appeasing SNP voters and winning their loyalties. Yet, as the disunity of the mainstream parties became more and more

---

[159] Analysis of the results of the October 1974 SES and the October 1974 BES show that between 8 percent and 9 percent of those who supported the SNP in the February 1974 General Election voted for Labour in the October election. According to these surveys, there was no return of SNP voters to the Conservatives. Although the small sample size could lead to anomalous results, there is wider support for this general pattern. Calculations from Miller and Brand 1981; calculations from Crewe et al. 1975b.

[160] The October 1974 SES and the October 1974 BES provide different estimates of the percentage of individuals who defected from the Conservative Party to the SNP during the October 1974 General Election; the former is lower than the latter. Ibid.

[161] The average yearly data is based on monthly polls starting in October 1974. Herald System 3 Polls, cited on http://www.alba.org.uk/polls/pollwestminsteryearly.html.

obvious, public opinion shifted back toward the SNP – as expected.[162] In the next year, public support for the SNP increased and approached a new high.[163] The impact of the Conservative and Labour parties' policy appeasement on issue voters was being undermined by the parties themselves.

1977–79. How did the electoral environment change after 1976, when the Conservatives rejected their pro-devolution pretense and officially embraced an adversarial stance? What effect did the mainstream parties' resulting accommodative-adversarial strategic combination have on issue salience, ownership, and voter behavior? Consistent with the PSO theory's expectations for an accommodative-adversarial strategy, the perceived salience of the devolution issue increased in this electoral period. As compared with 15 percent of those surveyed about the October 1974 General Election, 22 percent of survey respondents stated that the issue of a Scottish government was "extremely important" to their voting decision in the 1979 General Election; an additional 36 percent characterized it as being "fairly important."[164] The issue of devolution was attaining a public prominence that seemed to mirror the amount of attention the topic received within the corridors and committee rooms of Westminster.

The mainstream parties' strategies also affected the perceived ownership of the issue. In this battle of opposing forces, the Conservatives sought to reinforce the devolution image of the SNP – as well as their own *anti-devolution* title – against Labour elite, at least some of whom were attempting to steal the niche party's title. Although the SNP's hold on the issue was weakened, it still emerged as the only credible owner of the pro-devolution issue. Of those who favored devolution, 30 percent named the SNP as their preferred party according to the 1979 Scottish Election Study.[165] And its strong pro-devolution stance was clear to 94 percent of the survey respondents.[166]

The same cannot be said of the Labour Party. The contradictory strategies pursued by Labour elite had ramifications for voters' perceptions of the party's policy stance and issue ownership. Even after the Labour government sponsored the only bills to date on the creation of a Scottish Assembly, only 43 percent of those polled perceived Labour to be in favor of a Scottish Assembly.[167] Given this percentage, it is not surprising that voters were unsure of which devolution title, pro-devolution or anti-devolution, the party was vying for. While 40 out of 111, or 37 percent, of devolution supporters indicated their preference for Labour – a percentage higher than that received by the SNP – an almost equal number of

---

[162] The dip and then rise in SNP support as the credibility of Labour's devolution scheme rose and then fell runs counter to the expectations of Chhibber and Kollman (2004).

[163] The monthly data on which the yearly numbers in Figure 7.6 are based show that the consistent increase in SNP support was especially concentrated toward the end of 1976 and the beginning of 1977.

[164] Calculations from Miller and Brand 1981.

[165] Ibid.

[166] Ibid.

[167] Ibid.

anti-devolution respondents, 31 out of 111, or 28 percent, also named Labour as their preferred party.[168] No doubt a result of its severe internal divisions, the Labour Party's schizophrenic image rendered it incapable of being a credible owner of either issue position. Primed pro-devolution issue voters would have been unlikely to flock to Labour on the basis of that issue.

As expected based on their adversarial tactics, the Conservatives continued to be seen as the party least supportive of devolution, with only 14 percent of pro-devolution respondents favoring them.[169] Because 42 percent of SES respondents who were opposed to devolution preferred Thatcher's party, the Conservatives were judged the unambiguous opponent of devolution and winner of the *anti-devolution* ownership title.

These conclusions about issue ownership are reinforced by additional data from the 1979 Scottish Election Study. Of those surveyed, 63 percent named the SNP as the party most responsible for "moves towards" the creation of a Scottish Assembly.[170] This opinion was shared by a plurality of respondents in each partisan group. Because of the inconsistencies in Labour's accommodative efforts, less than 20 percent of respondents held Labour responsible for the Scottish devolution policy; voters recognized the Labour Party's role in defeating its own devolution bills! In accordance with our expectations, the Conservatives were deemed responsible for Scottish devolution by less than 2 percent of respondents.

If support for a niche party depends on two conditions – that its issue remains salient and that it is perceived to be the credible issue owner – then this period should have seen issue voters abandoning the mainstream parties for the SNP; an ACAD strategy where AD > AC should result in the electoral strengthening of the niche party. From the end of 1976 through the fall of 1977, this expectation was met; public support for the SNP, as measured by Herald System 3 monthly opinion polls, reached an all-time high.[171] Miller (1980: 100) highlights the role of Labour in this defection:

Perhaps it is coincidence, but as soon as Tam Dalyell and 70 Labour MPs published their letter threatening to vote against a guillotine motion on the devolution bill, support started to flow back to the SNP and its popularity hit a second peak just after the guillotine defeat on February 22, 1977.

But the opposite pattern emerges in 1978 and 1979. Figure 7.6 reveals a sharp drop-off in support for the SNP during this period. This downward trend is reflected in the results of the 1979 General Election. In that election, the SNP captured only 17.3 percent of the vote and two seats. According to the 1979 SES, although the SNP attracted 2 percent of the Conservatives' October 1974 Scottish electorate and 6 percent of Labour's, the SNP lost 20 percent of its

---

[168] Ibid.
[169] Only 11 percent of all 1979 SES respondents identified the Conservative Party as being pro-devolution. Calculations from Miller and Brand 1981.
[170] Ibid.
[171] http://www.alba.org.uk/polls/pollwestminster74.html.

October 1974 electorate to the Conservatives and 8 percent to the Labour Party, for a net loss of voters to the mainstream parties.[172]

These percentages seem to indicate that the owner of a salient issue was losing its issue supporters – an observation counter to the predictions of the PSO theory. A closer examination of the survey data reveals, however, that issue-based voters supportive of devolution were not, in fact, all abandoning the SNP. Of those 1979 SES respondents who recalled voting for the SNP in October 1974 and were, as of 1979, "very much" or "somewhat" in favor of a Scottish Assembly, only 6 percent defected to the Tories. Although a higher percentage of these pro-devolutionists (9 percent) defected to Labour in the 1979 General Election, the SNP at the same time gained 8 percent of the former Labour voters who were supportive ("very much" or "somewhat" in favor) of a Scottish elected body.[173] Since Labour's October 1974 electorate was larger than the SNP's, these statistics imply that the SNP, if anything, was gaining pro-devolution voters in 1979.

This analysis suggests that the SNP's significant vote loss was a product of other factors. The failure of the Scottish referendum to meet the requisite 40 percent requirement and the SNP's subsequent role in bringing down the Labour government no doubt depressed enthusiasm for devolution in general and support for the SNP in particular. The SES provides evidence of these attitudes toward the niche party: 45 percent of SES respondents in 1979 stated that the SNP has "not been good for Scotland," and 43 percent reported that the SNP has "delayed devolution."[174]

Perhaps more important for the defection of former SNP voters, however, was an underlying shift in the distribution of voter preferences away from the devolutionist pole. Pro-devolution voters were sticking with or defecting to the SNP as my PSO theory predicts, but survey data indicate that there was a decline in the overall number of pro-devolution voters – the potential population of SNP voters.[175] In October 1974, 65 percent of survey respondents supported greater devolution. By 1979, that percentage had fallen to 46 percent.[176] This shift hides a more significant change in voter policy positions. As Figure 7.7 shows, especially in comparison to Figure 7.4, the modal category for Labour and Conservative

---

[172] Calculations from Miller and Brand 1981. A similar pattern of the SNP's net vote loss emerges from the results of the 1979 British Election Study. According to it, the SNP lost 13 percent of its October 1974 voters to the Conservatives and 17 percent to Labour and gained back no former Conservative voters and only 4 percent of Labour's October 1974 voters. Calculations from Crewe, Särlvik, and Robertson 1979.

[173] Calculations from Miller and Brand 1981.

[174] Ibid.

[175] This shift in voter distribution during competition runs counter to the standard assumption underlying this and every spatial account of party competition. While the causes of this shift are the subject of another book, recent work on party competition in the United States (e.g., Gerber and Jackson 1993) has raised the possibility that parties may be able to change voters' policy preferences. In other words, perhaps these voter shifts are a result of the mainstream parties' strategies.

[176] There was an even more pronounced change in attitude toward the Scottish Assembly: the percentage of those favoring a Scottish Assembly fell from 78 percent in October 1974 to 53 percent in 1979. Calculations from Miller and Brand 1981.

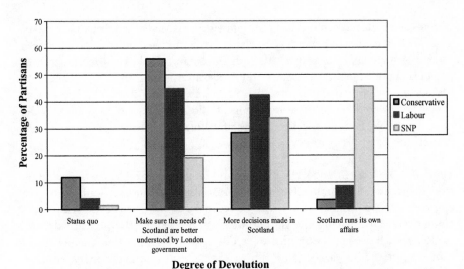

FIGURE 7.7. Partisan Preference Distribution on How to Govern Scotland, 1979. *Source:* Scottish Election Study 1979.

partisans, and survey respondents in general (not shown here), changed from support for more decisions being made in Scotland (i.e., some form of political and legislative decentralization) to support for more awareness of the needs of Scotland by the central government (a nebulous position short of devolution). Although the 1979 electorate was not flocking in larger numbers to the Conservative Party's status quo position, partisans from both parties were less likely to support the idea of regional autonomy or independence; between October 1974 and 1979, the percentage of partisan respondents wanting Scotland to "run its own affairs" dropped by more than half.[177] The shift away from devolution in general ("More decisions" and "Run its own affairs") occurred in all partisan groups but to a much greater extent among Conservative and Labour identifiers.

How did these shifts in partisan and voter distribution affect a vote for the SNP? The panel dimension of the 1979 Scottish Election Study allows us to examine individual-level shifts in devolution preferences between October 1974 and 1979. Consistent with the aforementioned shift in partisan preferences, those who voted SNP in October 1974 were more likely to express support for devolution when interviewed in 1974 than when re-interviewed in 1979. Eighty-nine percent of October 1974 SNP voters preferred devolution when asked in 1974 as opposed to only 61 percent of those 1974 SNP voters when the question was asked five years later.

This change in policy preference is correlated with an SNP voter's likelihood of defecting. Data from the 1979 SES indicate that respondents who voted for the SNP in October 1974 but defected to the Conservatives or Labour in 1979 were more likely than those who remained loyal to the niche party to favor

[177] Ibid.

policies short of independence, a policy position associated with the SNP. Likewise, SNP defectors in general were also more likely to be opposed to a Scottish Assembly than SNP loyalists. Although the small sample sizes in these comparisons should make us cautious about overinterpreting the results, the data are consistent with the idea that the SNP was losing voters, not because its devolution issue was irrelevant or because it did not maintain ownership of the issue, but rather because the preferences of its former voters no longer coincided with its own.

1979–87. Starting in 1979, the Labour and Conservatives parties moved away from these active accommodative and adversarial stances toward a joint dismissive approach. As was similarly observed between 1970 and 1973, the parties were consciously downplaying the significance of the issue to the political debate. In doing so, however, the parties were not calling into question the perceived ownership of the devolution issue. Thus, whereas a successful dismissive strategy should decrease the interest of average issue voters in the niche party's issue, it will not necessarily deter fans of the issue from maintaining their support for its owner. Indeed, when dismissive tactics follow an unsuccessful attempt at issue co-optation, it is likely that the niche party will retain both its title as issue owner and many of its past issue voters. The PSO theory therefore expects a decrease in issue salience and some decline in voter flow to the SNP, but not the complete elimination of the niche party's electorate.

Between 1979 and 1987, the issue of devolution vanished from newspaper headlines and party pronouncements. Just as the public and political parties were not discussing the issue, social scientists and pollsters also seemed to judge the topic largely irrelevant to the lives of Scotsmen. The question about the devolution issue's importance to voting decisions was dropped from the British Election Studies of 1983 and 1987. Polls commissioned by Gallup and the Scottish newspaper *The Herald* also eliminated the devolution topic from their closed-ended salience questions.[178] Although survey designers are always confronted with tradeoffs, their decision to omit one of the defining Scottish issues from their questions is significant. Indeed, this action reveals the issue's low salience (or at least the perception thereof) in the public arena.

Just as there was a lack of direct information on devolution issue salience between 1979 and 1987, there was a lack of data on the perceived ownership of the issue. During this period, no survey asked a devolution ownership question. One could infer from the percentage of parties' manifesto sentences devoted to the issue during this period that the SNP remained the strongest proponent of the position. However, whether the public also recognized the niche party as the most credible and dedicated issue owner is not known.

Given the general disregard for and de-emphasis of the devolution issue in these two electoral periods, did the SNP lose issue-based voters, as predicted? In both the 1983 and 1987 General Elections, the SNP attracted fewer voters than it had during the 1970s. In addition, the SNP was plagued by high rates

---

[178] *Gallup Political and Economic Index*, various years; *The Herald*, various years.

of abstention. According to the 1983 British Election Study, 25 percent of the SNP's 1979 electorate did not participate in the 1983 election. These observations suggest that voters were either casting their ballots for other parties on the basis of different and more salient issues or, faced with the "irrelevance" of the devolution issue, withdrawing from the political scene altogether. In either case, as shown in Figures 7.3 and 7.6, the electoral support of the SNP was adversely affected by the dismissive stances of the mainstream parties.

1987–97. But, the devolution issue and its niche party proponent did not die away. Consistent with my expectations, the adversarial and accommodative strategies that the Conservative and Labour parties adopted catapulted the devolution issue into the Scottish and British political debate after 1987. As indicated by the topics covered in national and regional surveys, devolution regained its place as one of Scotland's central issues in the period between 1987 and 1997. The questions on the importance of a Scottish Assembly were once again asked of survey respondents to the Scottish Election Study and other established national and regional opinion polls. In the run-up to the 1992 General Election, a MORI poll reported that 33 percent of Scots surveyed "saw the government of Scotland as among the most important issues which would decide their vote."[179] Although this number is less than the almost 60 percent of Scottish respondents who, in 1979, claimed that the devolution issue was fairly or extremely important to them, it certainly heralded the return of the issue to the agenda. By 1997, the significance of the issue was near 1970s levels.[180] Of those answering the 1997 SES, 17 percent reported that the Scottish Parliament was an extremely important issue in deciding their vote (see Figure 7.5).[181] An additional 33 percent said that the issue was important to that process.

With issue voters once again paying attention to devolution, which party was perceived to be the policy's most credible advocate? Surveys administered between 1992 and 1997 did not ask respondents to identify the most preferred party on, let alone the owner of, the devolution issue. However, because support for devolution is a prerequisite for issue ownership, information about the perceived policy positions of the mainstream and niche parties will at least give us an idea of which parties were in contention. According to the British and Scottish Election Studies, the Labour Party was seen as a strong supporter of Scottish decentralization by an ever-increasing percentage of Scottish respondents across the decade. From 1979, when the percentage of respondents associating Labour with devolution was 68 percent, the figure increased to 76 percent in 1992 and 77 percent in 1997.[182] Yet, despite a slight decline over this same period from 93 percent in 1979 to 88 percent in 1997, the SNP still retained its position as the most highly recognized advocate of devolution. We can also conclude that the Conservatives – as predicted – were not seen as competitors for the title of

---

[179] 1992 MORI poll cited in Butler and Kavanagh 1992: 139.
[180] The devolution issue salience question was not asked in the 1992 British Election Study.
[181] Calculations from McCrone et al. 1999.
[182] Calculations from Heath 1993; calculations from McCrone et al. 1999.

devolution party. Seventy-one percent of respondents in 1992 and 67 percent in 1997 perceived the Tory devolution policy to be that of the status quo, or no elected body.[183] Thus, Labour and the SNP were left alone in their battle for control of the issue, with the SNP refusing to cede its ground.[184]

Based on the salience of devolution and the SNP's persistent, although somewhat weakened, ownership of the issue, it comes as no surprise that the electoral strength of the Nationalists increased during the 1990s. In both general elections, the SNP experienced a net gain of voters, in particular voters who had defected from the Labour Party and, to a lesser extent, the Conservative Party.[185] According to their survey responses, these voters switched parties mainly for programmatic reasons. The 1997 SES reveals that mainstream party defectors to the SNP were three times more likely to say that the Scottish Parliament issue was critical to their voting decisions than those voters who remained loyal to the mainstream parties.[186] Moreover, in both 1992 and 1997, mainstream party defectors to the SNP expressed greater support for devolution than mainstream party loyalists.[187] This evidence is consistent with the claim that these individuals voted for the devolution issue owner.

While the electoral results match my theory's expectations based on the observed changes in issue salience and ownership, they are not consistent with the predicted effects for an accommodatively dominant ACAD strategy within a given electoral period. The question thus becomes why the more intense and unified co-optative efforts of the Labour Party from 1987 to 1997 failed to overwhelm the effects of the Conservatives' adversarial tactics. How did the SNP survive this strong accommodative attack?

---

[183] Ibid.

[184] Although founding members of the Scottish Constitutional Convention and proponents of the Scottish Parliament, the Liberal Democrats were not perceived by the electorate to be credible competitors for devolution issue ownership. More survey respondents professed ignorance of their position than of any other major party's. Twenty-five percent of survey respondents in 1992 said they did not know what it was. The percentage increased to 34 percent in 1997! Calculations from Heath 1993; calculations from McCrone et al. 1999.

[185] In 1992, the SNP received support from 10.3 percent of 1987 Labour voters and 6.4 percent of 1987 Conservative voters and only lost 4.4 percent and 2.6 percent of its 1987 voters to Labour and the Conservatives, respectively (calculations from Heath 1993). In 1997, the SNP received votes from 6.1 percent of 1992 Labour voters and 5.5 percent of 1992 Conservative voters. No 1992 SNP voters defected to the Tories, and 12.9 percent defected to Labour (calculations from McCrone et al. 1999). In both elections, the number of mainstream party voters switching to the SNP exceeded the number of SNP voters switching to the mainstream parties.

[186] Forty-one percent of mainstream party defectors (and 51.5 percent of Labour defectors) to the SNP in 1997 said that the issue was "extremely important," as opposed to only 13.6 percent of mainstream party loyalists. Recall that the salience question was not asked in the 1992 British Election Study.

[187] Of the 1987 Labour and Conservative voters who defected to the SNP in 1992, 92 percent were supportive of further devolution to Scotland as compared with 67 percent of those 1987 Labour and Conservative voters who remained loyal to the mainstream parties in 1992 (calculations from Heath 1993). In 1997, 94 percent of mainstream party defectors to the SNP supported greater Scottish devolution as opposed to 76 percent of 1992 mainstream party voters who remained loyal. Calculations from McCrone et al. 1999.

The answer to this puzzle in 1992 and 1997 lies in the behavior of the Labour and Conservative parties in the twenty years *prior to 1987*. As was argued in Chapter 2 and demonstrated in the case of the French Front National in Chapter 6, accommodative strategies are time-sensitive. Failure to appropriate an issue soon after the niche party's electoral debut, whether due to a lack of mainstream party credibility or a delay in its strategies, results in the reputational entrenchment of the niche party as its most credible proponent. In the Scottish case, the inability of the Labour Party to present a unified devolution policy in the 1970s – not to mention its role in the failure of the 1979 referendum – allowed the SNP to continue to be recognized as *the* devolution party.

Once the window of opportunity had closed, Labour's efforts to prioritize this issue in the 1990s were insufficient to wrest control from the SNP. The salience of the devolution issue increased as a result of the mainstream parties' actions, but its ownership did not change. Survey evidence from 1997 reveals that the vast majority of voters of all parties (including Labour) did not always trust Labour to work in Scotland's interest, on this issue or others.[188] The SNP, on the other hand, had gained the trust of the majority of Scottish voters, SNP and Labour voters alike.[189] The inconsistencies of Labour's strategic past had a lasting effect on the credibility, and thus effectiveness, of its more recent accommodative behavior. The SNP was able to overcome current mainstream party attacks because of the contradictions in past ones.

AN ALTERNATIVE HYPOTHESIS: WAS LABOUR ACCOMMODATING THE WRONG ISSUE POSITION?

Drawing on archival and survey evidence, this chapter has argued that the electoral success of the SNP was the product of weak accommodative strategies combined with strong adversarial ones. Labour's co-optative tactics were rendered ineffective at seizing the devolution issue and its voters from the SNP because they were sabotaged by internal party divisions, divisions encouraged in part by the Tories' adversarial stance. But there is another possibility. Perhaps Labour's efforts fell short – that is, the SNP electorate was not able to be co-opted – because the Labour Party was not directly targeting the policy preferences of the SNP voters. In particular, proponents of this hypothesis might claim that there was a qualitative difference between the degree of devolution preferred by supporters of this nationalist party and the home rule alternative offered by Labour.

An examination of the SNP's policy pronouncements and the public's perception of its issue position lends some credence to this claim. In its October 1974 manifesto (SNP 1974: 2), the niche party called for "self-government for

---

[188] Only 13 percent of SES 1997 respondents thought that the Labour Party could always be trusted to work in Scotland's interest. Among Labour voters, that percentage was only slightly higher, at 22 percent. Calculations from McCrone et al. 1999.

[189] Fifty-five percent of all respondents said that the SNP could always be trusted to look out for Scotland's interests. Seventy-eight percent of 1997 SNP voters and 54 percent of Labour voters shared this opinion. Ibid.

Scotland" through "a Parliament entrusted with the sovereign rights of the people of Scotland." When it became clear from Labour's 1975 white paper that Scotland would be offered only limited decentralization, the 1976 SNP Party Conference voted to welcome the assembly proposal, but only after reaffirming that it saw the assembly as a first step; the SNP Party Conference made clear that the party's aim was full independence (Miller 1981: 244). Over the next twenty years, gradualists within the SNP gained more power, and the party emphasized the more realistic goal of greater Scottish decentralization within the United Kingdom. The platform of independence was never fully rejected, however, and it re-emerged in 1997 when, with the election of a Labour government, the creation of a Scottish Parliament with significant legislative and even some financial powers seemed likely.

Despite variation in the devolution preferences of the SNP elite, there was little variation in the Scottish electorate's perception of the niche party. Ninety-two percent of Scottish respondents identified the SNP as being pro-devolution in October 1974, with 88 percent associating the SNP with the more extreme version of devolution, namely wanting Scotland to "run its own affairs." Five years later, the percentages were almost identical.[190] Confirming the association between Scotland running its own affairs and independence, 87 percent of respondents to a more specific survey question identified an independent Scotland as the preferred constitutional option of the SNP. And perceptions changed little over the next twenty years. Eighty-seven percent of the respondents to the 1992 British Election Study and 79 percent of the respondents to the 1997 Scottish Election Survey identified the SNP's position as being in favor of independence.[191] These results varied only slightly by partisanship group.

While the SNP was clearly seen as a party of independence, the Labour Party of the 1970s and 1990s explicitly rejected Scottish independence. As has been discussed in this chapter, Labour's proposals under the Wilson and Callaghan governments offered limited devolution. Much to the chagrin of some Labour devolutionists, the white paper and the subsequent Scotland and Wales Bill of 1976 and Scotland Bill of 1978 proposed the creation of an assembly without taxing capabilities. The Labour Party increased the powers of this proposed body when the subject was revisited in the 1990s. But it was made clear through countless party pronouncements that this was a proposal for regional governance, not the dissolution of the United Kingdom.

These differences in party objectives and reputations seem to substantiate the claim that Labour failed because it was unwilling to meet the regional independence demands of the SNP. But this alternate explanation loses its force when we look at the preferences of the niche party's voters and partisans. In contrast to

---

[190] Ninety-four percent of respondents said that the SNP was pro-devolution with 88 percent further specifying that "Scotland run its own affairs" was the SNP's preference for governing Scotland. Calculations from Miller and Brand 1981.

[191] These percentages represent the sums of two possible responses: "Independent from the UK and EC" and "Independence within the EC."

the general public's monolithic perception of the SNP as an independence party, the policy preferences of SNP voters and identifiers were much more diverse. Only 47 percent of the SNP's October 1974 voters favored the independence option; 41 percent preferred the lesser form of devolution (more decisions made in Scotland) advocated by Labour.[192] Of the voters who supported the SNP in 1979 – the supposedly "hard core" who refused to be co-opted by Labour in the 1979 election – 40 percent favored the lesser form of devolution associated with the Callaghan government's Scotland Bill. These percentages remained the same in the 1990s. In 1992 and 1997, 38 percent and 34 percent of SNP voters, respectively, favored a Scottish Assembly. More telling, such levels of support for limited devolution even extended to SNP partisans – those who self-identified with, and presumably had a stronger attachment to, the niche party.[193] Therefore, we can conclude that many SNP voters and partisans espoused positions consistent with Labour's offerings and should have been susceptible to Labour's accommodative efforts.

That voters and partisans did not choose Labour or defected to the SNP from Labour implies that they were motivated by factors beyond mere policy position. Survey evidence rules out the possibility that these voters were not issue-driven. The voting decisions of SNP voters were more likely to be influenced by the issue of the Scottish Parliament than those of the average voter. In addition, pro-devolution and antisecessionist former Labour voters who defected to the SNP said that the issue of the Scottish Parliament was very important to their voting decisions.[194] This was not the case for pro-devolution voters who remained loyal to Labour. The data presented previously suggest that the critical factor driving these voters to support the SNP was its ownership of the devolution issue. Consistent with my PSO theory, issue voters defected to the SNP because of the lack of Labour Party credibility on the devolution issue.

CONCLUSION

Starting as little more than a minor regional pressure group in the early 1960s, the Scottish National Party became a major political actor determining the governmental fortunes of the mainstream parties on the Scottish and British political scenes. As this chapter has shown, the niche party's electoral success was not the natural manifestation of a deep-seated and distinctive regional identity. Nor was it simply the result of objective regional economic disparities. Although the SNP did benefit from a plurality system that offered an advantage to geographically concentrated parties, its electoral rise under an unchanging electoral

[192] Calculations from Miller and Brand 1981.
[193] Thirty-three percent of SNP partisans in October 1974 and 38 percent in 1979 preferred the lesser form of devolution. In 1992 and 1997, those percentages were 43 percent and 29 percent, respectively.
[194] In 1979 and 1997, the years for which this calculation can be made, former Labour voters defecting to the SNP were four times more likely than Labour loyalists to rate the issue as very important to their voting decisions. Calculations from Miller and Brand 1981; McCrone et al. 1999.

system owed more to the reactions of the mainstream parties given this institutional context than to the institutions alone.

As with the French Front National, the success of the Scottish National Party can be attributed to the strategies, specifically the accommodative and adversarial strategies, of proximal and distant mainstream parties. In the 1970s and 1990s, the Labour and Conservative parties proved critical to keeping the niche party's issue on the national political agenda. According to the PSO theory, with issue voters primed to vote on the basis of the devolution issue, the recipient of their votes would turn on issue ownership. The tactics of the mainstream parties encouraged the flow of pro-devolution voters to the SNP by reinforcing the niche party's reputation as the most credible issue proponent. In the case of the Labour Party, the strengthening of the SNP's claim as issue owner was the unfortunate side effect of a weak accommodative strategy undermined by anti-devolution Labour factions and a lack of party discipline between 1973 and 1979. This process was aided by the deliberate adversarial tactics of the Conservatives after 1976, which bolstered the SNP and the devolution issue in order to encourage the fragmentation of Labour's devolution coalition and the defection of Labour's voters. By the time the Labour Party pursued a unified and intense accommodative strategy that outshined the Tories' adversarial strategy, the window of opportunity for issue-ownership transfer had long since closed. The SNP's reputation as devolution issue owner had become entrenched, and, as a result, it had become a major player in the Scottish political system.

In uncovering the strategic moves of the Labour and Conservative parties and their effects on the vote share of the SNP, this chapter has also demonstrated that strategic choice, although constrained, is not eliminated. Mainstream parties have choices to make in each electoral period. Rather than pursuing the same strategy continuously across the niche party's life-span, the Labour and Conservative parties adopted tactics that varied with the ebb and flow of the SNP's relative electoral threat. Internally costly active strategies were abandoned for dismissive ones when Scottish seats were no longer in danger or were not critical for securing and maintaining the party's control of the government. Active accommodative and adversarial strategies were brought back when the niche party threat rose again. In an extreme instance of strategy shifting, the Conservative Party even experimented with a policy about-face after it failed to be viewed as a credible competitor with Labour for the title of devolution issue owner. In this particular case, the high costs of switching between contradictory policy positions, which typically render such moves irrational, were largely negated by the internally inconsistent and, thus, unpersuasive accommodative strategy of the Labour Party. In sum, this case shows that not only is the effectiveness of mainstream party strategies dependent on the behavior of other, nonproximal mainstream party actors, but the choice of niche-targeted strategies also turns on the tactics of the other political players. Competition between unequals affects, but is also affected by, competition between equals.

8

Cross-National Comparisons and Extensions

Why did the Green Party in Britain lose support across the 1990s as the electorate became more environmentally minded? How did the Front National overcome the institutional barriers to minor parties to become the number three party in France? Why did the support of the "institutionally advantaged" SNP wax and wane between 1970 and 1997?

The goal of Chapters 5, 6, and 7 has been to examine the electoral fortunes of these niche parties and find answers to these puzzles. In each case, the in-depth evidence has highlighted the insufficiency of the standard institutional and sociological explanations. Rather, examination of party documents, survey data, and interviews with party officials has demonstrated the central role of mainstream parties in determining the electoral highs and lows of each niche party. British and French mainstream parties have adopted strategies to deliberately manipulate the vote share of these green, radical right, and ethnoterritorial parties in order to improve their own electoral position vis-à-vis their mainstream party opponent. And as the survey data have confirmed, these mainstream parties have benefited from a more potent set of tactics than previously recognized; they have altered niche party support not just by shifting their positions on the niche party's issue but also by influencing the perceived salience and ownership of the issue.

The goal of this chapter is to further test the explanatory range of the PSO theory of party competition. To this end, I begin by placing the findings of these case studies in context by comparing them to other cases of niche party fortune in Britain and France. Recall that the Green Party, the Front National, and the SNP were chosen for in-depth analysis because, out of the set of niche parties competing in Britain and France (countries that are "hard cases" for my strategic theory), they maximized variation on the dependent variable. That the conclusions from the three case studies are consistent with the findings of the statistical analyses of niche party vote across Western Europe in Chapter 3 boosts our confidence in the explanatory power of the PSO theory of party competition. But it is also necessary to confirm that conclusions drawn from these cases hold for other parties in these countries – parties that have experienced different electoral results and have been subjected to different tactics; this is the focus of the first section of this chapter. I then test the generalizability of the PSO theory by applying my analysis of party competition and niche party performance to cases beyond Western Europe. I explore the extent to which mainstream party strategies were critical to the electoral boost of the Green Party in the United States and the electoral failing of the One Nation party in Australia.

FROM THREE TO SIX: UNDERSTANDING NICHE PARTY FORTUNES
ACROSS FRANCE AND BRITAIN

Despite their restrictive electoral environments, Britain and France saw the emergence and electoral participation of a range of single-issue parties between 1970 and 2000. Green, radical right, and ethnoterritorial parties competed in each country; the names of these parties and their electoral fortunes are summarized in Table 8.1.[1] Although the countries share this similarity, the electoral experiences of their niche parties have varied both across countries and within. As discussed in Chapters 5 through 7, support for the environmental party was undermined in Britain while the French radical right party and the Scottish ethnoterritorial party flourished. And the evidence presented in those chapters and summarized in Table 8.1 shows that mainstream party strategies were largely responsible for these electoral outcomes.[2] But what explains the electoral fortunes of the other British and French niche parties? And do our conclusions about the power of the PSO theory change in light of these additional cases?

Table 8.1 provides some clues to the answers to these questions. Based on the case study chapters, we have already been able to conclude that the electoral fortunes of niche parties do not depend solely on the country in which they compete. From this table, it is now clear that variation in niche party success is also not simply a function of the type of niche party. Whereas this book has explored the success of the Front National in France and Scottish National Party in Britain, their counterparts in the other country – namely the National Front in Britain and the UDB in France – were far from electoral successes. Only the Greens suffered the same fate in both countries, but even the shape – the level and timing of vote highs and lows – of their electoral trajectories was different.[3]

[1] Several ethnoterritorial parties emerged in each country, each competing in a different region, but in the interest of space, only the SNP and UDB are discussed here. As discussed in Chapter 3, the other cases of ethnoterritorial parties contesting multiple national legislative elections between 1970 and 2000 are the Plaid Cymru in Wales (Britain) and the Unione di u Populu Corsu in Corsica (France).

[2] While this presentation conveys the general flavor of the established parties' strategies, it drastically simplifies the series of strategic interactions between each mainstream party and niche party. As seen in the cases presented in Chapters 5 to 7, these interactions took place over multiple electoral periods – anywhere from four to eight, depending on the niche party involved. And although the parties' strategies did not change after every electoral period, there was no case in which the behavior of a party was constant across the life-span of a niche party.

[3] Several French environmental parties emerged between 1970 and 1980. Les Verts was officially created in 1984 out of environmental parties that developed in the 1970s. A second official green party – la Génération Écologie – was formed in 1990. Here I am discussing the combined threat of these two environmental parties.

TABLE 8.1. *Electoral Outcomes of Mainstream Party Strategies across British and French Niche Party Cases*

Niche Parties		Observed Strategic Combinations	Strategy with Higher Intensity	Predicted Electoral Outcome	Observed Electoral Outcome	
					Success	Failure
Green Parties	**Britain:** *Green Party*	ACAC	–	Failure		✓
	France: Les Verts / La Génération Écologie	ACAD	AC	Failure		✓
Radical Right Parties	**Britain: National Front**	ACAD	AC	Failure		✓
	France: *Front National*	ACAD	AD	Success	✓	
Ethnoterritorial Parties	**Britain:** *SNP*	ACAD	AD	Success	✓	
	France: UDB	ACAD	AC	Failure		✓

Note: The italicized cases are the subjects of Chapters 5 through 7.

Likewise, these electoral trajectories cannot be explained by the standard institutional and sociological theories. The similar institutional characteristics of the two countries cannot account for why the electoral fortunes of the niche parties varied within and across the countries. The institutional theories fail to explain why, for example, the French Greens were contained while their compatriot, the French Front National, rose to electoral glory; why the British National Front languished as an ideologically similar French Front National was able to exploit the anti-immigration position for its own electoral gain; or why, when electoral rules benefit geographically concentrated niche parties, the Scottish National Party maintained its electoral threat whereas its Breton counterpart across the Channel lost much of its popular audience twenty years ago.

Electoral differences within the set of radical right parties and the set of ethnoterritorial parties suggest the possible relevance of sociological factors.[4] Perhaps the British National Front emerged under unfavorable economic circumstances, while the French Front National benefited from more propitious ones. An examination of the economic health of the two countries does indeed reveal that Britain enjoyed relatively low levels of unemployment during the 1970s when the NF first contested elections whereas France faced high levels of unemployment during the mid to late 1980s when the FN emerged.[5] According to sociological theories, these factors could account for the differences in the radical right parties' trajectories.

While somewhat compelling, this story is not without contradictions. Sociological theories claim that niche party support will track changes in economic indicators. But if this is so, then why did the vote level of the French Front National not fall along with the unemployment rate in the early 1990s? As shown in Figure 6.2, the FN's support only grew stronger. The case of the British National Front poses similar problems for sociological explanations. As the economic conditions in Britain deteriorated over the course of the 1980s, the niche party *lost*, rather than gained, votes. In neither case, then, are these theories able to fully explain the electoral trajectories of the niche parties.

Similarly, the sociological theories seem to offer some explanation for the differential success of the ethnoterritorial parties, but they cannot fully account for the trajectories of the SNP and UDB. The findings of the regression analyses in Chapter 3 suggest that the success of ethnoterritorial parties follows the logic proposed by the overtaxed development theory as opposed to the internal colonialism

---

[4] Sociological variables have also been shown to play a role in the similar electoral fortunes of the green parties in Britain and France. Recall from the results of the pooled and green-party-specific regressions in Chapter 3 that GDP per capita is significantly and positively correlated with green party vote in general. There was some evidence from the bivariate correlations discussed in Chapter 5 that this measure of economic prosperity is also correlated with the vote of the British Green Party. Similarly, support for the green parties in France is positively and significantly correlated with GDP per capita. It should be noted, however, that green party vote share and these economic variables do not always trend together. The constantly rising GDP per capita in these countries cannot account for the early dips in support for the French Greens and the decline of the Greens in both Britain and France at the end of the 1990s.

[5] *OECD Statistical Compendium CD-ROM* 2000.

argument. And a comparison of the relative regional GDPs per capita in Scotland and Brittany reveals that the SNP was competing in a more economically prosperous region relative to the country as a whole than the more electorally marginal UDB. But, a comparison of the relative unemployment rates would suggest the opposite; following the logic of the overtaxed development theory, the Breton party, which was competing in a region with lower unemployment rates relative to the national average than the SNP, should have been more electorally advantaged than the Scottish party – a prediction that runs counter to reality.[6]

A shift of focus from the economically based sociological theories to the more culturally based explanations does not eliminate these disparities. If ethnoterritorial parties are supposed to be favored in areas with deep-seated and distinctive cultural and linguistic traditions, then why was the SNP – a party that emerged in a region lacking a distinctive identity – electorally successful while a party that was based on a strong regional identity that distinguished it from the rest of France was electorally marginalized? These theories are insufficient to explain why the SNP succeeded while the UDB failed. The answer to these and other puzzles of niche party success lies, rather, in the strategic behavior of the mainstream parties.

The Green Parties of Britain and France: Different Strategies with Similar Outcomes

A comparison of the Green Party trajectories in Britain and France reveals how mainstream party tactics can produce similar outcomes out of dissimilar electoral situations. With the majority of British voters supporting greater environmental protection (Jones 1989/1990: 50) and with voters from both mainstream parties defecting to the Green Party, the Labour and Conservative parties both adopted costly accommodative strategies to undermine the niche party's equal threat.

In contrast, the French Greens followed the more typical pattern of drawing support largely from the center-left mainstream party. Fearing vote loss in the 1981 presidential and legislative elections, the Socialists tried to woo ecological voters with promises of greater environmental protection. When the green party threat diminished between 1981 and 1988, the PS switched to dismissive tactics. However, with an increase in the defection of Socialist voters to the Greens after 1988, the PS adopted an intense accommodative campaign. In addition to emphasizing environmental protection policies, including organizing a twenty-four-country environmental protection summit at the Hague (O'Neill 1997: 189), the Socialists pursued organizational tactics to capitalize on the strong environmental credibility of the green parties. The Socialist Rocard and Cresson governments created the first environmental ministry and appointed a Green Party leader as its first minister.[7] And the PS formed an electoral pact with Les Verts for

---

[6] Also recall from Chapter 7 that correlations between SNP vote and relative measures of economic variables were not statistically significant.

[7] In 1988, Brice Lalonde, a 1988 Green Party presidential candidate, was named junior minister for the environment. In 1991, Lalonde became the first person to be minister of the environment. O'Neill 1997: 191. Interview with Brice Lalonde, Paris, France, February 9, 1999.

the 1997 legislative elections (Spoon 2005). As articulated by the former Prime Minister Laurent Fabius, "the PS must become the number one ecology party in France."[8] The Socialists' hope was to become green, at least by association.

The unthreatened RPR countered the Socialists' actions with adversarial tactics, including repealing the moratorium on nuclear weapons testing on the Pacific island of Mururoa Atoll, calling for the creation of more highways,[9] and even eliminating the position of environmental policy expert from its organization.[10] Although it was not internally divided over its stance on the environmental issue or toward the Greens, the RPR never prioritized the issue enough to exceed the intensity of the PS's accommodative tactics.[11]

Whereas dissimilar electoral situations led to different mainstream party strategies, these strategic interactions both resulted, as expected, in green party electoral decline. In each country, the mainstream parties called attention to the issue of the environment. By their accommodative actions, the center-left parties in both countries were able to loosen the niche parties' control of issue ownership. In Britain, Labour won the ownership title by convincing the electorate that its environmental credibility was greater than that of both the niche party and its mainstream party opponent. In France, the Socialists did not win environmental ownership outright, but did manage to become more green in the eyes of the voters by co-opting green party leaders and allying with a green party that already had that credibility.[12] As expected when issue salience is heightened and issue ownership (in whole or part) is transferred away from the niche party, many environmental voters abandoned the single-issue parties in favor of the mainstream party accommodator,[13] and green party support declined in Britain and France.

Radical Right Parties of Britain and France: Opposite Intensities Lead to Opposite Outcomes

In contrast to the environmentalist parties' common fate, the radical right and ethnoterritorial parties in these two countries achieved different electoral

---

[8] Archives de l'OURS, "Motions nationales d'orientation: Congrès de Rennes, 15–18 mars 1990," *La Poing et la Rose* 130 (1990).

[9] Archives du CEVIPOF, Professions de Foi, 1993.

[10] Service de Presse du RPR, "Organigramme," 1997.

[11] The RPR's preoccupation with the Front National during the 1980s and 1990s contributed to the low priority assigned to its strategy on the environmental issue.

[12] The Socialists' green image increased throughout the 1990s. Although the majority of respondents still considered the French Greens (Les Verts and La Génération Écologie) the owner of the environmental protection issue in 1994 – an expected outcome given the Socialists' years of dismissive tactics – the Socialists captured second place and were considered the most green of the mainstream parties (calculations from Schmitt et al. 2001). This image strengthened by 1999 when a BVA survey reported that the adjective French voters most associated with the political Left was "ecological," and the person they deemed best represented this "environmental" Left was Socialist Lionel Jospin; Jospin was cited by 66 percent of those surveyed whereas Voynet, the leader of Les Verts, was named by only 21 percent (BVA poll 1999).

[13] Direct evidence of this mechanism is revealed in the results of the 1995 French National Election Study. Those 1993 Green Party supporters who defected to the PS in 1995 were more likely to name the PS presidential candidate Jospin as the owner of the environmental issue than those who continued to vote Green. Calculations from Lewis-Beck et al. 1996.

outcomes. In each case, the mainstream parties' basic strategic responses were the same; they could be characterized as battles of opposing forces, where one party employed accommodative tactics while the other adopted adversarial tactics. However, the different intensities of these constituent tactics toward the radical right or the ethnoterritorial parties in these two countries led, within each pair of niche parties, to success in one instance and failure in another.

As discussed in Chapter 6, the emergence of an anti-immigrant party in France prompted responses from both mainstream parties. With the Front National posing a smaller (but not nonexistent) threat to the PS than the RPR, the nonproximal Socialists launched a multifaceted adversarial strategy that included programmatic, organizational, and institutional tactics designed to use the FN as a weapon against their Gaullist opponents. Plagued by internal party division and indecision, the RPR only began to implement accommodative tactics toward the threatening FN as of 1986. Even then, however, the RPR's message was still too divided to overpower the unified adversarial tactics of the Socialists.

Internal division similarly affected the British mainstream parties' choice of strategies toward the British National Front, but, in this case, the more ambivalent player was the adversarial Labour Party. In a situation less cut and dried than in the voter distributions presented in Chapter 4, both mainstream parties risked losing voters in marginal and safe seats in the local and Westminster elections regardless of how they reacted to the niche party. After dismissing the National Front in the early 1970s when it was not a threat and then trying to retain anti-immigrant voters while courting ethnic minorities when it became one, the Tories abandoned their half-hearted adversarial efforts in the mid-1970s.[14] Under the leadership of Margaret Thatcher, the Tories began to actively employ anti-immigrant rhetoric, such as invoking images of Britain being "swamped" by immigrants, and adopted the restrictive immigration policies called for by the radical right party.[15]

Even less decisive than the Conservatives, the British Labour Party struggled between choosing an adversarial tactic that would consolidate its pro-immigrant vote and would undermine the efforts of the Conservatives, and an accommodative tactic that would help prevent the further defection of anti-immigrant workers to the NF and "out-trump the Tories" on the immigration issue.[16]

---

[14] Between the 1970 and October 1974 General Elections, the National Front increased its number of MP candidates from ten to ninety (Butler and Butler 2000: 178), and its vote increased almost tenfold from 11,449 to just under 114,000 (calculations from Outlaw 2005). Whereas the lack of statistical or survey data makes exact figures unobtainable, the National Front drew enough votes from the Conservative Party to allow Labour to win one extra seat in the 1970 General Election and one in each of the 1974 General Elections. Although seemingly inconsequential for a country with 635 parliamentary seats, this figure does not include the significant number of local elections in 1973 and 1974 in which the defection of Tories to the National Front altered the electoral outcome in specific seats.

[15] In a famous January 1978 television interview that Margaret Thatcher gave on "World in Action," she described the immigration problem as a flood, using the imagery that was commonplace in the radical right party's literature and speeches. Taylor 1982: 144.

[16] Richard Crossman (1976: 149) explained the temptation for Labour to adopt an accommodative strategy: "[I]t has been quite clear that immigration can be the greatest potential loser for the Labour Party. . . . We felt we had to out-trump the Tories by doing what they would have done and so transforming their policy into a bipartisan policy."

Demonstrating how reputation constrains the viability of strategic choices, the Labour Party's limited efforts to capture the anti-immigrant title proved futile, and thus the party eventually settled on an adversarial strategy. By then, however, Labour's actions were not enough to overpower the strong xenophobic messages and legislative proposals of the Conservatives.

Analyses of survey and electoral evidence in these cases confirm the predictions of the PSO theory. In France, where the coherence and timeliness of the adversarial tactics exceeded those of the accommodative tactics, the window of ownership opportunity was quickly closed; the ownership of the anti-immigration issue was largely retained by the radical right party; and the FN's electoral support increased. When the conditions were reversed, as in Britain, the accommodative party, aided by the inconsistent tactics of its mainstream party opponent, was able to pry the title of issue owner away from the niche party – surprisingly, without also acquiring the racist reputation.[17] Lacking ownership of the anti-immigration issue position, the British National Front found its support evaporating.

Ethnoterritorial Parties of Britain and France: Different Strategic Intensities and Different Outcomes

In the cases of the Scottish National Party and the Union Démocratique Bretonne, the mainstream parties also pursued accommodative-adversarial strategies, but the intensities of the individual tactics were opposite to those observed against the radical right parties. As discussed in Chapter 7, Labour's attempts to co-opt the SNP's pro-devolution message and win back defecting voters were undermined in part by its extreme party disunity. United party support for the creation of a Scottish Parliament would only emerge very late in the interaction, at the end of the 1980s. The Conservatives, although initially divided over an unsuccessful accommodative strategy, adopted a strong adversarial strategy as of 1977 in order to use the SNP to challenge Labour's electoral strength.

With an average regional vote of only 0.62 percent, the Union Démocratique Bretonne posed much less of a direct menace to the established parties than its Scottish counterpart. However, given that strategic decisions turn on the *relative* threat of the niche party and that interaction with niche parties provides opportunities for hurting a mainstream party opponent, it is not surprising that the French mainstream parties actively responded to the ethnoterritorial party. Support for the UDB cost the Socialists votes in local and national elections in Brittany – a region in which the Socialists needed to increase their electoral

---

[17] According to the 1979 British Election Study, 61 percent of respondents named the Conservative Party the "most likely to keep immigrants out." Only 2 percent named the Labour Party. Furthermore, the Conservatives' title of issue owner was agreed on by the majority of both Tory and Labour voters. Sixty-seven percent of Conservative voters and 54 percent of Labour voters named the Tory Party. The Labour Party was named by 1 percent of Conservative voters, but also by only 4 percent of Labour voters. Thirty percent of Conservative voters and 38 percent of Labour voters found there to be no difference between the parties. Calculations from Crewe et al. 1979.

support as part of their plan for national governmental power. Moreover, the eth-noterritorial party was publicizing an issue that challenged the idea of a strong central state – a central tenet of the dominant Gaullist Party. Thus, in an attempt to strengthen itself while weakening the Gaullist Party, the Socialists began to court regionalist voters by adopting the policies and even the language of the Breton party (Monnier 1998: 28).[18] Like its Leftist counterpart in Scotland, the PS featured an institutional reform at the center of its intense accommodative strategy: the creation of directly elected regional assemblies with some degree of policy autonomy.

The Gaullists, although not unscathed by the emergence of this regionalist party, lost few voters to the UDB.[19] But, in light of the PS's strong decentralization strategy, the RPR adopted adversarial tactics; seeing this as an opportunity to prevent the Socialists' co-optation of regionalist party support and to use the UDB as a weapon to retain governmental dominance, the RPR opposed UDB calls for regional autonomy.[20] The strategy was not the central priority of the RPR during the 1970s and early 1980s, though. And, in the end, the RPR was not legislatively strong enough to prevent the Socialist government's passage of decentralization reforms.

As a result of these mainstream party strategies, the SNP became electorally successful while the UDB was marginalized. By the time the Labour Party coalesced around a strong pro-devolution strategy in the late 1980s, the effectiveness of its accommodative tactics was already weakened. Years of Labour division over devolution policy during a period when the Tories reinforced the SNP's ownership of Scottish devolution meant that subsequent Labour tactics could not undermine the niche party's hold on issue ownership or lead to the recapturing of issue voters.

Unfettered by internal party divisions and able to overpower the weaker adversarial tactics of the RPR, the accommodative French Socialists captured the title of decentralization issue owner from the UDB by the 1980s.[21] This reputation was further reinforced by the adoption of the Deferre reforms in 1982, creating

---

[18] The Socialist accommodative strategy also included the formation of electoral pacts with the UDB, whereby UDB candidates agreed to step down in the second round of national- and local-level legislative elections in order to boost the support of the Socialist candidates. Archives de la Documentation Française, Dossier Partis politiques, Mouvements autonomistes et régionalistes, 1983–6, Jean Guisnel, "L'UDB menacée d'implosion," *Libération*, March 1, 1984.

[19] The UDB emerged just as the Gaullists' hold on the once-safe seats of Brittany was weakening.

[20] Indicative of the statements made by the RPR against the UDB, Chirac argued that "regional power was romanticism which can lead to the worst excesses." He also is quoted as saying that "only dreamers and irresponsible people could demand elected regional assemblies." Both quotes are from Archives de la Documentation Française, Dossier Partis politiques, Mouvements autonomistes et régionalistes, 1972–5, "Giscard Halts Regional Plans," *The Guardian*, October 2, 1975.

[21] While there is a startling lack of survey material about the perceived ownership of the decentralization issue, anecdotal evidence strongly suggests that the Socialists had been able to pry the title away from the small regionalist party. The decentralization policy was recognized as being one of the most important policies proposed and enacted by the PS (Safran 1989: 124). And even UDB officials observed that the PS had become seen by their fellow Bretons as the main party of regionalization (Monnier 1998: 29).

directly elected, albeit somewhat emasculated, regional assemblies. By placing decentralization at the center of the 1981 electoral campaign and the legislative agenda of Mitterrand's first term, the Socialists were also boosting the salience of the issue. French and Breton voters were primed to vote on the basis of decentralization and to shift support to the PS issue owner.[22] The consequence was the further marginalization of an already small party.[23] As politicians and scholars remarked at the time, the UDB became the sacrificial lamb of the Socialists' decentralization policy.[24]

While this discussion can only begin to summarize the nature and effects of competition between the mainstream parties and the French Greens, the British National Front, and the Union Démocratique Bretonne, it shows that these cases exhibit causal relationships consistent with my theories of strategic interaction and strategic choice and also found in the empirical analyses of Chapters 3 and 5 through 7. Despite the restrictiveness of the French and British institutional and sociological environments, mainstream parties employed costly tactics to shape the electoral fortunes of niche party opponents. The relative electoral threat of the niche parties influenced the strategies that the dominant parties enacted against them. But with the salience- and ownership-altering characteristics of strategies enabling competition to reach beyond ideological neighbors, mainstream parties were not limited to undermining the support of niche parties directly threatening their vote. Rather, mainstream parties could also boost the electoral support of those single-issue parties who threatened the vote of their mainstream party opponents.[25]

As these comparisons across niche party cases emphasize, the effectiveness of these tactics did not turn on whether the niche party target was flora-loving or immigrant-hating, British or French. The difference between niche party success and failure depended on the nature and intensity of multiple mainstream parties' tactics, which in turn depended on the parties' ability to overcome internal division and decision-making impasses.

---

[22] Phlipponneau 1981: 91; 1986: 146.

[23] The UDB's vote share dropped after the election of the PS government in 1981 and the passage of the Deferre reforms in 1982. Following a regional vote share of 1.2 percent in 1981, the party saw its vote fall to less than 0.5 percent in each of the next three elections. The UDB's vote increased to 1.27 percent in 1997, largely the mechanical effect of an increase in the number of candidates it ran rather than the popularity of each candidate or the issue of decentralization. Indeed, the UDB's per candidate average in 1997 was lower than it had been in 1973, when its overall regional support level was a mere 0.43 percent. Calculations from BDSP; http://elections.figaro.net/popup_2004/accueil.html.

[24] This statement was made by a Breton political activist quoted in Archives de la Documentation Française, Dossier Partis politiques, Mouvements autonomistes et régionalistes, 1983–6, Michel Alleno, "Les autonomistes bretons déçus du socialisme," *Le Matin*, November 19, 1984.

[25] The third option of undermining a niche party's vote by downplaying the salience of its issue – i.e., a dismissive tactic – was also employed by mainstream parties against all three of the comparison cases. It was used against the French Greens, the British National Front, and the UDB in the years before their electoral prominence and, in the latter two cases, in the years following the mainstream parties' active strategies to further encourage the decline of the niche party.

EXTENSIONS OF THE THEORY: PARTY COMPETITION IN OTHER
ADVANCED INDUSTRIAL DEMOCRACIES

Although this study focuses on competition between mainstream and niche parties in Western Europe, the niche party phenomenon is not limited to this region.
Indeed, over the last three decades, party systems in advanced industrial democracies around the world have faced political and electoral challenges like those
seen in Western Europe. From Australia, New Zealand, and Japan to Canada and
the United States, partisan identification has declined, and, in most cases, voter
volatility has increased (Dalton 2000: 25; Dalton et al. 2000: 41). The electoral
grasp of the once oligopolistic mainstream parties has weakened. Adding to their
insecurity, and in some cases causing it, is a set of new political competitors. Many
of these new parties are just variants of the existing economically oriented actors,
but examples of green, radical right, and ethnoterritorial niche parties have also
surfaced in these countries, making their voices heard.

The existence of these electoral and political circumstances in other democracies invites the question of whether my theories of party competition and strategic
choice are applicable to arenas outside Western Europe. If the preconditions for
a modified spatial explanation of party interaction and strategic choice exist –
namely that established parties face single-issue parties proposing new, noneconomic issue dimensions that often cross-cut the traditional cleavage of party
competition – then my hypotheses should hold. While testing the validity of my
models across all advanced industrial democracies is a subject for another book,
a brief examination of a few cases will speak to the generalizability of my theories
and findings. In keeping with the research design, I examine mainstream party–
niche party interaction in crucial country cases. My focus is on the U.S. Green
Party and the Australian radical right party, One Nation. In the next two sections,
I will examine the institutional, sociological, and strategic factors associated with
the main theories of niche party vote to try to understand why Green Party vote
increased in the United States and the vote share of One Nation declined in
Australia.

United States: A Mainstream Party Strengthening
Green Party Support

The inclusion of the United States in an analysis of mainstream party–niche
party interaction may, at first glance, seem puzzling. Indeed, the United States
has been held up as a primary example of a stable two-party system (Sartori 1976).
Yet third party competitors are not new to the American political scene. According to Hirano and Snyder (2007), during the late nineteenth and early twentieth
centuries, third party candidates regularly contested elections for the U.S. House
of Representatives and the U.S. Senate. As data from Rosenstone et al. (1996:
Appendix A) show, minor party presidential candidates are even more plenti-
ful throughout U.S. history, with candidates from an average of more than ten
different minor parties contesting each presidential election from 1972 to 1992.

Whereas the majority of these parties are variants of the economically focused mainstream players, some niche parties have emerged over the past twenty years.[26] The Green Party has participated in state legislative elections since 1986 and congressional elections since 1992.[27] Starting in 1996, the party began presenting presidential candidates.[28] Although the most renowned example, the Green Party is not the only niche party to have developed in the United States. Indeed, it has been joined by various ethnoterritorial parties at the state and local levels, including the Puerto Rican Independence Party.

The mere development of niche parties, however, does not ensure that the new actors pose electoral threats to the dominant mainstream party players. If any advanced industrialized country is considered to have a hostile institutional climate for new parties, it is the United States. According to institutional arguments, the combination of a plurality electoral system with presidentialism discourages voter support of minor parties at every level. Even the presence of a federal state structure cannot eliminate this disincentive because, as Shugart and Carey (1992) argue, voters are unlikely to support a party – presumably at local, state, or national levels – if that party has little chance of getting its candidate elected to the highest governmental office. So, just as the institutional environments of Britain and France render them crucial cases, the institutions of the United States should also make it stand out as a least-likely place to see niche parties flourish or to see mainstream parties react with costly strategies to those structurally disfavored niche parties.

And yet, any observer of the 2000 presidential election knows how actively – vociferously and intensively – the mainstream parties responded to a Green Party candidate who threatened to determine the outcome of the close contest.[29] With a larger percentage of Democratic partisans and former Clinton voters attracted to the pro-environmental position of the Greens than Republican partisans and former Dole supporters,[30] the Democratic Party launched a co-optative

---

[26] Until recently, most proponents of new issues, such as immigration, have worked as pressure groups within existing parties. This approach accounts for the lack of an independent radical right party in the United States. But the Green Party and the few ethnoterritorial parties that have emerged have traded this role for the chance to become independent political and electoral forces.

[27] http://www.greens.org/elections.

[28] Ralph Nader was the Greens' presidential candidate in 1996, winning less than 1 percent of the popular vote. Cannon 2000: 26.

[29] Consistent with many cross-national studies that include both the United States and the parliamentary democracies of Western Europe, North America, and Australasia (see the voter turnout study of Wattenberg 2000), I compare electoral outcomes from the most important set of elections. Whereas in the parliamentary democracies, these are the fortunes of parties in the parliamentary elections, in the United States, these are the electoral outcomes of parties' candidates in the presidential elections. In their focus on minor parties in the United States, Rosenstone et al. (1996) likewise restrict their analysis to the presidential performance of these parties.

[30] According to the 2000 American National Election Study (ANES) pre-election survey administered in September 2000, 48.8 percent of Democratic partisans prioritized environmental protection over job creation versus 33.5 percent of Republican partisans. Similarly, 51.5 percent of former Clinton voters versus 40.1 percent of former Dole voters reported in 2000 that they prioritized

strategy against the niche party and its candidate, Ralph Nader.[31] Although most standard spatial accounts of party competition also would expect a threatened mainstream party to act accommodatively toward the environmental competitor, it is clear from the behavior of the other established party that the logic of my PSO theory was at work instead. Whereas the menaced Democrats tried to establish their ownership of the environmental issue and retain potential Green voters,[32] the relatively untouched Republican Party followed an even more intense adversarial strategy. While Al Gore proclaimed himself to be the environmental candidate and proposed vast increases in federal spending on energy and environmental conservation,[33] George W. Bush emphasized his antigreen roots. Bush proclaimed that he would not ratify the Kyoto protocol on limiting greenhouse gases and called into question the finding linking pollution to global warming.[34] Bush proposed significantly reducing governmental regulations on environmental protection and allowing drilling for oil in formerly protected areas of the Arctic National Wildlife Refuge (Wald 2000). As he and others emphasized repeatedly, the Republican Party was opposed to the Green Party's positions on environmental protection (Jehl 2000; Wald 2000).

With these actions, the Republicans were signaling to environmental voters that Nader, not Gore, was the credible green candidate. To aid in this process, a Republican group – the Republican Leadership Council – even paid for and ran pro-Nader television advertisements highlighting Nader's environmental record (Meckler 2000).[35] The Green Party's candidate was being used by the Republicans as a weapon – a weapon that all political observers felt would undermine the Democrats' support. And as evidenced by their popularization of the slogan "a vote for Nader is a vote for Bush," the Democrats correctly perceived the effect of their opponent's adversarial strategy.

The outcome of the presidential election may be very familiar to the reader: George W. Bush lost the popular vote but won the presidency by a very small

environmental protection over job creation. Both of these sets of calculations were made using the survey question with the standard response format asked of only the face-to-face (FTF) respondents. This is consistent with the advice of Bowers and Ensley (2003) in response to the potential problems caused by combining the results of the standard and experimental-format questions asked of both face-to-face and telephone respondents.

[31] Gore reportedly changed the focus of his electoral campaign due to Nader's threat. Moberg 2000.

[32] The loss of environmental votes to Nader in certain states, such as California and Florida, was of particular concern to the Gore campaign (Leonhardt 2000; Maier 2000).

[33] Gore proposed to spend $171 billion on the environment and energy over the next decade. Bush, on the other hand, called for only $14.5 billion to be spent over the next five years. Wald 2000: A44.

[34] Presidential debate transcript at http://www.debates.org/pages/trans2000b.html.

[35] Institutional aspects of the Republican Party's adversarial strategy against Nader would become more prominent four years later. In addition to continuing to promote anti-environmental policies in the run-up to the 2004 presidential election, the Republican Party collected signatures for Nader's ballot drives and helped with his legal battles to get ballot access (Alberts 2004). Republican supporters also donated money to Nader's campaign ("'The New Nader Raiders:' Latest FEC Reports Show More Evidence of GOP Support to Nader," 2004).

and contested margin of electoral college votes.[36] However, what became of the Green Party? Did its electoral score match the PSO theory's predictions for an accommodative-adversarial strategic combination in which the adversarial tactics were stronger? Moreover, did the strategies work by altering issue salience and ownership as expected? In other words, do my hypotheses hold up in this institutionally least-likely case?

It is important to note that the format of presidential elections changes the nature of party competition slightly. With attention focused on individual candidates more than in parliamentary systems – even those conducted by plurality rules – personality and the policy reputation of the specific candidate play a greater role in party interaction and vote outcomes. Although Nader was the Green Party's chosen candidate, he was not a longtime party member. Moreover, unlike the single-issue environmental party, he was also associated with a wider set of issues, including a consumer movement that predated his involvement with the Green Party.

That said, an analysis of this competition between unequal political candidates reveals some of the same mechanisms behind party competition and strategic choice discussed earlier in the niche party cases in the nonpresidential systems of Western Europe. First, the election day results suggest the power of an adversarially dominant accommodative-adversarial strategic combination. Although the Green Party candidate did not meet his personal goal of 5 percent,[37] Nader won a significant number of votes; he netted 2.9 million votes, or 2.7 percent of the popular vote. Not only was this impressive for a third party presidential candidate in the United States,[38] but it also signified an important increase in Green Party voter support over Nader's paltry gain of 0.72 percent of the vote in the 1996 presidential election (*Political Database of the Americas*).

And, as predicted, the Green candidate's strength came at the expense of the Democratic candidate. An analysis of the 2000 American National Election Study (ANES) reveals that Nader was drawing voters disproportionately from the Democrats: 41 percent of Nader supporters in 2000 had voted for the Democratic candidate, Bill Clinton, in 1996 while only 13 percent had voted for the Republican candidate, Bob Dole.[39] These figures are consistent with the

---

[36] Bush received 47.8 percent of the popular vote and 271 electoral college votes whereas Gore received 48.3 percent of the popular vote and 267 electoral college votes.

[37] Nader was striving for that support level in order to qualify for federal funding in the next presidential election.

[38] This percentage of popular support had only been surpassed by three minor party or independent candidates since World War II; as one of the three candidates, Ross Perot achieved this distinction twice, once in 1992 with 18.9 percent of the vote and once in 1996 with 8.4 percent (Rosenstone et al. 1996: Appendix A; http://psephos.adam-carr.net/countries/u/usa/pres/1996.txt).

[39] Based on the admittedly small sample of Nader voters in the ANES, Nader drew 31 percent of his vote from repeat third-party voters – those having supported Ross Perot in 1996. The percentages cited are for the combined face-to-face and telephone samples of the 2000 ANES. In light of concerns about combining these two samples raised by Bowers and Ensley (2003), I have followed their suggestion and rerun the analysis for just the standard ANES face-to-face respondents. For this sample, the percentages change, but the overall conclusions remain the same: Nader voters

conclusion reached by exit polls that, in the absence of a Green Party candidate, "half of Mr. Nader's voters would otherwise have supported Mr. Gore."[40]

Voter defection to Nader in 2000 represented only 1.6 percent of Clinton's 1996 electorate,[41] but the importance of these votes to the Democrats should not be underestimated. Analyses (e.g., Stone and Rapoport 2001; White 2001; Wlezien 2001) have shown that the Green Party cost Gore wins in the states of New Hampshire and Florida.[42] Had these two states and their twenty-nine electoral college votes been picked up by Gore, the White House would have remained in Democratic hands. With these repercussions, it is clear that the Green Party's threat had increased in this electoral period over the previous one – an outcome unexpected by institutional theories.

The Economy Helps, but Strategies Emerge as a Major Factor in Green Party Strength. The Green Party's vote and threat increases were not unexpected by all competing theories. Consideration of sociological conditions in the United States in the run-up to the 2000 election leads to a fairly sanguine prognosis for niche party support. Unemployment had fallen since the last presidential election, and the levels of GDP per capita and postmaterialism had risen.[43] According to sociological theories, these factors should encourage voters to more readily support non-materialist issues and their parties.

Thus, one cannot dismiss the applicability of sociological factors to this case of niche party support. However, the explanatory power of this approach is called into question by further examination of the trends in the sociological theories' variables of interest. In the United States in recent times, both GDP per capita and postmaterialism have been increasing monotonically. By the logic of the sociological theories, Green Party support levels should also be increasing during this period. But the results of the subsequent presidential election of 2004 run counter to this prediction. A decline in the Green Party's fortune in that election suggests that, while the economy may be facilitating the electoral success of the niche party, other factors also play a role.

are still much more likely to have voted for Clinton than Dole in 1996. However, one needs to be cautious about placing too much weight on the results of this subsample given that the number of included Nader voters drops by almost half. Calculations from Burns et al. 2005.

[40] Quote in the text from "The Spoiler," *The Economist*, November 11, 2000. From an analysis of counterfactuals, Magee (2003) arrives at a slightly lower estimate; he predicts that if Nader had not run, Gore would have received 32–40 percent of Nader votes and Bush, 14–17 percent.

[41] Calculations using the combined FTF and telephone samples from Burns et al. 2005. The result for the FTF sample alone is 1.5 percent. For the telephone sample, it is 1.7 percent.

[42] Nader received more than 97,488 votes in Florida in 2000, and Bush won that state by only 537 votes. In New Hampshire where Bush won by 7,211 votes, Nader received more than 22,000 votes.

[43] Unemployment and GDP per capita (as measured in U.S. dollars with current prices and PPPs) are from the *OECD Factbook 2006: Economic, Environmental and Social Statistics*. Although they arrive at different percentages of postmaterialists in the United States, both the General Social Surveys (Davis et al. 2006) and the World Values Surveys (cited in Dalton 2006: 88) exhibit similar trends in postmaterialism values.

As argued throughout this book, those other factors are mainstream party strategies and, specifically, strategies that follow a modified spatial logic.[44] The fact that Gore voters defected to Nader cannot be explained by standard spatial models, which would focus solely on the accommodative tactics employed by the environmentally proximal Democratic Party. This flow of voters can be understood only by also considering the role of the nonproximal Republican Party and the power of its adversarial tactics, as argued by the PSO theory.

Mainstream Party Manipulation of the Salience and Ownership of the Environmental Issue. The Republican Party was no doubt aided by the sociological permissiveness of the political climate, but evidence of the expected changes in the salience and ownership of the environmental issue further supports my claim that Nader's results were the product of mainstream party behavior. As predicted by the PSO theory, the perceived salience of the environment increased in the run-up to the 2000 presidential election. Gallup Polls chart a steady increase in the importance of the environmental issue for presidential voting decisions, from 23 percent of respondents reporting it extremely important in January 2000 to 26 percent in April and 28.6 percent in July.[45] This increase in the perceived importance of the environment is consistent with findings from Pew polls from before and after the election. In January 2000, prior to the active start of the presidential campaign, the percentage of people calling for the environment to be highly prioritized was 54 percent.[46] Just two months after the 2000 election, and at a time when the election was still fresh in the minds of voters and politicians and still in the news, 63 percent of those surveyed felt that protecting the environment should be a top priority for the government.[47] These increases in issue importance correspond to the implementation of active mainstream party strategies during 2000.

The limited availability of survey questions on the ownership of the environmental issue hinders the testing of this aspect of the modified spatial mechanism. A close look at the available measures reveals some information about the issue credibility of the political parties. As predicted, the public did not view the parties as being equally "green." According to an ABC News Poll from July 2000, Gore was trusted to do a better job of protecting the environment than Bush.[48] Evidence from the ANES supports this conclusion. Asking respondents about the relative positions of the two mainstream parties rather than issue ownership per se, the 2000 ANES finds that Gore was perceived to be much

[44] Hirano and Snyder (2007) similarly find evidence for the central role of U.S. mainstream party strategies in the electoral decline of leftwing, third parties since the 1930s.
[45] http://institution.gallup.com.
[46] "Some Final Observations on Voter Opinions," 2000.
[47] "Clinton Nostalgia Sets in, Bush Reaction Mixed," 2001.
[48] Of the ABC News Poll respondents, 56 percent chose Gore. This view was shared by the majority of supporters of Gore, Buchanan, and Nader. Bush supporters, on the other hand, named Bush as the issue owner. Calculations from ABC News 2001.

more supportive of environmental protection and environmental regulation than Bush.[49] ANES respondents shared this opinion regardless of their political affiliations.[50]

The survey evidence confirms Gore's "green" image relative to his Republican counterpart, but did Gore capture the title of environmental issue owner, stealing it from Nader and the Green Party? Neither the ABC News Poll nor the ANES asked any questions about the environmental credibility or position of Nader, alone or relative to Gore.[51] But the available data suggest Nader and the Green Party maintained some control of issue ownership. Those ABC News Poll respondents who thought that the environment was a very important issue were slightly more likely than those who did not, to reply either that they did not know who owned the issue or that neither candidate owned it.[52] Given the findings (Converse 1964; Holbrook et al. 2004; Iyengar 1990; Zaller 1986) that those who prioritize an issue are more likely to be informed about it and, by extension, its ownership, this seems to raise some modest doubts about Gore's monopoly of the issue. Combine this with the fact that prospective Nader voters were also more likely than others to state that neither mainstream party owned the issue or they did not know who did, and it seems that the Green Party was able to retain at least some claim to the title of issue owner.[53]

This brief analysis reveals the ability of mainstream party tactics to boost the electoral attractiveness of a niche party under even the most unfavorable institutional conditions. Democratic efforts to keep all issue-based voters from supporting the seemingly irrelevant niche party were stymied by the stronger adversarial actions of the Republicans under sociologically advantageous conditions.[54] The Green Party prevailed because voters were primed by the mainstream parties

---

49 Based on the face-to-face respondent sample in the 2000 ANES, 56 percent of respondents said Gore prioritized the environment "somewhat more" to "much more" than jobs. Only 17 percent said the same about Bush. Unfortunately, no comparative questions were asked about the positioning of Nader. Calculations from Burns et al. 2005.

50 Interestingly, the gap between the two candidates on the prioritization of environmental protection versus jobs was found to be greatest among strong Republican partisans. Ibid.

51 Such questions were also absent from the National Annenberg Election Study 2000; the Knowledge Networks data used in Hillygus (2007); and the Voter News Service Exit Polls.

52 The percentage of respondents who said "neither" or "don't know" to the question on issue ownership was 10.2 percent of those who said the environment was very important versus 8.6 percent of everyone else surveyed. Calculations from ABC News 2001.

53 According to the ABC News Poll, 12.5 percent of prospective Nader voters said "neither" or "don't know" as opposed to 8.9 percent of everyone else surveyed. Ibid.

54 Research by Burden (2005) and Hillygus (2007) highlights the fact that many voters who favored Nader did not ultimately vote for the Green Party candidate on election day. There was significant attrition throughout the course of the campaign. That said, there were approximately 2.9 million who did – a number significantly higher than the 685,000 who voted for the same candidate four years earlier. And a November 2000 Pew Research Center survey finds that 82 percent of those who did vote Green were motivated by the issue stance of Nader. With regard to these voters, Gore's accommodative strategy of ownership co-optation failed, a failure largely driven by the adversarial behavior of Bush rather than any innate anti-environmental characteristics of Gore. "Some Final Observations on Voter Opinions," 2000.

to care about the environment, and, thanks to Bush's adversarial tactics, enough voters seemed to perceive Nader to be the most credible issue proponent.[55]

Australia: Niche Party Containment by Mainstream Party Tactics

Just as mainstream party tactics were critical to the electoral strengthening of the Green Party's candidate in the United States, the behavior of the established parties in Australia ensured the decline of the relatively successful radical right party, One Nation. From the perspective of the dominant, institutional theory of new party success, what is surprising in this case is not only that the mainstream parties pursued costly tactics to alter the new party's electoral share, but also that the niche party's support declined.

This unusual combination of puzzles stems from an institutional environment that has both similarities to and differences from those discussed in depth in this volume. Like the British, French, and American systems, the Australian electoral system is highly disproportional; with a district magnitude of one and the requirement that the winning candidate capture a majority of votes, the electoral system favors larger parties, and minor parties have very little chance of winning seats (Lijphart 1994: ch. 2). Unlike those countries, however, Australia uses the Alternative Vote (AV), or preferential voting, system. Because votes for unpopular parties are not wasted, just reallocated to the next party ranked on the ballot, the disincentives for voting for minor parties are lower in the AV system than in plurality systems (Cox 1997; Farrell 2001). Add to the AV system Australia's federalism and its parliamentary system, and institutional theories would expect niche party vote to be higher in this country than in countries like the United Kingdom or even France, but lower than in countries using PR.

However, institutionalists would not expect Australian mainstream parties to incur significant costs to react to niche parties. Under the AV system, smaller parties' votes are typically reallocated to stronger (and often mainstream) parties. Moreover, the national election outcomes produced under AV since the 1970s closely resemble those that would have been produced under plurality rules (see Bean 1986, 1997). With votes being funneled to the mainstream parties anyhow, the larger parties have little incentive to adopt costly tactics to respond to the new parties. Thus, although niche party vote is expected to be higher than that seen in Britain and France, Australia similarly emerges as a least-likely institutional environment in which a theory of the mainstream party determinants of niche party support should apply.

An examination of the niche party phenomenon in Australia challenges these expectations of modest niche party success and, as will be shown later, indifferent mainstream parties. While several green parties and one radical right party have formed, few have achieved significant levels of support. In the first three elections after its formation, the national Green Party only managed to capture an average

---

[55] Even in the face of scare tactics about the electoral dangers of voting Green, environmentally concerned Democrats cast their ballots for, seemingly, the credible issue owner – Ralph Nader.

of 0.8 percent of the vote. Although the party's support level would increase to 5 percent in 2001, even this score seems low given that there are few disincentives for minor party voting. The anti-immigration party, One Nation, fared much better, gaining 8.4 percent of the legislative vote in 1998.[56] By 2001, however, its vote fell to 4.3 percent, a drop unexpected by institutional theories in this particular institutional environment or in any environment in which institutions do not change.

As the next pages will demonstrate, this example of niche party decline provides an interesting illustration of the power of mainstream party strategies to decrease the competitiveness of a niche party in a somewhat permissive electoral environment. In 1996, the issue of immigration control and a plea for the preservation of a white Australia propelled Pauline Hanson – a former Liberal candidate who was elected as an Independent – into the political spotlight and into the House of Representatives.[57] She formed the radical right One Nation party a year later, and, by 1998, One Nation had solidified and expanded its support. With individuals attracted to One Nation on the basis of its position against immigration and multiculturalism,[58] the party captured an average of 22.7 percent in the Queensland state election in June 1998 and won 8.4 percent in the October 1998 federal elections for the House of Representatives, with a peak district vote of more than 30 percent (Markus 2001: 238–9).

The majority of One Nation's votes came from former supporters of the Liberal Party–National Party coalition. According to data from the 2001 Australian Election Study (AES), these voters accounted for 54 percent of One Nation's 1998 vote, while 23 percent had previously supported Labor.[59] Officials in the Liberal Party perceived the threat to them as being even greater than this survey suggests; a former chief of staff to Liberal leader John Howard reportedly stated that former Coalition voters comprised 80 percent of One Nation voters (Markus 2001: 244). Although votes for minor parties are typically less threatening to mainstream parties under AV than plurality rules, the magnitude of One Nation's support had the potential to determine the outcome in marginal districts (Markus 2001: 244).

Concerned about the resonance of Hanson's message with the electorate, the Australian mainstream parties responded, originally to Hanson and then, after

---

[56] One Nation gained a seat in the Senate for the state of Queensland in 1998 and again in 2001.

[57] Pauline Hanson originally ran as the Liberal legislative candidate from Queensland. But two weeks before the election, she was stripped of the Liberal moniker because of her racist comments. In light of the Liberals' subsequent adoption of her positions, this initial disowning is ironic.

[58] Goot argues that "Respondents in the 1998 Australian Election Study who said that they had voted for One Nation appear to have been driven by their attitudes to Aborigines, their concerns about immigration, and their general political alienation." Consistent with my definition of niche party, Goot suggests that there is little evidence that these voters supported Hanson primarily because of her position on the economic issue of globalization. Goot n.d., "The Australian Party System, Pauline Hanson's One Nation, and the Party Cartelisation Thesis." Additional evidence of the immigration basis of One Nation party support is presented in Gaylord 2001.

[59] As reported in Markus (2001: 244), "the remainder either supported minor parties or had not previously voted."

1997, to her One Nation party. The Liberal Party adopted an accommodative strategy that would help stem the flow of its voters to the radical right party. Despite calls from the Labor Party, Prime Minister Howard refused to denounce as racist the anti-immigrant stance expressed by Hanson in her maiden, or first, speech to Parliament. Indeed, to quote Robert Manne (1998 quoted in Markus 2001: 101),

> when Hanson spoke of Australia being swamped by Asians or of Aborigines being Australia's new privileged class, Howard's response was not to deplore the arrival of a new politics of race but to applaud the arrival of a new era of free speech.

The Liberal Party combined this silence with anti-immigration and anti-multiculturalist policies. As part of a coalition government with the National Party, the Liberal Party reduced the number of immigrants – specifically Asian immigrants – allowed to enter the country, passed legislation that limited the claims of the Aboriginal population, and disbanded the Bureau of Immigration, Multicultural and Population Research. These actions, begun in 1996, resembled the policy demands made by Pauline Hanson that same year in her inaugural speech to Parliament.[60] Although changes to the immigration and multiculturalism policies had been discussed prior to the emergence of the Pauline Hanson–One Nation phenomenon, the intensity of the eventual reforms and their timely adoption were in no small part a reaction to the popularity of Hanson and the radical right party.

In response to the disapproval of Howard's policies among formerly Liberal immigrant voters, the Liberal Party did flirt with some antiracist adversarial tactics shortly before the 1998 federal elections.[61] Questions about the sincerity of the Liberal Party's co-optative efforts mitigated their vote-reducing effect in the 1998 elections, most likely contributing to One Nation's strong showing in its first national-level elections.[62] However, the Liberals' accommodative efforts intensified in the next electoral period as popular support for One Nation increased again.[63] In the run-up to the 2001 elections, the Liberal Party and the

---

[60] Markus (2001: 99–100) notes, "Hanson called for the abolition of targeted benefits for Aboriginal people, the abolition of multiculturalism and the reintroduction of a racially discriminatory immigration policy to save Australia from being 'swamped by Asians.'" In the Howard government's plan, this last goal was accomplished by shifting the emphasis of the country's immigration policy from family reunification to the attraction of skilled and English-speaking immigrants (Money 2001: 13).

[61] Money (2001) reports that the Liberal Party started a $5 million antiracist campaign. See also Barber 1998.

[62] It should be noted that, although Pauline Hanson had been in office since 1996 and the party had existed since 1997, the 1998 federal elections were the first national-level elections that One Nation contested. The strategies of the Liberal Party, in combination with the tactics of the Labor Party, are expected to have influenced the niche party's results under these circumstances, but one cannot judge their effects relative to One Nation's nonexistent past national electoral performances. This analysis of the validity of the PSO theory, therefore, will center on the niche party's vote in the 2001 federal elections, its second national contest.

[63] As early as October 19, 1998, sixteen days after the elections, there was concern that One Nation would stage a comeback at both the national and state levels (Robinson 1998). According to

Howard government adopted more extreme and controversial policies similar to Hanson's proposals, such as restricting visa access and even preventing asylum-seeking boatpeople from landing on Australian soil (Gaylord 2001). The goal of these tactics was clear. As reported by *The Economist*,

Rather than denouncing the emergence four years ago of the anti-immigration, isolationist One Nation party, led by Pauline Hanson, a former Liberal member, Mr. Howard has been preoccupied with how he could win over the disgruntled voters to whom she appealed.[64]

The Labor Party reacted differently to the One Nation threat. Like the British Labour Party in the case of the National Front, the Australian Labor Party received support both from voters who were in favor of greater protection for immigrants and from those who preferred more restrictive immigration practices (Jackman 1998). With the former group being larger and with Labor losing fewer voters to One Nation than the Liberals, an adversarial strategy offered the Labor Party the possibility of shoring up the support of the pro-immigrant group while using the niche party as a weapon against the Liberals.

Consistent with this prediction of my strategic choice theory, the Labor Party launched an adversarial campaign against Pauline Hanson and One Nation (Brennan and Mitchell 1999). The party and its leader, Kim Beasley, were quick to denounce the racist statements of Pauline Hanson after her election and maiden speech to the House of Representatives in 1996, thereby reinforcing her credibility as the owner of the issue. Against the criticisms of both One Nation and the Liberal government, Labor over the next five years defended its creation of the multicultural and antiracist framework defining the Australian state. For example, it once again repeated its commitment to apologize to Aborigines, especially members of the "stolen generation," for their treatment by the Australian government and vowed to strengthen multiculturalism by, in part, returning the Australian Office of Multicultural Affairs to the prime minister's department – its location prior to its demotion by the Liberal government.[65]

But the intensity of Labor's adversarial tactics, which contributed to One Nation's strong vote in 1998, was undermined in the last few months before the 2001 legislative elections. In a move inconsistent with previous party pronouncements, the Labor Party called for the further restriction of immigration to Australia, including the detainment of asylum seekers (Holloway 2001). Seemingly a reaction to the popularity of the Liberal government's ban on the admission of boat refugees (Holloway 2001), especially among the anti-immigrant segment of Labor's electorate,[66] this shift in position toward the accommodation of One

---

Newspoll surveys, support for One Nation remained fairly constant for the first three months after the 1998 elections, then dropped to new lows. It rose sharply nine months before the 2001 elections (www.newspoll.com.au).

[64] "Third Time Lucky?" 2001.

[65] "ALP Woos Ethnic Vote," 1998; Australia, Ministry of Immigration 1998.

[66] See Jackman (1998) on the division within the Labor electorate over the issue of race and immigration.

Nation was not rational for the party. Such policy inconsistency, according to my theory, would be costly on two fronts. First, niche party supporters would not view the accommodative strategy as credible, and so few would vote for Labor on this basis. It is also unclear whether such an eleventh-hour about-face would allow Labor to retain voters who supported this position. Second, the Labor Party would lose longtime supporters who favored multiculturalism. Indeed, electoral results show that both of these negative outcomes occurred in the 2001 elections.[67]

But what happened to One Nation in 2001? The combination of the Liberal Party's strong and fairly consistent accommodative tactics with Labor's half-hearted attempts first to demonize Hanson and then later to embrace her restrictive immigration position contributed to the decline in the electoral threat of the niche party. In the 2001 elections, One Nation received only 4.3 percent of the vote, down from 8.4 percent only three years earlier, and Pauline Hanson lost her bid for a seat in the Senate. Data from the 2001 AES reveal this shift at the level of individual voters: only 48 percent of respondents who voted for One Nation in 1998 did so again in 2001. As expected, the Liberal Party was the major beneficiary of the niche party's defectors, winning 53 percent of them.[68] Its coalition partner, the National Party, captured 13 percent of defecting One Nation voters, and the Labor Party received 22 percent. As noted in the preceding text, this movement is consistent with the partisan origins of the One Nation voters. Thus, in contrast to the expectations of the institutionalist theories, the niche party was not maintaining its support in an environment where Duverger's wasted vote theorem did not apply. One Nation issue voters were, rather, returning to the parties from which they came.

Sociological conditions also fail to offer a clear explanation for this drop in One Nation support. On the one hand, the end of the 1990s was characterized by low levels of immigration – a condition consistent with low levels of radical right support. On the other hand, the unemployment rate ended its almost decade-long fall and began to rise the year of the 2001 elections; sociological theories associate this latter condition with an increase in radical right support.[69] The combination of rising unemployment with the high levels of anti-immigration sentiment that had been prevalent in Australia for a decade (Markus 2001: 207–9) created a climate that would seem more ripe for radical right party success, or at least persistent levels of niche party support, than failure.[70]

---

[67] As Holloway (2001) reports, "Older blue collar Labor voters drifted to the Coalition over the issue while younger, inner city voters defected to the Greens."

[68] Those voters who had more recently supported One Nation in the subnational state elections followed similar patterns of defection in the 2001 federal elections. The Liberals received the largest percentage of defectors (57 percent), with 11 percent and 18 percent of One Nation defectors voting for the National Party and Labor Party, respectively. Calculations from Bean et al. 2002.

[69] Immigration data from Markus (2001: 23–6). Unemployment data from *OECD Economic Outlook* 2006.

[70] The constancy of Australia's high level of anti-immigrant sentiment between the early 1990s and 2001 leads sociological approaches to predict constant radical right party vote, *ceteris paribus*.

A clearer explanation for the observed decline in One Nation's vote emerges from strategic approaches. Both the standard spatial theory and my PSO theory correctly predict the flight of One Nation voters to the accommodating Liberal Party. However, the reasons for this voter defection go beyond the mere relocation of parties on an issue dimension. Rather, as the evidence presented in the next section suggests, the Australian mainstream parties altered the electoral competitiveness of One Nation by manipulating issue salience and ownership – the mechanisms unique to my modified spatial approach. Voters were primed to think about immigration and, finding the Liberals to be its owner, cast their ballots for that mainstream party.

Evidence of Issue Salience and Ownership Manipulation in Australia. Although the topic of immigration was not new to the Australian electorate, it had not previously been considered one of the more pressing concerns facing the nation. Between 1993 and June 2001, immigration was ranked, on average, thirteenth out of fourteen very important issues by respondents to Newspoll surveys.[71] But in the run-up to the 2001 elections, the Liberals' and Labor's active tactics boosted the perceived salience of the issue. Newspoll surveys reveal that immigration jumped to a rank of nine out of fifteen by September 2001 as 50 percent of those surveyed said that it would be very important for determining their vote in the federal elections.[72] The popularity of the immigration issue is also demonstrated in the findings of the 2001 AES. With almost half of those who responded deeming immigration to be an extremely important issue, the issue earned the rank of six out of twelve issues.[73] The related issue of refugees and asylum seekers ranked fifth. If one looks at the percentage of AES respondents who named either immigration or refugees and asylum seekers as the *most* important issue during the campaign, the issues ranked first. According to some analysts, immigration "all but crowded out domestic issues from the campaign" (Gaylord 2001).

The importance of the issue seemed to be increasing as a result of the mainstream parties' active strategies. What effect did these tactics have on immigration ownership? Were the more intense accommodative tactics of the Liberals between 1998 and 2001 able to overcome the inconsistent adversarial strategies of the Labor Party to wrest issue credibility away from One Nation? As in the American case, the available survey questions on issue ownership do not provide ideal measures for testing this hypothesis. For example, One Nation is never included as a possible response to the ownership question. But these survey

---

[71] Over twenty-one surveys, the issue fluctuated between the rank of eleven and fourteen out of fourteen issues. Those issues were health and medicare; leadership; family issues; the environment; welfare and social issues; taxation; unemployment; interest rates; women's issues; inflation; immigration; industrial relations; Aboriginal and Native title issues; balance of payments (ended September 1998); and education (added in May 1999). Newspoll surveys reported in *The Australian* and quoted in Marcus 2001: ch. 7 and www.newspoll.com.au.

[72] This was the last Newspoll data point in this series before the elections. A fifteenth issue of defense was added to the list of fourteen issues as of January 2001. Data from www.newspoll.com.au.

[73] Calculations from Bean et al. 2002.

questions do allow us to get a sense of the struggle between the parties for control of the immigration issue.

Starting in 1993, Newspoll surveys asked respondents which party – the (Liberal-National) Coalition, the Labor Party, or someone else – would "best handle immigration."[74] From 1993 until the emergence of One Nation in 1997, the Liberal-National Coalition typically captured the plurality of responses, with an average margin of 9 percentage points over the Labor Party.[75] However, in the polls taken after the formation of One Nation, the size of the Liberals' margin was smaller, and there was a noticeable increase in the percentage of respondents who said that "someone else" owned the issue. Over the next four years, the overall percentage of respondents naming "someone else" would fluctuate, increasing sharply before the 1998 elections and dropping to slightly below its average before the 2001 elections. Although we cannot be certain about which party respondents were thinking when answering "someone else," examination of respondent answers by voting intention strongly suggests that we were witnessing changes in One Nation's issue ownership.[76] In September of 1998, 75 percent of One Nation supporters, as opposed to 12 percent of all respondents, named "someone else" as the party best handling immigration.[77] By September 2001, that percentage had dropped to 59 percent, as opposed to 9 percent of all respondents.

These changes were accompanied by a rise in the perceived ownership of the Liberal-National Coalition right before the 2001 elections. Despite having received an average of only 33 percent of all responses since the formation of One Nation, or a 4 percentage point margin over Labor, the Coalition emerged as the strongest party on immigration ownership in September 2001 with a score of 43 percent and a margin of 18 percentage points over Labor. And more significantly for this analysis, this increase in the Coalition's issue ownership was recognized by One Nation supporters. From September 1998, when only 10 percent of One Nation supporters named the Coalition, the percentage would jump to 24 percent in September 2001.[78] Thus, although we cannot be certain of One Nation's loss of issue ownership because of the absence of any label identifying the niche party in the ownership question, these survey results indicate that the Liberal-National Coalition was perceived to be the title winner by the

---

[74] From 1993 until September 1998, the Australian Democrats were included as a choice in the issue-ownership question. Data from Newspoll Market Research and *The Australian* newspaper.

[75] Calculations of data from Newspoll Market Research at www.newspoll.com.au and *The Australian* newspaper.

[76] I would like to thank Cassandra Marks and Sol Lebovic at Newspoll Market Research for their help with access to the disaggregated results of the Newspoll surveys run in *The Australian* newspaper.

[77] This was the first survey in which "One Nation" supporters were identified separately from "Other" supporters.

[78] This represents an increase over the average of 16 percent among One Nation supporters from September 1998 to September 2001. Data from Newspoll Market Research and *The Australian* newspaper.

respondents in general and, even more telling, by an ever-growing population of One Nation supporters.

The question remains, however, what title did the Liberal-National Coalition win? Although the Newspoll question does not specify whether the title is for the anti- or pro-immigration issue owner, the fact that One Nation supporters were identifying the Coalition suggests that it was being judged the owner of the anti-immigration stance. This claim is substantiated by data from the 2001 AES on the perceived position of the Liberals. According to that study, respondents who named the Liberal-National Coalition as their closest party on the immigration issue were more likely to favor reducing immigration, more likely to view immigrants as increasing crime and taking jobs away from Australians, and less likely to see immigrants as being good for the economy than those who were located closest to the Labor Party, the other party option presented.[79]

And, more importantly for testing the issue-ownership hypothesis, this anti-immigration position of the Liberal-National Coalition was similar to that associated with One Nation and its potential electorate (Bean et al. 2002; Goot and Watson 2000). Understandably, many One Nation partisans and voters reacted to the lack of a One Nation option in the 2001 AES closest-party question by responding "there is no difference between the parties" or "I don't know." Yet, among those One Nation partisans who named one of the two listed parties as the closest party on immigration, the Coalition was chosen by an overwhelming margin over Labor. The Coalition was also the party named closest by 48 percent of voters who supported One Nation in 1998 – the target audience of the Liberals' strategy in 2001.[80] Even Pauline Hanson acknowledged the similarities between the two parties' policy stances when she complained that the Liberals were stealing her policies ("Third Time Lucky?" 2001). Thus, while we cannot conclude with certainty from this data that the Liberal Party was able to wrest sole control of the anti-immigration issue from One Nation, the survey findings do indicate that the Liberal Party was actively challenging the niche party for this title (and the associated issue voters) and having some success.

This brief analysis demonstrates that even when institutional conditions are more propitious, the electoral success of single-issue parties is not guaranteed. Indeed, established party competitors can use accommodative tactics to steal both the niche party's issue position and its voters. While this conclusion is consistent with the hypotheses of the standard spatial model, evidence from the Australian case suggests that another strategic mechanism is at work. As predicted by my PSO theory of party interaction, John Howard's party was able to "neutralise Mrs. Hanson politically" ("Third Time Lucky?" 2001) by boosting the salience

---

[79] In the AES question asking respondents to identify the party closest to their own views on immigration, the respondents were given the following response options: "Labor," "Liberal-National Coalition," "There is no difference," and "Don't know."

[80] As expected, that percentage was even higher (94 percent) among those 1998 One Nation voters who defected to the Liberals in 2001. Calculations from Bean et al. 2002.

of the immigration issue and challenging One Nation's sole control of the anti-immigration position.

CONCLUSION

Regardless of whether party competition between unequals takes place in Western Europe, North America, or Australasia; under restrictive or slightly more permissive electoral rules; in presidential or parliamentary systems; or even between proximal or distant competitors, these comparative cases show that mainstream parties have been able to shape the electoral fortunes of their niche party opponents. Just as in the electorally restrictive institutional environments of France and Great Britain, mainstream parties in the United States and Australia defied the expectations of the institutionalists and pursued costly tactics toward parties with minimal chances of attaining office or governmental control. In line with my strategic choice theory, the adoption of strategies turned on the threat to the mainstream party's relative electoral strength posed by each niche party. This concern even determined party behavior in Australia, where, as a result of the Alternative Vote system, the mainstream parties' tolerance for minor party support was expected to have been even higher.

This comparison of cases within and across regions also highlights the explanatory power of strategic theories and specifically my PSO theory of niche party fortune. The tactics of mainstream parties in the United States ensured the electoral strengthening of a green party in an electorally restrictive environment whereas those of their counterparts in Australia led to the electoral decline of a radical right party in an institutionally more permissive climate. The success of the U.S. Green Party under these conditions suggests that the failure of green parties in both Britain and France cannot simply be dismissed as being "overdetermined" by similarly restrictive electoral environments. Rather, the U.S. case shows that niche party fortune depends on the behavior of mainstream and – *contra* standard spatial models – especially nonproximal mainstream parties.

Further evidence supporting the PSO theory, the details from this case and the others examined in this chapter demonstrate that the effects of mainstream party strategies are not limited to changing the relative policy positions of the parties. The adversarial tactics of the Republicans reinforced the U.S. Green Party's vote by shoring up the salience of the environmental issue and the Green Party's ownership of it. The strong accommodative tactics of the French Socialists and the Australian Liberals succeeded in undermining the vote of the UDB and One Nation, respectively, by stealing the title of issue owner away from the niche party. Similar issue salience- and ownership-altering processes underlay the ability of the British Conservatives and French Socialists to reduce the vote share of the National Front and the Greens. The patterns revealed in these cases are consistent with the findings in Chapters 5 through 7 and the statistical analyses of Chapter 3, thus increasing our confidence that the fortunes of niche parties – whether they are from Europe or other advanced industrial democracies – and the mechanisms by which they are produced follow the predictions of the PSO theory.

9

Conclusions

Broader Lessons of Competition between Unequals

Since the 1970s, the political systems of Western Europe have undergone a major transformation. Competition between mainstream parties has been interrupted by the emergence of niche parties, actors that are fundamentally different from their mainstream opponents. The new parties' rejection of the economic focus of politics and their introduction of new and controversial issues have threatened the content of the political debate and the very partisan alignments that ensure mainstream parties' electoral and governmental dominance.

Yet, although they have transformed political arenas across the region, niche parties have experienced wide variation in their electoral success. Hoping to explain why some green, radical right, or ethnoterritorial parties floundered while others flourished, scholars have turned to the institutional and sociological characteristics of the particular political environments. According to these theories, parties fail under restrictive electoral rules or unfavorable economic and societal conditions. Niche party success, therefore, occurs under the opposite conditions: for example, when PR rules are in effect or, in the case of radical right parties, when unemployment and immigrant populations are high.

As the analyses in this book suggest, however, the electoral successes and failures of green, radical right, and ethnoterritorial parties are not merely the reflection of the institutional and sociological environment. Rather, this study finds answers to the puzzle of niche party performance in a factor that has been largely ignored in this literature: party competition. To the extent that institutional and sociological variables underlie a party's success, they are not neutral, exogenously determined variables. The institutions – such as electoral rules or a state's federalist structure – are chosen by mainstream parties, and as my British and French case studies demonstrate, they can be an explicit part of a mainstream party's strategy toward a niche party. Similarly, the relationships between objective economic conditions and voter support for a particular party are not intrinsic; they are fostered or undermined by political actors.

This study brings parties back into the analysis of party success and failure. The book's central argument is that niche party fortunes are the product of party competition. Specifically, their electoral lows and highs are influenced by the strategies of the most powerful set of political actors – the electorally and governmentally dominant mainstream parties. While strategic explanations are hardly new to political science, my argument rests on a reconception of party competition and party strategies. In contrast to the standard spatial explanation designed to account for interaction between mainstream parties, competition between unequals is not defined as parties simply shifting their policy stances on a given set of issue dimensions. Instead, I argue, mainstream parties have access to a wider and more effective range of tools with which to undermine, but also boost, niche party support. In the rest of this chapter, I summarize the book's major conclusions and then explore the theoretical implications of my story of competition between unequal parties for institutional change, competition between equals, and party systems in general.

A STRATEGIC EXPLANATION OF NICHE PARTY SUCCESS AND FAILURE

To understand how and why mainstream parties manipulate – diminish and enhance – the electoral strength of these new party competitors, this book moves beyond the basic tenets of spatial theory. Contrary to the standard assumptions of spatial models, research has shown that the importance of issue dimensions can fluctuate during campaigns and that voters are not indifferent between parties promising the same policy positions. Based on these findings, a new conception of party strategies is necessary. In addition to shifting their policy stances on issue dimensions, parties, I argue, can alter the attractiveness of themselves and others by changing the salience and ownership of those issues for political competition.

The implications of this reconception of party strategy are significant, especially for the nature of competition between political unequals. The two standard tactics of policy convergence and divergence are replaced by three – dismissive, accommodative, and adversarial tactics. Mainstream parties, thus, have more tools with which to undermine or boost niche party vote levels. Moreover, competition is no longer limited to interaction between ideologically proximal parties. Adversarial tactics allow mainstream parties to increase the vote share of a niche party on the other flank of an issue dimension, whereas dismissive tactics allow mainstream parties to decrease niche party support levels without even needing to take or publicize a stand on the niche party's issue.

Two consequences follow. If ideological proximity is not necessary for party competition, then a niche party's fortune will be the product of the strategies of *multiple* mainstream parties. Second, the possibility of targeting a niche party anywhere in the political space means that mainstream parties can increase the electoral support of new parties that threaten the vote of their mainstream party opponents. In other words, niche parties are either targets themselves or weapons used to hurt other parties.

While the issue salience- and ownership-altering dimensions of strategies increase their power and their range of use, they also introduce constraints to strategic effectiveness. Not only is the success of party strategies dependent on their consistency over time – as in all strategic models – but their success now also depends on their timing. An established party's ability to undermine a niche party ultimately rests on its implementation of accommodative tactics prior to the reputational entrenchment of the niche party as the only credible issue promoter. Mainstream party hesitation, whether it stems from internal party factionalism or a decentralized party organizational structure, fosters niche party success.

In addition to demonstrating that an alternate conception of strategies is in use and that these strategies have new implications – opportunities and challenges – for party competition between unequals, this study has explored the conditions under which mainstream parties adopt and implement these strategies. The case studies confirm that the strategic choice of an established party is not driven by the oft-studied national vote share of the new party. As the active responses of the British, French, and U.S. mainstream parties demonstrate, established parties are motivated to react to niche parties even in institutionally restrictive electoral environments and even when niche parties draw only small numbers of voters nationwide. Strategic choice turns on the threat that a niche party is posing to one mainstream party relative to another and, in the plurality systems under investigation, the geographic concentration of that threat. But as Chapter 4 argues and the case studies illustrate, strategies are not adopted in a vacuum. A party's choice of tactics is constrained by the anticipated or observed strategic maneuvers of other political actors, not to mention the past policy decisions of the strategizing party and the capacity of the strategizing party to overcome internal division and decision-making impasses.

The predictions of my theories of strategic interaction and strategic choice are strongly supported by quantitative and qualitative evidence from Western Europe, and Great Britain and France in particular. The cross-sectional time-series analyses of 149 strategic interactions between mainstream and niche parties in seventeen countries between 1970 and 1998 confirm that mainstream party tactics play a central role in accounting for the electoral lows and highs of the neophyte parties. As shown by the results of Model IIa in Table 3.5,[1] three sets of tactics reduce niche party support: when both mainstream parties act dismissively (DIDI), when one is dismissive and the other is accommodative (DIAC), and when the accommodative tactics of one mainstream party are stronger than the adversarial tactics of the other (ACAD when AC > AD). Niche party support increases under three other strategic combinations: when one mainstream party is dismissive and the other is adversarial (DIAD), when both are adversarial (ADAD), and when one party's adversarial tactics are stronger than the accommodative tactics of another mainstream party (ACAD when AD > AC). The regression analyses

---

[1] The analysis of ethnoterritorial party vote presented in Table 3.11 reinforces these findings. In Model VI, three sets of tactics (DIDI, DIAC, and ACAD when AC > AD) reduce ethnoterritorial party vote, and one set (ACAD when AD > AC) increases it; DIAD and ADAD tactics were not observed in this population of cases. Recall that, although it has the expected negative sign, the ACAC strategic variable is not statistically significant in the pooled green and radical right party model (Model IIa) or the ethnoterritorial party model (Model VI).

also provide some evidence that hesitation undermines the vote-reducing effects of accommodative tactics.

Although there was some variation in the strength of these findings across niche party types, no other set of factors (institutional or sociological) emerges as a stronger predictor of green, radical right, and ethnoterritorial party support. Moreover, these results challenge the standard spatial model's positional conception of party strategies and competition. By highlighting the power of the strategies of both proximal and distant mainstream parties, the statistical findings suggest that strategies are working, as I argue, by altering the salience of the niche party's issue and the attractiveness and ownership of its position on that issue.

The case studies add context, substance, and additional explanatory power to the statistical relationships. In-depth analyses of survey and electoral data on the salience and ownership of the niche parties' issues corroborate my inferences from the statistical analyses about the modified spatial nature of party strategies: namely, parties are competing by shifting the importance of new issue dimensions and the perceived credibility of parties on them.

In a manner not possible in the statistical analyses, these case studies also shed light on the degree to which a strategy's effectiveness can be constrained. They confirm the theory's claims that delays in the implementation of tactics and contradictions in party policy, typically stemming from party disunity, undermine the power of strategies to affect issue ownership and thus niche party support.[2] But it also becomes clear, from the SNP case study in particular, that the common modeling assumption of fixed voter policy preferences made by this and most other theories of party competition (e.g., Downs 1957; Enelow and Hinich 1984) does not always hold and that the success of strategies is affected by shifts in the distribution of voters on the niche party's new issue.[3]

These in-depth examinations of competition between unequals also serve as a test of the theory of strategic choice advanced in Chapter 4. Information from party archives and interviews with politicians reveals the motivations behind the strategic behavior of the established parties as well as any impediments to their ability to adopt and implement particular tactics. From this book's examination of seventy-six data points (the thirty-four observations of individual mainstream party strategic choice in these three sets of British and French mainstream party–niche party interaction plus the forty-two observations underlying the five cases discussed briefly in Chapter 8), we can conclude that tactics are, as predicted, a

---

[2] The regression analyses only tested the effect of hesitation and, even then, only on DIAC and ACAC tactics.

[3] In contrast to the theoretical literature, some empirical work on party competition, especially in Western Europe, has noted the variability of voter distribution over time, mostly with regard to the Left-Right scale (see Adams 2001; Adams, Clark, Ezrow, and Glasgow 2004; Budge 1994). Less is known, however, about the causes of these shifts in public opinion. The limited existing research on the origins of voter preferences (e.g., Gerber and Jackson 1993; Jackson 2003) suggests that an answer lies, in part, in the behavior of parties. Additional research is needed, but it would not be surprising to find that the shifts in voter preferences on the devolution issue in Scotland in the 1970s (discussed in Chapter 7) were the result of mainstream party tactics on that issue – a new issue with which voters were unfamiliar.

function of the relative electoral threat of the niche party in a given institutional environment, subject to other mainstream parties' behavior and the strategizing party's own organizational and reputational constraints.

LARGER THEORETICAL IMPLICATIONS

The distinct nature of competition between political unequals has been the focus of this study. However, in affirming the general hypotheses of my PSO theory of party competition, this analysis does more than demonstrate how powerful mainstream parties have been able to determine the competitiveness and vote of their single-issue niche party opponents. It also has ramifications for work on institutional change, party competition in general, and party system stability.

Strategies toward Niche Parties as Drivers of Institutional Change

The modified spatial conception of strategies introduces the idea that political parties are not limited to shifting their policy positions in order to compete for votes. Although much of the emphasis of this analysis has been on the position-, salience-, and ownership-altering dimensions of issue-based tactics, this book has also discussed how mainstream parties have access to organizational and institutional tools. For example, mainstream parties form coalitions with niche parties or make niche party leaders into cabinet members to attract voters by convincing them of the reputational credibility of the mainstream party on the new issue.

Although they do not challenge issue ownership like issue-based and organizational tactics, institutions – such as electoral rules or state structure – likewise become tools for undermining or promoting niche party support. Not only does this mean, *contra* standard institutional theories, that institutions cannot be assumed to be exogenous to party competition, but it also suggests a new explanation for cases of institutional change. For instance, the adoption of decentralization has been explained in the larger literature by a range of factors, from a party's ideological drive to locate power in the hands of the people (Sawer 1969) to a state's need to increase efficiency by satisfying regionally or sectorally specific preferences (Alesina et al. 1999). Those who conceive decentralization as an explicit political strategy have argued that national parties will devolve power (political and/or fiscal) to subnational governments either when the power of the subnational party elite is greater than that of the national party elite (Garman, Haggard, and Willis 2001), or when the national party is electorally weak and hopes to shore up subnational support (O'Neill 2005). In either case, decentralization is intended to produce subnational benefits for the party (or its dominant subnational elite).

My study of competition between unequals shows, however, that national parties will adopt decentralization reforms even when they face opposition from their subnational elite and even when they do not expect the transfer of powers to benefit them electorally at the subnational level. The British Labour Party, for example, pushed for decentralization even though the Scottish members of the party were originally opposed to the proposal and even though Labour was expected to be (and was) disadvantaged electorally in elections to those new subnational governments. Rather, as seen in Chapter 7 on the SNP and in the discussion in Chapter 8 on the UDB, decentralization was a means of reinforcing a party's *national* electoral strength by appeasing supporters of a threatening ethnoterritorial party.[4]

Similarly, this study finds that changes to electoral rules may also be designed to alter the competitiveness of niche parties. The French Socialists adopted PR for the 1986 election with the express hope of driving up Front National votes at the expense of the RPR.[5] The emerging work on the adoption of new electoral systems (Andrews and Jackman 2005; Boix 1999) does frame such decisions as strategic moves by mainstream parties to shore up their future support, but it has overlooked the significance of minor parties as the means of accomplishing this – either directly as the intended victim of the institutional change or indirectly as the weapon to undermine the electoral strength of mainstream party opponents.[6] In the former case, this myopia may only change the details of the story told about institutional change (e.g., the number and motivations of the actors); in the latter, the failure to recognize the role of third parties may lead, in some cases, to different predictions about the timing and nature of the electoral change.[7]

Challenges to Models of Party Competition

A second set of implications of this study of niche party success speaks to general theories of party competition. This book contends that niche parties are fundamentally different from mainstream parties and that mainstream parties consequently have access to a wider and more effective range of strategies to use against them. As I have highlighted, these findings challenge the standard conception of mainstream party tactics. But they have even broader implications for existing theories of party interaction.

First, they call into question the common modeling supposition that political actors are interchangeable. Formal models of party interaction assume the

[4] O'Neill (2005: ch. 7) does acknowledge the role of subnational regionalist pressure in changes to state structure, but she only describes it as applying to cases of political decentralization, not to the instances of joint political and fiscal decentralization that have characterized Spain, Belgium, and, to a lesser extent, Scotland.

[5] Similarly, the RPR's decision to reinstate a two-round plurality system for the next election was likely affected by its desire to minimize the support of the FN.

[6] Benoit (2004) is something of an exception. Although his discussion of the French electoral system change in 1986 does not acknowledge the role of the Front National as the Socialists' weapon against the RPR, his general model of electoral change does at least include all parties in a given political system.

[7] Inclusion of minor and niche parties in models of electoral change is of particular importance in explaining more-recent institutional changes.

existence of several parties, where each typically is distinguished only by its policy positions.[8] It is also assumed that parties in these models have access to the same tactics and are equally affected by those tactics, *ceteris paribus*. Niche parties challenge these assumptions. They stand out from other parties on the basis of their single-issue status. Because they are limited to competing on their one issue dimension, they are more susceptible to strategies than multi-issue mainstream parties, which can always shift focus to a new issue. This vulnerability is further exacerbated by the niche party's relative immobility on that one dimension.

We should not conclude, however, that niche parties are helpless. First, although niche parties may not achieve their office- or vote-seeking goals because of powerful mainstream party strategies, they may succeed in policy terms. Accommodative tactics result, after all, in the mainstream party's adoption of the niche party's policy objectives. Second, it may be possible for niche parties to improve their fortunes as office-seeking actors. Although there is little evidence of this currently, perhaps in the future niche parties will be able to overcome their strategic limitations by reinventing themselves as mainstream parties. For now at least, the standard modeling assumptions of party interchangeability fail to capture the characteristics of mainstream party–niche party competition.

The same modeling limitations appear to hold true for competition involving other nonmainstream parties. Research by Adams et al. (2006) shows that communist parties, in addition to green and radical right parties, differ from mainstream parties in that they are less likely to alter their policy stances.[9] To the extent that the communists do move closer to the median voter, they are punished.[10] Not only does this result run counter to the expectations of the standard spatial model, but these scholars find that it is opposite to the electoral effects of similar shifts by mainstream parties. As this book and the growing strategic literature on nonmainstream parties (e.g., Adams et al. 2006; Ezrow forthcoming) suggest, recognizing that different types of party exist and that they have important effects on the outcomes of party competition is critical to accurately modeling party interaction.

The emergence of niche parties introducing new and previously unpoliticized issues poses a potential challenge to another central modeling assumption. Models of party interaction (e.g., Downs 1957; Enelow and Hinich 1984) typically assume that parties compete on a known set of political dimensions that remain

[8] Two exceptions to this trend involve the growing subfield that incorporates valence dimensions of party qualifications into spatial models (e.g., Ansolabehere and Snyder 2000; Groseclose 2001; Schofield 2003) and the literature that distinguishes parties by their office/vote-seeking and policy-seeking goals (e.g., Adams and Merrill 2006).

[9] Of the nonmainstream parties that Adams et al. (2006) examine, the majority (six out of ten) are communist parties, three are radical right parties, and one is a green party.

[10] The implication of this finding – that nonmainstream parties profit electorally from extreme positions – is verified by Ezrow (forthcoming). From an analysis of a larger set of communist, green, and radical right parties in Western Europe, he concludes that policy extremism on the Left-Right dimension benefits nonmainstream parties, whereas, consistent with the expectations of the standard spatial theory, it hurts mainstream parties.

constant, both during the interaction and over time. Whereas mainstream parties can use dismissive tactics to downplay the niche party and its new issue, thereby retaining the existing content of the political arena, the established parties' use of more active tactics does change the effective dimensions of party competition during interaction. By adopting either an accommodative or an adversarial strategy, the mainstream party is prioritizing the niche party's issue dimension and "adding" it to the mainstream political debate. Contrary to the standard modeling assumptions, therefore, the shape of the policy space in competition between unequals is both variable and endogenous to party competition.

That mainstream parties incorporate the niche party's new issue into the dominant political debate during party competition also means that the "success" of a niche party's issue is distinct from niche party electoral success. Immigration and the environment have become mainstream political topics in most Western European countries even though many of the niche parties that introduced them have been marginalized or eliminated through accommodative tactics. In many cases, these topics are kept in the public eye by their mainstream party issue owners who continue to use them to attract voter support. Even if these issues are not the most important topics in a given election, their recurrent discussion in party manifestos and presence in public opinion survey questions demonstrate that strategies directed against short-term niche party threats may also have a lasting impact on the content of the mainstream political debate.

Challenges to the Nature and Stability of Party Systems

The incorporation of a new issue dimension is not the only manner in which competition between unequals can shape the long-run competition between mainstream party equals. A third theoretical implication of this study concerns the nature and stability of the party system. The literature on party systems in developed countries tends to assume the relative constancy of the effective number of parties in the system, barring any changes to institutions or critical upheavals (Duverger 1954; Sartori 1976). This book provides another mechanism for changes to party systems. In shaping the vote of niche parties, mainstream party strategies can affect the very survival of the mainstream parties and the stability of the party system. Accommodative tactics bolster the electoral strength of the strategizing mainstream party by undermining the vote of a threatening niche party. Mainstream party dominance and party system stability are facilitated by the elimination of new competitors.

But this study has also shown that mainstream party strategies can lead to a different outcome. Unique to the PSO theory of party competition, adversarial tactics can turn nonproximal niche parties into weapons against mainstream party opponents. Even though the electoral success of a mainstream party typically depends on the party's attractiveness on multiple policy dimensions, such single-issue adversarial tactics have been responsible for the loss of mainstream parties' legislative seats and even governmental turnover. The latter situation unfolded in Austria in 1999 where, after facing three electoral periods of joint adversarial strategies, the radical right FPÖ became the second most popular party. The Socialists were forced from office as the FPÖ and the conservative ÖVP formed a coalition government.[11] Examples are not restricted to Western Europe, as demonstrated by the role of the Republicans' adversarial tactics toward Green Party candidate Ralph Nader in the defeat of Democrat Al Gore in the 2000 U.S. presidential election.

While mainstream parties employing adversarial strategies seek to benefit from the electoral weakening of their mainstream counterparts, their success can come at the expense of party system stability.[12] As seen in the Austrian and U.S. cases, the intense adversarial tactics that highlight uncompromising policy differences between parties resulted in the extreme polarization of the electorate and political system. In the Austrian case, years of mainstream party demonization of the radical right party also damaged the sustainability and effectiveness of the mainstream party–niche party government.[13] And the potential costs could be even greater. At the extreme, adversarial strategies could result in party system realignment through the elimination of the mainstream party opponent and its replacement with the niche party.[14]

With such consequences, mainstream party strategies against niche parties are not just means to counteract a set of single-issue political actors; these everyday tactics have effectively become tools in the much larger political processes of party system change. Party competition between unequals therefore sheds light not only on the fortunes of niche parties, but also on competition between equals and the very nature of party politics.

[11] The Socialists received the highest percentage of vote in the 1999 legislative elections. Although their adversarial tactics contributed to the flight of ÖVP voters to the FPÖ, the Socialists' refusal to form a coalition government with the radical right party led to their exclusion from the coalition government. As this case demonstrates, adversarial tactics may undermine the vote of a mainstream opponent, but, at the same time, they may also hurt the *strategizing* party's chances at office. Such was also the case in the 2002 French presidential election when electoral support for the FN's Jean-Marie Le Pen – boosted by years of Socialist adversarial tactics – surpassed that for the then-prime minister and Socialist presidential candidate, Lionel Jospin. Jospin was eliminated from the race, and Le Pen and Gaullist Jacques Chirac advanced to the second round. It should be noted that Jospin's electoral position was also hurt by the proliferation of leftist presidential candidates holding issue positions similar to his.

[12] And as the Austrian example demonstrates, adversarial tactics can even exact unanticipated costs on the "successful" strategizing mainstream party.

[13] This damage to the effectiveness of the FPÖ-ÖVP government was compounded by anti-FPÖ sanctions issued by the European Union.

[14] This latter case highlights the dangers of the adversarial tactic: an adversarial mainstream party has helped to replace its mainstream opponent with a niche party whose policy position it may abhor even more.

References

Collections of Public and Private Papers

Archives du CEVIPOF, Paris, France
Archives de la Documentation Française, Paris, France
Archives de la FNSP, Institut d'Etudes politiques, Paris, France
Archives du Ministère de l'Intérieur, Archives Nationales, Fontainbleau, France
Archives de l'OURS, Paris, France
Archives du Premier Ministre, Archives Nationales, Fontainbleau, France
Conservative Party Archives, Bodleian Library, Oxford, UK
Labour Party Archives, National Museum of Labour History, Manchester, UK
Service de Presse du RPR, Paris, France

Statistical Data

ABC News. 2001. *ABC News Poll, July 2000* (computer file). ICPSR version. Horsham, PA: Taylor Nelson Sofres Intersearch (producer), 2000. Ann Arbor, MI: Inter-university Consortium for Political and Social Research (distributor).

Banque de Données Socio-Politiques (BDSP). *Résultats électoraux, par circonscription, 1971–97* (computer file). http://cdsp.sciences-po.fr/page.php?&idRubrique=votesFrance&lang=FR.

Bean, Clive, David Gow, and Ian McAllister. 2002. *Australian Election Study, 2001* (computer file). Canberra: Social Science Data Archives, The Australian National University (distributor).

Binghamton Election Results Archive. http://www.binghamton.edu/cdp/era/index.html.

British Election Results. http://www.laws.qmw.ac.uk/election.

Burns, Nancy, Donald R. Kinder, Steven J. Rosenstone, Virginia Sapiro, and the National Election Studies. 2005. *American National Election Study, 2000: Pre- and Post-Election Survey* (computer file). 3rd ICPSR version. Ann Arbor: University of Michigan, Center for Political Studies (producer), 2001. Ann Arbor, MI: Inter-university Consortium for Political and Social Research (distributor).

Butler, David and David Stokes. 1974. *Political Change in Britain: 1966–1970 British Election Study Panel* (computer file). Colchester, UK: ESRC Data Archive.

BVA poll. 1999. "L'identité des gauches." October. http://www.bva.fr/archives/gauches.html.

Centre d'Etudes de la Vie Politique Française and Centre d'Informatisation des Données Socio-Politiques. 1995. *French National Election Study 1988* (computer file). Paris, France: Centre d'Etudes de la Vie Politique Française/Grenoble, France: Centre d'Informatisation des Données Socio-Politiques (producers), 1988. Grenoble, France: Centre d'Informatisation des Données Socio-Politiques (distributor).

———. 1997. *French National Election Study 1978* (computer file). Paris, France: Centre d'Etudes de la Vie Politique Française/Grenoble, France: Centre d'Informatisation des Données Socio-Politiques (producers), 1978. Grenoble, France: Centre d'Informatisation des Données Socio-Politiques (distributor).

Centre d'Etudes de la Vie Politique Française, Centre d'Informatisation des Données Socio-Politiques, and Centre de Recherches Administratives, Politiques et Sociales. 2001. *French National Election Study 1997* (computer file). Paris, France: Centre d'Etudes de la Vie Politique Française/Grenoble, France: Centre d'Informatisation des Données Socio-Politiques/Lille, France: Centre de Recherches Administratives, Politiques et Sociales (producers), 1997. ICPSR version. Ann Arbor, MI: Inter-university Consortium for Political and Social Research (distributor).

Chrique, Philippe. 1997. *Legidoscope: Trend Surveys of French Public Opinion and Media Usage, September 1992–May 1993* (computer file). ICPSR version. Paris, France: Institute Française d'Opinion Publique (producer), 1993. Ann Arbor, MI: Inter-university Consortium for Political and Social Research (distributor).

Crewe, Ivor, Bo Särlvik, and James Alt. 1970. *British Election Study, 1964–1966–1970 Panel* (computer file). Ann Arbor, MI: Inter-university Consortium for Political and Social Research (distributor).

———. 1975a. *British Election Study, February 1974, cross-section* (computer file). Ann Arbor, MI: Inter-university Consortium for Political and Social Research (distributor).

———. 1975b. *British Election Study, October 1974, cross-section* (computer file). Ann Arbor, MI: Inter-university Consortium for Political and Social Research (distributor).

Crewe, Ivor, Bo Särlvik, and David Robertson. 1979. *British Election Study, May 1979, cross-section* (computer file). Ann Arbor, MI: Inter-university Consortium for Political and Social Research (distributor).

Davis, James A., Tom W. Smith, and Peter V. Marsden. 2006. *General Social Surveys, 1972–2004: Cumulative File* (computer file). ICPSR04295-v2. Chicago: National Opinion Research Center (producer), 2005. Storrs, CT: Roper Center for Public Opinion Research, University of Connecticut/Ann Arbor, MI: Inter-university Consortium for Political and Social Research (distributors).

van der Eijk, Cees, Erik Oppenhuis, and Hermann Schmitt. 1994. *European Election Study, 1989* (computer file). Amsterdam, the Netherlands: Steinmetz Archive/SWIDOC, European Election Study Research Group (producer), 1993. Amsterdam: Steinmetz Archive and Ann Arbor, MI: Inter-university Consortium for Political and Social Research (distributors).

Eurostat Statistics. 2003. Reinberg, Germany: DSI Data Service and Information.

Gallup Political and Economic Index. Various years. London: DOD's Publishing and Research.

Gallup Political Index, 1989–90. 1989–90. London: Social Surveys.

Heath, Anthony. 1983. *British Election Study, 1983* (computer file). Colchester, UK: ESRC Data Archive.

———. 1989. *British Election Study, 1987* (computer file). Colchester, UK: ESRC Data Archive.

———. 1993. *British Election Study, 1992* (computer file). Colchester, UK: ESRC Data Archive.

Heath, Anthony, R. Jowell, J. K. Curtice, J. A. Brand, and J. C. Mitchell. 1996. *British General Election Cross-Section Survey, 1992* (computer file). ICPSR version. London: Social and Community Planning Research (producer), 1992. Colchester, UK: ESRC Data Archive/Ann Arbor, MI: Inter-university Consortium for Political and Social Research (distributors).

Heath, Anthony, R. Jowell, J. K. Curtice, and P. Norris. 2000. *British General Election Cross-Section Survey, 1997* (computer file). 2nd ICPSR version. London: Social and Community Planning Research (producer), 1998. Colchester, UK: The Data Archive/Ann Arbor, MI: Inter-university Consortium for Political and Social Research (distributors).

Herald System 3 Polls. http://www.alba.org.uk/polls/pollwestminsteryearly.html.

Inglehart, Ronald, Karlheinz Reif, and Anna Melich. 1994. *European Communities Studies, 1970–1992: Cumulative File* (computer file). 3rd ICPSR version. Ann Arbor: Ronald Inglehart, University of Michigan (producer), 1994. Ann Arbor, MI: Inter-University Consortium for Political and Social Research (distributor).

Inglehart, Ronald, et al. 2000. *World Values Surveys and European Values Surveys, 1981–1984, 1990–1993, and 1995–1997* (computer file). ICPSR version. Ann Arbor, MI: Institute for Social Research (producer), 1999. Ann Arbor, MI: Inter-university Consortium for Political and Social Research (distributor).

Lewis-Beck, Michael, Nonna Mayer, Daniel Boy, et al. 1996. *French National Election Study, 1995* (computer file). ICPSR version. Iowa City: Michael S. Lewis-Beck, University of Iowa, Department of Political Science/Paris, France: Nonna Mayer and Daniel Boy, et al., Centre d'Etude de la Vie Politique Française (producers), 1995. Ann Arbor, MI: Inter-university Consortium for Political and Social Research (distributor).

McCrone, David, Alice Brown, Paula Surridge, and Katarina Thomson. 1999. *British Election Study: Scottish Election Survey 1997* (computer file). ICPSR version. London: Social and Community Planning Research (producer), 1998. Colchester, UK: ESRC Data Archive/Ann Arbor, MI: Inter-university Consortium for Political and Social Research (distributors).

Miller, William L. and Jack A. Brand. 1981. *Scottish Election Study, 1979* (computer file). Colchester, UK: The Data Archive (distributor). SN: 1604.

MORI Polls. http://www.ipsos-mori.com/political/trends.shtml.

Newspoll Market Research. Various years. "Political Surveys," in *The Australian*. http://www.newspoll.com.au.

OECD. 1987. *Historical Statistics: 1960–1985*. Paris: OECD.

———. 1999. *Economic Outlook: Historical Statistics, 1960–1997*. Paris: OECD.

———. 2000. *OECD Statistical Compendium CD-ROM*. Paris: OECD Electronic Editions.

———. 2006. *Economic Outlook 2006*. Paris: OECD.

———. 2006. *OECD Factbook 2006: Economic, Environmental and Social Statistics*. Paris: OECD.

Outlaw, Iain. 2005. *British Election Data by Constituency*. http://www.psr.keele.ac.uk/area/uk/outlaw/sheetindex.htm.

Pierce, Roy. 1996. *French Presidential Election Survey, 1988* (computer file). ICPSR version. Ann Arbor: Roy Pierce, University of Michigan (producer), 1995. Ann Arbor, MI: Inter-university Consortium for Political and Social Research (distributor).

Political Database of the Americas. United States: 1996 Presidential Election (Internet). Georgetown University and the Organization of the American States. http://www.georgetown.edu/pdba/Elecdata/USA/pres96.html.

Robertson, David. 1977. *British Election Study, October 1974* (computer file). Colchester, UK: ESRC Data Archive.

Schmitt, Hermann, Cees van der Eijk, Evi Scholz, and Michael Klein. 2001. *European Election Study, 1994* (computer file). Koeln, Germany: Zentralarchiv fuer Empirische Sozialforschung/Mannheim, Germany: European Election Study Research Group (producers), 1996. Koeln, Germany: Zentralarchiv fuer Empirische Sozialforschung/Ann Arbor, MI: Inter-university Consortium for Political and Social Research (distributors).

Other Primary and Secondary Sources

Achen, Christopher H. 1982. *Interpreting and Using Regression*. Newbury Park, CA: Sage Publications.

Adams, James. 2001. *Party Competition and Responsible Party Government*. Ann Arbor: University of Michigan Press.

Adams, James, Michael Clark, Lawrence Ezrow, and Garrett Glasgow. 2006. "Are Niche Parties Fundamentally Different from Mainstream Parties?: The Causes and Electoral Consequences of Western European Parties' Policy Shifts, 1976–98." *American Journal of Political Science* 50 (3): 513–29.

Adams, James and Samuel Merrill III. 2006. "Why Small, Centrist Third Parties Motivate Policy Divergence by Major Parties." *American Political Science Review* 100 (3): 403–17.

Adams, James, Samuel Merrill III, and Bernard Grofman. 2005. *A Unified Theory of Party Competition: A Cross-National Analysis Integrating Spatial and Behavioral Factors*. Cambridge: Cambridge University Press.

Agasøster, Bodil. 2001. "A Framework for Analysing Local Party Policy Emphases in Scotland," in *Estimating the Policy Positions of Political Actors*, ed. Michael Laver. London: Routledge. 76–89.

Alberts, Sheldon. 2004. "Republicans' New Ally: Ralph Nader." *The Gazette* (October): 24.

Aldrich, John H. 1995. *Why Parties? The Origin and Transformation of Party Politics in America*. Chicago: University of Chicago Press.

Alesina, Alberto. 1988. "Credibility and Policy Convergence in a Two-Party System with Rational Voters." *American Economic Review* 78: 796–806.

Alesina, Alberto, Reza Baqir, and William Easterly. 1999. "Public Goods and Ethnic Divisions." *Quarterly Journal of Economics* 114 (November): 1243–84.

"ALP Woos Ethnic Vote." *The Sydney Morning Herald* (Sydney, Australia), September 22, 1998.

Alt, James. 1984. "Dealignment and the Dynamics of Partisanship in Britain," in *Electoral Change in Advanced Industrial Democracies*, eds. Russell J. Dalton, Scott C. Flanagan, and Paul Allen Beck. Princeton: Princeton University Press. 298–329.

Amorim Neto, Octavio and Gary Cox. 1997. "Electoral Institutions, Cleavage Structures and the Number of Parties." *American Journal of Political Science* 41 (1): 149–74.

Anderson, Christopher J. 1998. "Parties, Party Systems, and Satisfaction with Democratic Performance in the New Europe." *Political Studies* 46: 572–88.

Andrews, Josephine and Robert Jackman. 2005. "Strategic Fools: Electoral Rule Choice under Extreme Uncertainty." *Electoral Studies* 24 (1): 65–84.

L'Année politique, économique et sociale en France. Various years. Paris: Editions du Moniteur.

Ansolabehere, Stephen D. and James M. Snyder Jr. 2000. "Valence Politics and Equilibrium in Spatial Election Models." *Public Choice* 103: 327–36.

Argelaguet, Jordi. 2006. "Esquerra Republicana de Catalunya: The Third Pole within Catalan Politics," in *Autonomist Parties in Europe: Identity Politics and the Revival of the*

Territorial Cleavage. vol. 1, eds. Lieven De Winter, Margarita Gómez-Reino, and Peter Lynch. Barcelona: ICPS. 143–65.

Aron, Debra J. and Edward P. Lazear. 1987. "Competition, Relativism, and Market Choice." *Working Papers in Economics E–87–56*, Hoover Institution (December).

———. 1990. "The Introduction of New Products." *American Economic Review* 80 (2): 421–6.

Atkins, Ralph. 1991. "A Withering Party Finds the Political Grass not so Green." *Financial Times* (April 12): sec. I, UK News, p. 6.

Australia. Ministry of Immigration. 1998. "Labor's Immigration Policy Disappointing Shame: Ruddock." MPS 135/98. September 25. http://www.minister.immi.gov.au/media_releases/ruddock_media98/r98135.htm.

Bale, Tim. 2003. "Cinderella and Her Ugly Sisters: The Mainstream and Extreme Right in Europe's Bipolarising Party Systems." *West European Politics* 26 (3): 67–90.

Balfour, Sebastian. 1996. "'Bitter Victory, Sweet Defeat': The March 1996 General Elections and the New Government in Spain." *Government and Opposition* 31: 275–87.

Barber, Peter. 1998. "Libs Have Switched Tack on Aborigines, Survey Shows." *AAP Newsfeed* (September 28).

Barberà, Òscar and Astrid Barrio. 2006. "Convergència i Unió: From Stability to Decline?" in *Autonomist Parties in Europe: Identity Politics and the Revival of the Territorial Cleavage*, vol. 1, eds. Lieven De Winter, Margarita Gómez-Reino, and Peter Lynch. Barcelona: ICPS. 101–41.

Barjon, Carole. 1997. "Les droites face au FN." *Le Nouvel Observateur* (March 27–April 2).

Bartolini, Stefano and Peter Mair. 1990. *Identity, Competition, and Electoral Availability: The Stabilisation of European Electorates, 1885–1985.* Cambridge: Cambridge University Press.

Bean, Clive. 1986. "Electoral Law, Electoral Behaviour and Electoral Outcomes: Australia and New Zealand Compared." *Journal of Commonwealth and Comparative Politics* 24: 57–73.

———. 1997. "Australia's Experience with the Alternative Vote." *Representation* 34 (2): 103–10.

Beaufays, J. 1988. "Belgium: A Dualist Political System?" *Publius: The Journal of Federalism* 18 (2): 63–73.

Beck, Nathaniel and Jonathan Katz. 1995. "What to Do (And Not to Do) with Time-Series Cross Section Data." *American Political Science Review* 89: 634–48.

———. 1996. "Nuisance vs. Substance: Specifying and Estimating Time-Series-Cross-Section Models." *Political Analysis* 6: 1–36.

———. 2001. "Throwing Out the Baby with the Bathwater: A Comment on Green, Yoon, and Kim." *International Organizations* 55: 487–95.

Bélanger, Éric. 2003. "Issue Ownership by Canadian Political Parties since 1953." *Canadian Journal of Political Science* 36: 539–58.

Bennie, Lynn, Jack Brand, and James Mitchell. 1997. *How Scotland Votes.* Manchester, UK: Manchester University Press.

Benoit, Kenneth. 2004. "Models of Electoral System Change." *Electoral Studies* 23 (3): 363–89.

Benoit, Kenneth and Michael Laver. 2006. *Party Policy in Modern Democracies.* London: Routledge.

Benoit, Kenneth, Michael Laver, and Slava Mikhailov. 2007. "Mapping Policy Preferences with Uncertainty: Measuring and Correcting Error in Comparative Manifesto Project Estimates." Paper presented at the Annual Meeting of the Midwest Political Science Association, Chicago, IL, April 12–15.

Betz, Hans-Georg. 1990. "Politics of Resentment: Right-Wing Radicalism in West Germany." *Comparative Politics* 23 (1): 45–60.

Betz, Hans-Georg and Stefan Immerfall, eds. 1998. *The New Politics of the Right*. New York: St. Martin's Press.

Blatt, David S. 1996. "Immigration Politics and Immigrant Collective Action in France, 1968–1993." PhD diss., Cornell University.

Boix, Carles. 1999. "Setting the Rules of the Game: The Choice of Electoral Systems in Advanced Democracies." *American Political Science Review* 93 (3): 609–24.

Bowers, Jake and Michael J. Ensley. 2003. "Issues in Analyzing the Data from the Dual Mode 2000 American National Election Study." *National Election Studies Technical Report*. http://www.umich.edu/~nes.

Bowler, Shaun. 1990. "Voter Perceptions and Party Strategies: An Empirical Approach." *Comparative Politics* 23: 61–83.

Boy, Daniel and Elisabeth Dupoirier. 1993. "Is the Voter a Strategist?" in *The French Voter Decides*, eds. Daniel Boy and Nonna Mayer. Ann Arbor: University of Michigan Press. 149–65.

Brady, David W. and Craig Volden. 1998. *Revolving Gridlock: Politics and Policy from Carter to Clinton*. Boulder, CO: Westview Press.

Brand, Jack. 1979. *The National Movement in Scotland*. London: Routledge and Kegan Paul.

Bréchon, Pierre. 1995. *La France aux urnes: Cinquante ans d'histoire électorale*. Paris: La documentation Française.

Brennan, Geoffrey and Nicole Mitchell. 1999. "The Logic of Spatial Politics: The 1998 Queensland Election." *Australian Journal of Political Science* 34 (3): 379–90.

Brown, Alice, David McCrone, Lindsay Paterson, and Paula Surridge. 1999. *The Scottish Electorate: The 1997 General Election and Beyond*. London: Macmillan Press.

Brubaker, Rogers. 1992. *Citizenship and Nationhood in France and Germany*. Cambridge, MA: Harvard University Press.

Budge, Ian. 1994. "A New Theory of Party Competition: Uncertainty, Ideology, and Policy Equilibria Viewed Comparatively and Temporally." *British Journal of Political Science* 24: 443–67.

Budge, Ian and Dennis J. Farlie. 1977. *Voting and Party Competition*. London: John Wiley and Sons.

———. 1983a. *Explaining and Predicting Elections*. London: George Allen and Unwin.

———. 1983b. "Party Competition-Selective Emphasis or Direct Confrontation?" in *Western European Party Systems: Continuity and Change*, eds. Hans Daalder and Peter Mair. London: Sage Publications. 267–306.

Budge, Ian, Hans-Dieter Klingemann, Andrea Volkens, Judith Bara, and Eric Tanenbaum, eds. 2001. *Mapping Policy Preferences: Estimates for Parties, Electors, and Governments, 1945–1998*. Oxford: Oxford University Press.

Budge, Ian, David Robertson, and Derek Hearl, eds. 1987. *Ideology, Strategy and Party Change: Spatial Analysis of Post-War Election Programs in 19 Democracies*. Cambridge: Cambridge University Press.

Budge, Ian and Derek W. Urwin. 1966. *Scottish Political Behaviour: A Case Study in British Homogeneity*. London: Longmans.

Burden, Barry C. 2005. "Minor Parties and Strategic Voting in Recent U.S. Presidential Elections." *Electoral Studies* 24: 603–18.

Bürklin, Wilhelm. 1987. "Governing Left Parties Frustrating the Radical Non-established Left: The Rise and Inevitable Decline of the Greens." *European Sociological Review* 3: 109–26.

Butler, David. 1995. *British General Elections since 1945*. 2nd ed. Oxford: Blackwell.

Butler, David and Gareth Butler. 2000. *Twentieth Century British Political Facts, 1900–2000*. London: Macmillan Press.

Butler, David and Dennis Kavanagh. 1974. *The British General Election of February 1974*. London: Macmillan Press.

———. 1975. *The British General Election of October 1974*. London: Macmillan Press.

———. 1980. *The British General Election of 1979*. London: Macmillan Press.

———. 1984. *The British General Election of 1983*. London: Macmillan Press.

———. 1988. *The British General Election of 1987*. London: Macmillan Press.

———. 1992. *The British General Election of 1992*. London: Macmillan Press.

Butler, David and Anthony King. 1966. *The British General Election of 1966*. London: Macmillan Press.

Butler, David and Michael Pinto-Duschinsky. 1971. *The British General Election of 1970*. London: Macmillan Press.

Campbell, Angus, Philip E. Converse, Warren E. Miller, and Donald E. Stokes. 1960. *The American Voter*. New York: John Wiley and Sons.

———. eds. 1966. *Elections and the Political Order*. New York: John Wiley and Sons.

Camus, Jean-Yves. 1996. "Origine et formation du Front National (1972–1981)," in *Le Front National à découvert*, eds. Nonna Mayer and Pascal Perrineau. Paris: Presses de la Fondation Nationales des Sciences Politiques. 17–36.

Cannon, Angie. 2000. "Nader's Glad He Might Be the Spoiler." *U.S. News and World Report* (October 30): 26.

Caramani, Danièle. 2000. *Elections in Western Europe since 1815: Electoral Results by Constituencies*. New York: Grove's Dictionaries.

———. 2004. *The Nationalization of Politics: The Formation of National Electorates and Party Systems in Western Europe*. Cambridge: Cambridge University Press.

Carlisle, Kenneth, MP. 1984. *Conserving the Countryside: A Tory View*. London: Conservative Political Centre.

Carr, Robert. 1973. *Runnymede Trust Bulletin* 42 (April): 3.

Carter, Elisabeth. 2005. *The Extreme Right in Western Europe: Success or Failure?* Manchester, UK: Manchester University Press.

Carton, Daniel. 1995. "Jospin favorable à la réprésentation proportionnelle." *Le Monde* (March 10).

Castles, Francis G. and Peter Mair. 1984. "Left-Right Political Scales: Some 'Expert' Judgments." *European Journal of Political Research* 12: 73–88.

Chandra, Kanchan. 2001. "Cumulative Findings in the Study of Ethnic Politics." *APSA-CP Newsletter* (Winter): 7–11.

Chhibber, Pradeep K. and Ken Kollman. 2004. *The Formation of National Party Systems: Federalism and Party Competition in Canada, Great Britain, India and the United States*. Princeton, NJ: Princeton University Press.

Chiche, Jean and Nonna Mayer. 1997. "Les enjeux de l'élection," in *L'électeur à ses raisons*, eds. Daniel Boy and Nonna Mayer. Paris: Presses de la Fondation Nationale des Sciences Politiques.

Chirac, Jacques. 1988. *La Décennie du Renouveau*. Paris: RPR.

"Clinton Nostalgia Sets In, Bush Reaction Mixed." 2001. Washington, DC: Pew Research Center for the People and the Press. http://people-press.org/reports/print.php3?PageID=131.

Colomer, Josep M. 1999. "The Spanish 'State of Autonomies': Non-Institutional Federalism," in *Politics and Policy in Democratic Spain*, ed. Paul Heywood. London: Frank Cass. 40–52.

Conservative Party. Various years. *The Campaign Guide*. London: Conservative and Unionist Central Office.

————. Various years. *Verbatim Report of the Annual Conservative Party Conference*. London: National Conservative and Unionist Associations.

————. 1983. *The Conservative Manifesto 1983*. London: Conservative Research Department.

————. 1986/1987. *Protecting the Environment*. London: Conservative Central Office.

————. 1987. *The Next Moves Forward: The Conservative Manifesto 1987*. London: Conservative Research Department.

Converse, Philip E. 1964. "The Nature of Belief Systems in Mass Publics," in *Ideology and Discontent*, ed. David Apter. New York: Free Press. 206–61.

————. 1975. "Public Opinion and Voting Behavior," in *Handbook of Political Science, vol. 4*, eds. F. Greenstein and N. Polsby. Reading, MA: Addison-Wesley. 75–169.

Conversi, Daniele. 1997. *The Basques, the Catalans and Spain*. Reno: University of Nevada Press.

Cornford, James and Daniel Dorling. 1997. "Crooked Margins and Marginal Seats," in *British Elections and Parties Review*, vol. 7, eds. Charles Pattie, David Denver, Justin Fisher, and Steve Ludlam. London: Frank Cass. 74–90.

Cox, Gary W. 1997. *Making Votes Count*. Cambridge: Cambridge University Press.

Craig, F. W. S. 1977. *Britain Votes 1: British Parliamentary Election Results 1974–1977*. Chichester, UK: Parliamentary Research Services.

————. 1980. *Britain Votes 2: British Parliamentary Election Results 1974–1979*. 2nd ed. Chichester, UK: Parliamentary Research Services.

————. 1984. *Britain Votes 3: British Parliamentary Election Results 1983*. 3rd ed. Chichester, UK: Parliamentary Research Services.

Crossman, Richard. 1976. *Diaries of a Cabinet Minister*. London: Hamish Hamilton and Jonathan Cape.

Curtice, John and Michael Steed. 1992. "The Results Analysed," in *The British General Election of 1992*, eds. David Butler and Dennis Kavanagh. London: Macmillan Press. 322–62.

Dale, Iain, ed. 2000. *Labour Party General Election Manifestos, 1900–1997*. London: Routledge.

Dalton, Russell J. 1996. *Citizen Politics: Public Opinion and Political Parties in Advanced Industrial Democracies*. 2nd ed. Chatham, NJ: Chatham House Publishers.

————. 2000. "The Decline of Party Identifications," in *Parties without Partisans: Political Change in Advanced Industrial Democracies*, eds. Russell J. Dalton and Martin P. Wattenberg. Oxford: Oxford University Press. 19–36.

————. 2006. *Citizen Politics: Public Opinion and Political Parties in Advanced Industrial Democracies*. 4th ed. Washington, DC: CQ Press.

Dalton, Russell J., Ian McAllister, and Martin P. Wattenberg. 2000. "The Consequences of Partisan Dealignment," in *Parties without Partisans: Political Change in Advanced Industrial Democracies*, eds. Russell J. Dalton and Martin P. Wattenberg. Oxford: Oxford University Press. 37–63.

Dalyell, Tam. 1977. *Devolution: The End of Britain?* London: Jonathan Cape.

Dao, James. 2000. "The 2000 Election: The Green Party: Some Nader Supporters Seem Shaken, Not Stirred, by Result." *New York Times* (November 10): A29.

De Winter, Lieven. 1998. "Conclusion: A Comparative Analysis of the Electoral, Office and Policy Success of Ethnoregionalist Parties," in *Regionalist Parties in Western Europe*, eds. Lieven De Winter and Huri Türsan. London: Routledge. 204–47.

De Winter, Lieven and Huri Türsan, eds. 1998. *Regionalist Parties in Western Europe*. London: Routledge.

Denver, David. 1994. *Elections and Voting Behaviour in Britain*. 2nd ed. New York: Harvester Wheatsheaf.

Dewachter, Wilfried. 1987. "Changes in a Particratie: The Belgian Party System from 1944 to 1986," in *Party Systems in Denmark, Austria, Switzerland, the Netherlands, and Belgium*, ed. Hans Daalder. New York: St. Martin's Press. 285–364.

"Les dirigeants politiques et le FN." 1998. *Revue Politique et Parlementaire* 995: 65–74.

Downs, Anthony. 1957. *An Economic Theory of Democracy*. New York: Harper Collins.

Drucker, H. M. and Gordon Brown. 1980. *The Politics of Nationalism and Devolution*. London: Longman.

Duhamel, Olivier and Jérôme Jaffré. 1990. "Huit leçons de 1989," in *L'Etat de l'Opinion 1990*, eds. Olivier Duhamel and Jérôme Jaffré. Paris: Editions du Seuil.

Duverger, Maurice. 1954. *Political Parties: Their Organization and Activity in the Modern State*. London: Methuen.

Eaton, B. and C. Lipsey. 1975. "The Principle of Minimum Differentiation Reconsidered: New Developments in the Theory of Spatial Competition." *Review of Economic Studies* 42: 27–49.

Eckstein, Harry. 1975. "Case Study and Theory in Political Science," in *Strategies of Inquiry: Handbook of Political Science, Vol. 7*, eds. Fred I. Greenstein and Nelson W. Polsby. Reading, MA: Addison-Wesley Publishing Company. 79–137.

Ecology Party. 1979. *The Ecology Party*. Exeter, UK: Devon Ecology Party.

Elazar, Daniel J. 1995. "From Statism to Federalism: A Paradigm Shift." *Publius* 25 (2): 5–18.

Ellis, James. 1998. "Voting for Markets or Marketing for Votes? The Politics of Neoliberal Economic Reform." PhD diss., Harvard University.

Enelow, James M. and Melvin J. Hinich. 1984. *The Spatial Theory of Voting: An Introduction*. Cambridge: Cambridge University Press.

"L'Extrême Droite." 1985. in *L'Etat de l'Opinion 1985*, ed. SOFRES. Paris: Gallimard.

Ezrow, Lawrence. Forthcoming. "On the Inverse Relationship between Votes and Proximity for Niche Parties." *European Journal of Political Research*.

Farrell, David M. 2001. *Electoral Systems: A Comparative Introduction*. New York: Palgrave.

Faux, Emmanuel, Thomas Legrand, and Gilles Perez. 1991. *Plumes de l'ombre*. Paris: Editions Ramsey.

———. 1994. *La main droite de Dieu*. Paris: Editions du Seuil.

Fearon, James D. and Pieter van Houten. 2002. "The Politicization of Cultural and Economic Difference: A Return to the Theory of Regional Autonomy Movements." Unpublished ms.

Frankland, E. Gene. 1990. "Does Green Politics Have a Future in Britain? An American Perspective," in *Green Politics One*, ed. Wolfgang Rüdig. Edinburgh, UK: Edinburgh University Press. 7–28.

Franklin, Mark N., Thomas T. Mackie, Henry Valen et al. 1992. *Electoral Change: Responses to Evolving Social and Attitudinal Structures in Western Countries*. Cambridge: Cambridge University Press.

Friedrich, Robert J. 1982. "In Defense of Multiplicative Terms in Multiple Regression Equations." *American Journal of Political Science* 26: 797–833.

Front National. 1993. *300 mesures pour la renaissance de la France*. Paris: Editions Nationales.

Fysh, Peter and Jim Wolfreys. 1998. *The Politics of Racism in France*. New York: St. Martin's Press.

Gallagher, Tom. 2000. "Exit from the Ghetto: The Italian Far Right in the 1990s," in *The Politics of the Extreme Right*, ed. Paul Hainsworth. London: Pinto Press. 64–86.

Garman, Christopher, Stephan Haggard, and Eliza Willis. 2001. "Fiscal Decentralization: A Political Theory with Latin American Cases." *World Politics* 53 (January): 205–36.

Gaspard, Françoise. 1995. *A Small City in France*. Cambridge, MA: Harvard University Press.

Gaylord, Becky. 2001. "No Afghan Refugees Down Under, Please." *Business Week* (December 3): 4.

Gerber, Elizabeth and John Jackson. 1993. "Endogenous Preferences and the Study of Institutions." *American Political Science Review* 87: 639–56.

Gibbons, John. 1999. *Spanish Politics Today*. Manchester, UK: Manchester University Press.

Giesbert, Franz-Olivier. 1990. *Le Président*. Paris: Seuil.

Givens, Terri. 2005. *Voting Radical Right in Western Europe*. Cambridge: Cambridge University Press.

Golder, Matt. 2003a. "Electoral Institutions, Unemployment and Extreme Right Parties: A Correction." *British Journal of Political Science* 33: 525–34.

———. 2003b. "Explaining Variation in the Electoral Success of Extreme Right Parties in Western Europe." *Comparative Political Studies* 36: 432–66.

Gomez-Reino Cachafeiro, Margarita. 2002. *Ethnicity and Nationalism in Italian Politics: Inventing the Padania Lega Nord and the Northern Question*. Burlington, VT: Ashgate.

Goot, Murray. n.d. "The Australian Party System, Pauline Hanson's One Nation, and the Party Cartelisation Thesis." Unpublished ms. http://www.pol.mq.edu.au/publications/Hanson.htm.

Goot, Murray and Ian Watson. 2000. "One Nation's Electoral Support: Where Does It Come From, What Makes It Different, and How Does It Fit?" http://pol.mq.edu.au/pub/AJPH-Hanson.htm.

Gordin, Jorge P. 2001. "The Electoral Fate of Ethnoregionalist Parties in Western Europe: A Boolean Test of Extant Explanations." *Scandinavian Political Studies* 24 (2): 149–70.

Gourevitch, Peter Alexis. 1979. "The Re-emergence of 'Peripheral Nationalisms': Some Comparative Speculations on the Spatial Distribution of Political Leadership and Economic Growth." *Comparative Studies in Society and History* 21: 303–22.

Gras, Christian and Georges Livet, eds. 1977. *Regions et regionalisme en France*. Paris: Presses universitaires de France.

Greenberg, Joseph and Kenneth A. Shepsle. 1987. "The Effects of Electoral Rewards in Multiparty Competition with Entry." *American Political Science Review* 81: 525–37.

Groseclose, Tim. 2001. "A Model of Candidate Location When One Candidate Has a Valence Advantage." *American Journal of Political Science* 45 (4): 862–86.

Guiraudon, Virginie. 2001. "Immigration Policy in France." *U.S.-France Analysis* (July). http://www.brook.edu/dybdocroot/fp/cusf/analysis/immigration.htm.

Gundle, Stephen and Simon Parker, eds. 1996. *The New Italian Republic*. London: Routledge.

Gunther, Richard, Giacomo Sani, and Goldie Shabad. 1988. *Spain after Franco*. Berkeley: University of California Press.

Hainsworth, Paul. 2000. "The Front National," in *The Politics of the Extreme Right: From the Margins to the Mainstream*, ed. Paul Hainsworth. London: Pinter. 18–32.

Harmel, Robert and John Robertson. 1985. "Formation and Success of New Parties: A Cross-National Analysis." *International Political Science Review* 6 (4): 501–23.

Harmel, Robert and Lars Svasand. 1997. "The Influence of New Parties on Old Parties' Platforms." *Party Politics* 3 (3): 315–40.

Hechter, Michael. 1975. *Internal Colonialism: The Celtic Fringe in British National Development, 1536–1966*. Berkeley: University of California Press.

Hermsen, Hanneke and Anders Verbeek. 1992. "Equilibria in Multiparty Systems." *Public Choice* 73: 147–66.

Hillygus, D. Sunshine. 2007. "The Dynamics of Voter Decision Making Among Minor Party Supporters: The 2000 U.S. Presidential Election." *British Journal of Political Science* 37 (2): 225–44.

Hine, David. 1982. "Factionalism in West European Parties: A Framework for Analysis." *West European Politics* 5 (1): 36–53.

Hinich, Melvin and Michael Munger. 1997. *Analytical Politics*. Cambridge: Cambridge University Press.

Hirano, Shigeo and James M. Snyder Jr. 2007. "The Decline of Third-Party Voting in the United States." *The Journal of Politics* 69 (1): 1–16.

Holbrook, Allyson et al. 2004. "Attitude Importance and the Accumulation of Attitude-Relevant Knowledge in Memory." Paper presented at the Annual Meeting of the American Political Science Association, Chicago, IL.

Holloway, Grant. 2001. "Australian Prime Minister Wins Third Term." *CNN.com* (November 11). http://www.cnn.com/2001/WORLD/asiapcf/auspac/11/10/aust.pollwait.html.

Holmes, Colin. 1991. *A Tolerant Country? Immigrants, Refugees and Minorities in Britain*. Boston: Faber and Faber.

Hooghe, Lisbet. 1991. *A Leap in the Dark: Nationalist Conflict and Federal Reform in Belgium*. Ithaca, NY: Western Societies Program, Cornell University.

Hossay, Patrick. 2004. "Recognizing Corsica: The Drama of Recognition in Nationalist Mobilization." *Ethnic and Racial Studies* 27 (3): 403–30.

Hotelling, H. 1929. "Stability in Competition." *Economic Journal* 39: 41–57.

http://www.alba.org.uk

http://www.debates.org/pages/trans2000b.html

http://www.election.demon.co.uk/changes.html

http://elections.figaro.net/popup_2004/accueil.html

http://www.electionworld.org/france.htm

http://www.europeangreens.org

http://www.greens.org/elections

http://institution.gallup.com

http://www.jura.uni-sb.de/law/GG/gg2.htm

http://www.les-verts.org

http://www.margaretthatcher.org/speeches/displaydocument.asp?docid=107346

http://parties-and-elections.de/france.html

http://psephos.adam-carr.net/au/distribution-senate.txt

Huber, Evelyne, Charles Ragin, and John Stephens. 1993. "Social Democracy, Christian Democracy, Constitutional Structure and the Welfare State." *American Journal of Sociology* 99 (3): 711–49.

Huber, John D. 1996. *Rationalizing Parliament: Legislative Institutions and Party Politics in France*. Cambridge: Cambridge University Press.

Huber, John and Ronald Inglehart. 1995. "Expert Interpretations of Party Space and Party Locations in 42 Societies." *Party Politics* 1 (1): 73–111.

Hug, Simon. 2001. *Altering Party Systems*. Ann Arbor: University of Michigan Press.

Ignazi, Piero. 1992. "The Silent Counter-Revolution: Hypotheses on the Emergence of Extreme Right-Wing Parties in Europe." *European Journal of Political Research* 22: 3–34.

———. 2003. *Extreme Right Parties in Western Europe*. Oxford: Oxford University Press.

Immergut, E. M. 1992. *Health Politics: Interests and Institutions in Western Europe*. Cambridge: Cambridge University Press.

Inglehart, Ronald. 1977. *The Silent Revolution*. Princeton, NJ: Princeton University Press.

———. 1984. "The Changing Structure of Political Cleavages in Western Society," in *Electoral Change in Advanced Industrial Democracies*, eds. Russell J. Dalton, Scott C. Flanagan, and Paul Allen Beck. Princeton, NJ: Princeton University Press. 25–69.

———. 1997. *Modernization and Postmodernization*. Princeton, NJ: Princeton University Press.

Ivaldi, Gilles. 1998. "Le Front National à l'assaut du système." *Revue Politique et Parlementaire* (July/August): 5–22.

Ivarsflaten, Elisabeth. 2005. "The Vulnerable Populist Right Parties: No Economic Realignment Fuelling Their Electoral Success." *European Journal of Political Research* 44: 465–92.

Iversen, Torben. 1994a. "The Logics of Electoral Politics: Spatial, Directional and Mobilizational Effects." *Comparative Political Studies* 27 (2): 155–89.

———. 1994b. "Political Leadership and Representation in West European Democracies: A Test of Three Models of Voting." *American Journal of Political Science* 38 (1): 45–74.

Iyengar, Shanto. 1990. "Shortcuts to Political Knowledge: The Role of Selective Attention and Accessibility," in *Information and Democratic Processes*, eds. John Ferejohn and James Kuklinski. Urbana: University of Illinois Press.

Jackman, Simon. 1998. "Pauline Hanson, the Mainstream, and Political Elites: The Place of Race in Australian Political Ideology." *Australian Journal of Political Science* 33 (2): 167–86.

Jackman, Robert W. and Karin Volpert. 1996. "Conditions Favouring Parties of the Extreme Right in Western Europe." *British Journal of Political Science* 26: 501–21.

Jackson, John. 2003. "Electoral Competition with Endogenous Voter Preferences," in *Computational Models in Political Economy*, eds. Kenneth Kollman, John Miller, and Scott Page. Cambridge, MA: MIT Press. 109–42.

Jaffré, Jérôme. 1985. "L'humeur de Francis: L'année politique: les dix leçons de 1984," in *Opinion politique*, ed. SOFRES. Paris: Gallimard. 105–11.

Janda, Kenneth. 1980. *Political Parties: A Cross-National Survey*. New York: The Free Press.

Jehl, Douglas. 2000. "The 43rd President: Interior Choice Sends a Signal on Land Policy." *New York Times* (December 30): A5.

Joffrin, Laurent. 1987. *Un coup de jeune: portrait d'une génération morale*. Paris: Seuil.

Johnson, Stanley, MEP. 1981. *Caring for the Environment*. London: Conservative Political Centre.

Johnston, Jack and John DiNardo. 1997. *Econometric Methods*. 4th ed. New York: McGraw-Hill.

Jolly, Seth. 2006. "Determinants of Regional Party Success in Western Europe." Unpublished ms., Duke University.

Jones, Bill. 1989/90. "Green Thinking." *Talking Politics* 2 (2): 50–4.

Jones, J. Barry and Michael Keating. 1982. "The Resolution of Internal Conflicts and External Pressures: The Labour Party's Devolution Policy." *Government and Opposition* 17 (3): 279–92.

Katz, Richard and Peter Mair. 1995. "Changing Models of Party Organization and Party Democracy." *Party Politics* 1 (1): 5–28.

Keating, Michael. 1998. *The New Regionalism in Western Europe: Territorial Restructuring and Political Change*. Cheltenham, UK: Edward Elgar.

Keating, Michael and David Bleiman. 1979. *Labour and Scottish Nationalism*. London: Macmillan Press.

Keeler, John T. S. and Martin A. Schain. 1996. "Introduction: Mitterrand's Legacy, Chirac's Challenge," in *Chirac's Challenge: Liberalization, Europeanization, and Malaise in France*, eds. John T. S. Keeler and Martin A. Schain. New York: St. Martin's Press. 1–20.

Keesing's Record of World Events, CD-ROM. 1999. Bethesda, MD: Keesing's Worldwide.

Kellas, James G. 1971. "Scottish Nationalism," in *The British General Election of 1970*, eds. David Butler and Michael Pinto-Duschinsky. London: Macmillan Press. 446–62.

———. 1989. *The Scottish Political System*. 4th ed. Cambridge: Cambridge University Press.

Kellner, Peter. 1989. "Decoding the Green Message." *The Independent* (July 7): Home News p.6.

Kennedy, Peter. 1992. *A Guide to Econometrics*. Cambridge, MA: MIT Press.

King, Anthony, ed. 2001. *British Political Opinion 1937–2000*. London: Politico's.

King, Gary. 1998. *Unifying Political Methodology: The Likelihood Theory of Statistical Inference*. Ann Arbor: University of Michigan Press.

Kingdon, John W. 1995. *Agendas, Alternatives and Public Policies*. New York: Harper Collins.

Kitschelt, Herbert. 1988. "Left-Libertarian Parties: Explaining Innovation in Competitive Party Systems." *World Politics* 40 (2): 194–234.

———. 1989. *The Logics of Party Formation: Ecological Politics in Belgium and West Germany*. Ithaca, NY: Cornell University Press.

———. 1994. *The Transformation of European Social Democracy*. Cambridge: Cambridge University Press.

———. 1995. *The Radical Right in Western Europe*. Ann Arbor: University of Michigan Press.

———. 2000. "Linkages between Citizens and Politicians in Democratic Polities." *Comparative Political Studies* 33 (6/7): 845–79.

Klingemann, Hans-Dieter, Andrea Volkens, Judith Bara, Ian Budge, and Michael McDonald. 2006. *Mapping Policy Preferences II: Estimates for Parties, Electors and Governments in Eastern Europe, European Union and OECD 1990–2003*. Oxford: Oxford University Press.

Knutsen, Oddbjørn. 1998. "Expert Judgements of the Left-Right Location of Political Parties: A Comparative Longitudinal Study." *West European Politics* 21 (2): 63–94.

Kofman, Eleonore. 1982. "Differential Modernization, Social Conflicts and Ethno-Regionalism in Corsica." *Ethnic and Racial Studies* 5: 300–12.

Kreuzer, Marcus. 1990. "New Politics: Just Post-Materialist? The Case of the Austrian and Swiss Greens." *West European Politics* 13: 12–30.

Laakso, Markku and Rein Taagepera. 1979. "'Effective' Number of Parties: A Measure with Application to West Europe." *Comparative Political Studies* 12 (1): 3–27.

Labour Party. 1970. *Now Britain's Strong – Let's Make It Great to Live In*. London: Labour Party. http://www.psr.keele.ac.uk/area/uk/man/lab70.htm.

———. 1977. *Statements to Annual Conference by the National Executive Committee*. London: Labour Party.

———. 1982. *Labour's Programme, 1982*. London: Labour Party.

———. 1990. *An Earthly Chance*. London: Labour Party.

———. 1992. *It's Time to Get Britain Working Again*. London: Labour Party.

———. Various years. *Report of the Annual Labour Party Conference*. London: Labour Party.

Lagrange, Hugues and Pascal Perrineau. 1989. "Le syndrome lepéniste," in *Le Front national à découvert*, eds. Nonna Mayer and Pascal Perrineau. Paris: Presses de la Fondation Nationale des Sciences Politiques. 228–46.

Laible, Janet. 2001. "Nationalism and a Critique of European Integration: Questions from the Flemish Parties," in *Minority Nationalism and the Changing International Order*, eds. Michael Keating and John McGarry. Oxford: Oxford University Press. 223–45.

Lancelot, Alain. 1983. *Les élections sous la Cinquième République*. Paris: Presses Universitaires de France.

———. 1998. *Les élections nationales sous la Cinquième République*. 3rd ed. Paris: Presses Universitaires de France.

Laver, Michael, Kenneth Benoit, and John Garry. 2003. "Extracting Policy Positions from Political Texts Using Words as Data." *American Political Science Review* 97 (2): 311–31.

Laver, Michael and John Garry. 2000. "Estimating Policy Positions from Political Texts." *American Journal of Political Science* 44: 619–34.

Laver, Michael and W. Ben Hunt. 1992. *Policy and Party Competition*. New York: Routledge.

Laver, Michael and Norman Schofield. 1998. *Multiparty Government: The Politics of Coalitions in Europe*. Ann Arbor: University of Michigan Press.

Leonhardt, David. 2000. "The Election: Was Buchanan the Real Nader?" *New York Times* (December 10): D4.

Levi, Margaret and Michael Hechter. 1985. "A Rational Choice Approach to the Rise and Decline of Ethnoregional Political Parties," in *New Nationalisms of the Developed West: Towards Explanation*, eds. Edward A. Tiryakian and Ronald Rogowski. Boston: Allen and Unwin. 128–46.

Lewis-Beck, Michael S. 1984. "France: The Stalled Electorate," in *Electoral Change in Advanced Industrial Democracies*, eds. Russell J. Dalton, Scott C. Flanagan, and Paul Allen Beck. Princeton, NJ: Princeton University Press. 425–48.

———. 1993. "Introduction to the English Edition: The French Voter – Steadfast or Changing?" *The French Voter Decides*, eds. Daniel Boy and Nonna Mayer. Ann Arbor: University of Michigan Press. 1–13.

Lijphart, Arend. 1975. "The Comparable-Cases Strategy in Comparative Research." *Comparative Political Studies* 8 (2): 158–77.

———. 1984. *Democracies: Patterns of Majoritarian and Consensus Government in Twenty-One Countries*. New Haven, CT: Yale University Press.

———. 1990. "The Political Consequences of Electoral Laws, 1945–85." *American Political Science Review* 80: 481–96.

———. 1994. *Electoral Systems and Party Systems: A Study of Twenty-Seven Democracies, 1945–90*. Oxford: Oxford University Press.

———. 1999. *Patterns of Democracy: Government Forms and Performance in Thirty-Six Countries*. New Haven, CT: Yale University Press.

Loughlin, John and Sonia Mazey. 1995. "Introduction," in *The End of the French Unitary State? Ten Years of Regionalization in France (1982–1992)*, eds. John Loughlin and Sonia Mazey. London: Frank Cass. 1–9.

Lubbers, Marcel, Mérove Gijsberts, and Peer Scheepers. 2002. "Extreme Right-Wing Voting in Western Europe." *European Journal of Political Research* 41: 345–78.

Lynch, Peter. 2002. *SNP: The History of the Scottish National Party*. Cardiff, UK: Welsh Academic Press.

Mackie, Thomas T. and Richard Rose. 1991. *The International Almanac of Electoral History*. 3rd ed. Washington, DC: CQ.

———. 1997. *A Decade of Election Results: Updating the International Almanac*. Glasgow, UK: Centre for the Study of Public Policy, University of Strathclyde.

Mackintosh, John P. 1975. *A Parliament for Scotland*. Tranent, UK: Berwick and East Lothian Labour Party.

———. 1998. "The New Appeal of Nationalism." Excerpted in *A Diverse Assembly*, ed. Lindsay Paterson. Edinburgh, UK: Edinburgh University Press. 64–71.

Magee, C. S. 2003. "Third-Party Candidates and the 2000 Presidential Election." *Social Science Quarterly* 84: 574–95.

Maier, Timothy. 2000. "The Voter Turnout Will Swing Election." *Insight on the News* (October 30).

Mair, Peter. 1997. *Party System Change: Approaches and Interpretations*. Oxford: Clarendon Press.

———. 1999. "New Political Parties in Established Party Systems: How Successful Are They?" in *Elites, Parties and Democracy*, eds. Erik Beukel, Kurt Klaudi Klausen, and Poul Erik Mouritzen. Odense, Denmark: Odense University Press. 207–24.

Markus, Andrew. 2001. *Race: John Howard and the Remaking of Australia*. Crows Nest, New South Wales, Australia: Allen and Unwin.

Mayer, Nonna and Pascal Perrineau. 1996. "Conclusion: L'introuvable équation Le Pen," in *Le Front national à découvert*, eds. Mayer and Perrineau. Paris: Presses de la Fondation Nationale des Sciences Politiques, 381–91.

Mayer, Nonna and Mariette Sineau. 2002. "France: The Front National," in *Rechtsextreme Parteien*, eds. Helga Amsberger and Brigitte Halbmayr. Leverkusen, Germany: Leske and Budrich. 42–91. http://www.elections2002.sciences-po.fr/Enjeux/pdf/FN%20-%20VD%202001.pdf.

Mazzoleni, Oscar. 1999. "La Lega Ticinesi: Vers l'Integration?" *Swiss Political Science Review* 5 (3): 79–95.

McCormick, John. 1991. *British Politics and the Environment*. London: Earthscan.

McCrone, David. 1992. *Understanding Scotland*. London: Routledge.

McGann, Anthony J. and Herbert Kitschelt. 2005. "The Radical Right in the Alps: Evolution of Support for the Swiss SVP and Austrian FPÖ." *Party Politics* 11 (2): 147–71.

McLean, Robert. 1992. *Labour and Scottish Home Rule*. Pt 2. West Lothian, UK: Scottish Labour Action.

McRoberts, Kenneth. 2001. *Catalonia: Nation Building without a State*. Oxford: Oxford University Press.

Meckler, Laura. 2000. "GOP Group to Air Pro-Nader TV Ads." *The Washington Post* (October 27). http://www.washingtonpost.com/wp-srv/aponline/20001027/aponline115918_000.htm.

Meguid, Bonnie M. 2001. "Stability in the Face of Change: The Strategic Role of Mainstream Political Parties in the Maintenance of Western European Political Landscapes." Unpublished ms.

———. 2005. "Competition Between Unequals: The Role of Mainstream Party Strategies in Niche Party Success." *American Political Science Review* 99 (3): 347–59.

Mill, John Stuart. *A System of Logic* (London: John W. Parker, 1843; New York: Longman, Green and Co., 1970).

Miller, William L. 1979. "What Was the Profit in Following the Crowd? The Effectiveness of Party Strategies on Immigration and Devolution." Glasgow, UK: Centre for Public Policy, University of Strathclyde.

———. 1980. "The Scottish Dimension," in *The British General Election of 1979*, eds. David Butler and Dennis Kavanagh. London: The MacMillan Press. 98–118.

———. 1981. *The End of British Politics? Scots and English Political Behaviour in the Seventies*. Oxford: Clarendon Press.

Mitchell, James. 1990. *Conservatives and the Union: A Study of Conservative Party Attitudes to Scotland*. Edinburgh, UK: Edinburgh University Press.

Mitchell, James and Jonathan Bradbury. 2001. "Devolution: New Politics for Old?" *Parliamentary Affairs* 54: 276–88.

Mitterrand, François. 1988. *Une Lettre à Tous les Français*. Paris: Parti Socialiste.

Moberg, David. 2000. "Ralph's Way: Will His Strategy Work?" *In These Times* (October 30).

Money, Jeannette. 1999. *Fences and Neighbors: The Political Geography of Immigration Control*. Ithaca, NY: Cornell University Press.

———. 2001. "Xenophobia and Xenophilia: Pauline Hanson and the Counterbalancing of Electoral Incentives in Australia." *People and Place* 7 (3): 7–19.

———. 2005. "Immigrants and the Host Polity: Immigrant Voters as an Electoral Counterweight to Extreme Right Parties," in *International Migration and Security*, eds. Elspeth Guild and Joanne van Selm. London: Routledge. 82–98.

Monnier, Jean-Jacques. 1998. *Histoire de l'Union Démocratique Bretonne*. Lannion, France: Presses Populaires de Bretagne.

Mouvement des Jeunes Socialistes. 2001. *Le Livre Noir 1998–2001*. Paris: MJS.

Mudde, Cas. 1999. "The Single-Issue Party Thesis: Extreme Right Parties and the Immigration Issue." *West European Politics* 22 (3): 182–97.

Mueller, Dennis. 1989. *Public Choice, II*. Cambridge: Cambridge University Press.

Müller, Wolfgang and Kaare Strøm. 1999. "Conclusions: Party Behavior and Representative Democracy," in *Policy, Office or Votes?*, eds. Wolfgang Müller and Kaare Strøm. Cambridge: Cambridge University Press. 279–309.

Müller-Rommel, Ferdinand, ed. 1989. *New Politics in Western Europe*. Boulder, CO: Westview Press.

———. 1996. "The New Challengers: Explaining the Electoral Success of Green and Right-Wing Populist Parties in Western Europe," in *Les petits partis*, eds. Annie Laurent and Bruno Villalba. Paris: L'Harmattan. 119–41.

———. 1998. "Ethnoregionalist Parties in Western Europe," in *Regionalist Parties in Western Europe*, eds. Lieven De Winter and Huri Türsan. London: Routledge. 17–27.

Murphy, A. 1995. "Belgium's Regional Divergence: Along the Road to Federation," in *Federalism: The Multiethnic Challenge*, ed. Graham Smith. New York: Longman. 73–100.

Nairn, Tom. 1977. *The Break-Up of Britain*. London: New Left Books.

Narud, Hanne Marthe and Audun Skare. 1999. "Are Party Activists the Party Extremists? The Structure of Opinion in Political Parties." *Scandinavian Political Studies* 22 (1): 45–65.

"'The New Nader Raiders:' Latest FEC Reports Show More Evidence of GOP Support to Nader." 2004. *Common Dreams Progressive Newswire* (October 27). http://www.commondreams.org/news2004/1027-06.htm.

Newell, James L. 1998. "The Scottish National Party: Development and Change," in *Regionalist Parties in Western Europe*, eds. Lieven De Winter and Huri Türsan. London: Routledge. 105–24.

———. 2000. "Italy: The Extreme Right Comes in from the Cold." *Parliamentary Affairs* 53 (3): 469–85.

Newman, Saul. 1996. *Ethnoregional Conflict in Democracies*. Westport, CT: Greenwood Press.

Norris, Pippa. 1995. "May's Law of Curvilinear Disparity Revisited: Leaders, Officers, Members and Voters in British Political Parties." *Party Politics* 1 (1): 29–47.

———. 2005. *Radical Right: Voters and Parties in the Electoral Market*. Cambridge: Cambridge University Press.

Norton, Philip. 1980. *Dissension in the House of Commons, 1974–1979*. Oxford: Clarendon Press.

Oakley, Robin. 1990. "Environmental concern may damage Conservative Vote." *The Times* (February 12): Home news.

O'Neill, Kathleen. 2005. *Decentralizing the State: Elections, Parties and Local Power in the Andes*. Cambridge: Cambridge University Press.

O'Neill, Michael. 1997. *Green Parties and Political Change in Contemporary Europe: New Politics, Old Predicaments*. Brookfield, VT: Ashgate.

Ordeshook, Peter C. and Olga V. Shvetsova. 1994. "Ethnic Heterogeneity, District Magnitude and the Number of Parties." *American Journal of Political Science* 38 (1): 100–23.

Palfrey, Thomas. 1984. "Spatial Equilibrium with Entry." *Review of Economic Studies* 51: 139–56.

Parti socialiste. 1981. *110 Propositions*. Paris: PS.

———. 1998. *Livre Noir des Alliances de la Droite avec le Front national*. Paris: PS.

Paterson, Lindsay. 1998. *A Diverse Assembly*. Edinburgh, UK: Edinburgh University Press.

Peacock, Alan. 1977. "The Political Economy of Devolution: The British Case," in *The Political Economy of Fiscal Federalism*, ed. Wallace E. Oates. Lexington, MA: D.C. Heath. 49–63.

Pedersen, Mogens. 1979. "The Dynamics of European Party Systems: Changing Patterns of Electoral Volatility." *European Journal of Political Research* 7 (1): 1–26.

Pereira, Juan Montabes, Carmen Ortega Villodres, and Enrique G. Pérez Nieto. 2003. "Electoral Systems and Electoral Success of Regionalist Parties in Western Europe." Paper presented at the ECPR Joint Sessions, Edinburgh, UK.

Perrineau, Pascal. 1996. "Les étapes d'une implantation électorale (1972–1988)," in *Le Front National à découvert*, eds. Nonna Mayer and Pascal Perrineau. Paris: Presses de la Fondation Nationale des Sciences Politiques. 37–62.

———. 1997. *Le Symptôme Le Pen: radiographie des électeurs du Front National*. Paris: Fayard.

Petrocik, John. 1996. "Issue Ownership in Presidential Elections, with a 1980 Case Study." *American Journal of Political Science* 40 (3): 825–50.

Phlipponneau, Michel. 1981. *Décentralisation et régionalisation: la grande affaire*. Paris: Calmann-Lévy.

———. 1986. *Géopolitique de la Bretagne*. Rennes, France: Ouest-France.

Platone, François. 1994. "Public Opinion and Electoral Change," in *Developments in French Politics*, eds. Peter A. Hall, Jack Hayward, and Howard Machin. London: Macmillan. 55–76.

Posner, Daniel. 2004. "The Political Salience of Cultural Difference: Why Chewas and Tumbukas Are Allies in Zambia and Adversaries in Malawi." *American Political Science Review* 98 (4): 529–45.

Powell, G. Bingham, Jr. 2000. *Elections as Instruments of Democracy: Majoritarian and Proportional Visions*. New Haven, CT: Yale University Press.

Przeworski, Adam and John Sprague. 1986. *Paper Stones*. Chicago: University of Chicago Press.

Przeworski, Adam and Henry Teune. 1970. *The Logic of Comparative Social Inquiry*. New York: John Wiley.

Rabinowitz, George and Stuart Elaine Macdonald. 1989. "A Directional Theory of Issue Voting." *American Political Science Review* 83: 93–121.

Rabinowitz, George, Stuart Elaine Macdonald, and Ola Listhaug. 1991. "New Players in an Old Game: Party Strategy in Multiparty Systems." *Comparative Political Studies* 24 (2): 147–85.

Rae, Douglas. 1971. *The Political Consequences of Electoral Laws*. New Haven, CT: Yale University Press.

Ramsay, Robert. 1983. *The Corsican Time-Bomb*. Manchester, UK: Manchester University Press.

Reece, Jack E. 1977. *The Bretons against France*. Chapel Hill: University of North Carolina Press.

Reif, K. and H. Schmitt. 1980. "Nine Second-Order National Elections." *European Journal of Political Research* 8: 3–44.

République Française. Various years. *Journal Officiel: Débats de l'Assemblée Nationale*.

République Française, Ministère de l'Intérieur. 1988. *Les élections législatives de 1988*. Paris: La Documentation Française.

Riker, William H. 1962. *The Theory of Political Coalitions*. New Haven, CT: Yale University Press.

———. 1982a. *Liberalism Against Populism*. San Francisco: W. H. Freeman.

———. 1982b. "The Two-Party System and Duverger's Law: An Essay on the History of Political Science." *American Political Science Review* 76 (4): 753–66.

———. 1986. *The Art of Political Manipulation*. New Haven, CT: Yale University Press.

———. 1996. *The Strategy of Rhetoric*. New Haven, CT: Yale University Press.

Robertson, David. 1976. *A Theory of Party Competition*. London: John Wiley and Sons.

Robinson, Gwen. 1998. "Howard Cabinet Aims to Woo Rural Australia." *Financial Times* (October 19): 4.

Rohrschneider, Robert. 1993. "New Party Versus Old Left Realignments: Environmental Attitudes, Party Politics and Partisan Affiliations in Four Western European Countries." *Journal of Politics* 55 (3): 682–701.

Rosenstone, Steven, Roy L. Behr, and Edward H. Lazarus. 1996. *Third Parties in America.* Princeton, NJ: Princeton University Press.

RPR. 1980. *Atout France.* Paris: Editions Roudil.

———. 1997. *Fiches argumentaires sur le Front National.* Paris: RPR.

———. 1998. *Parti Socialiste, Front national: Les Liaisons Dangereuses.* Paris: RPR Service des études.

Rüdig, Wolfgang and Mark N. Franklin. 2000. "Whatever happened to . . . the British Greens?" Paper presented at the Annual Meeting of the APSA, Washington, DC, August 31–September 3.

Rüdig, Wolfgang, Mark N. Franklin, and Lynn G. Bennie. 1996. "Up and Down with the Greens." *Electoral Studies* 15 (1): 1–20.

Rudolph, Joseph R., Jr. and Robert J. Thompson. 1989. "Pathways to Accommodation and the Persistence of the Ethnoterritorial Challenge in Western Democracies," in *Ethnoterritorial Politics, Policy, and the Western World*, eds. Joseph R. Rudolph, Jr. and Robert J. Thompson. Boulder, CO: Lynne Rienner. 221–40.

Rydgren, Jens. 2004. *The Populist Challenge.* New York: Berghahn Books.

Safran, William. 1989. "The French State and Ethnic Minority Cultures: Policy Dimensions and Problems," in *Ethnoterritorial Politics, Policy, and the Western World*, eds. Joseph R. Rudolph, Jr. and Robert J. Thompson. Boulder, CO: Lynne Rienner. 115–57.

Samuels, David. 2002. "Presidentialized Parties: The Separation of Powers and Party Organization and Behavior." *Comparative Political Studies* 35: 461–83.

Sanders, David. 1999. "The Impact of Left–Right Ideology," in *Critical Elections: British Parties and Voters in Long-Term Perspective*, eds. Geoffrey Evans and Pippa Norris. London: Sage.

Sani, Giacomo and Giovanni Sartori. 1983. "Polarization, Fragmentation and Competition in Western Democracies," in *Western European Party Systems: Continuity and Change*, eds. Hans Daalder and Peter Mair. London: Sage Publishing. 307–40.

Särlvik, Bo and Ivor Crewe. 1983. *Decade of Dealignment: The Conservative Victory of 1979 and Electoral Trends in the 1970s.* Cambridge: Cambridge University Press.

Sartori, Giovanni. 1976. *Parties and Party Systems: A Framework for Analysis.* Vol I. Cambridge: Cambridge University Press.

———. 1986. "The Influence of Electoral Systems: Faulty Laws or Faulty Method?" in *Electoral Laws and their Political Consequences*, eds. Bernard Grofman and Arend Lijphart. New York: Agathon. 43–68.

Sawer, Geoffrey. 1969. *Modern Federalism.* London: Watts.

Schain, Martin. 1994. "Immigration and Politics," in *Developments in French Politics*, eds. Peter A. Hall, Jack Hayward, and Howard Machin. London: Macmillan. 253–68.

Schlesinger, Joseph A. and Mildred S. Schlesinger. 1990. "The Reaffirmation of a Multi-party System in France." *American Political Science Review* 84 (4): 1077–1101.

Schofield, Norman. 2003. "Valence Competition in the Spatial Stochastic Model." *Journal of Theoretical Politics* 15: 371–84.

Scottish National Party. 1966a. *SNP and You.* Edinburgh, UK: SNP.

———. 1966b. *The Wasted Years.* Edinburgh, UK: SNP.

———. 1974. *October 1974 Manifesto.* Edinburgh, UK: SNP.

Selten, R. 1978. "The Chain Store Paradox." *Theory and Decision* 9: 127–59.

Shaked, Avner. 1975. "Non-existence of Equilibrium for the Two-Dimensional Three Firms Location Problem." *Review of Economic Studies* 42: 51–6.

Shepsle, Kenneth A. 1991. *Models of Multiparty Electoral Competition*. New York: Harwood Academic Publishers.

Shields, James G. 1997. *"La Politique du Pire*: The Front National and the 1997 Legislative Elections." *French Politics and Society* 15 (3): 21–36.

Shugart, Matthew and John M. Carey. 1992. *Presidents and Assemblies: Constitutional Design and Electoral Dynamics*. Ithaca, NY: Cornell University Press.

Silverman, Maxim. 1992. *Deconstructing the Nation: Immigration, Racism and Citizenship in Modern France*. London: Routledge.

Skach, Cindy. 1999. "Divided Minority Government and Democracy." PhD diss., Oxford University.

Smelser, N. J. 1967. "Notes on the Methodology of Comparative Analysis of Economic Activity," in *Transactions of the Sixth World Congress of Sociology*. Vol. II. Evian, France: International Sociological Association.

SOFRES. 1988. "Le Pen," in *L'Etat de l'Opinion 1988*, eds. Duhamel and Dupoirier. Paris: Editions du Seuil. 131–42.

Solesbury, William. 1976. "Issues and Innovation in Environmental Politics in Britain, West Germany, and California." *Policy Analysis* 2 (1): 1–38.

"Some Final Observations on Voter Opinions." 2000. Washington, DC: Pew Research Center for the People and the Press (December 2000). http://people-press.org/reports/print.php3?PageID=135.

"Spending Favored over Tax Cuts or Debt Reduction." 1998. Washington, DC: Pew Research Center for the People and the Press (January 1998). http://people-press.org/reports/print.php3?PageID=608.

"The Spoiler." 2000. *The Economist* (November 11): 42.

Spoon, Jae-Jae. 2005. "Winning Elections or Representing Interests? The Multi-Faceted Strategies of the French Greens, 1997–2002." PhD diss., University of Michigan.

Steed, Michael. 1971. "An Analysis of the Results," in *The British General Election of 1970*, eds. David Butler and Michael Pinto-Duschinsky. London: Macmillan Press. 386–415.

———. 1974. "The Results Analysed," in *The British General Election of February 1974*, eds. David Butler and Dennis Kavanagh. London: Macmillan Press. 313–39.

Stokes, Donald E. 1963. "Spatial Models of Party Competition." *American Political Science Review* 57: 368–77.

———. 1966. "Spatial Models of Party Competition," in *Elections and the Political Order*, eds. Angus Campbell, Philip E. Converse, Warren E. Miller, and Donald E. Stokes. New York: John Wiley and Sons. 161–79.

Stone, Walter and Ronald Rapoport. 2001. "It's Perot Stupid! The Legacy of the 1992 Perot Movement in the Major-Party System, 1994–2000." *PS: Political Science and Politics* (March): 49–58.

Strøm, Kaare. 1990. "A Behavioral Theory of Competitive Political Parties." *American Journal of Political Science* 34: 565–98.

Swank, Duane H. 1992. "Politics and the Structural Dependence of the State in Capitalist Democracies." *American Political Science Review* 86 (1): 38–54.

Swank, Duane and Hans-Georg Betz. 1995. "Right-Wing Populism in Western Europe: The Impact of Structural Change, Political Institutions and Economic Performance on Party Electoral Fortunes in 16 Nations." Paper presented at the Annual Meeting of the American Political Science Association, Chicago, IL.

———. 1996. "Internationalization and Right-Wing Populism in Western Europe." Paper presented at the Conference on Globalization and Labor Markets, University of California, Los Angeles.

———. 2003. "Globalization, the Welfare State and Right-Wing Populism in Western Europe." *Socio-Economic Review* 1 (2): 215–45.

Taagepera, Rein and Matthew Shugart. 1989. *Seats and Votes: The Effects and Determinants of Electoral Systems*. New Haven, CT: Yale University Press.

Taggart, Paul. 1996. *The New Populism and the New Politics*. New York: St. Martin's Press.

Taylor, Stan. 1982. *The National Front in English Politics*. London: Macmillan Press.

Thatcher, Margaret. 1993. *The Downing Street Years*. London: Harper Collins.

"Third Time Lucky?" 2001. *The Economist* (November 3): 71.

Tiersky, Ronald. 1994. *France in the New Europe: Changing Yet Steadfast*. Belmont, CA: Wadsworth.

Trilling, Richard J. 1976. *Party Image and Electoral Behavior*. New York: John Wiley and Sons.

Tsebelis, George. 1990. *Nested Games: Rational Choice in Comparative Politics*. Berkeley: University of California Press.

UDB. 1964. "Un nouveau parti: L'Union Démocratique Bretonne." *Le Peuple breton* 1 (1): 1.

United Kingdom. Department of the Environment. 1990. *This Common Inheritance*. Cm. 1200. London: HMSO.

———. 1996. *Ethnicity in the 1991 Census*. Vol. 1. London: HMSO.

Van der Brug, Wouten, Meindert Fennema, and Jean Tillie. 2000. "Anti-Immigrant Parties in Europe: Ideological or Protest Vote." *European Journal of Political Research* 37: 77–102.

Van Houten, Pieter. 2003. "Fiscal Autonomy and Party Politics in Catalonia." Paper presented at the PSA Conference, Leicester, UK.

Volkens, Andrea. 2001. "Quantifying the Election Programs: Coding Procedures and Controls," in *Mapping Policy Preferences: Estimates for Parties, Electors, and Governments, 1945–1998*, eds. Ian Budge, Hans-Dieter Klingemann, Andrea Volkens, Judith Bara, and Eric Tanenbaum. Oxford: Oxford University Press. 93–109.

von Beyme, Klaus. 1985. *Political Parties in Western Democracies*. Aldershot, UK: Gower.

Wald, Matthew L. 2000. "From Social Security to Environment, the Candidates' Positions." *New York Times* (November 5): A44.

Walker, Martin. 1977. *The National Front*. Glasgow, UK: Fontana.

Ware, Alan. 1996. *Political Parties and Party Systems*. New York: Oxford University Press.

Wattenberg, Martin P. 2000. "The Decline of Party Mobilization," in *Parties without Partisans: Political Change in Advanced Industrial Democracies*, eds. Russell J. Dalton and Martin P. Wattenberg. Oxford: Oxford University Press. 64–76.

Watts, Ronald. 1996. *Comparing Federal Systems in the 1990s*. Kingston, ON: Institute of Intergovernmental Relations, Queen's University.

Weil, Patrick. 1991. *La France et Ses Étrangers*. Paris: Calmann-Levy.

Whale, John. 1975. "Secret Papers Cast Doubts on Scottish and Welsh Assemblies." *The Sunday Times* (September 28): 4.

White, John. 2001. "The Election in Perspective: Two Nations, Four Parties," in *America's Choice 2000*, ed. William Crotty. Boulder, CO: Westview Press. 180–206.

Whitney, Craig. 1997. "A Convention Draws French for Far-Right and Against It." *New York Times* (March 30): A10.

Willey, Joseph. 1998. "The Formation and Success of New Political Parties in Established Democracies." PhD diss., SUNY Binghamton.

Wlezien, Christopher. 2001. "On Forecasting the Presidential Vote." *PS: Political Science and Politics* (March): 25–31.

Woldendorp, Jaap, Hans Keman, and Ian Budge. 1998. "Party Government in 20 Democracies: An Update (1990–95)." *European Journal of Political Research* 33 (1): 125–64.

Young, Robin. 1990. "Thatcher in Attack on 'Airy-Fairy' Greens." *The Times* (March 17): Home news.

Ysmal, Collette. 1984. "Le RPR et l'UDF Face au Front National: Concurrence et Connivences." *Revue politique et parlementaire* 86: 6–20.

———. 1995. "La Droite modérée sous la pression du Front National." *French Politics and Society* 13 (2): 1–9.

Ysmal, Colette and Roland Cayrol. 1996. "France: The Midwife Comes to Call," in *Choosing Europe?* eds. Cees van der Eijk and Mark N. Franklin. Ann Arbor: University of Michigan Press. 115–36.

Zaller, John. 1986. "The Effects of Political Involvement on Public Attitudes and Voting Behavior." Paper presented at the Annual Meeting of the American Political Science Association, Washington, DC.

———. 1992. *The Nature and Origins of Mass Opinion*. Cambridge: Cambridge University Press.

Zariski, Raphael. 1960. "Party Factions and Comparative Politics: Some Preliminary Observations." *Midwest Journal of Political Science* 4: 27–51.

———. 1989. "Ethnic Extremism among Ethnoterritorial Minorities in Western Europe: Dimensions, Causes and Institutional Responses." *Comparative Politics* 21 (3): 253–72.

Zolberg, Aristide R. 1977. "Federalization without Federalism in Belgium," in *Ethnic Conflict in the Western World*, ed. Milton J. Esman. Ithaca, NY: Cornell University Press. 103–42.

Index

accommodative strategy. *See also*
  accommodative-accommodative
  (ACAC) strategy; accommodative-
  adversarial (ACAD) strategy;
  adversarial-adversarial (ADAD)
  strategy
  British Liberal Democrats and, 139–41
  Conservative Party and, 124–8, 131,
    211–12
  cost of, 94, 127
  definition of, 24, 24n5
  Gaullist Party and, 164, 166–8, 171–3,
    176–9, 183
  Labour Party and, 128–30, 131–2,
    212–14, 219–20, 229–30
  policy position and, 28
  timeliness and, 37–8
accommodative-accommodative (ACAC)
    strategy
  British Green Party and, 133–6
  effects of, 59
  issue ownership and, 232
  issue salience and, 232–3
  niche party as equal threat and, 103
accommodative-adversarial (ACAD)
    strategy
  coding of, 50
  effects of, 34
  Front National and, 183
  issue ownership and, 186, 236–7
  issue salience and, 185, 236
  One Nation and, 268
  radical right parties and, 66
  SNP and, 219, 241–3

unequal niche party threat and, 102
U.S. Green Party and, 260
Adams, James, 15, 279
adversarial strategy
  Conservative Party and, 216–19, 221–2,
    227–9
  cost of, 94
  definition of, 24
  French Socialist Party and, 158–63,
    168–9, 173–5, 179–81
  nonproximal parties and, 32–3
  policy position and, 29
  purpose of, 102
  timeliness and, 37
adversarial-adversarial (ADAD) strategy,
    59, 63, 104
AGALEV, Belgium, 69
Ahrens, Dani, 129
Aldrich, John H., 104
Alleanza Nazionale, Italy, 44n10
Alternative Vote system, 264
Amorim Neto, Octavio, 52
anti-immigration stance. *See* Front
    National (FN), France
AP/PP (Conservative Party), Spain, 79–82
Australia, One Nation, 264–72
Austria, 41, 281

Barre, Raymond, 172
Basque parties, 79–82
Beasley, Kim, 267
Beck, Nathaniel, 54, 56
Belgium, 69, 70
Benoit, Kenneth, 44, 49

Kathleen Thelen, *How Institutions Evolve: The Political Economy of Skills in Germany, Britain, the United States, and Japan*

Charles Tilly, *Trust and Rule*

Daniel Treisman, *The Architecture of Government: Rethinking Political Decentralization*

Lily Lee Tsai, *Accountability without Democracy: How Solidary Groups Provide Public Goods in Rural China*

Joshua Tucker, *Regional Economic Voting: Russia, Poland, Hungary, Slovakia and the Czech Republic, 1990–1999*

Ashutosh Varshney, *Democracy, Development, and the Countryside*

Jeremy M. Weinstein, *Inside Rebellion: The Politics of Insurgent Violence*

Stephen I. Wilkinson, *Votes and Violence: Electoral Competition and Ethnic Riots in India*

Jason Wittenberg, *Crucibles of Political Loyalty: Church Institutions and Electoral Continuity in Hungary*

Elisabeth J. Wood, *Forging Democracy from Below: Insurgent Transitions in South Africa and El Salvador*

Elisabeth J. Wood, *Insurgent Collective Action and Civil War in El Salvador*